D0875951

Democracy in Decline

Rhode Island's
Constitutional Development
1776–1841

Democracy in Decline

Rhode Island's
Constitutional Development
1776–1841

Patrick T. Conley

Providence · Rhode Island Historical Society · 1977

RHODE ISLAND HISTORICAL SOCIETY
Officers:
Duncan Hunter Mauran, *President*
Dennis E. Stark, *Vice-President*
James F. Twaddell, *Vice-President*
David W. Dumas, *Secretary*
Talbot Rantoul, *Assistant Secretary*
George H. Cicma, *Treasurer*
John H. Drury, *Assistant Treasurer*
Albert T. Klyberg, *Director*
Clifford P. Monahon, *Director Emeritus*

Publications Committee:
Stuart C. Sherman, *Chairman*
Henry L. P. Beckwith, Jr.
Mrs. Philip Davis
Wendell D. Garrett
Charles E. Neu
Norman W. Smith
Gordon S. Wood
Nancy Fisher Chudacoff, *Ex Officio*

Copyright © Rhode Island Historical Society 1977
All rights reserved
Printed in the United States of America
Library of Congress Catalog Card Number: 77-76314
ISBN 0-917012-09-7

No part of this publication may be reproduced or
transmitted in any form or by any means, electronic
or mechanical, including photocopying, recording, or
any information storage or retrieval system without
permission in writing from the publisher except by a
reviewer who wishes to quote brief passages for a review
to be included in a magazine, newspaper, or broadcast.

Set in Baskerville type with Bulmer titles
Design: Elizabeth Heitzmann

to
Aunt Mary
Uncle Tom
and
Aunt Julia

8 0 0 3 8 1   LIBRARY
ALMA COLLEGE
ALMA, MICHIGAN

Chari?
ALMA COLLEGE
ALMA, MICHIGAN

Foreword

For a long while, students of government have been impressed by the strong influence that constitutions have exerted upon society. Some basic laws have affected not only the growth and direction of political party systems, but also have been responsible for landscaping the contours of economic and social systems as well. In few instances have constitutional considerations been so responsible for shaping the history of an American state as they have for Rhode Island.

It would be foolhardy to discount totally the implications of Rhode Island's natural endowment of bountiful Narragansett Bay and its less bountiful hinterland, or the impact of its size — early circumscribed by powerful neighbors — or its initial attraction to misfits and outcasts, or finally its precociousness in the development of an industrial state. More pervasive than all these influences and at the same time interacting powerfully among them have been the forces, practices, and prohibitions of the Rhode Island colonial charter of 1663 and its successor document, the state constitution of 1843.

The fascinating story of how a colony of contentious individualists managed to govern themselves and survive against enemies within and without is an important part of the following monograph by Professor Patrick T. Conley. Beyond that tale is the first clear, cogent and coherent analysis of the constitutional tragedy that devolved into the crisis known as the Dorr Rebellion.

Rhode Island's colonial charter served the agricultural and maritime economy of the late seventeenth century and most of the eighteenth century quite handily; under its provisions most farmers and merchants experienced a relatively evenhanded justice and an open opportunity for political participation in the affairs of a liberal society. After the Revolution, shifts in population upset the fixed ratio of representation in the Assembly; and large numbers of propertyless, immigrant mill workers who arrived during the nineteenth-century transformation to an industrial economy could not be accommodated in a political system where only property owners could vote. The old colonial charter — that contained no provisions for amendment — became a prescription for minority rule of a very oppressive variety; labor strife and religious bigotry added volatile ingredients. The resulting flash of the Dorr Rebellion produced the constitution of 1843. Although Rhode Island may have entered the nineteenth century in 1790 with the success of Samuel Slater's textile factory, it clearly failed to leave the eighteenth century behind until the grip of its colonial charter was finally broken.

Dr. Conley's work is an important publication for our Rhode Island Historical Society; it represents not only a landmark constitutional and legal historical study, but also offers truly fundamental insights to the total Rhode Island experience. Conley sheds new light on Roger Williams's approach to typology and on nineteenth-century issues of reapportionment and equal rights; he is the first historian to give adequate notice to the emotional and effective employment of religious prejudice as a factor behind the Law and Order party's opposition to constitutional reforms proposed by Thomas Wilson Dorr.

We are pleased — as a means of fulfilling our Society's charter — to have played a part in seeing this work published.

Albert T. Klyberg, *Director*
Rhode Island Historical Society

Contents

Foreword by Albert T. Klyberg   vii

Abbreviations   x

Illustrations   xi

Tables   xi

Preface   xiii

I The Colonial Background
    CHAPTER 1   The Lively Experiment   7
    CHAPTER 2   The Munificent Charter   21

II The Revolutionary Era
    CHAPTER 3   The Conservative Revolution   57
    CHAPTER 4   Paper Money and Party Politics   74
    CHAPTER 5   Rhode Island and Disunion   107

III Reapportionment
    CHAPTER 6   Economic Transformation and
                Political Polarization   145
    CHAPTER 7   George Burrill: Federalist Reformer   162
    CHAPTER 8   The First Convention   184

IV Equal Rights

CHAPTER 9   Free Suffrage   217

CHAPTER 10   Workingmen, Constitutionalists and the Convention of 1834   236

CHAPTER 11   The Constitutional Party in Decline   269

CHAPTER 12   The Forceful Effort   290

V Epilogue

CHAPTER 13   The Dorr Rebellion and Its Legacy   309

Bibliography   381

Index   417

ABBREVIATIONS

DC	Dorr Correspondence, Rider Collection
D Mss.	Dorr Manuscripts, Rider Collection
DP	Dorr Papers, Rider Collection
JCC	*Journals of the Continental Congress* (ed. W. C. Ford)
JHL	John Hay Library, Brown University
Misc. Mss. RIHS	Miscellaneous Manuscripts, Rhode Island Historical Society
PAC	Papers Relating to the Adoption of the Constitution of the United States
RICC	*Rhode Island in the Continental Congress* (comp. W. R. Staples)
RICR	*Records of the Colony of Rhode Island. . . .* (ed. J. R. Bartlett)
RIGA, Records	Records of the Rhode Island General Assembly
RIGA, Reports	Reports to the Rhode Island General Assembly
RIHS	Rhode Island Historical Society
RIHS Mss.	Rhode Island Historical Society Manuscripts
RISA	Rhode Island State Archives
Schedules	*Schedules* [Acts and Resolves] *of the Rhode Island General Assembly*

Illustrations

Ballot on the People's Constitution,
December 1841   *opposite Dorr quotation*

Roger Williams   6

Country Party "Prox" of 1786   56

Rhode Island Mill Village   144

Map of Rhode Island in 1840 showing expanding,
declining, and static communities, selected mill villages
and political preferences of the towns.   153

Thomas Wilson Dorr   216

Native American Broadside, March 1842   308

Tables

TABLE 1   Rhode Island in 1782 — Population, Ratio of
Representation, Value of Rateable Property   65

TABLE 2   The Population of Rhode Island and its
Towns, 1790–1840   155

TABLE 3   Rate of Population Growth, 1790–1840   156

TABLE 4   Ratio of Representatives to Population —
1790–1840   159

TABLE 5   State Estimates of Rateable Property 1796,
1823, 1849   161

TABLE 6   Vote by Towns on the Proposed Constitution
of 1824   211

Preface

Among American historians there exists a prevailing belief that a gradual expansion of democracy (the ability of a citizen to vote, hold office, and otherwise participate fully in the political process) occurred during the three generations between the beginning of the American Revolution and the end of the administration of President Andrew Jackson. According to this view such reforms as the removal of diminution of property qualifications for voting and officeholding, adherence to the principle of equal representation in the apportionment of state legislatures, a transfer in the selection of presidential electors from the legislature to the people, the framing of popularly oriented, written state constitutions, the creation of the national nominating convention, the practice of rotation in office, the enthusiastic acceptance of the "spoils" system and the system of party politics, a decline in deferential voting, increased citizen participation in elections and the popularization of campaign techniques, made government not only *for* the people but *of* and *by* the people as well. The thesis of the present study is that Rhode Island — the home of the "otherwise minded" — was a blatant exception to this trend. In that contrary state the base of democracy contracted markedly — Rhode Island was a democracy in decline. At the time of the American Revolution the smallest state possessed the greatest autonomy and the broadest democracy in the new Union; by 1841 it had "degenerated into a freeholding aristocracy" or a "landed oligarchy," according to such reformers as Thomas Wilson Dorr. This situation even prompted some advocates of change to exclaim that the American Revolution, by removing appeals to a higher authority from the arbitrary actions of the legislature, had made Rhode Island's non-voters "less free." Repeated and unsuccessful attempts to reverse this development, with their related frustrations, furnish the prologue to the Dorr Rebellion — the central political and constitutional episode in Rhode Island history. This volume attempts to describe the antecedents and the causes of that political upheaval. Hopefully this constitutional survey of Rhode Island's formative years will serve as a useful backdrop not only for understanding the rebellion but also for writing a long-range history of Rhode Island constitutionalism from the adoption of the still-operative basic law of 1842 to the present day.

This study has relied heavily upon the vast and valuable but seldom explored Sidney S. Rider Collection at Brown University's John Hay Library. It has also made ample use of more than a score of important collections of unpublished primary materials relating to local history housed at the Rhode Island Historical Society, some of which were previously unconsulted. In addition, I have examined nearly all the major Rhode Island newspapers printed during the period which this study treats, and drawn upon the copious resources of the Rhode Island State Archives including such important public documents relating to this topic as the acts, resolves, reports, proceedings, and journals of the General Assembly. The Newport Historical Society, the John Carter Brown Library, and the Library of Congress have also yielded valuable documents, and the town meeting records of Rhode Island's communities were a mine of information. Of course, the published primary and secondary materials relating to Rhode Island history were consulted with great profit, as were a number of hitherto neglected doctoral dissertations and master's theses on various aspects of the state's development.

An attempt has been made to view Rhode Island history within the broader context of national affairs and to assess the impact of national trends and movements on the state's constitutional history. I have also addressed myself, but necessarily in a cursory fashion, to such current historiographical issues as the thought of Roger Williams, the validity for Rhode Island of the socioeconomic interpretation of the colonial and revolutionary eras, and the nature and sources of Jacksonian reform.

My indebtedness is large. The contribution of Albert T. Klyberg, the able and progressive director of the Rhode Island Historical Society, was invaluable. The energetic managing editor of *Rhode Island History,* Noel P. Conlon, also rendered expert assistance as copy-editor and vigilant proofreader. Mary T. Quinn, the knowledgeable state archivist, and her gracious successor, Mrs. Phyllis Peloquin, were most helpful. Always accommodating were the highly efficient personnel of the John Hay Library of Brown University. The Reverend Cornelius P. Forster, O.P., Dean of the Graduate School and Chairman of the History Department at Providence College, provided constant encouragement and gentle prodding, while Providence College itself provided a generous faculty research grant. My colleagues, Mr. Matthew J. Smith, archivist of Providence College, and Dr. James B. Morris read the manuscript and saved me from several grammatical and stylistic lapses, as did the late Mr. William H. Edwards, prominent Providence attorney and a specialist in legal and constitutional history. Professor Joseph Norton, a former student and a fellow worker in the historical vineyards of early Rhode Island, furnished me with several valuable leads. The Rhode Island Bicentennial Commission endorsed this project allowing Glenn LaFantasie and Paul Campbell of the Commission staff to render expert editorial assistance and Elizabeth Heitzmann to practice her talent for book design. Most of the typing chores were capably performed by Virginia Mary Conley. The late Dr. Aaron I. Abell of the University of Notre Dame, an inspiring and kindly teacher, guided this study in its initial stages. Dr. Marshall Smelser directed it to completion in its dissertation form and imparted to me whatever skills I possess as a researcher. To all these benefactors I freely and gratefully acknowledge my debt. Hopefully the reader will find this volume worthy of their efforts.

Providence, December 27, 1976

Democracy in Decline

1776   1841.

Adoption of the Constitution of Rhode Island.

PEOPLE'S TICKET.

I am an American citizen, of the age of twenty-one years, and have my permanent residence or home in this State.

I am   qualified to vote under the existing laws of this State.

I vote for the CONSTITUTION formed by the Convention of the People, assembled at Providence, and which was proposed to the People by said Convention on the 18th day of November, 1841.

A ballot prepared for the December 27-29, 1841 referendum on the People's Constitution. The second sentence contains a space for the insertion of a statement by the voter of his political status under the charter regime. The inclusive dates symbolize the reformers' belief that they were reviving and invoking the revolutionary principles of 1776 (from the "prox" collection, Rhode Island Historical Society).

We have seen that our government was in its origin a democracy; and continued such, by assent of the King of England, to the time of the Revolution; that the whole people succeeded to the sovereignty of the State; that, for the reasons given, they omitted to exercise it in the formation of a constitution; that our government has degenerated into a freeholding aristocracy; that safety and self respect forbid a longer delay in the work of reform; and that the people are now proceeding, in an unobjectionable and appropriate mode, to adopt such measures as justice requires. And in so doing, they will relieve the freeholders from the absurd position in which a portion of them, at least, have placed themselves in attempting to resist the course of popular rights. They tell us that the people have no authority to make a constitution; that the legislature have no authority; and that the freeholders have no authority, because they cannot move an inch until authorized by the legislature! In this distressing difficulty, rather than that the authority of the State should evaporate and be entirely lost, the people have consented to step in and to take the case into their own hands and do substantial justice to all the parties who are concerned. . . . I trust the result will be the adoption of a constitution that shall be worthy of our venerated ancestors and transmit the blessings of their "ancient democracy" and of well-ordered and rational liberty to their remotest descendants.

> from Thomas Wilson Dorr's speech on the right of the
> people of Rhode Island to form a constitution,
> delivered in the People's Convention, November 18, 1841

I. The Colonial Background

Roger Williams made his "errand into the wilderness" in 1636 to establish a "lively experiment" in religious liberty and church-state separation. The charter of 1663, obtained through the influence of Williams and Dr. John Clarke, remained the basic law of Rhode Island until May, 1843 (from a painting by Peter Frederick Rothermel, Rhode Island Historical Society).

CHAPTER ONE

The Lively Experiment

I

Roger Williams is the first significant figure in Rhode Island constitutional history. The fact that Williams, contrary to widely accepted assumptions, was basically a theologian rather than a political theorist,[1] does not detract from his importance during

---

[1] The so-called "Progressive" historians writing during the second quarter of this century viewed Williams as primarily a political thinker and the first great hero of the American democratic tradition. They inordinately minimized Williams's religious thought and erroneously believed that his thirst for "religious toleration was only a necessary deduction from the major principles of his political theory." The chief among those historians viewing Williams in this romantic light were: Vernon L. Parrington, *Main Currents in American Thought* (New York, 1927), I, 62–75; James E. Ernst, *The Political Thought of Roger Williams* (Seattle, 1929); and Samuel H. Brockunier, *The Irrepressible Democrat: Roger Williams* (New York, 1940). Recent scholars, most notably, Mauro Calamandrei, "Neglected Aspects of Roger Williams' Thought," *Church History*, XXI (Sept., 1952), 239–259; Perry Miller, *Roger Williams; His Contribution to the American Tradition* (Indianapolis, 1953); Alan Simpson, "How Democratic Was Roger Williams?" *William and Mary Quarterly*, 3rd Ser., XIII (Jan., 1956), 53–67; Sacvan Bercovitch, "Typology in Puritan New England: The Williams-Cotton Controversy Reassessed," *American Quarterly*, XIX (Summer, 1967), 166–191; Richard

the formative period of Rhode Island constitutional development, because his theological excursions often took him into the
domain of politics. As Edmund Morgan has observed: "However theological the cast of his mind, he wrote most often, most
effectively, and most significantly about civil government." [2]

Master Williams was the most contrary of those independent-
minded and strong-willed ministers who departed from centrifu-
gal Massachusetts Bay to find an intellectual and religious refuge
in the New England wilderness. A decree of banishment had
been issued against the polemical Williams in October 1635,
chiefly because of his violent attack upon the cornerstones of the
fledgling Massachusetts regime — the theology of the covenant
and the principle of non-separation.[3] In addition, the outspoken
"seeker" had raised the question of whether the Bay colonists had
any right to the land they occupied because their ownership was
not based upon purchase from the Indians. He was even so bold
as to declare that the King's authority to grant such control
rested upon a "solemn public lie." Finally, he condemned the decree of the magistrates that required all "unregenerate" inhabitants who were not freemen to take a resident's oath to support

M. Reinitz, "Symbolism and Freedom: The Use of Biblical Typology as
an Argument for Religious Freedom in Seventeenth Century England
and America" (unpublished doctoral dissertation, University of Rochester, 1967); and John Garrett, *Roger Williams: Witness Beyond Christendom* (New York, 1970), have properly offered a theological interpretation of his thought and writings. Ola Elizabeth Winslow, *Master Roger
Williams* (New York, 1957) is the most balanced biography of the controversial Williams. The best study of Williams's ideology is the succinct
and penetrating Edmund S. Morgan, *Roger Williams: The Church and
the State* (New York, 1967), hereafter cited as Morgan, *Williams.* Morgan suggests the principal reason for the erroneous identification of Williams as primarily a political theorist: "Williams' every thought took its
rise from religion. But in his writings . . . Williams was more often concerned with ecclesiastical and political institutions than with theology."
Morgan, *Williams,* pp. 86–87. For a summary of the divergent views of
Williams see LeRoy Moore, Jr., "Roger Williams and the Historians,"
Church History, XXXII (Dec., 1963), 432–51; and Nancy E. Peace,
"Roger Williams—A Historiographical Essay," *Rhode Island History,*
XXXV (Nov., 1976), 103–13.

[2] Morgan, *Williams,* pp. 86–87.

[3] Miller, p. 24.

the colony and its government. Williams's iconoclastic posture left no alternative to the Massachusetts magistrates but to banish him, for they could have scarcely carried out their "holy experiment" if they allowed the recusant reverend to remain.[4]

A vital area of disagreement between Williams and the builders of the Bay Colony was that Williams considered some religious doctrines propounded by the Puritans to be a prostitution of theology. His alternative to the orthodox Puritan approach was not only a cause for his exile, it is also essential to a full understanding of his notions of religious freedom and the separation of church and state — principles which found their expression in Rhode Island's basic law.

Roger Williams's challenge to covenant theology revolved around a method of interpreting the Bible, specifically the relation of Old Testament to New, which is called typology. Williams's version of the typological method was based upon a belief that everything in the Old Testament is merely a prefiguration of the New Testament, that each event in the history of Israel could be understood only when it came to fruition in the life of Christ, and that the Old Testament had no independent significance. In his typological rendition each occurrence in the Old Testament was an archetype, a pale rehearsal for an event in the New Testament which was its key and its antitype. Williams's typology was allegorical in nature and attacked both the literal and historical character of the Old Testament.

This complex method of Biblical exegesis in its practical application to the life of Massachusetts Bay had important consequences. Among other things, Williams's method of interpreting the Scriptures was at variance with the historical mode of typological interpretation upon which covenant theology rested. Orthodox typology held that the Old Testament was simultaneously a literal *and* spiritual work. On the former level, Israel's scrip-

---

4 Edmund S. Morgan, *The Puritan Dilemma: The Story of John Winthrop* (Boston, 1958), pp. 115–133, and Irwin H. Polishook, "Unorthodoxy in Massachusetts: A History of the Banishment of Roger Williams from Massachusetts and Its Consequences" (unpublished master's thesis, Brown University, 1958).

tural theocracy provided the eternal pattern of civil justice, while
spiritually Israel as the Promised Land prefigured Christ. Orthodox typology thus intermingled the Church and the civil state,
and supported the Puritan contention that the Christian magistrates of Massachusetts Bay could enforce religious conformity
by basing their actions on similar powers exercised by the Biblical Israelites.[5] Williams's brand of typology, being of a purely
spiritual nature, disputed the Massachusetts Puritan belief that
any political or social arrangement could be legitimized by reference to a similar arrangement described in the Old Testament.
Specifically, Williams denied the right of the Massachusetts magistrates, basing their actions on those of the Israelites, to use the
civil power to enforce religious conformity. It was Williams's contention that the events and the laws of Israel, having found completion in the New Testament, were, without exception, purely
moral and ceremonial, and not to be emulated by seventeenth-
century New Englanders.

A crucial issue in the typological debate between Williams and
John Cotton was the meaning of Christ's Incarnation — the dividing line between the Old and New Testaments. Cotton believed
that from this pivotal event to the millennium, or "Second Coming" of Christ, the Church and State should continue united as
they had in the past. He and the Bay Puritans viewed the history
of redemption as an essentially unchanged covenant of grace.
Conversely, Williams interpreted Christ's Incarnation as the historical moment when God had changed the nature of His Kingdom radically. For Williams, the Crucifixion clearly revealed that
the nature of Christian life until the millennium demanded im-

---

[5] Perry Miller has contended that the early Puritans "eschewed" and
rejected typology. Bercovitch has persuasively argued that they accepted
this method of Biblical exegesis but utilized it differently than did Williams. Bercovitch states that the Cotton-Williams clash was not a disagreement between "a typologist and a Puritan, but an opposition between two different typological approaches." Williams's approach, in
the Augustinian tradition, was purely spiritual and in the allegorical
mode; Cotton's method, in the Eusebian tradition, was both spiritual
and literal and thus in the historical mode. See Bercovitch, pp. 166–81,
especially pp. 167, 175–78.

placable opposition between Christ and the world — between spirit and flesh. A knowledge of Williams's and Cotton's divergent views on the significance of Christ's birth and death makes more comprehensible Cotton's attachment to a union of the civil and the spiritual, and Williams's abhorrence of such a connection.[6]

Another crucial theological disagreement between Williams and the Massachusetts Puritans stemmed from their divergent views of the Ten Commandments. These divinely revealed injunctions were divided into two "tables"; the first table (commandments one through four) was concerned with God and the worship of God, and was called "ceremonial"; the second (commandments five through ten) was to govern human relations and was called "moral." John Cotton and his associates contended that the function of judges and kings in the Old Testament state of Israel, whereby they enforced both tables, continued to be valid. According to this interpretation the task of enforcing the first table (*viz.* worship of God) resided with civil magistrates and ministers acting in concert. Williams believed that Jesus had abrogated this Hebraic system. He contended that Christ had set forth new laws of worship which had stripped judges, kings, and civil magistrates of their right to enforce ceremonial provisions of the first table. These matters now belonged purely to the spiritual realm. "Soul liberty," which pertained to the first table, was exclusively an affair of private conscience; the magistrate had no jurisdiction whatsoever in this sphere.[7]

As a result of these exegetical efforts, Williams concluded that the temporal power exercised over the religious sphere in the Old Testament was merely the archetype of spiritual power in the

---

[6] For the place of the Incarnation in the development of Williams's thought see Jesper Rosenmeier, "The Teacher and the Witness: John Cotton and Roger Williams," *William and Mary Quarterly,* 3rd Ser., XXV (July, 1968), 408–31. Rosenmeier agrees with Bercovitch on the adherence of the Puritans to the typological approach. A recent, but undocumented and unconvincing minimization of the influence of the Old Testament on Puritan life and thought (including government) is Eugene R. Fingerhut, "Were the Massachusetts Puritans Hebraic?" *New England Quarterly,* XL (Dec., 1967), 521–31, especially 525–27.

[7] Garrett, pp. 176–191.

New, and thus, whenever the modern state attempted to enforce conformity of religious belief, it was acting in an unjustifiable manner, and its leaders were assuming that the Old Testament was a model with independent significance. That false assumption, asserted Williams, had and would lead to persecution, religious wars, and even damnation.[8] This obsession with religious persecution and its baneful effects upon both spiritual and civil life occupies a prominent place in Williams's thought.[9]

The fiery minister's typological approach had as its logical corollary liberty of conscience, and it contributed substantially to Williams's dogma of the separation of church and state. It is important to note that the theologically obsessed Williams sought this separation not to protect the State from the dominance of the Church, but to free the Church and the individual conscience from the interference and coercions of the State. Williams's religious creed thus led him into the political sphere where he was essentially a traditionalist who believed in stability and deference. "So far as the political order was concerned, Williams had really only one revolutionary statement to make. He denied that the state had any responsibility for the only form of life which has absolute importance — the life of the soul." [10] As an example of

---

[8] Miller, pp. 32–43, 149–54, 183–87; Bercovitch, *passim*. The best statement of Williams's typological doctrine can be found in his *Bloudy Tenent of Persecution* in *The Complete Writings of Roger Williams* (New York, 1963), III, especially 282–425. The first six volumes of this edition are an exact reprint of the scarce Narragansett Club Edition of Williams's works (Providence, 1866–1874). The seventh volume in this reprint edition contains those treatises by Williams that were discovered after publication of the Narragansett Club Edition, plus an excellent introductory essay on Williams by Perry Miller. I have used the reprint edition; it is hereafter cited Williams, *Writings*.

[9] W. K. Jordan, *Development of Religious Toleration in England* (Cambridge, Mass., 1932–40), III, 472–507, contains an analysis of Williams's views on religious liberty that the author calls an "inferential by-product of Williams's epical holy war against the evils of persecution." *Ibid.*, p. 488.

[10] Simpson, pp. 54–56. Williams, according to Edmund Morgan, believed that there was one thing government could do to advance Christ's kingdom — "government could protect the free exercise of conscience in religion." Morgan, *Williams,* p. 140.

how strongly Williams felt about State domination of the Church, in one burst of vituperation the polemical theologian asserted that such a condition would render the Church "the garden and spouse of Christ, a filthy dunghill and whore-house of rotten and stinking whores and hypocrites." [11] Let it not be said that Williams took the issue of separation lightly!

It is exceedingly difficult to ascertain whether Roger Williams's passionate dedication to religious liberty, freedom of conscience, and separation of church and state flowed from his typological approach, or whether his typology was merely a means and a device used to demonstrate the validity of principles already espoused. While the former view is probably correct, the logical progression of Williams's beliefs is less important to the student of Rhode Island constitutional history than the conclusions that he reached.

Among the most significant of these conclusions were: (1) any attempt by the state to enforce religious orthodoxy "stinks in God's nostrils," because it perverts God's plan for the regeneration of souls, and it is productive of persecution and religious wars; (2) God had not favored any particular form of government, and it is therefore to be inferred that forms of government will vary according to the nature and disposition of the people governed; (3) political and especially religious diversity was inevitable; (4) the human conscience must be completely emancipated through the establishment of religious freedom and the separation of church and state.[12]

Historian Perry Miller has said of Williams that "he exerted little or no direct influence on theorists of the Revolution and the Constitution, who drew on quite different intellectual sources, yet as a figure and a reputation he was always there to remind Americans that no other conclusion than absolute religious freedom was feasible in this society." [13] Williams's influence and im-

---

[11] *Bloody Tenent Yet More Bloody,* Williams, *Writings,* IV, 122.

[12] Simpson, pp. 56–62.

[13] Miller, p. 254. Williams's indirect influence on the founding fathers may have been considerable, because many of the framers were greatly impressed by the liberality of the Rhode Island charter.

pact on Rhode Island's basic law is another matter, however, for the royal charter of 1663 bears the indelible impress of his fundamental beliefs.

II

Williams began his religious experiment in 1636 on lands purchased from the Indians at the head of Narragansett Bay near the confluence of two small streams. Here Williams and his tiny band established a settlement that they optimistically called Providence. During this town's early months it was governed by a primitive arrangement consisting of a fortnightly meeting of the "masters of families" who considered matters relating to the "common peace, watch and planting." [14]

As the number of settlers increased, a formal government became necessary. Presumably, in 1637, Williams and the initial settlers drafted articles of self-incorporation. Then a mutual compact creating a "town fellowship" was entered into by the original "masters of families" and an agreement to obey these "householders" and all whom "they shall admit into the same fellowship and privilege" was signed by thirteen other inhabitants who were either unmarried or minors. These documents were the fundamental papers of Providence town government. The principal features of both the fellowship and submission compacts were the vesting of administrative control in a majority of the "householders" and the all-important proviso that such control was to be exercised "only in civil things." [15]

---

[14] Roger Williams to John Winthrop, [n.d., *ca.* Sept., 1636], Williams, *Writings,* III, 3–5. Since most of the early records of Providence were destroyed in King Philip's War, this letter constitutes the fullest available account of the early months of Providence plantation.

[15] Roger Williams to John Winthrop, [n.d., *ca.* Sept. 1636], Williams, *Writings,* VI, 3–7. In this letter Williams expressed his intention to institute the above-described system. The "householders" compact has been lost, but the submission agreement or compact is printed in Horatio Rogers, George M. Carpenter, and Edward Field, eds., *The Early Records of the Town of Providence* (Providence, 1892–1915), I, 1. Hereafter cited as *Providence Early Records.* The latter is substantively the same as the proposed document in Williams's letter to Winthrop. The

In the formative period of the Providence plantation Williams's political posture was not as liberal as his religious views. His plan for the temporary submission of new inhabitants, his unfulfilled desire to reserve unto himself a veto over the admission of new settlers, and his establishment of a closed corporation of landed proprietors are examples of this political caution.[16] Williams's position is understandable, however, for it appears that he did not wish his experiment in religious freedom to be extinguished by the influx of those who were hostile to his efforts — a fate then befalling the Calverts in Maryland.

Disagreements arising from these restrictions on Providence settlers necessitated a strengthening of the loose compact of 1637, and a plantation agreement was adopted in August 1640. This instrument provided for the election of five "disposers," who were charged with the disbursement of land to selected inhabitants, management of the common stock, and the arbitration of local disputes. In addition, the agreement allowed a broader par-

wording of the preserved submission compact indicates that a "householders" agreement had been adopted. There is considerable confusion over the date and the circumstances surrounding the adoption of these compacts. The most authoritative accounts of the founding of Providence contain conflicting views. Cf. *Providence Early Records,* I, 1; Howard M. Chapin, ed., *Documentary History of Rhode Island* (Providence, 1916–19), I, 44–46, 96–98; Charles McLean Andrews, *The Colonial Period of American History* (New Haven, 1936), II, 7–8; Howard K. Stokes, *The Finances and Administration of Providence* (Baltimore, 1903), pp. 4–8; John R. Bartlett, ed., *Records of the Colony of Rhode Island and Providence Plantations in New England* (Providence, 1856–65), I, 14, hereafter cited as *RICR;* and Williams, *Writings,* VI, 5, note 1.

[16] Roger Williams to John Winthrop [n.d., *ca.* Sept. 1636], Williams, *Writings,* VI, 6 (veto); *Providence Early Records,* III, 90–91 (land distribution). On Williams's political conservatism see Edmund S. Morgan, "Miller's Williams," *New England Quarterly,* XXXVIII (Dec., 1965), 521–22; Simpson, *passim;* Rosenmeier, pp. 419–20; and Garrett, pp. 30–31, 182. These writers have correctly observed that despite Williams's belief in spiritual freedom, the founder of Providence in his capacity as a civil ruler insisted that the inherently evil flesh be kept under tight control to prevent chaos. Williams, these historians persuasively contend, was not a political radical, but rather a traditionalist whose views were authoritarian. The most recent statement of this position is Robert d. Brunkow, "Love and Order in Roger Williams' Writings," *Rhode Island History,* XXXV (Nov., 1976), 115–26.

ticipation by the inhabitants in town affairs, and it clearly reaffirmed and endorsed "liberty of Conscience." [17] Thus did Williams and his Providence associates give early and repeated expression to their conviction that the state should not interfere in
matters of religious concern.

While Providence was still in its infancy the Narragansett
region became the refuge of other nonconformists. In 1638, a
group of religious exiles, mostly Antinomians, led by William
Coddington, established the community of Portsmouth on the
northern tip of the island of Rhode Island on land which they
had purchased from the Indians through the intercession of
Roger Williams.[18] The outcasts of Portsmouth, in Biblical fashion, elected Coddington "Judge" of their little community.

It was evident from the outset, however, that the forceful Coddington did not share Williams's concern for the absolute separation of church and state.[19] For this and other reasons Antinomian leader Anne Hutchinson, Samuel Gorton, and other disgruntled settlers staged a coup against Coddington and deposed
him in April 1639. Undaunted, Coddington led his followers to
the southern end of the island where he established the settlement of Newport. Here he was chosen "Judge" with a double
vote.[20]

---

[17] *Providence Early Records,* XV, 2–5. The compact contained a total
of twelve provisions. Affixed to it are thirty-nine signatures including
those of two women and twelve of the thirteen original signers of the
submission agreement of 1637. These latter had evidently been elevated
to full privileges and participation in the community. *Ibid.,* I, 1 and XV,
5. That liberty of conscience was possessed by Providence women is evidenced not only by the signatures of two females on this compact but,
more dramatically, by the famous Verin case of 1638. *RICR,* I, 16–17;
Roger Williams to John Winthrop, May 22, 1638 and [September or
October, 1638], Williams, *Writings,* VI, 94–96, 120–25.

[18] Chapin, I, 59–60.

[19] *RICR,* I, 52; Chapin, I, 40–60; Clarence S. Brigham, ed., *The
Early Records of the Town of Portsmouth* (Providence, 1901), pp. 1–4.

[20] *RICR,* I, 87. Lloyd A. Robson, "Newport Begins," published serially in *Newport History,* 1964–1967, is the best study of Newport's origins, while Carl Bridenbaugh, *Fat Mutton and Liberty of Conscience,
Society in Rhode Island, 1636–1690* (Providence, 1974) is the best account of Newport's first half-century.

Although Coddington had been bested he was not beaten, for within a year he had cleverly engineered a consolidation of the two island towns under a common administration of which he was governor. This new political entity proclaimed itself a democracy in 1641 and guaranteed religious liberty to all. Because title to the entire island of Rhode Island was in his name, Coddington began to entertain thoughts of creating a domain of his own distinct from the Providence plantation. This ambitious plan constituted the most serious internal obstacle to the creation of a united colony during Rhode Island's formative years.[21]

Partially to thwart Coddington's feudal aspirations, but principally to forestall the exorbitant land claims of the incipient New England Confederation, Roger Williams journeyed to a troubled England in 1643 to secure a patent that would unite the settlements of Providence, Portsmouth, and Newport into a single colony and confirm the settlers' claims to the land which they held by Indian purchase.[22] Williams obtained the desired patent from Robert Rich, the Earl of Warwick, and his parliamentary Committee on Foreign Plantations. Significantly, the patent lacked the royal seal, for Charles I had already begun to lose power and control to the parliamentary opposition. The patent, dated March 14, 1643,[23] was the first legal recognition of the Rhode Island towns by the mother country. It authorized the

---

[21] Andrews, II, 8–11; Chapin, I, 105–06; Dennis Allen O'Toole, "Exiles, Refugees and Rogues: The Quest for Civil Order in the Towns and Colony of Providence Plantations, 1636–1654" (unpublished doctoral dissertation, Brown University, 1973), and Sidney V. James, *Colonial Rhode Island: A History* (New York, 1975), pp. 13–32, 48–74.

[22] On the relations between the New England Confederation and the Rhode Island settlements see Harry M. Ward, *The United Colonies of New England 1643–90* (New York, 1961), especially pp. 136–156.

[23] Prior to 1752 the Old Style or Julian calendar was used in England and her colonies. Under that calendar the year technically began on March 25. In 1752 the present New Style or Gregorian calendar was adopted by England and an eleven-day adjustment was made in the transition from Old Style to New. I have used the Old Style dates as they appear on the original records for the pre-1752 period of Rhode Island history. Under the New Style system the date of the patent would be March 24, 1644, because only a ten-day transitional adjustment was required during the seventeenth century.

union of Providence, Portsmouth, and Newport under the name
of "the Incorporation of Providence Plantations in Narragansett Bay in New England," and it granted these towns "full
power and authority to govern and rule themselves" and future
inhabitants by majority decision, provided that all regulations
that were enacted were "comformable to the laws of England"
so far as the nature of the place would permit. This initial patent
specifically conferred political power upon the inhabitants of the
towns. The repeated emphasis of the document upon "civil government" gave implicit sanction to the separation of church and
state, whereas the use of words "approved and confirmed" rather
than "grant" in conjunction with the right to the land was a
vindication of Williams's questionable contention that the Indian
deeds were valid. Williams's adroitness and diplomacy had won
the day, and he was greeted with great enthusiasm when he returned to Providence, patent in hand, in September 1644.[24]

While Williams was in England volatile Samuel Gorton, a
free-thinking man with a proclivity for disputation and passion
for the common law, had succeeded in developing a mainland
settlement to the south of Providence which he eventually called
Warwick. Here, as in Providence, liberty of conscience prevailed.
Although his new settlement was not mentioned in the patent, the
beleaguered Gorton sought and eventually secured inclusion of
his town under its protective provisions.[25]

---

[24] Chapin, I, 214–17 contains the State Paper Office copy of the
patent that is the most accurate draft; Andrews, II, 23–26. The eminent
historian, Edward Channing, *History of the United States* (New York,
1905–25), I, 383–85, 393–96, perceptively questions both the validity of
the land purchases and the "legal standing" of the patent. Channing
contends that the patent "was issued before the battle of Naseby and
while affairs in England were in an extremely critical condition, and when
it would be absurd to regard Parliament as exercising sovereign authority."
Ibid., p. 94. Howver, Oliver Cromwell, in his capacity as Lord Protector,
confirmed the patent in 1655, *RICR,* I, 317.

[25] Andrews, II, 11–17; *Early Records of the Town of Warwick* (Providence, 1926), are fragmentary and disorganized and shed little light on
the founding of that settlement. More valuable on both Warwick's origins
and Gorton's thought is Samuel Gorton, *Simplicity's Defense against
Seven-Headed Policy*, ed. William R. Staples (Providence, 1835). This is
Vol. II, *Collections Rhode Island Historical Society.*

The two island towns of Portsmouth and Newport also embraced the legislative patent and representatives of the four communities met initially on Aquidneck Island in November 1644. After this and three subsequent sessions, they held the momentous Portsmouth Assembly of May 1647 to organize a government and to draft and adopt a body of laws. According to Charles McLean Andrews "the acts and orders of 1647 constitute one of the earliest programmes for a government and one of the earliest codes of law made by any body of men in America and the first to embody in all its parts the precedents set by the laws and statutes of England." [26]

The assembly that drafted this code was attended by a majority of the freemen of the four towns. Upon assembling, the delegates agreed that they were "willing to receive and to be governed by the laws of England together with the way of Administration of them, so far as the nature and constitution of this plantation will admit." However, they further declared that the form of government for the colony was "democraticall," in that it rested on "the free and voluntary consent of all, or the greater part of the free inhabitants." [27] This claim was vindicated by the first list of colonial freemen, published in 1655. When compared with the population figures of the towns, it revealed that one-half the adult male residents in Providence, two-thirds in Portsmouth and Newport, and nearly ninety percent in Warwick had the right to vote and hold office.

At the landmark 1647 assembly, officers were elected, a system of representation established, and a legislative process—containing provisions both for local initiative and popular referen-

---

[26] Andrews, II, 26; The first meeting of the General Assembly under the Patent was probably held in November, 1644 on Aquidneck. The famous 1647 Assembly was apparently the fifth such gathering, but the first for which records have been preserved. "Early Sessions of the General Assembly," *Rhode Island Historical Society Collections*, XIV (Jan., 1921), 7–10 is an article that shows (contrary to popular opinion) that the 1647 conclave was not the initial session of the colonial assembly.

[27] *RICR*, I, 147–48, 156; *Providence Early Records*, XV, 9–10; and O'Toole, pp. 537–38. Gorton's town of Warwick, although not mentioned in the Williams Patent of 1643, was given "the same privileges as Providence," by the 1647 assembly. *RICR*, I, 148.

dum — was devised.[28] Then was enacted the remarkable Code, an elaborate body of criminal and civil law prefaced by a bill of rights.[29]

Finally, for the administration of justice, the productive 1647 Assembly established a General Court of Trials having jurisdiction over all important legal questions. The president, who was the chief officer of the colony, and the assistants representing their respective towns, were to comprise this high tribunal. By inference, the existing town courts were to possess the jurisdiction heretofore exercised in matters of minor and local importance. The Code and the court system of 1647 served as the cornerstones of the judicial establishment of Rhode Island both as colony and state.[30] Thus did the four original towns and their inhabitants combine to create a fairly systematized federal commonwealth and deal a paralyzing blow to the forces of decentralization.

---

[28] *RICR*, I, 147–49. The initiative provision was annulled in 1650 (*RICR*, I, 228–29), and the referendum was repealed in 1664 (*RICR*, II, 21).

[29] *RICR,* I, 157–90.

[30] *RICR*, I, 191–208; John T. Farrell, "The Early History of Rhode Island's Court System," *Rhode Island History,* IX (July, 1950), 65–71; IX (October, 1950), 103–117; X (January, 1951), 14–25; Edward C. Stiness, "The Struggle for Judicial Supremacy," in Edward Field, ed., *State of Rhode Island and Providence Plantations at the End of the Century: A History* (Boston, 1902), III, 89–105. The original records of this court are preserved in a manuscript volume entitled "Rhode Island Colony Records, 1646–1669" in the Rhode Island State Archives (RISA). They were published as *Rhode Island State Records: Records of the Court of Trials of the Colony of Providence Plantations, 1647–1662* (Providence, 1920) and *Rhode Island Court Records . . . 1662–1670* (Providence, 1922) by Howard M. Chapin of the Rhode Island Historical Society.

CHAPTER TWO

The Munificent Charter

I

The union of 1647 did not long endure, for ambitious William Coddington, after a brief flirtation with the New England Confederation, succeeded in securing from the Council of State in 1651 a commission that contravened the Patent of 1643 by granting to Coddington exclusive ownership and proprietary rights to the islands of Aquidneck (Rhode Island) and Conanicut (Jamestown). A determined group of Newporters opposed this powergrab, and they dispatched Dr. John Clarke to England to obtain a recision of this extraordinary commission. Clarke sought the aid of the influential Williams and the two men made the tedious journey to the mother country. As a result of the intercession on Williams's behalf by Sir Henry Vane and Oliver Cromwell, the Council of State responded by annulling the Coddington commission and reaffirming the patent of 1643. Williams, after a brief immersion in English domestic affairs, returned to Rhode Island in 1654 and immediately began to counteract the divisive forces within the settlement. He was determined to reunite and consolidate the four towns, and by mid-1657 his efforts produced an encouraging degree of cohesion.[1]

There were still stormy seas ahead for the Rhode Island ship of state, for no sooner had a semblance of internal unity and stability been created than there arose two external dangers, one of which menaced the colony's landed possessions and the other its very existence. The first danger resulted from the claims of the Atherton land company to the area that now comprises Washington County; the second and greater threat arose from the restoration in 1660 of the Stuart dynasty to the throne of England. The Restoration rendered doubtful the legal validity of the parliamentary Patent of 1643 and placed Rhode Island in a precarious position because of her close ties with the anti-monarchical Commonwealth and Protectorate of Cromwell.[2]

The apprehensive colony, fearful for its legal life, commissioned the able and diligent Dr. John Clarke to obtain royal confirmation of its right to exist. Clarke, who espoused principles of religious liberty similar to those of Williams, had remained in England upon completing his successful mission of 1651–52. After an exasperating delay stemming from Rhode Island's and Connecticut's conflicting claims to the Narragansett Country, Clarke, with the assistance of Connecticut agent John Winthrop, Jr., secured from Charles II the royal charter of 1663. This coveted document was immediately transported to Rhode Island where it was unanimously received by the grateful colonists in November 1663.[3]

---

[1] Andrews, II, 31–33; Richard LeBaron Bowen, *The Providence Oath of Allegiance and Its Signers, 1651–2* (Concord, New Hampshire, 1943), pp. 12–14, reproduces excerpts from papers in the British Record Office relative to Coddington's patent application. The title of Bowen's book is misleading, for the work is actually a detailed, scholarly, though antiquarian-type account of major political events in Rhode Island during the early 1650s. Cromwell again expressed support for the parliamentary patent in a letter to the colony dated March 29, 1655, *RICR,* I, 316–17.

[2] Andrews, II, 37, 41.

[3] *Ibid.,* pp. 41–47. A recent extensive account of the efforts of Clarke and Winthrop to secure the charter is Robert C. Black III, *The Younger John Winthrop* (New York, 1966), pp. 208, 226–32, 239–45. Winthrop's valuable assistance in obtaining the charter is stressed by Black, who also

The 6,500-word corporate instrument [4] devoted relatively brief space to organization of government, but it did provide for the offices of governor, deputy governor, and ten assistants. The original holders of these positions were named in the charter itself, but their successors were "to be from time to time, constituted, elected, and chosen at-large out of the freemen" of the colony ("company"). The charter also provided that certain "of the freemen" should be "elected or deputed" by a majority vote of fellow freemen in their respective towns to "consult," to "advise," and to "determine" the affairs of the colony in connection with the governor, deputy governor, and assistants. It specified that Newport was entitled to six of these "elected or deputed" representatives; Providence, Portsmouth, and Warwick received four each, and two were to be granted to any town which might be

---

contends that Winthrop's decision to compromise on the thorny question of Rhode Island's western boundary angered both the Atherton Company and the Connecticut legislature. *Ibid.,* pp. 255–58, 285–87, 298–302, 326–28. Connecticut had claimed all the land up to the western shore of Narragansett Bay and had actually been granted title to this so-called "Narragansett Country" in its charter of 1662. When Clarke protested, however, Winthrop reluctantly agreed to arbitrate. *Ibid.,* pp. 225, 241–242. An account which stresses Winthrop's membership in the acquisitive Atherton Company and his designs on the Narragansett lands is Richard S. Dunn, "John Winthrop, Jr. and the Narragansett Country," *William and Mary Quarterly,* 3rd Ser., XIII (Jan., 1956), 68–86; and Dunn, *Puritans and Yankees: The Winthrop Dynasty of New England, 1630–1717* (Princeton, N.J., 1962), pp. 108–147. On Clarke see the useful but uncritical Thomas W. Bicknell, *Story of Dr. John Clarke* (Providence, 1915). Clarke's views on the separation of church and state are expressed in his polemical *Ill Newes from New-England* (London, 1652) reprinted in the Massachusetts Historical Society *Collections,* 4th Ser., II (1854).

[4] There were two distinct forms of colonial government — the corporation and the province. Provinces were of two types, proprietary and royal, but in both power proceeded from above downward because the source of authority lay outside the province. The corporate colony was more democratic and self-governing for its power rested upon members of the corporation who were also freemen of the colony. Only Massachusetts (until 1691), Connecticut and Rhode Island became legally recognized corporations and thus self-sufficing political units. Cf. Herbert L. Osgood, "The Classification of Colonial Governments," *Annual Report of the American Historical Association for the Year 1895,* pp. 617–629.

established in the future. This apportionment was equitable in 1663, but its inflexibility would become a source of grave discontent.

The governor, deputy governor,[5] assistants and representatives or deputies were collectively called the "General Assembly." Each member of this body had one vote. The Assembly, with the governor presiding, was to meet at least twice annually in May and October. The only charter-imposed qualification for members was that they be freemen of the colony.

Rhode Island's legislature was endowed by the charter with extraordinary power. It could make or repeal any law, if such action was not "repugnant" to the laws of England, set or alter the time and place of its meeting, and grant commissions. It could exercise extensive powers over the judicial affairs of the colony, prescribe punishments for legal offenses, grant pardons, regulate elections, create and incorporate additional towns, and "choose, nominate and appoint such . . . persons as they shall think fit" to hold the status of freemen.

The royal charter also mandated annual elections for all at-large officers of the colony, provided for the raising and governing of a militia, conferred rights of fishery along the coast of New England, encouraged immigration to the colony, established acceptable boundaries (which included the Pawcatuck River as the western line of demarcation), and provided that the land within those boundaries be held "in free and common soccage." [6]

---

[5] The membership of the deputy governor in the Assembly is not clearly stated in the charter. One could interpret the charter's phraseology to include the deputy governor in the Assembly only in the absence or with the permission of the governor. Rhode Islanders, however, chose to give the deputy governor regular membership in the legislature.

[6] This summation, including the several quotations, is taken from the charter of 1663 as published in *RICR*, II, 1–21. The land held in "free and common soccage" was also held "as of the Manor of East Greenwich, in our county of Kent," according to the terms of the charter. The law of Kent was the law of Gavelkind under which real estate descended in equal portions to all male heirs. Rhode Island, before specifically banning the practice in 1770, sometimes utilized primogeniture in cases of intestacy, thus violating her charter. Stokes, pp. 34–35; Edward Cheyney,

An additional example of the charter's generous grant of governmental autonomy was the absence of a provision for appeal to the king in council in private causes. In this respect the Rhode Island charter furnished a principal exhibit supporting the theory of a royal animus against Massachusetts Bay, for although the absence of a general appeal clause appeared to foreclose recourse by private litigants to the king, the colony itself was granted the right of appeal "in all matters of publique controversy" with the other New England colonies. This provision was probably inserted because of the boundary claims of Rhode Island's avaricious neighbors and as a possible safeguard against the pressures of the powerful Bay Colony.[7]

The royal document also asserted, with language not unknown in other colonial charters, that inhabitants of the colony "shall have and enjoy all liberties and immunities of free and natural subjects . . . as if they . . . were born within the realm of England." This clause and its alleged violation would cause the mother country serious difficulties in a century hence.

Finally, the charter's most liberal and generous provision bestowed upon the inhabitants of the tiny colony "full liberty in religious concernments." The document commanded that

> Noe person within the sayd colonye, at any time hereafter, shall bee any wise molested, punished, disquieted, or called in question, for any differences in opinione in matters of religion, and

---

"The Manor of East Greenwich in the County of Kent," *American Historical Review,* XI (Oct., 1905), 29–35, contends that the charter phraseology that required land to be held "as of the Manor of East Greenwich" generally had "little if any real significance for the colonies." Cheyney's claim (as it applies to Rhode Island) is persuasively disputed by Sidney S. Rider, "The Meaning of the Phrase 'The Manor of East Greenwich in Our County of Kent,' in the Charter of Rhode Island in 1663," *Book Notes,* XXIII (Feb. 10, 1906), 17–27.

[7] Joseph Henry Smith, *Appeals to the Privy Council from the American Plantations* (New York, 1965), pp. 52–53, hereafter cited as Smith, *Appeals.* Smith says: "It is arguable that the operation of this clause would in effect amend the charters of contiguous colonies. For it would force an adversary to appear before the King whatever the terms of its charter, or permit Rhode Island to secure an *ex parte* hearing." Herbert L. Osgood, *The American Colonies in the Seventeenth Century* (New York, 1904–07), III, 170, shares Smith's opinion that a royal animus

doe not actually disturb the civill peace of our sayd colony; but
that all and everye person and persons may, from tyme to tyme,
and at all tymes hereafter, freelye and fullye have and enjoye
his and theire owne judgments and consciences, in matters of religious concernments, throughout the tract of lande hereafter
mentioned; they behaving themselves peaceablie and quietlie,
and not useing this libertie to lycentiousnesse and profanenesse,
nor to the civill injurye or outward disturbeance of others; any
lawe, statute, or clause, therein contayned, or to bee contayned,
usage or custome of this realme, to the contrary hereof, in any
wise, not withstanding.[8]

This guarantee of absolute religious liberty was a vindication of
Williams's beliefs and royal recognition of the fundamental principles upon which the Providence Plantation was founded — absolute freedom of conscience and complete separation of church
and state. As Williams observed, this liberality stemmed from the
king's willingness to "experiment" in order to ascertain "whether
civil government could consist with such liberty of conscience." [9]
This was the "lively experiment" upon which the government of
Rhode Island was based.

---

against Massachusetts Bay "furnished a strong reason . . . for the
grant of the Rhode Island charter."

[8] *RICR,* II, 5–6.

[9] Williams to Major Mason, June 22, 1670, Williams, *Writings,* VI,
346. Williams explained to his Connecticut correspondent the circumstances surrounding the granting of the charter as follows: "The King's
Majesty winks at Barbadoes, where Jews and all sorts of Christian and
Antichristian persuasions are free, but our grant, some few weeks after
yours sealed, though granted as soon, if not before yours, is crowned with
the King's extraordinary favor to the colony, as being a banished one, in
which his Majesty declared himself that he would experiment, whether
civil government could consist with such liberty of conscience. This his
Majesty's grant was startled at by his Majesty's high officers of State,
who were to view it in course before the sealing, but fearing the lion's
roaring, they couched, against their wills, in obedience to his Majesty's
pleasure." For the place of Rhode Island's charter as a landmark in the
development of the American tradition of church-state separation see
Anson Phelps Stokes, *Church and State in the United States* (New
York, 1950), I, 194–205, 442–43. For good discussions of the attempt
by Williams and John Clarke to reconcile religious liberty with civil order
see Theodore Dwight Bozeman, "Religious Liberty and the Problem of
Order in Early Rhode Island," *New England Quarterly,* XLV (March,
1972), 44–64, and Robert d. Brunkow, "Love and Order in Roger Williams' Writings," *Rhode Island History,* XXXV (Nov., 1976), 115–26.

With good reason the charter of 1663 won overwhelming approbation of the colonists and prompted nineteenth-century historian George Bancroft to remark (with only a modicum of hyperbole) that "no where in the world were life, liberty and property, safer than in Rhode Island." [10]

II

To the anxiety and chagrin of the colonists, their royal patent was neither safe nor secure, for Rhode Island's individualistic and sometimes defiant attitude prompted a number of attempts by English officials to have its charter repealed or at least made subject to more effective royal control. The first major onslaught came from Edward Randolph in 1685 during the formative stages of that abortive attempt at colonial consolidation — the Dominion of New England. Surprisingly, Rhode Island in 1686 submitted rather passively to Governor Edmund Andros of the dominion with one typical exception. Rhode Island concealed its charter, thus making it possible for it to claim, once the dominion was overthrown, that it had never actually surrendered its precious basic law.[11] This incident furnishes a good example of

---

[10] George Bancroft, *History of the United States from the Discovery of the American Continent* (Boston, 1834–75), II, 64. According to John E. Pomfret and Floyd M. Shumway the grant of religious liberty in the Rhode Island charter was conferred upon other colonies in the 1660s. They claim that "Freedom of conscience for colonists was not questioned despite the Act of Uniformity passed in England in 1662. Jamaica, New Jersey and the Carolinas, as well as Rhode Island, also received this boon." *Founding the American Colonies, 1583–1660* (New York, 1970), p. 227. Pomfret and Shumway, however, neglect to point out that, *except for Rhode Island,* "the term liberty of conscience so frequently used during this period went no further than to cover 'all persons professing the faith of the Lord Jesus Christ.' " Andrews, II, 311n.

[11] *Calendar of State Papers: Colonial Series, America and West Indies* (London, 1896–1939), 1685–1688, #279, #304, #632, #645, #750, #844, #857, #902, #925; hereafter cited as *CSP;* Robert A. Lindemann, "Important Factors in the Colonial History of Rhode Island Influencing Her Participation in the Revolutionary Movement," (unpublished doctoral

Rhode Island's standing policy toward the mother country — concession in words and resistance in deeds.

Despite the failure of the Dominion of New England, Randolph's suggested program of combining Rhode Island and Connecticut with other colonies to form one royal colony persisted well into the eighteenth century. Such a plan was advanced during King William's War as part of the mother country's general attempt to "tighten-up" her military and mercantile policy, and it was again suggested in 1723 by a home government impatient with Rhode Island and Connecticut because of their long unsettled boundary dispute.[12]

Another method of attacking the privileges and powers granted by the nearly autonomous corporate charter of Rhode Island consisted in disregarding or overriding certain of its provisions. These invasions of privilege were stubbornly resisted. For example, Massachusetts' royal governors William Phips during King William's War and Joseph Dudley during Queen Anne's War were unsuccessful in their attempts to assume active control over the colony's militia, despite official authorization. In 1704–05 Dudley endeavored to implement an opinion of the royal attorney general that governors might be appointed by the Crown

---

dissertation, Indiana University, 1952), pp. 5–9. Edward Randolph was a commercial and political agent of the Crown who made repeated suggestions for the reorganization of colonial administration from the time of his first arrival in Boston in 1676 until his death in 1703. The best works on this controversial figure are Michael G. Hall, *Edward Randolph and the American Colonies, 1676–1703* (Chapel Hill, North Carolina, 1960), and Robert N. Toppan and Alfred T. S. Goodrick, eds., *Edward Randolph: Including His Letters and Official Papers . . . 1676–1703,* 7 vols. (Boston, 1898–1909). The standard account of the dominion of New England is Viola F. Barnes, *The Dominion of New England* (New Haven, 1923). For the reaction of Rhode Island's General Assembly to the dominion (including an account of the hiding of the charter), and the reproduction of a number of documents relating to Rhode Island's role within the dominion, see *RICR,* III, 175–269. Also useful is Philip Haffenden, "The Crown and Colonial Charters, 1675–1688," *William and Mary Quarterly,* 3rd Ser., XV (July, 1958), 297–311; XV (Oct., 1958), 452–66.

[12] Lindemann, pp. 11–13; *CSP* 1695, #1964; 1697, #764; *RICR,* IV, 275.

in a charter colony in case of pressing danger, but this bold maneuver also failed.[13]

During the imperial reorganization of the 1690s, reports of Rhode Island's lack of participation in the first phase of the great Anglo-French confrontation for empire, rumors that the colony was countenancing piratical activities, and repeated refusals by the colony to recognize the commissions of some admiralty court officials prompted the strict and circumspect Board of Trade to authorize an investigation of Rhode Island's activities and government. The inquiry was conducted in 1699 by Richard Coote, Earl of Bellomont and governor of New York, Massachusetts, and New Hampshire (1699–1701). Bellomont was instructed to obtain copies of all the colony's laws and other public records "relating to the administration of that government." To this end the English investigator visited Rhode Island and then issued a scathing summary of conditions there. The people, he said, had a disdain for learning and were "shamefully ignorant." His report also disclosed an unjustified exercise of the judicial function by the General Assembly, violations of the Acts of Trade, usurpation of admiralty jurisdiction,[14] and the harboring of pirates.

[13] Lindemann, pp. 14–18; *CSP,* 1691, #1916; 1693, #591; 1694, #999; 1701, #1066, #1067; 1704, #23; Louise Phelps Kellogg, "The American Colonial Charter. A Study of English Administration in Relation Thereto, Chiefly After 1688," *Annual Report of the American Historical Association for the Year 1903* (Washington, 1904), I, 252–59. The decision of the attorney and solicitor general concerning Crown appointment of the governor is alluded to in *Acts of the Privy Council of England, Colonial Series . . . 1613–1783,* eds. William L. Grant and James Munro (Hereford, 1908–1912), VI, 87, hereafter cited as *Acts of the Privy Council.*

[14] Bellomont's complaint about Rhode Island's usurpation of admiralty jurisdiction stemmed from the colony's creation of its own admiralty court. This law establishing a colonial admiralty jurisdiction was notable in that it was invalidated by the Privy Council in 1704, because the council ruled that Rhode Island had exceeded her powers under the charter. I believe that this is the only Rhode Island statute ever disallowed by the Privy Council. See *Records of Vice-Admiralty Court of Rhode Island 1716–1752,* ed., Dorothy S. Towle, (Washington, 1936), pp. 81–98; Oliver M. Dickerson, *American Colonial Government, 1696–1765,* (New York, 1962), pp. 235–36; and Marguerite Appleton, "Rhode Island's First Court of Admiralty," *New England Quarterly,* V(1932), 148–58. The disallowance is printed in *Acts of the Privy Council,* II, 457.

Bellomont concluded his twenty-five point indictment, which listed many deviations from the directives of the charter, by asserting that "his Majesty is neither honored nor served by that government, as at present it is managed." [15]

Surprisingly, Bellomont's report did not lead to a rescinding of the Rhode Island charter, but it did furnish some ammunition for a more general attack on all corporate or proprietary charters in the period 1701–07. During these years the Board of Trade strenuously attempted to secure legislation that would nullify all such charters and replace them with royal patents. Among the leaders of the campaign against the five remaining non-royal mainland colonies, of which Rhode Island was avowedly the most recalcitrant, were Edward Randolph, Lord Cornbury, and Joseph Dudley.

After several unsuccessful efforts, the movement to vacate the charters temporarily collapsed in 1707 because of the European military disruptions, the pleadings of William Penn and Sir Henry Ashurst, the decline in influence of Cornbury and Dudley, and Whig opposition to expansion of royal power. A similar though isolated attempt to reduce all non-royal colonies was made in 1715, but it was unavailing principally because of the reluctance of the Whigs to accept an enlargement of royal prerogative, and their solicitude for vested interests.

During this period of travail and anxiety a small but influential group of men, who are called "the Rhode Island royalists" by historian Sidney James, lobbied with the crown to reestablish the government set up for Rhode Island under the Dominion for New England with themselves in control. This group which included John Fones and Francis Brinley, justices of the Dominion, merchant Peleg Sanford, Richard Smith, Jr. and other disappointed Narragansett proprietors, told royal officials that Rhode Island harbored pirates, abused the privilege of granting com-

---

[15] "Report of the Earl of Bellomont, on the Irregularities of Rhode Island," November 27, 1699, *RICR,* III, 385–88. This report, Bellomont's "Journal," and his correspondence with Rhode Island officials were copied from records of the State Paper Office by John Carter Brown and published in *RICR*, III, 385–400.

missions to privateers and violated the acts of trade. The allegations prompted Bellomont's investigation. Their subversive efforts were thwarted by Governor Samuel Cranston (1698–1727) whose outstanding accomplishment during his long tenure was "to bring his colony into a working relation with the imperial government in London while preserving its charter privileges." [16]

Thus did Rhode Island's charter survive the recurring crises of 1685–1723. Though the colony's basic law was threatened thereafter, by the Newport Tory Junto in 1764 and by the Crown on several occasions (principally because of controversial paper money emissions and the *Gaspee* incident of 1772), the charter remained intact, its liberality undiminished.[17]

III

Tenacious Rhode Island's struggle to retain her charter brought some compliance by the colony with the directives of the mother country. One such act of obedience was the codification of Rhode Island's laws. In 1698 Bellomont had been instructed to obtain a complete set of the colony's general statutes in the course of his

---

[16] Lindemann, pp. 20–36; Kellogg, pp. 252–341. Edward Hyde, Viscount Cornbury, was governor of New York and New Jersey, 1702–08; Joseph Dudley was royal governor of Massachusetts, 1702–15. An adequate account of Dudley's career is Everett Kimball, *The Public Life of Joseph Dudley* (New York, 1911). See also James, pp. 110–55.

[17] John Blanchard MacInnes, "Rhode Island Bills of Public Credit, 1710–1755," (unpublished doctoral dissertation, Brown University, 1952), pp. 321–381, 475–541, analyzes English response to Rhode Island's paper money policy. Gertrude Kimball, ed., *The Correspondence of the Colonial Governors of Rhode Island, 1723–1775* (Boston and New York, 1902–03), II, 438, reprints a letter from John Sherwood to Governor Wanton (1774) that alludes to the North ministry's intention to introduce a bill in Parliament which would vacate the colony's charter. Presumably this action was recommended because of the *Gaspee* affair. Lord Horsmanden, during his investigation of the *Gaspee* affair, made a recommendation to the Earl of Dartmouth that Rhode Island and Connecticut be consolidated under a royal governor, *RICR*, VII, 185. The Newport Junto posed a very serious threat to the charter because it launched an attack from within the colony itself. The royalist Junto objected to Rhode Island's factional politics and her resistance to the Sugar and Stamp Acts. See Walter F. Mullen, "Rhode Island and the

investigation. At first Rhode Island compiled mere "leaves of paper stitched indeed together," according to the Board of Trade.[18] Bellomont himself reported:

> Divers of their Acts and laws passed in the General Assembly, are not made and digested into any proper form or method, only framed by way of vote, and kept in loose scripts of paper not entered into any rolls or books; and oft times not to be found when inquiring is made for them at the office, that the people are at a loss to know what is law among them.[19]

This deplorable condition was remedied by the colony, however, for in 1705 a satisfactory manuscript digest was prepared. Then, in 1719, Rhode Island's first published compilation of her general laws appeared.[20]

The Digest of 1719 figures prominently in any discussion of the implementation of the famed guarantee of religious liberty contained in the charter of 1663. Although the royal charter had specifically stated that no person "'shall be in any wise molested, punished, disquieted, or called in question, for any differences of opinion in matters of religion," the 1719 code contained the following provision:

Imperial Reorganization of 1763–1766," (unpublished doctoral dissertation, Fordham University, 1965), pp. 175–85; David S. Lovejoy, *Rhode Island Politics and the American Revolution, 1760–1776* (Providence, 1958), pp. 48–51; Edmund S. Morgan, *The Gentle Puritan: A Life of Ezra Stiles, 1727–1795* (New Haven, 1962), pp. 219–25; Edmund S. and Helen M. Morgan, *The Stamp Act Crisis,* rev. ed., (New York, 1963), pp. 70–74; and Carl Bridenbaugh, *Silas Downer: Forgotten Patriot* (Providence, 1974), pp. 12–19.

[18] "The Board of Trade to the Governor and Company of Rhode Island," August 11, 1699, *RICR,* III, 376.

[19] November 27, 1699, *RICR,* III, 388.

[20] "Laws and Acts, Made from the First Settlement of Her Majesties Colony of Rhode Island and Providence Plantations" (1705), Rhode Island State Archives. A facsimile of this codification was published in 1896 by Sidney S. Rider, the noted Rhode Island historian and antiquarian. In 1895 Rider printed a facsimile of the 1719 published compilation which contains an excellent bibliographical and historical examination of all the folio digests (*viz.,* 1730, 1745, 1767, and the partial or supplementary digests of 1752 and 1772) of Rhode Island's colonial laws. These compilations of Rhode Island's laws will hereafter be cited as *Digest* with the appropriate year of publication.

> All Men *Professing Christianity,* and of Competent Estates, and
> of Civil Conversation, who acknowledge, and are Obedient to
> the Civil Magistrate, though of different Judgmnts in Religious
> Affairs (*Roman Catholicks only excepted*) shall be admitted
> Free-men, And shall have Liberty to Chuse and be Chosen Offi-
> cers in the Colony both Military and Civil.[21] (Italics mine.)

This act was allegedly passed in the March 1663 session of the
General Assembly. Its enactment then or at any time prior to
1719 is possible but highly improbable. In the original proceedings of the General Assembly for 1663 no such statute appears,
nor is it found in the preserved proceedings of any subsequent
session. Further, it is not contained in the manuscript "Laws and
Acts" of 1705.[22]

The passage of this restrictive "law" during 1663 is particularly implausible in view of the colonists' statutory enactment in
May 1664 of the religious guarantees of the charter. The fact
that Roger Williams was a member of the first assemblies renders the act's passage at that time even more doubtful.[23]

It can also be inferred that the controversial "law" was not
enacted at any time during the seventeenth century, because
Bellomont reported in his "Journal" on September 22, 1699, that
the Test Act was not enforced in the colony. If Rhode Island had
passed the alleged law of 1663 in defiance of her charter, it seems

---

[21] *Digest of 1719,* p. 3; *RICR,* II, 36–37. The best study of this dis-
puted law is Sidney S. Rider, *An Inquiry Concerning the Origin of the
Clause in the Laws of Rhode Island (1719–1783) Disfranchising Roman
Catholics* (Providence, 1889). This work is No. 1, 2nd Series, of *Rhode
Island Historical Tracts.* Rider's findings were accepted and summarized
in John Richard Meade, "The Truth Concerning the Disfranchisement
of Catholics in Rhode Island," *American Catholic Quarterly Review,*
XIX (Jan., 1894), 169–177. See also Patrick T. Conley and Matthew J.
Smith, *Catholicism in Rhode Island: The Formative Era* (Providence,
1976), pp. 7–9.

[22] The most detailed study of colonial Rhode Island, Samuel G.
Arnold, *History of the State of Rhode Island and Providence Plantations*
[1636–1790] (New York, 1859–60), II, 492, erroneously claims that the
discriminatory statute was included in the 1705 manuscript digest.

[23] *RICR,* II, 57. The Royal Commissioners in 1665 observed of Rhode
Islanders that "they allow liberty of conscience and worship to all who
live civilly." *Ibid.,* II, 127.

likely that she would have employed such a ready-made excuse as the Test Act to justify this violation.[24]

The discriminatory statute was inserted into the Digest of 1719 by the compilers of that volume to cater to the whims of the recent defenders of their charter, the English Whigs, whose anti-Catholic sentiments had been aroused by the Jacobite efforts in 1715–16 to place the Catholic Pretender on the English throne. In fact Jacobite uprisings had prompted the passage by Parliament of proscriptive legislation against "Papists" in June 1716.[25]

To Rhode Island's discredit this statute, enacted as part of the Digest of 1719, was reaffirmed by the Assembly in the digests of 1730, 1745, and 1767. Not until 1783 was the arbitrary disqualification of Catholics removed. The act which accomplished this, however, not only failed to recognize the true origins of the disabling "statute," it also neglected to define the civil status of those professing the Jewish faith.[26]

Other significant blemishes on the charter's guarantee of religious equality were the freemanship restriction imposed against Jews and the colony's refusal to naturalize adherents of the Jewish religion. Although Jews enjoyed freedom of worship,

---

[24] *RICR,* III, 390.

[25] The vigorous anti-Catholic nature of early eighteenth-century English Whiggism is evident in such writings as *Cato's Letters* and *The Independent Whig.* Cf. David L. Jacobson, ed., *The English Libertarian Heritage* (Indianapolis, 1965), pp. xvii–xlvii. See also Basil Williams, *The Whig Supremacy: 1714–1760,* 2nd ed. (Oxford, 1962), pp. 70–81, 150–51. Charles Butler, *Historical Memoirs of the English, Irish, and Scottish Catholics, Since the Reformation,* 3rd ed. (London, 1822), III, 165–178, contains a convenient summary and compilation of the acts against Roman Catholics passed during the reign of George I (1714–27).

[26] It should be noted that the Catholic population of colonial Rhode Island was negligible. See Robert H. Lord, John E. Sexton, and Edward T. Harrington, *History of the Archdiocese of Boston* (New York, 1944), I, 618, 667–68; Thomas F. Cullen, *The Catholic Church in Rhode Island* (North Providence, 1936), pp. 35–43; and Conley and Smith, pp. 4–7. There were no Catholic churches in Rhode Island colony. For an account of the small Jewish community in Newport see Max J. Kohler, "The Jews in Newport," *Publications of the American Jewish Historical Society,* No. 6 (1897), 61–80; and Morris A. Gutstein, *The Story of the Jews of Newport* (New York, 1936). The act of 1783 is printed in *RICR,* IX, 674–75.

none, however qualified or competent, was ever made a freeman of the colony of Rhode Island. On the issue of naturalization, both the Superior Court and the General Assembly in 1761–62 denied the citizenship petitions of Aaron Lopez and Isaac Elizer because they were non-Christians. The lower house of the Assembly further admonished them that adherents of their religion were "not Liable to be chosen into any Office in this Colony Nor allowed to give a Vote as a Freeman in Choosing others."[27]

The most careful student of Rhode Island Jewish history asserts that no evidence exists that anyone of the Jewish faith was ever naturalized in the colony of Rhode Island. But the rejection in the Lopez case, it should be noted, stemmed from the petitioner's political as well as religious affiliations. Lopez was closely associated with Nicholas Brown, an ally of Governor Stephen Hopkins. This prompted Hopkins's opponents in the Assembly, led by former governor Samuel Ward, to dismiss the Lopez petition.[28]

Although Jews suffered exclusion from citizenship, no explicit or formal barriers were erected by the colony against the naturalization of Catholics. On some occasions it appears that Catholic aspirants for citizenship were asked to abjure political allegiance to the Pope and the Stuart Pretender before their petition for naturalization was granted by the General Assembly. Portuguese Catholic Joseph Antunes was required to abjure when he sought citizenship in December 1750, but there is no evidence that his countryman James Lucena was compelled to adhere to such a procedure when he was naturalized in February 1761.[29]

---

[27] David C. Adelman, "Strangers: Civil Rights of Jews in the Colony of Rhode Island," *Rhode Island History,* XIII (July, 1954), 65–77. The quote is from the Assembly's decision on the petitions reproduced in Adelman. The originals are in the Rhode Island State Archives.

[28] Stanley F. Chyet, *Lopez of Newport: Colonial American Merchant Prince* (Detroit, 1970), pp. 34–41; Adelman, pp. 74–76; Arnold, II, 494–96; James B. Hedges, *The Browns of Providence Plantations: Colonial Years* (Cambridge, Mass., 1952), 94–99, 151–52; Lovejoy, *Rhode Island Politics,* pp. 76, 204. Lovejoy's study contains an excellent, detailed account of the famous Ward-Hopkins controversy.

[29] On Antunes see Records of the Rhode Island General Assembly, RISA, VII, (1746–1757), 223–24; hereafter cited RIGA Records. Lucena

Despite the aforementioned diversions from the charter,[30] religious liberty enjoyed by colonial Rhode Islanders seems to have been broader than that possessed by any of His Majesty's subjects including those within the realm of England itself. Though civil restrictions were imposed on some because of their religious affiliations, freedom of worship was never impaired in the Rhode Island colony.

IV

A summary of several developments in the implementation of the royal charter's administrative provisions is necessary for a proper understanding of the state's constitutional history. The

---

was ethnically a Jew, but like other Jews he was pressured into accepting Catholicism by the Portuguese government. What was most unusual about Lucena was that he maintained the Catholic attachment of his youth after his arrival in Rhode Island. Aaron Lopez and most other Jewish-Portuguese expatriates immediately embraced the Jewish religion once they had reached the safety of America. Chyet, pp. 14–17, 31, 34–35; Adelman, p. 72; *RICR,* VI, 262, 267. Arnold, II, 185, 494–96, gives as an undocumented example of Catholic naturalization, Stephen Decatur, grandfather of the famous commodore, who was naturalized in 1753, *RICR,* V, 367. Lawrence Leland Lowther, "Rhode Island Colonial Government, 1732," (unpublished doctoral dissertation, University of Washington, 1964), pp. 22–23, after consulting an early biography of the commodore, suggests that Decatur was not a Genoese Catholic as Arnold states, but was probably a Huguenot. It is possible, however, that Francis Ferrari, another former subject of Genoa, naturalized in 1751, was a Catholic. *RICR,* V, 340.

[30] A final invasion of the civil liberties of a minority consisted in the colony's espousal of Negro slavery. Rhode Island in colonial times not only condoned slavery as did other northern colonies, it eagerly embraced it. The slave trade played a major role in Rhode Island's commercial development, and the institution of involuntary Negro servitude was firmly entrenched in the "Narragansett Country" of southern Rhode Island where a combination of the bylaws of South Kingstown and the general laws of the colony produced a slave code closely resembling that of eighteenth-century Virginia. On the eve of the Revolution the proportion of Negroes in Rhode Island was greater than that of any other New England colony. The royal charter was understandably silent on the subject of slavery because the institution was widely accepted in colonial America. The slave system which prevailed in eighteenth-century Rhode Island, however, was at variance with the liberal spirit of that

most important of these developments relate to legislative, judicial, and executive affairs, freemanship and suffrage.[31]

The most significant feature of Rhode Island's colonial government was the supremacy of the legislature. The General Assembly implemented and expanded the many prerogatives conferred upon it by the charter. Through its vast appointive power, its activities extended into every facet of Rhode Island life. The legislature was the focal point of government—the executive, the judiciary, and even the towns were subservient to it.[32]

---

document. On the colonial slave trade see Milton Longhorn, "The Rise of the Merchant Class in Rhode Island," (unpublished doctoral dissertation, University of Wisconsin, 1936), pp. 41–73; Hedges, pp. 70–85. On Rhode Island domestic slavery see William Davis Miller, "The Narragansett Planters," *Proceedings of the American Antiquarian Society,* XLIII (1933), 49–115; W. D. Johnston, "Slavery in Rhode Island, 1755–1776," *Publications of the Rhode Island Historical Society,* II, (1894), 109–164; Edward Channing, "The Narragansett Planters; A Study of Causes," *Johns Hopkins University Studies in Political and Social Science* (Baltimore, 1886), IV, 105–127; and Lorenzo Johnston Greene, *The Negro in Colonial New England* (New York, 1942), *passim.* In 1652, when the colony was temporarily split by Coddington's commission, the northern towns of Providence and Warwick, acting jointly, passed an anti-slave measure which limited the period of involuntary servitude to ten years, *RICR,* I, 243. After the reunion it apparently became inoperative because such sentiments were not shared by dominant Newport. The 1652 act has been cited as "the first legislative act of emancipation in the American colonies," Pomfret and Shumway, p. 221.

[31] In the following discussion the recurrent question of defining the boundaries established by the charter and the amorphous problem of local government have not been analyzed. The former plays a role in Rhode Island's constitutional history when persistent boundary disputes cause the exasperated mother country to recommend the absorption of Rhode Island by a larger colony, e.g., the dispute with Connecticut in 1723, *RICR,* IV, 275, 303–08; see also John Hutchins Cady, *Rhode Island Boundaries 1636–1936* (Providence, 1936); and especially James, pp. 75–93, 127–30, 138–46.

[32] The charter of 1663 effected far-reaching and important changes in the character and scope of local government and brought about a substantial diminution of local autonomy, especially in judicial and administrative areas. One of the earliest acts of the new colonial government annulled the local referendum statute (*RICR,* II, 27). Under the royal charter the general government became "legally, and very soon *de facto,* the supreme legislative assembly and the rights to local government which the towns exercised were derived wholly from it. No further charters

Although the authority of the Assembly was substantial, it was not unlimited. The king, his Privy Council, and Parliament were external if seldom used checks, and the charter's proviso that colonial statutes be not "repugnant" to the laws of England was another legal curb. The most powerful barriers to legislative omnipotence, however, were the freemen themselves. The frequency of elections, at least semiannually for deputies and annually for the governor, deputy governor, and assistants, kept the Assembly, and especially the lower house, close to the thinking and desires of the electorate. In addition, the oft-employed practice of submitting important questions to the freemen of the several towns before final determination and action shows the solicitude of the Assembly for public opinion and approbation. By this common procedure the legislature would direct the freemen at their town meeting to "instruct" or inform their deputies of the position to be taken on pending legislation.[33]

---

were issued to the towns during the colonial period. All of the governmental rights were granted to them in the form of separate statutes. Most of such statutes were permissive and seem to have been enacted at the request of the town, but a sufficiently large number were mandatory and evidenced the full sovereignty of a central government." Stokes, pp. 62–63. The question of home rule is not treated in this study; it does not become a major reform issue until the late nineteenth century. Cf. Amasa M. Eaton, *Constitution-Making in Rhode Island* (Providence, 1899), pp. 34–67. Eaton was a pioneer in the home rule movement. His statement that the charter of 1663 "made no change in the relation of the towns to the colony" (*Ibid.*, p. 64) does not accord with law or experience, but neither did the charter make the towns mere "creatures" of the state and deny them any inherent right of local self government as the Rhode Island Supreme Court questionably asserted in *City of Newport v. Horton,* 22 R.I. 196 (1900) and *City of Providence v. Moulton,* 52 R.I. 236 (1932). The best studies of town government in colonial Rhode Island are Lowther, pp. 45–127; Stokes, pp. 1–130, and William E. Foster, "Town Government in Rhode Island," *Johns Hopkins University Studies in Political and Social Science* (Baltimore, 1886), IV, 69–104.

[33] Deputies were regularly elected semiannually at town meetings in April and August prior to the regular May and October sessions of the Assembly. An act mandating annual elections for deputies was passed in June 1733 but repealed the following December. *RICR,* IV, 484–85; RIGA, Records, V, 124, 147; and Kenneth Colegrove, "New England Town Mandates; Instructions to the Deputies in Colonial Legislatures,"

In a survey such as this, the manifold functions of the legislature cannot be detailed, but certain procedural and structural innovations affecting that body must be mentioned. Among these were establishment of a general council and the adoption of a bicameral system. Soon after reception of the charter, the governor, deputy governor, and assistants combined to form an executive body known as the general council. The only reference in the charter to such an agency was the authorization for the governor, or deputy governor, and a majority of assistants to provide for the defense of the colony when the Assembly was not in session. The charter does not employ the term "council" in referring to these officials. The council device may have come into use because the charter modeled the government of Rhode Island after that of a trading company or corporation, whose executive body was a council. Massachusetts practice may also have served as a precedent. For whatever reason, the general council was created to supervise colony affairs when the Assembly was not sitting. Its decisions were usually of an interim nature, often labeled temporary and subject to confirmation or rejection at the next session of the full Assembly.[34]

A major structural change within the legislature itself occurred in 1696. In that year the seeds of bicameralism implanted in the colony's basic law reached maturity with the formal statutory division of the General Assembly into an upper house composed of governor, deputy governor, and ten assistants elected on an at-large basis and a lower house consisting of deputies elected from the towns according to the rigid six-four-two ratio established by the charter.[35]

Publications of the Colonial Society of Massachusetts, XXI (Dec., 1919), 441–49.

[34] Lowther, p. 7.

[35] *RICR,* III, 313. For early attempts at bicameralism see *RICR,* II, 124, 157, 181. During the eighteenth century there were two significant irregularities in the designation or selection of assistants. In 1722 when Kingstown was divided into North Kingstown and South Kingstown, raising the number of municipalities to ten, the two new towns were guaranteed by statute that they should have one assistant each, *RICR,* IV, 316. This privilege became increasingly unfair as more towns were

Another important aspect of the colony's governmental machinery was her judicial system. By its general charge to the legislature "to appoint, order and direct, erect and settle, such places and courts of jurisdiction, for the hearing and determining of all actions, cases, matters and things . . . as they shall think fit," the charter did not fundamentally alter the judicial structure of 1647. The general court of trial was retained, and in 1664 the Assembly ordered that its sessions be held semiannually with the governor or deputy governor, and at least six assistants presiding. Several inferior courts were from time to time created.

Because legislative and judicial functions were for a time combined in the same body of men (namely, the governor, deputy governor, and assistants), the General Assembly often exercised functions now considered the exclusive domain of the judicial branch. For example, it heard and often reversed appeals and petitions from the judgment of the general courts of trial, and almost any part of the judicial process was open to its inspection and possible correction. The nature of its involvement in judicial affairs appeared to Lord Bellomont (and many observers since) to have been a usurpation of power not justified by the charter.[36]

To trace the complex and sometimes inscrutable evolution of Rhode Island's colonial court system would require a lengthy volume. Perhaps it was this complexity that prompted John Russell Bartlett to exclude most of the court proceedings from his

---

created. Also, when an assistant's position became vacant the General Assembly filled the post. This practice was authorized by a 1664 statute (*RICR*, II, 83–84). However, the charter stipulated that vacancies in the ranks of the assistants be filled by the governor, deputy governor, assistants *and company* (*RICR*, II, 11) and this provision renders at least questionable the election of assistants exclusively by the Assembly on numerous occasions, *e.g., RICR*, III, 523–24; V, 65. In 1738 the legislature elected a deputy governor to fill a vacancy caused by the death of an incumbent. *RICR*, IV, 545.

36 Bellomont's "Report," *RICR*, III, 386. In defense of the Assembly it should be noted that its judicial role in colonial Rhode Island was similar to that played by the English House of Lords. Plural office-holding was not unique to colonial Rhode Island. It was a relatively common condition which existed prior to the ascendancy of the separation of powers principle. See Ellen E. Brennan, *Plural Office-Holding in Massachusetts, 1760–1780* (Chapel Hill, N.C., 1945).

published *Records* of the Colony of Rhode Island.[37] In the compass of this study only the structural landmarks of that development can be mentioned.

Of primary importance was the rearrangement of the court system in 1729, through the use of three counties (Newport, Providence, and King's) as units of judicial administration.[38] The lowest tribunal in this county-based structure was the local court of the justice of the peace. This agency, which was in continuous session, had original jurisdiction in minor matters and bound over more serious offenders to the higher court having jurisdiction. On the next level were the courts of general sessions of the peace and the courts of common pleas. The former, established in each county, were conducted by all the local justices of the peace or any five of them, and were empowered to try all criminal cases, capital crimes excepted. Their sessions were semiannual and their decisions could be appealed to the highest court. They in turn exercised appellate jurisdiction over all petty offenses originally triable by a justice of the peace.

The courts of common pleas were civil courts conducted by "judicious" persons chosen by the Assembly from their respective counties. These appointees, upon their selection, were elevated to justiceship of the peace. The jurisdiction of these courts, which was both original and appellate, extended to the trial of nearly all civil actions arising in the county. Their business was conducted semiannually together with the courts of general sessions. These courts while nominally distinct from the courts of general sessions were usually conducted by the same personnel.[39]

---

[37] A comparison of Bartlett's ten published volumes with manuscript records in Rhode Island State Archives reveals numerous omissions of court proceedings, especially those of the eighteenth century. A number of these records have been subsequently published. Cf. Farrell, IX, 65–66, for a convenient listing.

[38] *RICR*, IV, 427–28. The original counties, Providence and Newport, were created in 1703 and had judicial functions within the old system. *RICR*, III, 477.

[39] There was considerable overlapping of personnel in the lower courts. For example, judges of courts of common pleas presided in justice of the peace courts for criminal cases and in general sessions of the peace courts as well as in the courts of common pleas. See diagrams of Rhode

At the apex of the county system was the Superior Court. Held at Newport, it consisted of the governor, deputy governor, and assistants. The Superior Court possessed original jurisdiction in certain major cases, but its primary function consisted in reviewing appeals from decisions of the courts of general sessions and the courts of common pleas. Petitions from decisions of the Superior Court, however, were often entertained and acted upon by the ubiquitous General Assembly and occasionally appeals from the court's verdict were accepted by the king in council.[40]

In 1741, a so-called Court of Equity was erected to hear and determine all appeals in personal actions from judgments of Superior Court. The act constituting this tribunal declared that "the judgment and determination of said court shall be final, saving an appeal to his Majesty in council in those cases wherein the law hath already provided." This court was abolished in 1743.[41]

Another noteworthy development in colonial judicial admin-

Island's county-based court system in Lowther, pp. 181, 192. The judiciary act of 1729 provided that judges and clerks of the courts of common pleas and the courts of general sessions should serve for good behavior. In 1733 the act was amended to provide for the annual election of these officials by the General Assembly. *RICR,* IV, 484; *Digest of 1745,* p. 171; and Francis I. McCanna, "A Study of the History and Jurisdiction of Rhode Island Courts," *Journal of the American Irish Historical Society,* XXII (1923), 170–95.

[40] *RICR,* IV, 427–28; *Digest of 1730,* pp. 188–205; Lowther, pp. 174–192; Stiness, "Struggle for Judicial Supremacy," pp. 103–5. The full title of the Superior Court was the Superior Court of Judicature, Court of Assize and General Gaol Delivery. This name was changed in 1798 to the Supreme Judicial Court. It should be noted that the upper house of the Assembly, the general council, and the Superior Court (until 1746) were composed of the same group of men, *viz.,* the governor, deputy governor and assistants. This overlapping of functions was a salient feature of colonial Rhode Island's governmental structure; it extended to town government as well, because assistants were charged with the performance of administrative and judicial functions in the towns where they resided. Their multiple powers and duties (which included membership on the town council until 1733) are summarized in Stokes, pp. 62–79.

[41] *RICR,* V, 22, 76; *Acts of the Privy Council,* IV, 10. For the court's proceedings see Rhode Island Equity Court: File Papers, Sept. 1741–Dec., 1743, 7 vols. mss., RISA; and Zechariah Chafee, Jr. "Records of

istration came in February 1746, when the governor and assistants were removed from the bench of the Superior Court and replaced by one chief justice and four associates. Legislative influence was not significantly diminished at this juncture. Judges could still be members of the Assembly, so those deputies or assistants appointed to the bench usually retained their legislative posts. Furthermore all judges were subject to annual appointment by the Assembly.[42] During the session preceding the 1746 Superior Court Act, the legislature established a formal procedure for receiving, "hearing and determining" petitions praying relief from court decisions, thus strengthening and reaffirming its appellate powers which were similar to those possessed by the House of Lords.[43] These practices endured for the remainder of the colonial period. In fact, the petition process and the system of annual appointment persisted until the establishment of the state constitution in 1843.

A final important aspect of colonial Rhode Island's legal system was the process of appeal to the Privy Council. The absence in the royal charter of a provision for private appeal from the decision of the colony's courts was remedied by the mother country in 1699 when an order in council commanded that such appeals be allowed. Thereafter, Rhode Island became the most prolific source of appeals to the Privy Council not only because of the low minimum appealable amount established by the General Assembly for civil actions, but also because of the "litigiousness of the inhabitants," and the apparent deficiencies in the quality and capacity of the colony's courts.[44]

---

the Rhode Island Court of Equity, 1741–1743," *Publications of the Colonial Society of Massachusetts,* XXXV (1951), 91–118.

[42] *Digest of 1752,* pp. 27–30. Stiness, "Struggle for Judicial Supremacy," pp. 104–05, errs in placing the date of this change at 1767. In 1746 the fourth Rhode Island county, Bristol, was created, and it was enacted that the Superior Court should be held twice a year in every county. *RICR,* V, 208. Rhode Island's fifth and final county, Kent, was incorporated in 1750. *RICR,* V, 301–03.

[43] *Digest of 1752,* pp. 22–24.

[44] Smith, *Appeals,* pp. 140–42, 246–48, 270–71, 659; Harold D. Hazeltine, "Appeals from Colonial Courts to the King in Council, With

Although Rhode Island produced many appeals,[45] its attitude toward orders in council issued pursuant to those appeals was often defiant. The action of Rhode Island's Superior Court in the drawn-out appeal (1756–74) of *Freebody v. Brenton* was "probably the most notable example of colonial judicial recalcitrance." During this long controversy arising out of a mortgage cause, the colonial court evaded the directives of a 1769 order in council for nearly five years before reluctantly capitulating.[46]

The development of executive power under the charter of 1663 was comparable to growth of judicial autonomy — both were repressed by the powerful legislature. Apart from making the governor the presiding officer of the General Assembly and granting him the right to convene special sessions of that body, the charter bestowed few exclusive powers of significance upon the governor. He was little more than the executive agent of the Assembly and he had no appointive power, for that important prerogative resided in the legislature. Even the governor's charter-conferred position of commander-in-chief was carefully circumscribed by the Assembly.[47]

The most important effort by a colonial governor of Rhode Island to establish an executive prerogative at the Assembly's expense met with rejection. This rebuff came in 1732 when Governor Joseph Jenckes endeavored to assert the power to veto acts of the legislature. A paper money emission enacted by the

---

Especial Reference to Rhode Island," *Annual Report of the American Historical Association for the Year 1894,* pp. 299–350.

[45] Two students of the appellate process have uncovered nearly 70 appeals from Rhode Island to the king in council. There may have been some appeals that were not recorded. Hazeltine, p. 337; Lowther, p. 186. Lowther discovered nine appeals during the period 1725–35 of which Hazeltine was unaware. However, Lowther erroneously states that the total number of appeals was small when actually it was higher than in any other colony.

[46] Smith, *Appeals,* pp. 335–41, contains a detailed discussion of the case.

[47] Irwin H. Polishook, "Rhode Island and the Union, 1774–1790," (unpublished doctoral dissertation, Northwestern University, 1961), pp. 35–36 alludes to the *ad hoc* Council of War during the Revolution as an agency which restricted the governor's power as commander-in-chief.

General Assembly in 1731 met with Jenckes's attempted veto thereby precipitating a major quarrel over the colony's monetary policy in general and over the veto power of the governor in particular. When the Assembly rejected the veto, Jenckes, together with the royal collector of customs and seventeen merchants, appealed to the king and the Board of Trade. The petitions were referred to the attorney general and solicitor general who delivered this unusual decision:

> In this charter, no negative voice is given to the Governor, nor any power reserved to the Crown of approving or disapproving the laws to be made in this colony. . . . The presence of the Governor, or in his absence, of the Deputy Governor, is necessary to the legal holding of the General Assembly; yet, when he is there, he is a part of the Assembly, and included by the majority; and consequently, that acts passed by the majority of such Assembly, are valid in law, notwithstanding the Governor's entering his dissent at the time of passing thereof. . . . The Crown hath no discretionary power of repealing laws made in this province; but the validity thereof, depends upon their not being contrary, but as near as may be, agreeable to the laws of England, regard being had to the nature and constitution of the place, and the people.[48]

This opinion acknowledged not only the quasi-parliamentary nature of the colony's government, it also recognized that the Rhode Island General Assembly was among the most nearly autonomous legislative bodies in the British Empire.[49]

A final significant implementation of the charter, and the one which exerted the greatest impact on the nineteenth-century

---

[48] *RICR,* IV, 456–61; *CSP,* 1732, #191; Kellogg, p. 275; Lowther rather questionably makes this decision the focal point for his excellent study of Rhode Island government. The paper money controversy which forms the background for this decision is best covered in MacInnes, pp. 194–200, who also contends that Rhode Island's liberal charter gave her great freedom to emit paper money, thus securing for her economic advantages over neighboring colonies, pp. 547–70.

[49] In 1775 the Assembly stripped Governor Joseph Wanton of his power and refused to give him the oath of office (thus violating the charter) because of the governor's Loyalist leanings. Then they declared the office vacant and named the deputy governor to succeed him. Lovejoy, *Rhode Island Politics,* pp. 179–83.

movement for constitutional reform, concerned the creation of
freemen and their consequent power to vote. Contrary to widely
held opinion, the basic law of 1663 did not establish a specific
suffrage requirement. It simply empowered the Assembly to
"choose, nominate and appoint" freemen of the colony. However,
both the framers and recipients of the charter apparently considered the franchise a privilege to be exercised only by those who
had been elevated to the status of freemen, and indeed such was
the practice in both the towns and in the colony prior to 1663.[50]
Thus, under the royal charter freemanship remained a prerequisite for voting,[51] and the colonial legislature in 1664 declared
"that none presume to vote . . . but such whome this Generall
Assembly expressly by their writing shall admitt as freemen." [52]

In 1665 visiting royal commissioners informed Rhode Islanders
that it was "his Majestyes will and pleasure" that an oath of
allegiance be taken by every householder in the colony and that
"all men of competante estates and of civill conversation, who
acknowledge and are obediante to the civill magistrate, though
of differing judgments, may be admitted to be freemen, and have
liberty to choose and to be chosen officers both civill and military." [53] The Assembly promptly responded to the commissioners'
suggestions by enacting a statute which enabled those of "competent estates" to become freemen of the colony after taking a prescribed oath. Those not admitted to colony freemanship could

---

[50] *RICR,* I, 125, 217; Edwin Maxey, "Suffrage Extension in Rhode
Island Down to 1842," *American Law Review,* (1908), 541–48; Stokes,
pp. 26–9.

[51] Initially there was some doubt as to whether the "royall intention
. . . concerning the persons in whom the power emediately to elect doth
rest, or remayne; whether in the whole body of freemen, or in their representatives, the General Assembly." The doubt was of course resolved in
favor of the former. *RICR,* II, 28.

[52] *RICR,* II, 58. The most important acts relating to freemanship and
franchise in the period 1663–1775 are either reproduced or referred to
in *RICR* as follows: II, 28–29 (1664), 58 (1664), 113 (1665), 190
(1667); IV, 338 (1723), 550 (1738); V, 57 (1742), 73 (1743), 213
(1746); VI, 256–57 (1760), 270 (1761), 323 (1762), 343 (1762); VII,
24 (1770).

[53] *RICR*, II, 110.

not vote for "publicke officers" (i.e., governor, deputy governor, and assistants) or deputies, nor could they hold colonial office themselves.[54]

Many historians have failed to realize that a distinction existed between freemen of the towns and freemen of the colony, because most freemen had dual status.[55] The town freeman was empowered to vote for local officials such as the town council, sergeant, constable, and treasurer, but the suffrage statute of 1665 withheld from one who was only a freeman of a town the privilege of selecting deputies to the colonial Assembly. This restriction was not permanently removed until 1723.[56] In addition, a man who was merely a town freeman could not vote for general officers of the colony. An act of 1760 clearly stated that such votes were invalid and "shall be rejected and thrown out." [57]

According to the statute of 1665, a person became a freeman of the colony either by direct application to the Assembly or through being proposed by the chief officer of the town in which he lived. In the early years, some who petitioned the Assembly directly were not town freemen. A few were inhabitants of unincorporated territory such as the Block Island petitioners of 1665, while some held their land elsewhere in the colony than the town in which they resided. A person who was only a freeman of the colony was prohibited by statute from voting for local officials.[58]

In the normal course of events Rhode Islanders secured dual freemanship. They gained the right of inhabitancy and acquired a "competent estate" in the town where they had chosen to reside. Then they applied and were admitted to town freemanship

---

[54] *RICR,* II, 8, 113. There is at least one instance of the election of a man to town office who was not a freeman. Robert Curry was chosen town sergeant in 1718. *Providence Early Records,* XIII, 14.

[55] Notable exceptions are Lowther, pp. 12–44; Albert E. McKinley, *The Suffrage Franchise in the Thirteen English Colonies in America* (Philadelphia, 1905), Chapter XIV; and Howard K. Stokes, pp. 26–33.

[56] *RICR,* II, 113; IV, 338.

[57] *RICR,* VI, 257.

[58] *RICR,* II, 55, 58, 113, 147; *Digest of 1730,* p. 2, printed in Newport by James Franklin.

by their fellow townsmen of that status, and finally their names
were proposed or "propounded" to the General Assembly for admittance as freemen of the colony by the town's chief officer or the
town clerk. When a town freeman was proposed to the Assembly in this manner, his acceptance as a freeman of the colony
was practically assured. Once approved, his name was entered
in the records of the colony.[59]

In 1723 a statute was passed by the Assembly which set the
first specific landed requirement for town freemanship and, since
that status was the usual and nearly automatic prelude to colonial freemanship, the act is worthy of citation. This law stipulated that a person must be a "freeholder of lands, tenements, or
hereditaments in such town where he shall be admitted free, of
the value of one hundred pounds, or to the [rental] value of forty
shillings per annum, or the eldest son of such a freeholder." [60]

In 1729 the real estate requirement was increased to £200, in
1746 raised to £400, but by 1760 it had been reduced to £40
(ca. $134). These drastic and erratic changes were more the
result of inflationary and deflationary trends than of stringency
or fickleness of the General Assembly.[61]

The changes in land valuation requirements were often accompanied by provisions designed to eliminate fraud and elec-

---

[59] Stokes, pp. 25–26 and Lowther, pp. 12–44, contain an intelligent
description of the freemanship process.

[60] *Digest of 1730,* p. 131. Because the act of 1723 was the first colonial statute to connect *specifically* land and freemanship, many Rhode
Island historians have inferred that town freemen were not required to
hold land before that time. This is a false impression. Howard Stokes
after a thorough search through the Providence town papers asserts that
"The records of Providence contain many instances of the names of large
landholders who were not freemen: they contain many references to the
admission of freemen who were freeholders, but so far as I know not an
instance of the admission of a landless man to the rights of franchise."
Stokes, p. 33.

[61] *Digest of 1730,* p. 209; *Digest of 1752,* pp. 12–16; *RICR,* VI, 257.
See MacInnes, pp. 542–70, for the financial fluctuations. The £200 requirement imposed in 1729 was slightly restrictive in its intent and effect
because inflation of the late 1720s warranted an increase but not a
doubling of the freehold requirement. Lowther, pp. 29–33; Howard K.
Stokes, "Public and Private Finance," in Field, III, 201–209.

tion abuses. Since many people continued to vote after they had disposed of the property upon which they had been admitted, legislation was enacted in 1742 and 1746 to ban this practice and other types of chicanery.[62]

The last reform and revision of the colonial franchise laws in 1762 attacked further irregularities by denying the vote to those who owned only houses or tenements, but not the title in fee simple to the land upon which the structure stood. It also denied the franchise in the right of a wife's dower. Finally, this law was the first to specifically acknowledge the reserved right of townsmen to reject a freeholder proposed and duly qualified according to law. Henceforth, property did not *ipso facto* carry with it the right of admission.[63]

Freehold requirements and suffrage stipulations enacted by the legislature could cause the uncritical reader to assume that the franchise was a privilege enjoyed by a select minority. Such an inference would be erroneous. The real estate requirement for freemanship was not a measure of oppression or restriction in a rural, agrarian society where land tenure was widely dispersed. The suffrage statute of 1746 declared that the manner of admitting freemen was "lax" and the real estate qualification was "very low." [64] Authoritative students of Rhode Island's colonial history estimate that seventy-five percent of the colony's white adult male population were able to meet the specific freehold requirements from the time of their imposition in 1723 to the outbreak of the War for Independence.[65]

This fact, however, needs some qualification. Being allowed to

---

[62] *Digest of 1745,* pp. 252–53 (Act of 1742), *Digest of 1752,* pp. 12–16 (Act of 1746).

[63] *Schedules* [Acts and Resolves] *of the General Assembly for the Year 1762,* p. 192, hereafter cited as *Schedules; Digest of 1767;* pp. 78–89.

[64] *Digest of 1752,* p. 12.

[65] Lovejoy, *Rhode Island Politics,* pp. 13–18, makes his estimate for the period 1760–1776; Lowther, pp. 24–40, for the period up to 1754. In commercial Newport the percentage of freemen to white adult males was closer to fifty percent during the entire eighteenth century and, as Providence turned increasingly to commerce at mid-century, its ratio gradually declined. In other towns, all rural and agricultural, the ratio ranged from eighty to ninety-five percent. Lowther, pp. 37–40.

vote and to hold office was not synonymous with exercising those privileges. Normally less than half the freemen bothered to vote, and those that did often elected to office men from the upper socio-economic strata.[66] To coin a phrase, Rhode Island democracy was one of indifference and deference, but a democracy it was.[67]

Although the incentive to participate politically was not widespread, it was strong in some quarters as evidenced by the development of a system of two-party politics in the generation preceding the American Revolution. Opposing groups, one headed by Samuel Ward and the other by Stephen Hopkins, were organized with sectional overtones; generally speaking (though there were notable exceptions) the merchants and farmers of southern Rhode Island (Ward) battled with their counterparts from Providence and its environs (Hopkins). The principal goal

---

[66] Jackson Turner Main, *The Upper House in Revolutionary America, 1763–1788* (Madison, Wisconsin, 1967), pp. 182–87, notes, however, that deference played a lesser role in the Rhode Island legislature than in any other of the thirteen colonies. In speaking of the Rhode Island House of Magistrates (Senate), Main observes that "nowhere else did farmers' sons with little property have so much influence."

[67] For concurring conclusions see Lovejoy, *Rhode Island Politics,* pp. 16–17; Lowther, pp. 40–44; Joel Alden Cohen, "Rhode Island and the American Revolution: A Selective Socio-Political Analysis" (unpublished doctoral dissertation, University of Connecticut, 1967), pp. 4–8, 170–78; and Polishook, "Rhode Island and the Union," pp. 41–47, 53–56. See also the provocative article by J. R. Pole, "Historians and the Problem of Early American Democracy," *American Historical Review,* LXVII (April, 1962), 626–46, which stresses the role of "deference" in the selection of public officials during the colonial and early national period. Or, as John Adams phrased it: "Go into every village in New England, and you will find that the office of justice of the peace, and even the place of representative, which has ever depended only on the freest election of the people, have generally descended from generation to generation, in three or four families at most." Adams, *Defence of the Constitutions of the United States* . . . (Philadelphia, 1797), I, 110–111. A refinement of the concept of deference that utilizes the "central place theory" to explain geographical sources of political leadership in colonial New England is Edward M. Cook, Jr. "Local Leadership and the Typology of New England Towns, 1700–1785," *Political Science Quarterly,* LXXXVI (Dec., 1971), 586–608. Cook includes Exeter, Smithfield and South Kingstown in his analysis.

of these groups was to secure control of the powerful legislature in order to obtain the host of public offices — from chief justice to inspector of tobacco — at the disposal of that body.

The semi-permanent nature, relatively stable membership and explicit sectional rivalry of the warring camps has led one historian to describe the state's pre-Revolutionary political structure as one of "stable factionalism." Another, David Lovejoy, has boldly maintained that Rhode Islanders revolted from British rule not only "on the broad grounds of constitutional right to keep Rhode Island safe for liberty and property," but also to preserve "the benefits of party politics" — patronage and spoils.[68]

As noteworthy as the development of the party system in mid-eighteenth-century Rhode Island were the rules by which the political game was played. The charter provided the broad framework within which elections were conducted, but a succession of resourceful and imaginative politicians supplied the unique details through an intricate combination of custom and statute. Richard P. McCormick has correctly observed that the salient and most significant feature of Rhode Island government under the charter "was that the crucial electoral arena was the colony — later the state — as a unit." [69] The governor and deputy governor plus a secretary, an attorney general and a treasurer were elected annually in April on a colony-wide or at-large basis, as were ten "assistants" who comprised the upper house. Only the deputies, elected semiannually in April and August, were chosen on a local basis. Further, there was no county government; the county existed only as a unit of judicial administration. Thus there existed an obvious inducement to

---

[68] Lovejoy, *Rhode Island Politics,* pp. 20–30, 52–53, 194; Jack P. Greene, "Changing Interpretations of Early American Politics," in Ray Allen Billington, ed., *The Reinterpretation of Early American History: Essays in Honor of John Edwin Pomfret* (San Marino, California, 1966), pp. 176–77; Mack E. Thompson, "The Ward-Hopkins Controversy and the American Revolution in Rhode Island: An Interpretation," *William and Mary Quarterly,* 3rd ser., XVI (July, 1959), 363–375.

[69] Richard P. McCormick, *The Second American Party System* (Chapel Hill, N.C., 1966), p. 76.

form colony-wide parties in order to elect a full slate of general officers.

For these at-large contests Rhode Islanders devised a peculiar system known as "proxing." A "prox" was a ballot upon which a party placed the names of its at-large candidates. The elector in his town meeting on the third Wednesday in April took the prox of his choice (making any deletions or substitutions he deemed desirable) and signed it on the reverse side in the presence of the town moderator. The voter then submitted the prox to the moderator and that official forwarded it to the town clerk to be recorded. When this ritual was concluded, the proxies were sealed in a packet and taken to Newport by one of the town's state legislators for the start of the May session of the Assembly. On "election day," the first Wednesday in May, ballots were opened and counted by the incumbent governor in the presence of the incumbent assistants and newly elected deputies sitting jointly in "grand committee." The candidate having a *majority* of the total vote cast for his respective office was declared elected.

Under this system a party's success was dependent upon many procedural factors — upon how widely its printed prox could be distributed, upon how many new voters could be qualified by fraudulent transfers of land, upon the number of electors of the opposite persuasion who could be induced by bribes to abstain from voting. Rhode Island was also a democracy of corruption and chicanery.[70] The Rev. Andrew Burnaby perceptively ob-

---

[70] On Rhode Island's eighteenth-century electoral procedures, which in the main prevailed until the demise of the charter in 1843, see *Digest of 1767,* pp. 83–84; *Digest of 1798,* pp. 114–126; McCormick, *Second American Party System,* pp. 76–86; Lovejoy, *Rhode Island Politics,* pp. 21–30; Sidney S. Rider, "The Origin, Meaning and Duration of Existence in Rhode Island of the Political Word 'Prox,'" *Book Notes,* XXV (Dec. 26, 1908), 201–04. Although the charter required that the general officers be "newly chosen for the year ensueing, by such greater part of the sayd Company . . . as shall bee then and there present [at Newport]" (*RICR,* II, 11), the General Assembly ignored this provision because of the difficulties involved in traveling to Newport and passed an act in 1664 allowing proxy voting for general officers. *RICR,* II, 39–40, 62. Such a procedure had been in existence under the Union of 1647, *Ibid.,* II, 149, 217. In 1760 proxy voting, then quite common, was made man-

served in his travels through the colony in 1760 that the "men in power, from the highest to the lowest, are dependent upon the people, and frequently act without that strict regard to probity and honour, which ever ought invariably to influence and direct mankind." [71]

Rhode Island's political antics, not to mention its autonomy, scandalized many a squeamish observer. In the eyes of the colony's conservative critics, the land of Roger Williams, even on the eve of revolt, was "dangerously democratic," according to eighteenth-century standards. Chief Justice Daniel Horsmanden of New York, in a 1773 report to the Earl of Dartmouth during the *Gaspee* investigation, disdainfully described Rhode Island as a "downright democracy" whose governmental officials were "entirely controlled by the populace," and conservative Massachusetts Governor Thomas Hutchinson lamented to George III that Rhode Island was "the nearest to a democracy of any of your colonies." [72]

Because of such "democratic" conditions no protests were made nor reform measures attempted, in the generation prior to the War for Independence, indicating dissatisfaction with the suffrage requirements or with the charter-imposed system of

---

datory for all non-Newporters who were not members of the General Assembly because of the revelling which occurred in Newport at election time owing to the influx of freemen from elsewhere in the state. Such travel it was said also resulted "in a very great loss of peoples' time" during the planting season. *Ibid.,* VI, 256. See also Howard M. Chapin, "Eighteenth Century Rhode Island Printed Proxies," *American Collector,* I (1925), 54–59.

[71] Rev. Andrew Burnaby, *Travels Through the Middle Settlements in North America in the Years 1759 and 1760* (London, 2nd ed., 1775), p. 89.

[72] *RICR,* VII, 182–83. Peter Orlando Hutchinson, comp., *Diary and Letters of His Excellency Thomas Hutchinson, Esq.* (Boston, 1884), I, 172. Leonard Woods Labaree, *Conservatism in Early American History* (New York, 1948), pp. 26–27, contends that "the political equalitarianism of Rhode Island serves to emphasize the aristocratic and conservative tendencies of all the other colonies." On the *Gaspee* incident see William R. Leslie, "The Gaspee Affair: A Study of Its Constitutional Significance," *Mississippi Valley Historical Review,* XXXIX (September, 1952), 233–256.

legislative apportionment.[73] Rhode Islanders of the Revolutionary generation and their individualistic forebears were ever-
mindful that they enjoyed near-autonomy within the Empire and
broad powers of self-government within their colony. They were
also keenly aware that their self-determination flowed in large
measure from the munificent charter of Charles II.[74] Thus they
harbored a passionate attachment for the document and defended it against all comers. They allowed it to weather the
Revolutionary upheaval, and retained it as the basic law of the
state until 1843 — a point far beyond its useful life.

The liberality of the seventeenth-century charter prompted
Rhode Islanders to preserve and enshrine, or should we say, em-
balm it, until the patent became in the eyes of Thomas Wilson
Dorr and other political reformers of the nineteenth century a
despised and reactionary relic of a bygone age. This is the cruel
irony and the great tragedy of Rhode Island's constitutional
history.

---

[73] Lovejoy, *Rhode Island Politics,* pp. 14–15. An important factor
which militated against malapportionment was the periodic creation of
new towns by sub-dividing the existing ones. This "political cell-devision"
forestalled discontent over the fixed system of apportionment.

[74] See for example the comments of "William Freeborn" in the *Rhode
Island Gazette,* January 11, 1733 quoted in Lawrence H. Leder, *Liberty
and Authority: Early American Political Ideology, 1689–1763* (Chicago,
1968), pp. 63, 113.

II. The Revolutionary Era

TO RELIEVE THE DISTRESSED.

HIS EXCELLENCY

JOHN COLLINS, Efq;

GOVERNOR.

THE HONORABLE

DANIEL OWEN, Efq;

DEPUTY-GOVERNOR.

1. JOHN MATTHEWSON, Efq; Affiftant.
2. JOSEPH STANTON, jun. Efq; Affiftant.
3. JOHN WILLIAMS, Efq; Affiftant.
4. RICHARD SEARLE, Efq; Affiftant.
5. JAMES ARNOLD, Efq; Affiftant.
6. WILLIAM HAMMOND, Efq; Affiftant.
7. GIDEON CLARKE, Efq; Affiftant.
8. THOMAS G. HAZARD, Efq; Affiftant.
9. JOHN COOKE, Efq; Affiftant.
10. OLIVER DURFEE, Efq; Affiftant.

HENRY WARD, Efq; Secretary.
WILLIAM CHANNING, Efq; Attorney-Gen.
JOSEPH CLARKE, Efq; General-Treafurer.

Delegates to reprefent the State in Congrefs.

Honorable JAMES M. VARNUM, Efq; 1ft.
NATHAN MILLER, Efq; 2d.
GEORGE CHAMPLIN, Efq; 3d.
PELEG ARNOLD, Efq; 4th.

The Country party founded by Jonathan J. Hazard of Charlestown swept into power in 1786 on a paper money platform "to relieve the distressed" farmer. This rural-based organization became a bulwark of Antifederalism (from a "prox" or printed ballot, Rhode Island Historical Society).

CHAPTER THREE

The Conservative Revolution

I

In the fateful months following Lexington and Concord, Rhode Island and her twelve sister colonies moved toward the brink of separation from the Empire. Finally, in the belief that their natural rights, their rights of local self-government, their property rights, and their rights as Englishmen[1] had been denied or unjustly abridged, revolutionaries in each of these thirteen colonies took the decisive step — they declared their independence from England and proclaimed the creation of the United States of America.

---

[1] The charter of Charles II, in a not uncommon clause, guaranteed Rhode Islanders all the "liberties and immunities of free and natural subjects" of England. During 1765, aggrieved colonials in Rhode Island and elsewhere alleged that this provision was violated by the Stamp Act and its taxation without representation. In October 1769, England was again indicted by Rhode Island for failing to accord colonists the rights of Englishmen when the General Assembly adopted a Virginia resolution censuring the use of juryless and remote admiralty courts for trying those accused of violating the navigation acts. *RICR*, VI, 451–52, 602–04. For a good general discussion of the latter grievance see David S. Lovejoy, "Equal Rights Imply Equality: The Case Against Admiralty

Rhode Island's radicals were in the vanguard of the revolutionary movement.[2] They had the greatest degree of local self-government, and thus the most to fear and the most to lose from what many colonials considered the deliberate tyranny of the mother country.

On April 25, 1775, a week after the incidents at Lexington and Concord, the outgoing General Assembly authorized the raising of a 1,500-man "army of observation," despite the objections of Governor Joseph Wanton and Deputy Governor Darius Sessions.[3] On the first Wednesday in May the incoming Assembly met. A tabulation of the votes cast for general office in the town meetings of April 19 (the day of the Massachusetts outbreak) revealed that Wanton and Sessions had secured re-election. Notwithstanding, the Assembly chose Nathanael Greene as commander of their observation army. Wanton, in an attempt to obstruct military mobilization, feigned illness and absented himself from the May session. In Wanton's absence the army commissions could not be conferred. His running mate, Darius Sessions, anticipating trouble with the Assembly, declined to serve.

At this point the legislature, in a move of dubious legality, selected the militant Nicholas Cooke to fill the office of lieutenant-governor and heir apparent. Then, when Wanton finally made his appearance in June, the legislature declared that no one was "to administer the oath of office" to him. With Wanton effectively displaced, the Assembly directed Secretary Henry Ward to sign all military commissions, and Cooke immediately assumed the functions and eventually the title of chief executive when

---

Jurisdiction in America, 1764–1776," *William and Mary Quarterly*, 3rd Ser., XVI (October, 1959), 459–84.

[2] On May 17, 1774, less than two weeks after news of the Boston Port Bill arrived in Massachusetts, a Providence town meeting became the first group to advance proposals for a general congress of all the colonies for the purpose of bringing about united action in the emergency. On June 15, the Rhode Island General Assembly made the colony the first to appoint delegates to the anticipated Continental Congress. Edmund Cody Burnett, *The Continental Congress* (New York, 1941), pp. 19–20; *RICR*, VII, 246–47, 280–81.

[3] *RICR*, VII, 310–11.

Wanton was formally (and unconstitutionally) deposed in October 1775.[4]

In April 1776 Cooke was elected governor in his own right, and the Assembly with little opposition passed an act repudiating Rhode Island's allegiance to George III. This renunciation act of May 4 was a bold and defiant maneuver, but it did not constitute a declaration of independence from the Empire itself, despite the overwhelming popular and scholarly belief of succeeding generations that it severed the imperial ties.[5] For the next two-and-one-half months Rhode Islanders continued to describe their province as the "English Colony of Rhode Island and Providence Plantations." The oaths, writs, and commissions during this period clearly indicate a continued colonial status, and Governor Cooke, in a letter to General George Washington, accompanied by a copy of the controversial declaration, asserted that Assembly action upon the question of independence had been postponed pending a decision by the Second Continental Congress.[6]

---

[4] Correspondence between Wanton and the Assembly is printed in *RICR,* VII, 311, 332–37; Joel A. Cohen, "Lexington and Concord: Rhode Island Reacts," *Rhode Island History,* XXVI (October, 1967), 100–02. On Wanton's removal see *RICR,* VII, 392–93.

[5] For example, May 4 is called "Rhode Island Independence Day" and has been designated a legal holiday. *The Rhode Island Manual* (published biennially by the Secretary of State prints the renunciation measure under the title "An Act of Independence"). Historians have also accepted this popular but erroneous belief. Merrill Jensen contends that the colony's radicals "declared Rhode Island's independence of Britain two months before the radical party was able to achieve that end in the Continental Congress." Jensen, *The Articles of Confederation* (Madison, Wisconsin, 1963), p. 40. The act is found in *RICR,* VII 522–26. It passed the lower house by a margin of ten-to-one, with only six deputies in opposition. Nicholas Cooke to George Washington, May 6, 1776, *RICR,* VII, 545. Glenn W. LaFantasie presents a detailed examination of the May 4 act and the reasons why the Assembly did not declare independence. LaFantasie, "Act for All Reasons — Revolutionary Politics and May 4, 1776," *Rhode Island History,* XXXV (May, 1976), 39–47.

[6] *RICR,* VII, 522–23; Nicholas Cooke to George Washington, May 6, 1776, *Ibid.,* pp. 545–46. On May 7 Cooke explained the issue of independence to congressional delegate Stephen Hopkins: "Towards the close of the session, a vote passed the lower house for taking the sense of

When Congress did act, Rhode Island quickly responded. In Newport on Thursday, July 18, 1776, its Assembly, without conducting a popular referendum, approved the Declaration of Independence and pledged on behalf of its constituents to "support the said General Congress, with our lives and fortunes." The State of Rhode Island on that day asserted its statehood,[7] but a difficult and costly struggle intervened between that proclamation and England's reluctant ratification of Rhode Island's newly-assumed status.

That struggle — the American Revolution — wrought many political, economic, cultural, social, and ideological changes in those American states that rejected English rule. In fact, the nature and extent of these changes have long been the center of considerable historical debate. In Rhode Island, however, the internal political and constitutional alterations produced by the Revolution were minimal.

Many of the officers who presided over the colony's affairs in 1775 (Governor Wanton, of course, excluded) continued to hold important positions in 1783, the year the Treaty of Paris was declared definitive. Joseph Clarke was still general treasurer, and Henry Ward remained as secretary of state. Henry Marchant, attorney general in 1775, had become one of Rhode Island's delegates to the Confederation Congress. Assistant Peter Phillips

---

the inhabitants at large upon the question of independency. The upper house were of the opinion that although a very great majority of the Colony were perfectly ripe for such a question, yet, upon its being canvassed, several towns would vote against it, and that the appearance of disunion would be injurious to the common cause, and represented to the lower house that it was very possible the subject would be discussed in Congress before it would be possible to take the sense of the Colony in the proposed way and transmit it to the delegates, in which case they would be laid under the necessity of waiting for the sentiments of their constituents, and of course the Colony would lose its voice, and that the delegates when they should receive a copy of the *act renouncing allegiance,* and of the instructions, could not possibly entertain a doubt of the sense of the General Assembly; upon which the subject was dropped." (Italics mine). Cooke to Stephen Hopkins, May 7, 1776, in William R. Staples, comp., *Rhode Island in the Continental Congress* (Providence, 1870), p. 68, hereafter cited as *RICC.*

[7] *RICR,* VII, 581–82.

had become associate justice of the Superior Court, several assistants and deputies had been appointed justices of their county court of common pleas. Deputy Thomas Holden of Warwick had advanced to the position of brigadier general of militia in the county of Kent and Deputy William Bradford of Bristol had become speaker of the House. Several other deputies in the years immediately preceding the Revolution either served in the post-Revolutionary Assemblies or were replaced by relatives.[8] Rhode Island in 1783, as in 1775, was a white man's democracy in which the people often deferred to a coterie of traditional leaders. The War for Independence clearly did not produce an upheaval in the political personnel of the state. Nor did it markedly affect the structure of government.[9]

While the other rebellious provinces, Connecticut excepted,[10]

---

[8] Main, *Upper House,* pp. 182–83, notes "the striking similarity between the upper house [in Rhode Island] before and after the Revolution." Joel Alden Cohen, "Democracy in Revolutionary Rhode Island: A Statistical Analysis," *Rhode Island History,* XXIX (Feb.–May, 1970), 3–16, also denies the existence of a political upheaval.

[9] *RICR,* VII, 312–13, IX, 688–94. There was, however, a marked change in the composition of the upper House after the April 1775 elections. Four assistants were replaced, three others re-elected but resigned because of their opposition to the military measures being taken, and another was re-elected but died before taking office. *RICR,* VII, 239; Lovejoy, *Rhode Island Politics,* p. 182. Cohen, "Rhode Island and the Revolution," pp. 177–78, concludes that Rhode Island in 1783 was "politically democratic" but it was not "a popularly oriented democracy. Instead it appears to be a kind of eighteenth-century Whig democracy which was controlled by those who had 'a stake in society.' " Claude Blanchard, a French officer in Rochambeau's army, observed in 1780, however, that the education of the mechanic, the farmer and the merchant in Rhode Island is "very nearly the same; so that a mechanic is often called to their assemblies, where there is no distinction, no separate order." Gertrude Selwyn Kimball (ed.), *Pictures of Rhode Island in the Past, 1642–1833 by Travellers and Observers* (Providence, 1900), p. 84.

[10] Connecticut, like Rhode Island, was a self-governing colony with a very liberal, and, therefore, quite satisfactory charter. Connecticut retained her charter until 1818. For an account of that state's development from 1775 until the adoption of its first written constitution see Richard J. Purcell, *Connecticut in Transition, 1775–1818* (Middletown, Conn., 1963). Constitutional changes in the remaining states during this era of readjustment are discussed in Allan Nevins, *The American States*

scrapped their royally granted basic laws, Rhode Island tenaciously clung to the charter of Charles II.[11] In fact, an important motive underlying the revolutionary spirit of many Rhode
Islanders was the desire to preserve intact the liberal charter that
sustained their remarkable autonomy. As the leading student
of pre-Revolutionary Rhode Island has contended, "Rhode
Islanders went to war in April 1775, to force Great Britain to
recognize their self-governing colony." Then in mid-1776 they
first renounced royal allegiance and then proclaimed independence "as a final step in defense of their political self-suffi-
ciency." [12]

During and After the Revolution, 1775–1789 (New York, 1924), pp.
117–205; Benjamin F. Wright, "The Early History of Written Constitutions in America," in *Essays in History and Political Theory in Honor
of C. H. McIlwain* (Cambridge, Mass., 1936), pp. 344–71; William F.
Dodd, "The First State Constitutional Conventions, 1776–1783," *American Political Science Review,* II (Nov., 1908), 545–61; Gordon S.
Wood, *The Creation of the American Republic, 1776–1787* (Chapel
Hill, N.C., 1969), pp. 125 ff; and William C. Webster, "A Comparative
Study of the State Constitutions of the American Revolution," *Annals of
the American Academy of Political and Social Science,* IX(1897), 380–
420.

[11] Rhode Island made no changes of wording in its charter. It first
renounced allegiance to George III (May 4); then ratified the Declaration of Independence (July 18); and finally enacted a law (July 18)
providing that "the style and title of this government, in all acts and
instruments, whether of a public or a private nature shall be the State
of Rhode Island and Providence Plantations." *RICR,* VII, 581–82. One
implicit alteration of course, would be a nullification of the charter
directive that no law could be enacted contrary to the law of England.
Connecticut followed a more formal and detailed procedure in adapting
her colonial document to the needs of the newly emergent state. Purcell,
pp. 113–14. As Jackson Turner Main has observed "after every generalization concerning colonial politics one must mutter 'except Connecticut
and especially Rhode Island.'" *The Sovereign States, 1775–1783* (New
York, 1973), p. 101.

[12] Lovejoy, *Rhode Island Politics,* pp. 193–94. Lovejoy cites as other
motives prompting Rhode Island's revolt, the desire to safeguard property and to preserve "the benefits of party politics." He explains these
complex factors as follows: "To say that Rhode Islanders joined the
Revolutionary movement merely to preserve a liberal charter which sustained self-government does not do justice to the political genius of the
people of Rhode Island. Factional government, based on a number of

Reverence for the charter and attachment to the system it produced was so widespread that even Tory Governor Joseph Wanton, in opposing the army of observation, had based his argument in part upon it. "Your charter privileges are of too much importance to be forfeited," exhorted Wanton, as he admonished the Assembly regarding "the fatal consequences of levying war against the king." [13]

Despite the sacrosanct position of the charter, however, the exigencies of war did evoke repeated criticism in some quarters for one of its provisions — the apportionment clause. This criticism came from the country towns, particularly those on the remote western border and those in King's County (appropriately changed to Washington County in 1781).

As the war progressed, these relatively populous rural communities were forced to bear an unprecedented tax burden. The obligations of the country towns were accentuated between 1778 and 1780 because the valuations upon which the taxes were

---

local issues, was a stage in political growth which Rhode Island experienced earlier than most colonies owing to its large degree of political independence and the peculiar conditions which existed there. Government by faction was a stage in political growth which was characteristic of English politics as well at the same time. By 1760 Rhode Islanders had reached a surprising level of political maturity; in fact, their history in this period explains a good deal about political behavior in the eighteenth century and is significant if only for that. To say, too, that Rhode Islanders revolted to protect the wide area of freedom they were accustomed to enjoy does not really get to the bottom of the causes for resisting England. When Parliament, ministry, and King encroached upon self-government, they encroached upon a system of party politics which was not only mature but profitable. Self-interest was a spring for constitutional appeal, not hypocritically but naturally. Taxation and legislation by a Parliament in England — besides intruding on local political habits — intruded also on local property, and a defense of property, in good old Whig terms, was traditionally a defense of liberty. Sensitive to the real danger from abroad, Rhode Islanders joined their fellow colonists and revolted on the broad grounds of constitutional right to keep Rhode Island safe for liberty and property — and the benefits of party politics." See also Cohen, "Rhode Island and the Revolution," pp. 28–29.

[13] Message of Governor Wanton to the General Assembly of Rhode Island, May 2, 1775, *RICR*, VII, 332–33.

levied excluded those municipalities "in the possession of the enemy." Once-prosperous Newport, plus Middletown, Portsmouth, Jamestown and New Shoreham were thus exempted. Even after liberation these war-ravaged and depopulated Bay areas experienced a slow recovery and, therefore, were subjected to valuation estimates proportionately lower than those of prewar years. The country towns took up the slack, but only grudgingly and with difficulty.[14]

In the period 1777–1784 the rural communities protested against this new fiscal arrangement. Many of these protests included a demand for a "more equitable representation." The towns complained that their taxes had risen and that the war's financial burden weighed heavily upon them. In addition, some of these communities claimed a relatively sizeable population. Despite these circumstances, the number of deputies from the farming towns remained stationary — fixed by the charter. This "inequity" caused them to develop a resentment towards the Bay settlements, especially those enjoying greater representation. Portsmouth, in particular, was the object of their criticism. In 1782 it ranked 20th in population and 24th in the value of rateable property, but it had twice the representation in the Assembly of the mainland country communities.[15] The implication that this unequal representation had contributed to what the farmers considered an unjust levying of taxes by the Assembly made the rural areas even more dissatisfied.

---

[14] This development can be traced in the Committee Reports to the General Assembly, Rhode Island State Archives, III, 107; IV, 8, 13, 15, 19, hereafter cited Reports, RIGA. Some of these estimates are printed in *RICR,* IX, 169, 273.

[15] See Table #1.

TABLE 1

ᵃA valuation was not taken on New Shoreham (Block Island) because of British occupation.

ᵇIn 1781, Scituate was divided and Foster created out of its western sector.

SOURCE: "Rhode Island Census of 1782," Theodore Foster Papers, RIHS, Vol. XIV; *RICR,* IX, 520 (valuation given in pounds sterling).

TABLE 1

Rhode Island in 1782

Population, Ratio of Representation, and Value of Rateable Property

Towns and Counties	Deputies in the Gen. Assembly	Population	Ratio of Deputies to Population	Value of Rateable Property (in £)
Barrington	2	534	267	30,720
Bristol	2	1,032	516	65,240
Warren	2	905	453	39,000
BRISTOL COUNTY	6	2,471	412	134,960
Coventry	2	2,107	1,054	100,000
East Greenwich	2	1,609	805	79,600
West Greenwich	2	1,698	849	73,300
Warwick	4	2,112	528	175,100
KENT COUNTY	10	7,526	753	428,000
Jamestown	2	345	173	20,000
Little Compton	2	1,341	671	89,300
Middletown	2	674	337	34,000
Newport	6	5,530	922	153,000
New Shoreham[a]	2	478	239	NV
Portsmouth	4	1,350	338	55,000
Tiverton	2	1,959	980	110,500
NEWPORT COUNTY	20	11,677	584	461,800
Cranston	2	1,589	795	123,340
Cumberland	2	1,548	774	90,832
Foster[b]	2	1,763	882	76,000
Glocester	2	2,791	1,396	158,000
Johnston	2	996	498	64,200
North Providence	2	698	349	45,874
Providence	4	4,310	1,078	217,000
Scituate[b]	2	1,628	814	107,000
Smithfield	2	2,217	1,109	200,000
PROVIDENCE COUNTY	20	17,540	877	1,082,246
Charlestown	2	1,523	762	81,300
Exeter	2	2,058	1,029	102,870
Hopkinton	2	1,735	868	91,000
North Kingstown	2	2,328	1,164	148,650
South Kingstown	2	2,675	1,338	292,300
Richmond	2	1,094	547	70,360
Westerly	2	1,720	860	97,000
WASHINGTON COUNTY	14	13,133	938	883,480
RHODE ISLAND	70	52,347	748	2,990,486

The issue of taxation and the "equal representation" movement of the Revolutionary years were closely related. Rhode
Island's first wartime estimate of the value of rateable property
for the purpose of levying a tax was made in February 1777.
This estimate and the consequent £16,000 tax of March 1777
brought criticism not only from country towns but also from
Providence and Bristol.[16] This imposition, coupled with other
alleged irregularities by the Assembly, prompted the freemen of
Scituate to make the first request for charter revision. This request, dated April 28, 1777, was embodied in the town meeting's
instructions to Scituate's deputies in the General Assembly.

These instructions complained of a recent pay increase that
the state's legislators voted to themselves and protested against
the "great disproportion" between wages of officers and men in
the militia. More important, however, was the contention that
the colonial charter had become "void" when Rhode Island declared her independence from England. Further, the Scituate
freemen asked that the charter's apportionment system be discarded in favor of one based upon population and taxable
wealth. They "earnestly recommended" that the Scituate delegates use their "utmost influence to cause an act to be drawn
settling the form of government, having particular regard that
each town in this state be equally represented having regard to
the numbers of inhabitants, and value of estates in each town." [17]
Scituate had good reason to be aggrieved. Not only was it placed
eighth in the estimate of 1777; it also ranked third in population,
and an unenviable first in the number of inhabitants per
deputy.[18]

---

[16] Reports, RIGA, III, 107; *RICR,* VIII, 149–51.

[17] The original copy of these instructions is in the Rhode Island Historical Society Manuscripts, III, 11 (#500), hereafter cited RIHS Mss.
The Scituate Town Meeting Records, Town Clerk's Office, are practically barren for the period 1772–78. All subsequently cited town meeting records are in the municipal clerk's office of the respective town unless otherwise indicated.

[18] *Census of the Inhabitants of the Colony of Rhode Island and
Providence Plantations . . . 1774,* arranged by John R. Bartlett (Providence, 1858), p. 239; Reports, RIGA, III, 107.

Apparently little came of the Scituate request. Five months later, in the September 1777 session of the Assembly, a resolution was passed creating a five-man committee "to form a plan of government for this state." [19] This committee may have been created in response to Scituate's plea, but it never reported and the issue was temporarily postponed.

Scituate's disadvantageous position was slightly relieved by other means in 1781. In that year the town's western sector was set off and incorporated as the town of Foster. The principal effect of this political cell division was to halve Scituate's number of inhabitants per deputy, so that it approximated the state average.[20]

The next town to espouse the cause of equal representation was Glocester, another community whose population, ratio of deputies to inhabitants, and taxes were all high. On December 5, 1778, Glocester's freemen ordered her representatives to work for a system of apportionment which would give each town one deputy in the General Assembly. This request was also disregarded by the legislature.[21]

By early 1779, however, the Assembly showed signs of yielding to the agitation for a more equal allocation of deputies. In February, the House approved a proposal allowing each town two deputies. The upper chamber, however, suggested a representation of one or two men depending upon a town's wealth and population. The differences between the two houses could not be reconciled and again the movement was frustrated.[22]

This attempted alteration by the legislature prompted several newspaper articles in the *Providence Gazette* by a writer who referred to himself as "THE AMERICAN WHIG." "Whig" opposed any change in the form of government because of the turmoil it

---

[19] *RICR,* VIII, 304. Reports to the General Assembly contain no record of this committee's recommendations.

[20] *RICR,* IX, 460; see Table #1.

[21] Glocester Town Meeting Records, I, 140.

[22] Journal of the House of Deputies, 1778–79 (February 27, 1779); Journal of the Senate, 1777–1780 (February 28, 1779), RISA; RIHS Mss., III, 56.

could cause at this critical time. The Assembly evidently agreed, for it did not renew the proposals to modify the charter at its next session.[23]

In July 1780, as war costs mounted, the Assembly approved another estimate and prepared to impose another tax levy. This move produced immediate opposition and the estimate was revised in November. Yet several country towns complained or refused to cooperate, so a further revision was authorized at the May 1781 session. The grumbling continued, especially in Washington County; so the Assembly, in its valuation table of February 1782, made minor concessions to that area prior to imposing a state tax of £12,000 and a Continental levy of £6,000.[24]

The estimate and assessment of 1782 greatly aroused the freemen of Washington County. Particularly hard hit was South Kingstown whose valuation was set at a state high of £292,300, while Providence was a distant second with £217,000, and Portsmouth, with four Assembly votes, a remote twenty-fourth.[25]

A protest was in order, and on April 4, 1782, a convention composed of delegates from Westerly, Charlestown, Hopkinton, Exeter, Richmond and South Kingstown met at Little Rest (Kingston) and drafted resolutions requesting the General Assembly to devise a more equal mode of representation and taxation. The towns were especially aggrieved because communities that contributed less tax revenue than they, had "thrice & twice the number of voices in assessing the same."

Washington County communities unanimously recommended the calling of a constitutional convention composed of two delegates from each town.[26] South Kingstown enthusiastically approved these resolves in town meeting and instructed her deputies to work for their passage, but the influence of the Bay towns in

23 Cohen, ("Rhode Island and the Revolution," pp. 123–24) uncovered the articles of "the American Whig" in defense of the status quo. See the *Providence Gazette,* March 20 and April 24, 1779.

24 Reports, RIGA, IV, 15, 19, 21, 24, 37; *RICR,* IX, 169–70, 229–30, 260, 273–74, 279–80, 323, 397–98, 520–21.

25 See Table #1.

26 Charlestown Town Meetings, March 14 and April 17, 1782; Town Council and Probate Record, No. 3, 1767–1787.

the Assembly effectively prevented any positive response to the request of the Little Rest convention.[27]

Although the legislature was not responsive to the extreme demands of the towns aggrieved by the 1782 estimate, it was cognizant of their difficulties. In October 1782 it attempted to alleviate the distress by allowing the towns more time to collect the taxes which had been assessed.[28] This concession, while well-intended, did not solve the problem. In Glocester a few farmers attempted to divest the tax collector of some cattle he had confiscated from those who had refused to pay their rates. When these disgruntled rustics were arrested and placed on trial for their obstructionism, a mob, which included some Massachusetts men, rescued them. Before the situation got out of hand, Deputy Governor Jabez Bowen had the ringleaders captured and brought to trial. Most of the principal insurrectionists were heavily fined and ordered to jail until their fines were paid.[29] This quick action averted a minor Shay's Rebellion, but it left a residue of hard feelings in the country towns.

In February 1783 the Assembly made another attempt to lighten the tax load on Rhode Island's towns by placing an excise on certain enumerated foreign imports. In June this expedient was repealed and replaced with a general *ad valorem* impost of two per cent, but the revenue from this measure was insufficient to alleviate the financial plight of the state's municipalities. The legislature made an additional effort to aid the agrarian communities in October 1783 by revising upward the valuations for the island towns of Newport County. Despite this adjustment, farming towns on the mainland continued to shoulder the major tax burden.[30]

---

[27] South Kingstown Town Meetings, April 1 and April 29, 1782, Town Meeting Records, 1776–1836, pp. 146–48. On April 17, 1782 rural West Greenwich in Kent County instructed her deputies in the General Assembly to work for equal representation. Town Meeting Book No. 2, 1773–1811, RISA, pp. 91–92.

[28] *RICR,* IX, 606–07.

[29] Cohen, "Rhode Island and the Revolution," pp. 144–45.

[30] *Ibid.,* pp. 145–46; *RICR,* IX, 699, 718, 729–30; Elisha Dyer,

Reports of General Treasurer Joseph Clarke for 1782–86 reveal how burdened these towns were. South Kingstown, by far the most distressed, was continually deficient in its collections. In February 1786, on the eve of the paper money emission, the town was listed as delinquent for every levy since imposition of the 1782 estimate. Hopkinton, Richmond, and Coventry were also far in arrears, but in lesser amounts than South Kingstown, which owed £2,668 in back taxes.[31]

In early 1784 distress became acute. Two communities, Westerly and Hopkinton, feeling that a scarcity of currency was at the root of the problem, vainly urged the mercantile-controlled Assembly for an emission of paper currency.[32] Other hard-hit Washington County communities decided to call a second convention. This body met on April 1, 1784 in South Kingstown. As in 1782, it again demanded reapportionment. Further, it alleged that the present tax system was inequitable. To relieve the financial pressure upon the country towns it was urged that the impost be raised to five per cent.[33] Although several rural communities in other parts of the state officially expressed views similar to those advanced by the Washington County convention,[34] the

---

comp., *Valuation of the Cities and Towns in the State of Rhode Island* . . . (Prov., 1871), pp. 36–39.

[31] Reports, RIGA, IV, 74, 90, 94, 97, 101. For the condition of the taxes 1786–89, a period in which South Kingstown continued deficient despite the issuance of paper money, see Miscellaneous Manuscripts, Rhode Island Historical Society, R–346, hereafter cited Misc. Mss., RIHS. In early 1783 the General Assembly considered dividing South Kingstown in the same manner as it had bisected Scituate in 1781. This proposal was designed to solve the town's apportionment ills. However, South Kingstown strongly rejected this solution. Town Meeting Records, 1776–1836, pp. 161, 165–66.

[32] Cohen, "Rhode Island and the Revolution," p. 146.

[33] Resolves of the convention of 1784 are in Misc. Mss., RIHS, So 87, C 884 (Charlestown), and N874c. North Kingstown, South Kingstown, Exeter, Westerly, Hopkinton, Richmond, and Charlestown participated in the convention.

[34] Cohen, "Rhode Island and the Revolution," after examining town meeting records in other parts of the state, finds that Coventry, Foster, Johnston, Scituate, Smithfield, Warwick and West Greenwich took positions similar to the South Kingstown convention. See p. 147, footnote

Assembly remained cool to these protests. Their only concession was a raising of the impost by one-half of one per cent.[35]

After the convention of 1784 the equal representation movement temporarily abated only to revive in 1787 after country towns gained the ascendancy in the General Assembly. From beginning to end, however, this movement was not primarily one for constitutional reform *per se,* but rather a protest against oppressive taxation.

II

Although the War for Independence left the structure of Rhode Island government unchanged, despite the representation controversy, and though it failed to effect a drastic overturn in governmental personnel, it did prompt some legal and political changes within the state. The Revolution and the sentiments which it generated influenced legislation affecting Catholics and Negro slaves.

Whatever anti-Catholicism existed in Rhode Island was mollified by the assistance rendered to the struggling colonials by Catholic France and by the presence of large numbers of French troops in Newport under General Rochambeau, some of whom remained when the struggle was over. Thus, the General Assembly in February 1783 removed the arbitrarily imposed disability against Roman Catholics by giving members of that religion "all the rights and privileges of the Protestant citizens of this state." [36]

The most significant of the several Revolution-inspired statutes relating to Negroes was the emancipation act of 1784. With a preface invoking the sentiments of Locke, namely, that "all men are entitled to life, liberty and property," the gradual manumis-

---

#69. I have found statements of support in Misc. Mss., RIHS, F-811 (Foster) and Johnston (J-641).

[35] *RICR,* X, 48–49.

[36] *RICR,* IX, 674–75. The General Assembly was unaware that the Catholic disqualification had been inserted, without individual passage, in the *Digest of 1719,* for the 1783 measure purported to repeal the "Act of March, 1663." The Jews, also disfranchised in 1719, were not mentioned in the repeal statute.

sion measure gave freedom to all children born to slave mothers after March 1, 1784. Though this was an encouraging gesture it was not a complete abolition of slavery, for it failed to require emancipation of those who were slaves at the time of its passage.[37] One such individual, James Howland, remained technically and legally a slave until his death in 1859 on the eve of John Brown's raid.[38]

A side-effect of the Revolution that was to have important consequences for Rhode Island's political and constitutional development was the decline of Newport. Its exposed location, the incidence of Toryism among its townspeople, and its temporary occupation by the British, combined to produce both a voluntary and, at times, a forced exodus of its inhabitants. In 1774 its population was 9,209; by 1782 that figure had dwindled to 5,532. Conversely, the population of Providence, more sheltered at the head of the Bay, and a center of Revolutionary activity, remained stationary during these turbulent times.[39] The Revolution was a blow from which Newport never fully recovered. British occupation adversely affected both its population and its prosperity. From this period onward, numerical and economic ascendancy inexorably moved northward to Providence and the surrounding mainland communities.[40]

---

[37] *RICR,* X, 7. Other significant anti-slave statutes were a law of October 1779 which forbade the sale of Rhode Island slaves outside the state without their consent, *Ibid.,* VIII, 618; and a February 1778 measure which granted freedom to those slaves who enlisted in Rhode Island's "colored regiment," upon completion of their term of duty, *Ibid.,* VIII, 358–60. The Quaker influence on Rhode Island's anti-slave movement is discussed in Mack Thompson, *Moses Brown: Reluctant Reformer* (Chapel Hill, North Carolina, 1962), pp. 92–96, 175–202.

[38] Edwin W. Snow, *Report Upon the Census of Rhode Island: 1865* (Providence, 1867), p. xlvi.

[39] Population changes have been noted by comparing figures in Bartlett, *Census of 1774* with "Rhode Island Census of 1782," Vol. XIV, Theodore Foster Papers, RIHS.

[40] On the economic decline of Newport and Providence's rise see Lovejoy, *Rhode Island Politics,* pp. 193–94; Franklin Stuart Coyle, "The Survival of Providence Business Enterprise in the American Revolutionary Era, 1770–1785" (unpublished master's thesis, Brown University, 1960); Nancy Fisher Chudacoff, "The Revolution and the

The failure of political power to make as rapid a journey up the Bay, because of the charter's inflexible apportionment clause, became the source of increasing discontent and eventually prompted a number of calls for constitutional change. In the late eighteenth century, however, those càlls were sporadic and lacking in urgency. Only the equal representation movement posed a threat to any portion of the charter. Most Rhode Islanders apparently shared the opinion of David Howell, who made the following complacent observation in 1782, while serving as one of the state's popularly elected delegates to the Confederation Congress: "As you go Southward Government verges towards Aristocracy. In New England alone have we pure and unmixed Democracy and in Rhode Island & P.P. it is in its Perfection." [41]

With Howell's view evidently reflecting the sentiments of a majority of his fellow citizens, it is not surprising that during the decade of the 1780s the state's major constitutional disputes were not internal, but instead revolved around Rhode Island's relation to the central government, and especially to that system envisioned by the convention of 1787.

Town: Providence, 1775–1783," *Rhode Island History*, XXXV (Aug., 1976), 71–89; and Peter J. Coleman, *The Transformation of Rhode Island,* 1790–1860 (Providence, 1963) pp. 20–22. Coleman lists two factors preventing Newport's revival: it was no longer favorably located for sustained commercial expansion because its island location denied it access to mainland markets, and it suffered from "the exodus of entrepreneurial leadership that had made the town a great commercial center" (pp. 67–68).

[41] Howell to Welcome Arnold, August 3, 1782, quoted in Hillman Metcalf Bishop, *Why Rhode Island Opposed the Federal Constitution* (Providence, 1950), p. 11. This work is a pamphlet reprint of four articles by Bishop which appeared serially in *Rhode Island History,* VIII (1949).

CHAPTER FOUR

Paper Money and Party Politics

I

Rhode Island's initial response to a plan for a permanent central government was surprisingly cordial. Such a proposal was advanced by the *ad hoc* Continental Congress in 1777 and embodied in the Articles of Confederation that were drafted and debated by Congress, and placed before the rebellious states in late 1777. Delegate Henry Marchant bore this first national constitution to Rhode Island and urged its acceptance at a special session of the General Assembly in December. The question of adoption was deferred to the February 1778 session, but at that conclave Rhode Island promptly gave its assent unanimously. Three amendments were suggested, but these were merely recommendations and not prerequisites for ratification.

Rhode Island was uncharacteristically obliging because several of its towns were under British occupation and because it had incurred enormous military expenditures that might be partially absorbed by the new central government. Rhode Island instructed its delegates to ratify if eight other states should do so and, in the event that any alterations in the Articles were advanced, it empowered its delegates to accept whatever changes

were approved by nine of the states. Rhode Island further promised that it would be bound by any alterations agreed to in this
manner. No changes were made in the Articles, however, and the
state's representatives unhesitatingly signed the form of ratification in Philadelphia on July 9, 1778, hailing the document as
"the Grand Corner Stone" of the new nation.[1]

In the succeeding twelve years Rhode Island would seldom
act with such compliance toward the federal union. In fact, it
exhibited a recalcitrance in the national councils that proved
exasperating to many of its sister states. Rhode Island's initial
contrariness consisted in a flat rejection of the proposed continental impost of 1781, despite the efforts of Thomas Paine and
other prominent figures to enlist the state's support.

The impost proposal was advanced in the form of an amendment to the Articles which authorized Congress to levy a duty
of five percent on the value of all goods imported into the United
States. The revenue from this anticipated duty was to be applied
to the discharge of principal and interest on continental debts
arising from the war.[2]

After Rhode Island and others demurred, the frustrated Congress in 1783 revised this original program to meet some of the
objections offered by the measure's opponents. But Rhode Island
first ignored and then rejected this concession as well.[3] For reasons which shall be outlined, the merchants then gradually re-

[1] The foregoing discussion of the Articles is derived from *RICR*, VIII,
341, 362, 364–67; Jensen, *The Articles*, pp. 190–95; Edmund Cody Burnett, *The Continental Congress* (New York, 1941), pp. 341–44; Worthington C. Ford, *et. al.*, eds., *Journals of the Continental Congress, 1774–
1789* (Washington, 1904–37), XI, 638–39, 663, hereafter cited *JCC*.

[2] Bishop, pp. 5–14; Merrill Jensen, *The New Nation: A History of the
United States During the Confederation, 1781–1789* (New York, 1950),
p. 58; Nevins, pp. 630–37; Polishook, *Rhode Island and the Union*, pp.
53–80.

[3] Frank Greene Bates, *Rhode Island and the Formation of the Union*
(New York, 1898), pp. 72–99, *Columbia Studies in History, Economics
and Public Law* (Vol. X, No. 2). In 1785 Rhode Island took an un-
satisfactory first step towards adopting the impost plan of 1783 when the
Assembly passed a law imposing the duties as requested, but with un-
acceptable conditions. These included collection of the duties by state
agents, a limitation of $8,000 per year on the amount collected in Rhode

versed their stand and used their considerable influence to secure final approval of the impost by the General Assembly at its
February session, 1786.[4]

It had long been thought that Rhode Island's opposition to the
continental impost prior to 1786 was merely the result of extreme
individualism, an attachment to states' rights, and a fear of all
outside authority. Such a position contains some validity, but it
is simplistic and gives too much prominence to rhetoric. Further,
it overlooks the fact that the merchant class led the impost opposition, and this group, of course, was the same element which
vigorously fought for a new constitution — a measure that centralized power in the national government and diminished states'
rights to a far greater extent than any national duty.

True, the merchants in their campaign against the impost used
popular political and theoretical arguments. They did so, however, to conceal their real economic motives and to enlist the
support of the large farm population. Their rationalizations included the popular idea that all political power must be jealously
guarded and cautiously distributed, the notion that the impost
proposal would make Congress independent of the people, and
the admonition that the granting to Congress of a revenue independent of the states could destroy democracy by making that
body uncontrollable.[5]

An official statement reflecting these objections was presented
to the Congress itself as the unanimous resolutions of the General Assembly. This declaration contended that: (1) the impost
would be unequal, bearing hardest on the commercial states;
(2) this program was against the Rhode Island charter, because

---

Island which could be applied toward the payment of the nation's foreign
debts, and a proviso that any sum in excess of the $8,000 be used to dis-
charge that portion of the country's domestic debt which was held in
Rhode Island. *RICR*, X, 87–88. Allan Nevins calls this measure "a con-
glomerate, but almost wholly bad law, complying only in a small part
with the Congressional requirements. . . . It was simply a plan for state
revenue." Nevins goes on to show, however, that the ultimate responsibility for squelching the impost in 1786 rested with New York. Nevins,
pp. 630–42.

[4] Bates, p. 99. *Schedules,* February session, 1786, pp. 33–35.

[5] This political rhetoric is summarized by Bishop, pp. 6–12.

it admitted into Rhode Island officers unaccountable to the state government; and (3) the indefinite granting to Congress of an indefinite quantity of money would make the members thereof "independent of their constituents; and so the proposed impost is repugnant to the liberty of the United States." [6]

During the impost debate other formidable objections were advanced. One argument, which appealed to merchants and farmers alike, was that if the Rhode Island Assembly surrendered impost duties to Congress, a major source of state revenue would be sacrificed. In that event, state creditors would be left on a tenuous footing, and the burden of direct taxation (on real and personal property) to support state debts would be substantially increased. [7]

Another objection stemmed from the state's anxiety respecting the disposal of the western lands. David Howell, a leading foe of the impost, urged the Assembly not to yield the right to levy duties within Rhode Island's borders until the equal right to the public domain was established by Congress. As long as the western lands were still held by some states to the prejudice of others, Howell exhorted, a concession on the impost must not be made. [8]

The merchants, who spearheaded the attack on the continental duty, were primarily moved, however, by yet other considerations. Their real motives rested in large part upon the "peculiar nature of Rhode Island commerce." Before the Revolution, merchants of the colony lacked products for export because of the state's dearth of resources. Thus, the imaginative traders were forced to act as middlemen by importing foreign goods from abroad and reexporting these commodities at a profit. This situation, whereby the bulk of the articles imported into Rhode Island were exported either abroad or to other states, continued during the decade of the 1780s. The merchants' principal oppo-

---

[6] Jensen, *The New Nation*, p. 64. Quote is from the resolutions that are printed in *JCC*, XXIII, 788–89.

[7] Forrest McDonald, *We The People* (Chicago, 1958), p. 325.

[8] Bates, pp. 80, 87–88; David Howell to Governor Greene, July 30, 1782 in Staples, *RICC*, pp. 381–87. There is a wealth of significant documents on Howell and the impost controversy printed in Staples, *RICC*, 375 ff.

sition to the impost, therefore, stemmed from their belief that it would be detrimental to their trade. Since the plan of 1781 allowed no drawback on goods reexported (as opposed to those consumed within the state), Rhode Island merchants, in order to be competitive, would be compelled to absorb the five percent duty instead of adding it to the cost of the reexported articles.[9]

Although the merchants' campaign against the impost was initially successful, their triumph was far from an unmixed blessing, and they soon had occasion to regret their part in the impost's demise. Events proved that they had been uncharacteristically shortsighted, for after the first defeat of the national impost in 1782, several states resorted to tariffs of their own in an effort to obtain funds with which to pay the interest on their war debts. Because these levies generally excluded articles of American growth or manufacture, they did not directly hurt the farming interests. But these state duties did impose a heavy load on the Rhode Island merchant, who was obliged to pay not only the two-and-one-half percent *ad valorem* Rhode Island duty of 1784 on goods he imported,[10] but also a similar duty on wares he reexported to neighboring states. The tariff levies of adjacent Massachusetts and Connecticut were especially burdensome on Rhode Island commerce.[11]

The defeat of the impost backfired upon the merchants in a

---

[9] Bishop, pp. 8–9; James Blaine Hedges, *The Browns of Providence Plantations: Colonial Years* (Cambridge, Mass., 1952), pp. 323–25. Another factor contributing to Rhode Island's rejection of impost stemmed from the speculative activities of several Providence merchants (most notably Nicholas Brown) who exchanged rising value continental loan office certificates for the declining value securities of several states at a propitious moment when passage of the impost appeared imminent, and then worked for rejection of the impost in Rhode Island to effect a decline in the value of the relinquished continental securities and a sharp rise in the newly acquired state certificates. Nicholas Brown apparently made $30,000 by engaging in this bold bit of speculative legerdemain. McDonald, *We The People,* pp. 325–26; Hedges, pp. 314–23.

[10] *RICR,* X, 48–49.

[11] Bishop, pp. 12–13; Hedges, pp. 324–25; Donald E. McKiernan, "The Debtor-Creditor Struggle in Rhode Island, 1781–1790," (unpublished master's thesis, Rhode Island College, 1967), pp. 2–5.

second area as well. Without the impost, Congress lacked an adequate and independent source of revenue that would have eased its task of servicing the continental debt. The penury of Congress allowed it to pay only a fraction of the interest on that obligation, a circumstance which greatly depressed the value of its securities. As the continental loan office certificates were largely in the hands of the merchants, they came to see that an adequate revenue for the general government was essential to a rise in the worth of national securities. This belated realization contributed to Rhode Island's acceptance of the continental impost in 1786.[12]

A final product of their impost campaign was the persistence of a public opinion hostile to or at least suspicious of every attempt to increase the powers of the central government. Hillman Bishop has called this feeling (which has been variously described as states' rightism, individualism, separatism and democracy) "the chief result of the extensive propaganda campaign against the Impost." Bishop contends that "voters who had been led to believe that the small increase in the powers of Congress contemplated by the continental impost was a threat to democracy and liberty were certain to reject the Federal Constitution." [13] It should be emphasized, however, that the merchants' propaganda merely intensified and invigorated the political sentiments of Rhode Islanders, especially those in the agricultural country towns. Such appeals to democracy, liberty, and states

---

[12] Bishop, pp. 13–14; Hedges, pp. 325–26. By blocking the impost from 1781–86 and committing the state to pay the interest on continental securities, the merchants again actually worked against the forces of centralization that they were to champion from 1787 to 1790. E. James Ferguson has shown in his *The Power of the Purse: A History of American Public Finance, 1776–1790* (Chapel Hill, North Carolina, 1961), pp. 116–17, 142–45, that prior to 1787 "the nationalist cause was represented by the effort to vest the Revolutionary debt in Congress and give Congress the taxing power to support it, whereas state-oriented finance worked in a contrary direction." From 1781 to 1786 the Rhode Island mercantile community pursued fiscal policies which were contrary to those advocated by Robert Morris and other exponents of centralized authority. In the struggle over ratification they would come to rue their inconsistency.

[13] Bishop, p. 10.

rightism would never have been uttered if the majority of Rhode Islanders did not cherish these ideals, nor would such arguments have been so warmly embraced or enduring in their impact.

II

As the impost controversy reached its denouement in 1786, the infamous paper money era began. The sentiments and actions engendered both by the impost and the paper emission made fiscal matters the storm-center of Rhode Island political activity from 1781–91, and, as Forrest McDonald has perceptively stated, "only through an understanding of the intricacies of the state's financial history during the decade can the background of the contest over ratification be comprehended." [14]

The paper money agitation is even more complex, significant, and misunderstood than the impost controversy that preceded it. This currency plan was the offspring of Rhode Island's Revolutionary debt. By 1784, the state had put its financial house in order by "scaling" or adjusting its war obligations. The final figures revealed that the state government owed about £96,000 to private creditors. Of this total £50,000 was held by approximately 250 individuals in the form of six percent notes, and the balance by about 2,300 individuals (over half the voters in the state) in the form of four percent notes. The remaining computed debt was much larger, but it was charged against the national government. This included claims of the state government for uncompensated expenditures on behalf of Congress, and

---

[14] McDonald, *We The People*, p. 324. My summary of the paper money issue is based largely upon the persuasive interpretation of McDonald. This economic historian has revealed the complexities of Rhode Island's frenzied finance during the "critical era" by closely examining the pertinent documents relating to the paper money issue which are located in the Rhode Island State Archives. McDonald's insights are invaluable, but his narrative of the ratification process in Rhode Island is marred by numerous errors of fact. These misstatements will be corrected in succeeding footnotes. Old, written with an anti-paper animus, but still useful, is Elisha R. Potter, Jr. and Sidney S. Rider, *Some Account of the Bills of Credit, or Paper Money, of R. I. from 1710–1786*, Rhode Island Historical Tracts, ed. S. S. Rider, VIII (Providence, 1880).

claims of individuals for goods and supplies furnished to prosecute the war. These demands totaled £1,178,000 but the bulk of this sum would never be forthcoming.

There was another claim against the national Congress, however, that was quite significant. This debt took the form of continental loan office certificates amounting to £157,200 or $524,-000. Two-thirds of these securities were owned by Providence citizens, mostly merchants, and more than half by twelve men in that city. Among the big twelve merchant princes were John and Nicholas Brown, Zachariah and Philip Allen, Jabez Bowen, Welcome Arnold, and the powerful firm of Clarke and Nightingale. When final settlement certificates and other federal obligations were added to the loan office securities they produced a state total of $598,941 held by 411 individuals. Citizens of Providence and Newport owned $425,122 or 71 percent of this total.[15]

The enlightened self-interest of Rhode Island was so strong that it voluntarily assumed a portion of the continental debt burden by attempting to support the interest on those continental securities owned in the state. Mercantile influence in the Assembly prior to 1786 no doubt produced this fiscal concern. In fact while the merchants controlled the state government, vigorous efforts were made to collect those taxes that had been levied to meet the interest on the continental debt. Prior to 1786, Rhode Island's record of compliance with congressional requisitions was one of the best in the Union. Also, contrary to popular opinion, Rhode Island was not disposed to repudiate its state debt, largely because of the widespread distribution of its notes.

At first, the state's import duties alone (the impost of two percent *ad valorem* in 1783 and two-and-one-half percent in 1784) were nearly sufficient to service the debt; but soon, as the interest obligation increased, heavier direct taxes on real property became necessary. These levies steadily increased until they

---

[15] More money had been subscribed in the Rhode Island loan office during the Revolution, in proportion to the state's population, than had been subscribed in any other state except Pennsylvania. Bishop, p. 19. For Rhode Island's public debt holdings see Ferguson, pp. 280–82.

became oppressive. By 1786, many Rhode Island taxpayers, especially those in the country towns, had been caught in an absurd dilemma — they were losing their realty because of nonpayment of taxes levied on it for the purpose of supporting interest payments on their own state securities and the merchants' continental certificates.

At this critical juncture an aggrieved and resourceful South County politician, Jonathan J. Hazard, called "Beau Jonathan" by his colleagues, advanced an ingenious paper money plan. Hazard, a deputy from the coastal but agrarian and non-commercial community of Charlestown and that town's harried tax collector, gathered about him a forceful group of rural politicians. These men studied intently the records of the state's last pre-Revolutionary issue of paper money in 1750, then decided to adopt a similar program to solve Rhode Island's contemporary financial ills.

The paper money plan was to operate in the following manner: paper money, in an amount approximately equal to Rhode Island's war debt of £96,000, was to be printed and made legal tender for all public obligations and taxes. The paper would then be lent to those borrowers who could furnish good security — namely, real estate. Land, in fact, was the most desirable collateral both economically and politically because the right to vote was dependent upon its ownership.

Provisions would be made to prevent depreciation of the paper, for if it maintained its face value, the interest to be collected on it would be roughly equivalent to the interest owed by the state on its six and four percent certificates. If taxes were continued at existing levels, they would then be easier to pay because of the increased money in circulation. These taxes would be sufficient to retire the state debt at par in about seven years. If, however, the paper depreciated, it could be supported by increasing taxes fast enough to absorb the depreciation. If the tax revenues paid in this inflated money were used for debt service, the state would retire its debts in a much shorter time. Whether or not the paper depreciated, its issuance would relieve the current tax burden, and it would make the state, which was a debtor paying interest on nearly £100,000, also a creditor collecting interest on approximately the same amount.

By late 1785, Hazard and his associates had worked out the details of this well-conceived and imaginative scheme; during 1786 they set out to secure its implementation. In February they prompted the Assembly to request the towns to instruct their deputies regarding the desirability of a paper money issue. In March they attempted to gauge legislative sentiment with a motion to issue paper, but it was defeated in the lower house by a vote of 43 to 18, the same margin, incidentally, by which the impost was approved at the February session.[16]

Undaunted by this temporary setback, the paper money men stumped the state explaining the intricacies of the plan to disgruntled Rhode Island taxpayers. Hazard, a powerful orator, "subtle and ingenious in debate," led the educational campaign. This approach was most successful. In the April town meetings only the Bay towns of Providence, Portsmouth, and Newport instructed their delegates to oppose the issue. These meetings effected an overturn in the lower house by selecting thirty-eight new deputies to the General Assembly. In the general election John Collins of Newport, an advocate of paper money, won the governorship by a wide margin, as did a paper party deputy governor and five new assistants. These spring 1786 elections marked the coming to power of the pro-paper "Country" or "Land-

---

[16] At this time even some of the debt-ridden towns recoiled from the prospect of paper. For example, South Kingstown, the community with the greatest tax delinquency, declared against emission of paper currency "without a dissention" in town meeting on February 20 and reaffirmed this position at a special meeting one week later. By July 1786, however, they were vigorously supporting it. Town Meeting Records, 1776–1836, p. 218. For instructions given to the representatives of several other Rhode Island towns in February 1786 on the emission of paper money, see Papers Relating to the Adoption of the Constitution of the United States, pp. 40 ff., Rhode Island State Archives, hereafter cited PAC. Ironically, Charlestown's Town Meeting in February 1786 also voted against instructing its deputies to support emission. *Ibid.*, p. 59. The preserved instructions of Warwick, Cranston, Cumberland, Glocester, Smithfield, Coventry, Richmond, Tiverton, and Middletown indicate that they approved the paper money plan. *Ibid.*, pp. 40–63.

holders" party and the eclipse of mercantile control in the General Assembly.[17]

The victors, directed by deputy Hazard, wasted little time when the Assembly convened; their plans had been well laid. Within days they passed a law authorizing the issuance of £100,-000 in paper money according to the general outlines of the Hazard proposal. The act established, in effect, a land bank, where government-authorized paper bills, which had the capacity of legal tender, would be lent at the rate of four percent. These loans were to be well secured by mortgages on real property that was worth twice the nominal value of the currency lent. The duration of the loan was to be fourteen years with interest due for the first seven, and the principal repayable in equal annual installments during the second seven-year period.

The law contained numerous devices designed to maintain the par value of the paper. The most important and the most controversial were the provision making paper the legal tender for all debts public and private, and the infamous lodge money or "Know ye" clause which provided that if a private creditor should refuse to receive the paper, the debtor could discharge the debt by "lodging" or depositing the paper money with one of the judges of the county courts of common pleas. If the creditor declined to accept the "lodge money" after citation by the court, the judge was to issue public notice ("Know ye") that the tender had been made. Should the creditor remain adamant, the debt was declared cancelled after a three-month waiting period and the money was forfeited to the state.[18]

This plan encountered the inveterate opposition of the merchants, some of whom set out to discredit the issue and undermine faith in it through a palpably false propaganda campaign.

---

[17] McDonald, *We The People,* pp. 321–331. In March 1786 the merchant-controlled Assembly had granted a limited concession to the debtor interests by passing "An act for making real and certain enumerated articles of personal estates . . . liable under certain restrictions for the payment of debts upon execution." *RICR,* X, 182. This act fell short of the debtors' demands. It was repealed in June 1786. *Ibid.,* p. 205.

[18] RIGA, Records, XIII, 262–66.

The merchants, who regarded a hard-money policy as essential to economic stability, inaccurately charged that the emission was the work of radical agrarian debtors who wished to defraud creditors of their just compensation, and some of these merchants boldly borrowed large sums of the new paper to use as a fund for manipulating its value downward on the open market.[19]

The source of the merchants' discontent stemmed basically from the fact that the paper plan neglected the continental creditors, most of whom were members of the powerful mercantile establishment. The leaders of the "Country Party" were determined to pay the state debt, but they abandoned all responsibility for redeeming continental obligations. Their supporters in the western towns believed that this expense should be borne exclusively by Congress while a majority of freemen in the Bay communities (Providence, Newport, Bristol, and Warren excepted) felt it unjust that they were taxed to support these national securities while they received no money from either the state or Congress for war losses. That many of the continental securities had passed from the hands of their original owners, often farmers, into the hands of merchant-speculators, usually at a fraction of their face value, made direct taxation to support interest payments on these certificates even more objectionable.[20]

Another typical complaint was articulated in Smithfield's instructions to her deputies in April 1786. The town leaders contended that "there have been many examples where one year's interest hath been paid in silver, that was worth more than the principal was when loaned." [21] This incongruous situation, whereby the annual interest on the continental securities (raised by taxation and paid in specie) exceeded in value the depreci-

---

[19] The manipulation scheme is alluded to in Forrest McDonald, *E Pluribus Unum: The Formation of the American Republic, 1776–1790* (Boston, 1965), pp. 125–26.

[20] McDonald, *We The People*, pp. 330, 333–34. There was less speculation in the public debt in Rhode Island than in most other states. The "rate of transfer" was a relatively low 52 percent. Ferguson, 280–81.

[21] The Smithfield petition is in PAC, p. 54.

ated certificates themselves, was not to be tolerated by those who owned none.

Many merchants, however, and a sizable number of the freemen of Providence held continental loan office certificates. In fact, a dozen powerful and influential merchant-speculators in that town owned about half of the $524,000 in loan office securities held in the state.[22] No plan that ignored this debt could meet with the approval of Providence, nor could one which cut off the coveted specie that the merchants needed to satisfy their unrelenting foreign creditors. A principal source of this specie, of course, had been the interest paid in silver on the merchants' continental certificates.

The opposition to the paper plan in Newport was also formidable, but less strenuous than that manifested by Providence. The port towns of Bristol and Warren harbored hard money sentiments as well, but the remainder of the state, especially the interior towns, was firmly in the grip of the paperites as the May 1786 session drew to a close.[23]

The merchants issued vociferous denunciations of the paper money scheme. They alleged, without foundation, that since the paper would not be accepted outside the state, it would destroy Rhode Island's commerce. Their favorite tactic, however, was to depict the advocates of paper money as an unscrupulous band of dishonest debtors seeking to defraud their creditors. Because the anti-paper merchants controlled the principal means of communication, including the local press, this latter charge was often repeated and accepted as accurate both by contemporaries in other states and by historians.[24]

A man in large measure responsible for the dissemination of this anti-paper propaganda was journalist Peter Edes. This spokesman for the mercantile interest published a remarkable

---

[22] McDonald, *We The People*, pp. 334.

[23] Bates, pp. 123–29.

[24] Bates, for example, in his generally sound study, gives the following appraisal of the money plan: "Conceived in ignorance, and supported by folly and dishonesty, it had brought discord, repudiation and misery," p. 148.

series of articles in the pages of his *Newport Herald* reporting
on the proceedings of the General Assembly during the period
between the spring of 1787 and January 1790, when the legislature authorized a convention to ratify the Federal Constitution.
Edes's reports still provide the best existing description of the
legislative debates during the closing years of the confederation,
but they display a strong anti-paper and pro-Federalist bias.
Nonetheless they were frequently reprinted in newspapers
throughout the United States without proper caution that Edes's
indictment of the Country party was partial and distorted. Some
Federalist editors even embellished Edes's unflattering appraisal
of the paper money men. Francis Childs, publisher of the New
York *Daily Advertiser,* for example, reproduced one of Edes's
reports under the heading "Quintessence of Villainy." [25]

Contrary to the Newport editor's allegations, however, the
three most careful historians of confederation Rhode Island and
its paper issue persuasively maintain that the cancellation of
private debts was only a relatively insignificant by-product of
the scheme, not its essential purpose.[26] Forrest McDonald and
Hillman Bishop support this conclusion by alluding to the published announcements of lodge money deposits. Such deposits,
which represented all private debts cancelled by paper against
the wishes of the creditor, amounted to £17,000 out of a total
emission of £96,608 in paper bills. Actually, fewer than 300 different individuals, about two percent of the adult male population, were involved in the lodge money transactions in any
capacity. McDonald further demonstrates that "there is no foundation in fact for the commonly accepted generalization that the
paper-money movement in Rhode Island represented the actions
of large bands of debtor-farmers who were using depreciated
paper currency to pay obligations due to merchant-creditors."

---

[25] Edes's accounts have been collected by Irwin H. Polishook, ed.,
"Peter Edes's Report of the Proceedings of the Rhode Island General As-
sembly, 1787–1790," *Rhode Island History,* XXV (April, 1966), 33–42;
(July, 1966), 87–97; (Oct., 1966), 117–129; XXVI (Jan., 1967), 15–31.

[26] McDonald, *We The People,* pp. 332–33; Polishook, *Rhode Island
and the Union,* pp. 103–173; Bishop, pp. 15–25.

Both farmers and merchants involved themselves in the relatively few lodge money transactions; both availed themselves of this method of debt reduction.[27] The real motives behind the issuance of paper, for all but the most radical of the Country party, were tax relief and reduction of the state debt. The principal objections to the paper money program, as we have seen, stemmed from the abandonment by the Country party of all responsibility for continental obligations, and the plan's indirect curtailment of specie.

The propaganda of the merchants and their private manipulations helped to undermine popular faith in the new currency, and it depreciated rapidly. Thirty months following its issuance it had declined in worth at a steady rate until its market value was less than eight cents on the dollar. For two years it remained at this low level, then it rose to sixteen cents on the dollar, a value it held until all but a fraction of it was retired in 1800.[28] The depreciation, however, did not seriously impair the plan to retire state debts; in fact, it hastened the process.

In December 1786 the program of debt service began when the Assembly authorized the payment in paper of the first quarter of the state's six percent obligations. A March 1787 statute penalized those who refused to comply with this system by providing for the partial forfeiture of their securities and the interest thereon to the state if they failed to present their certificates to the general treasurer as directed.

The second quarterly payment on this debt was authorized in June 1787; the third in February 1788; and the final portion in March 1789. Meanwhile, in October and December 1788, authorization acts were passed allowing the holders of four percent notes to receive their compensation from the state. Thus, by mid-

---

27 McDonald, *We The People,* p. 333; Bishop, pp. 23–25, states that "many paper money supporters reprobated the action of those who lodged paper currency with the judges. Many who approved the use of paper money to liquidate the state debt did not approve the tendering of paper for debts originally incurred in gold." These moderates made paper money legal tender for private debts because they believed that this step was necessary in order to maintain the value of the emission.

28 McDonald, *We The People,* pp. 335–36.

1789 Rhode Island's entire debt had been liquidated, and the annual expenses of the debt-free government were reduced to less than £10,000. Forty percent of these expenses could be met by interest payments on the paper loaned, and the remainder supplied by import duties. To the delight and relief of all, especially the landholding farm population, the direct tax load had been abolished.

In retrospect, the paper plan must be considered a success, and the standard criticisms of the program must be adjudged inaccurate and undeserved. The state government benefited by retiring its pressing debt. The taxpayers also gained relief. So did the many holders of state securities, because the depreciated paper they received was worth more than the depreciated securities they had owned. The principal aims of the Country party had been effectively achieved. In addition, Rhode Island's interstate and foreign trade enjoyed an annual increase throughout the period of agitation, depite the merchants' apprehensions.[29]

But the controversial emission of '86 was a mixed blessing. Forrest McDonald in his perceptive defense of the paper plan lists two detrimental and unfortunate results of the scheme. The worst effect of the paper, says McDonald, was the great damage it did to the reputation of Rhode Island among its sister states. The dubious credit for this achievement must be shared by the Providence merchant princes and the irascible Peter Edes for, in their efforts to discredit the Country party, they further tarnished the already questionable reputation of their state as well. "Rogue's Island," the home of the dishonest debtor, was the image they presented to a condescending nation.

A second bad effect of the paper, asserts McDonald, was that

---

[29] *Ibid.* The schedule of debt retirement can be traced in RIGA, Records, XIII, 343, 359, 397, 429–30, 451, 478, 547, 569, 586–87. The taxes levied during this period were: £20,000 (June 1786), £20,000 (March 1787), £30,000 (Sept. 1787), £30,000 (June 1788), £20,000 (March 1789). *Ibid.,* 287–90, 359–62, 404, 407–08, 410–12, 527, 532–35, 589–92. McDonald errs when he states that "in 1788 the debts were retired in four quarterly installments." McDonald, *We The People,* p. 336. McDonald, *Ibid.,* p. 335 and Polishook, *Rhode Island and the Union,* pp. 168–70 agree regarding the increase in trade.

some private creditors suffered because £17,000 in depreciated bills were used to satisfy personal debts. These losses, of course, were far less significant than previously supposed, but this was little consolation to those creditors who were forced either to accept the lodged paper or forfeit it to the state.[30]

There were several other undesirable consequences of the paper controversy, however, that McDonald neglected to identify. First, the controversy caused hardship, privation, and subsequent reprisals which the disputants in the affair imposed upon one another. These recriminations engendered long-standing bitterness. For example, in the first weeks following the emission, merchants in the towns closed their stores rather than sell their goods for paper, while the farmers, who had mortgaged their lands to secure paper, sought to compel the townspeople to accept the money by withholding their produce from the market. Relations between town and country during this critical period were increasingly marked by suspicion and resentment.[31]

The debit side of the paper money ledger must also include mention of the bold, aggressive, and often unjust means employed by the Country party to implement and protect its program. A consideration of those means involves us with several issues relating directly to the state's constitutional development.

The most flagrant attempts made by the paper money men to defeat, coerce, or punish their opponents included: (1) the passage of a forcing act in June 1786 providing a heavy fine for non-acceptance of the paper or for contributing to its depreciation; (2) the addition of an amendment to this act in August 1786 providing for trial without jury or appeal for violators (this amendment was the law challenged in the famous case of *Trevett v. Weeden*); (3) an unsuccessful attempt to require a test oath binding the taker to make every effort to uphold the value of paper, and barring from public office all who refused to swear; (4) the revocation of recalcitrant Newport's city charter; and (5) a renewal of the equal representation movement, which

---

[30] McDonald, *We The People*, p. 336.
[31] Bates, pp. 126–28.

now offered the added prospect of weakening the mercantile opposition.

These maneuvers were those of a desperate faction, and they exhibited an unfortunate disregard for the rights of the minority opposition. It was, perhaps, these measures employed in conjunction with the paper emission that prompted many of the vehement denunciations of the Country party by the mercantile community.

The first maneuver was the forcing act of June 1786, which was designed to check the rapid depreciation of the paper bills. This statute stipulated that any person who refused to take these bills at par in exchange for any articles he offered for sale, or should make any difference in the prices between silver and paper money in any sale or exchange, or should attempt to depreciate or discourage the passing of these bills, would be fined one hundred pounds for the first offense. For the second violation, he would be fined the same amount and be rendered ineligible to vote or hold office in the state.[32]

This penal law apparently failed to achieve its intended effect because of delays in meting out penalties to violators, so a special August session of the legislature was convened which modified it with an ill-advised amendment. The August act lessened the monetary penalty on those refusing the paper, but it provided for the immediate trial of violators by a special court.

This supplementary statute stated that if any person refused to receive paper according to the requirements of the previous laws, the individual tendering the money should apply for relief to a justice of the Superior Court or to a judge of the Court of Common Pleas in the county where the offense was committed. The judge handling the complaint was then directed to summon the refusing party to appear before a *special* court within three days to stand trial, without benefit of jury. The judgment of this special court was to be final and conclusive; no appeal from its decision was allowed. If the accused was found guilty, he was to

---

[32] RIGA, Records, XIII, 279–80. McDonald, *We The People*, p. 332, gives the erroneous impression that this supplementary act was part of the original paper money statute.

pay the assessed fine plus costs or be committed to the county jail "till sentence be performed." [33]

Needless to say, this law provoked an uproar because of its disdain for procedural due process, and it was immediately defied. In Newport, where the anti-paper forces held a majority, John Weeden, a butcher, refused to accept the paper tender of John Trevett offered in payment for meat. Trevett entered a complaint against the recalcitrant butcher with the Chief Justice of the Superior Court, Paul Mumford, thus precipitating the case of *Trevett v. Weeden*.[34]

Two of Rhode Island's ablest lawyers sprang to Weeden's defense — Henry Marchant, former attorney general and a recent delegate to the Continental Congress, and General James Mitchell Varnum, member of Congress from Rhode Island. The trial was conducted, despite provisions of the penal law, at a special *session* of the Superior Court of Judicature, Rhode Island's highest tribunal.[35] It was held in Newport on September

---

[33] RIGA, Records, XIII, 297–99; *RICR*, X, 212–13. Those who passed this bold measure also approved a law at this session making the paper money a tender in payment of continental taxes. *RICR*, X, 211–12.

[34] Information on this case and the trial of the judges which followed can be found in Papers Relating to the Trevett versus Weeden Case, 1786, Miscellaneous Manuscripts, Newport Historical Society, Box 43, Folder 12 which contains three other writs summoning violators of the act to court; James M. Varnum, *The Case, Trevett against Weeden*. . . . (Providence, 1787), an account by Weeden's counsel; *Providence Gazette,* Sept. 30 and Oct. 7, 1786; *Newport Mercury,* Oct. 2, 1786; *RICR*, X, 215, 218–19; RIGA, Records, XIII, 315–17. The most convenient and accessible compilation of relevant material is John D. Lawson, ed., *American State Trials* (St. Louis, 1914–36), IV, 558–599, but this collection contains numerous inaccuracies.

[35] The August penal law which Weeden was accused of violating specified that *special* courts should try all cases arising under it. The Chief Justice summoned a special court to try the case. It convened on September 20, but "adjourned over into" the Superior Court which was sitting at its September term. The case, therefore, for reasons not fully known, was tried before the Superior Court. In the words of Varnum, the most accurate source for this case, "Mumford . . . caused a Special Court to be convened. But as the information was given during the [September] term of the [Superior] Court, it was referred into the term for consideration and final determination." Varnum, pp. 1–3. Many historians have failed to grasp the existence and significance of this subtle distinction,

22, 1786 with Chief Justice Mumford presiding. The case was highlighted by Varnum's speech for the defense, a brief which the most thorough student of the development of judicial supremacy considers one "which indicates perhaps better than any other document prior to the federal Convention, some of the ideas on which reliance was placed in accepting the principle of judicial review of legislative enactments."[36]

At the outset Varnum, a man of eloquence and imposing appearance, prayed that the Court would not take cognizance of Trevett's complaint because of three major objections to the act under which the charge was brought.[37] First, defense counsel contended that the August act under which Weeden stood accused had expired ten days after the rising of the Assembly. Faulty draftsmanship of the penal statute by the legislature gave this technical allegation much merit.[38]

Varnum informed the judges, however, that "we do not place our principal reliance upon this objection." He then embarked upon a more formidable avenue of attack, namely that by the statute "special trials are instituted, incontrollable by the Supreme Judiciary Court of the State." This was a gross violation of the long-standing principle that "the highest court of law,

---

including the most recent scholarly accounts: Irwin H. Polishook, "Trevett vs. Weeden and the Case of the Judges," *Newport History*, XXXVIII (April 1965), pp. 50–51, hereafter cited as Polishook, "Trevett vs. Weeden"; and William A. Curran, *"Trevett v. Weeden:* Its Place in Our History," *Rhode Island Bar Annual*, III (Oct. 1966), p. 24. No previous historian, it seems, has consulted the court record for the case, *viz.,* Superior Court of Judicature, Newport County, Record F (1772–1795), [September term, 1786], pp. 280–82, Newport County Court House, Office of the Clerk of the Superior Court.

[36] Charles Grove Haines, *The American Doctrine of Judicial Supremacy,* rev. ed. (Berkeley, California, 1932), p. 105. This is Vol. I of the *Publications of the University of California at Los Angeles in Social Sciences.* Benjamin Bourne, who later became Rhode Island's first United States Representative, also invoked the doctrine of judicial review in 1786 in a farcical case (arising out of the paper money dispute) which was never adjudicated. See the cursory allusion to Bourne's role by civic leader John Howland in his *Life and Recollections,* edited by Edwin M. Stone (Providence, 1857), pp. 101–04.

[37] *RICR,* X, 220; RIGA, Records, XIII, 316.

[38] Varnum, pp. 5–7.

hath . . . power to reverse erroneous judgments, given by inferior courts," and the duty to command, prohibit, and restrain "all inferior jurisdictions, whenever they attempt to exceed their authority, or refuse to exercise it for the public good." [39]

Finally Varnum attacked the measure for its failure to provide the accused with a jury trial. His arguments on this point were most effective. He made several allusions to the charter of Charles II and listed two principal causes of colonial discontent on the eve of the Revolution in the process of developing his position. "Trial by jury," asserted Varnum, "was ever esteemed a first, a fundamental, and a most essential principle, in the English constitution." This "sacred right" was transferred from England to America by numerous royal charters, including Rhode Island's basic law of 1663. He cited the charter provision giving colonists the right to "have and enjoy all liberties and immunities of free and natural subjects" of England as proof of this contention. These privileges and immunities were abridged by the Stamp Act levy and by England's use of admiralty jurisdiction. In fact, attempts of Parliament to deprive the colonists of trial by jury "were among the principal causes that united the colonies in a defensive war," contended the learned Revolutionary general.[40]

Now the Assembly had denied that long-cherished right of trial by jury, claimed Varnum. This was a clear usurpation, for the charter prohibited the Legislature from making laws "contrary and repugnant" to the general system of laws that governed the realm of England at the time of the grant. The Revolution, said Varnum, had made "no change" in this limitation of legislative power. Trial by jury, he contended, "is a fundamental right, a part of our legal constitution," and one with which the Assembly cannot tamper.

Then, after references to Coke and other legal authorities,

---

[39] *Ibid.,* pp. 7–9.

[40] Varnum's contention that English deprivation in certain instances of trial by jury for American colonials was a "principal" cause of the Revolution has been examined by Lovejoy, "Equal Rights Imply Equality," pp. 459–84.

Varnum espoused the doctrine of judicial review in his learned and forceful summation:

> We have attempted to show, that the act, upon which the information is founded, has expired: That by the act special jurisdictions are erected, incontroulable by the Supreme Judiciary Court of the State: And that, by the act, this court is not authorized or empowered to impannel a jury to try the facts contained in the information: That the trial by jury is a fundamental, a constitutional right — ever claimed as such — ever ratified as such — ever held most dear and sacred: That the Legislature derives all its authority from the constitution — has no power of making laws but in subordination to it — can not infringe or violate it: That therefore the act is unconstitutional and void. That this Court has power to judge and determine what acts of the General Assembly are agreeable to the constitution; and, on the contrary, that this Court is under the most solemn obligations to execute the laws of the land, and therefore cannot, will not, consider this act as a law of the land.[41]

Contrary to generally accepted belief, Rhode Island's highest court did not, on the basis of Varnum's appeal, declare the penal statute unconstitutional and void. It did, however, accede to Varnum's plea by denying jurisdiction over Trevett's complaint, for the Court unanimously decided "that the said complaint does not come under the cognizance of the Justices here present, and . . . it is hereby dismissed." [42] Presumably cognizance was denied because the justices heard the case in special session of the regular term and not as a special court as directed by the force act.

In the commotion that followed the trial, knowledge of the specific decision was somehow distorted, for the infuriated Assembly in special session issued a summons requiring the immediate attendance of the judges of the Superior Court to render their reasons for adjudging "an act of the supreme legislature of this state to be unconstitutional, and so absolutely void." [43] This may have been the justices' personal view, but it was not their formal decision.

---

[41] Varnum, pp. 10–36, especially p. 35.

[42] *RICR*, X, 215; RIGA, Records, XIII, 316.

[43] *RICR*, X, 215. Since Varnum prayed that the Court refuse to take cognizance of Trevett's complaint for three reasons, one of which was

In early October, after a two-week delay, Judges David Howell, Joseph Hazard, and Thomas Tillinghast appeared before the General Assembly to defend their course of action. Chief Justice Paul Mumford and Associate Justice Gilbert Devol were conveniently ill.

Both Tillinghast and Hazard, the latter a paper money supporter, stoutly defended the judgment which they had rendered. Howell did likewise in a speech that was much lengthier and more fully preserved. He asserted that the justices were accountable only to God and their own consciences for their decision. It was beyond the power of the General Assembly to judge the propriety of the Court's ruling, the angry Howell continued, for by such an act "the Legislature would become the supreme judiciary — a perversion of power totally subversive of civil liberty." Howell then contended for an independent judiciary so that judges would not be answerable for their opinion unless charged with criminality. In support of his position he made impressive citations from Montesquieu, Blackstone, Serjeant William Hawkins, and Bacon.

Showing little remorse or contrition for his act, Howell boldly informed the lawmakers that the Legislature had assumed a fact in their summons to the judges that was not justified or warranted by the records. The plea of Weeden, he pointed out, mentions the act of the General Assembly as unconstitutional, and so void, but the judgment of the Court simply was that the information was not cognizable before them. Hence it appears,

---

the alleged unconstitutionality of that portion of the penal act denying the accused a trial by jury, and the judges in disclaiming cognizance did accede to Varnum's request, it could be tenuously maintained that the Court by implication regarded the statutes unconstitutional. *RICR,* X, 220. However, the Court was not sitting as a special tribunal according to the provisions of the penal act, and this, assuredly, was the ground upon which the court refused cognizance. Polishook, ("Trevett vs. Weeden," p. 63), is only the most recent of many historians who have erroneously asserted that the court made a specific declaration of unconstitutionality. The original court record clearly shows that the action was dismissed. Superior Court of Judicature, Newport County, Record F (1772–1795), [September term, 1786], p. 282, Newport County Court House, Office of the Clerk of the Superior Court.

chided Howell, that the plea has been mistaken for the judgment. His personal opinion, however, was that the act was indeed unconstitutional, had not the force of law, and could not be executed.[44]

The response of the judges, especially that of Howell, did little to endear them to the General Assembly. Thus, the legislature declared its dissatisfaction with the judges' retorts and a motion was made to dismiss them from office. Before the vote on this imprudent suggestion was taken, a memorial signed by the three judges was introduced and read. They had anticipated the plan to remove them and they demanded as freemen and officers of the state the right of due process —"a hearing by counsel before some proper and legal tribunal, and an opportunity to answer to certain and specific charges . . . before any sentence or judgment be passed, injurious to any of their aforesaid rights and privileges." After the memorial was read, General Varnum addressed the House in defense of the Court.

This determined show of resistance caused the Assembly to waver. A motion was passed directing that the opinion of the Attorney General and other learned lawyers be obtained on the question of "whether constitutionally, and agreeably by law, the General Assembly could suspend, or remove from office the Judges of the Supreme Judiciary Court, without a previous charge and statement of criminality, due process, trial, and conviction thereon."

Attorney General William Channing (father of the famed Unitarian minister) and others consulted answered in the negative. Thus a large majority of the legislature agreed that "as the judges of said superior court, etc., are not charged with criminality in giving judgment upon the information, John *Trevett* against John *Weeden,* they are therefore discharged from any further attendance upon this Assembly on that account," and are allowed to resume their functions.[45]

---

[44] Varnum, pp. 37–43, summarizes the arguments of the judges.

[45] RIGA, Records, XIII, 317; *RICR,* X, 220; Varnum, pp. 44–53, contains a summary of the Assembly proceedings which followed upon the testimony of the judges.

The forcing statute that sparked the dispute was repealed in December,[46] but the Assembly gained some measure of satisfaction from the independent-minded Court when it declined to re-elect Howell, Hazard, Tillinghast, and Devol upon the expiration of their terms in May 1787. Chief Justice Mumford, who had failed to testify before the Assembly, either because of illness or discretion, was surprisingly retained. Congressional delegate Varnum and Attorney General Channing were also ousted because of their defiant stand, whereas Henry Goodwin, the state's counsel in the proceedings, was elevated by the Country party to the position vacated by Channing.[47]

The decision of the Rhode Island Superior Court in *Trevett v. Weeden* was not an authentic or technical precedent in the development of judicial review. Nor did the action of the Court prevent the implementation of the paper money program. Further, the effect of the case upon Rhode Island's long-range judicial development was slight. *Trevett v. Weeden* was a cause célèbre that produced great temporary excitement but made little permanent impact upon the operations of Rhode Island's governmental system. After 1786 the legislature exerted as much control over the state's courts as before. The dominant party continued to elect judges annually, despite the periodic protests of reformers, until the establishment of a written state constitution in 1843. The Assembly still entertained petitions from individuals adversely affected by legal decisions and often honored such petitions by overturning the judgment of the Supreme Court in cases of insolvency and by authorizing new trials in civil

---

[46] RIGA, Records, XIII, 345; *RICR,* X, 230–31, 242. The June forcing act was also repealed at this time, but the May emission act was amended to allow debtors to lodge money with any justice of *any* of the courts of common pleas. The May act had specified that the debtor had to lodge the money in the county wherein he resided. *RICR,* X, 226. In addition, the December session passed a statute providing that most personal actions for debt payment had to be commenced by creditors within two years after the debt was made or else the debt was not recoverable. This was a forcing act of sorts. It drew such stiff criticism that it was repealed in the March session, 1788. RIGA, Records, XIII, 344–45, 466, 473–74.

[47] *RICR,* X, 241–42.

suits. These practices were not terminated until 1856 when the state Supreme Court finally asserted its independence of the Assembly in the landmark case of *Taylor v. Place*. Until the *Taylor* decision, seventy years after *Trevett*, no state court dared challenge the Assembly; no Rhode Island justice gave official endorsement to the doctrine of judicial review.[48]

The real significance of the *Trevett v. Weeden* episode lies not in the formal action of the Court (which ducked the issue) but in the utterances of defense counsel James Mitchell Varnum and, to a lesser degree, in the *personal* observations of Justice David Howell. General Varnum's statement of the doctrine of judicial review was one of the most forceful and extensive arguments on that subject developed during this formative period.[49] Assuredly

---

[48] On the general course of Rhode Island judicial history from *Trevett v. Weeden* to *Taylor v. Place* see Stiness, "The Struggle for Judicial Supremacy," in Field, ed., III, 107–119; C. Peter Magrath, "Samuel Ames: The Great Chief Justice of Rhode Island," *Rhode Island History,* XXIV (July, 1965), 65–76; and Coleman, pp. 251–55, 285.

[49] Edward S. Corwin lists the case of *Trevett v. Weeden* among the "alleged precedents for judicial review antedating the Convention of 1787." Corwin, although aware that the court did not declare the penal act unconstitutional, makes the interesting point that the statute was "self-contradictory and impossible to be performed, since it required that those violating it be tried *without* a jury but *in accordance with* the 'Law of the Land.' " Corwin, *The Doctrine of Judicial Review,* pp. 71–74. On the significance of Varnum's argument in the development of judicial review Corwin makes the following observation: "Of the so-called 'precedents' for judicial review antecedent to the Convention of 1787, the one which called forth the most elaborate argument on theoretical grounds and which produced the most evident impression upon the membership of the convention, was the Rhode Island case of *Trevett v. Weeden*. . . . The feature of the case which is of immediate pertinence is the argument which is evoked against the act on the part of the attorney for the defendant, James Varnum." Varnum developed "the theory of a law superior to legislative enactments." His argument, in the tradition of Coke and Locke, "kept alive, even after the fires of revolution had cooled, the notion that the claim of law to obedience consists in its intrinsic excellence rather than its origin. Again, it made rational the notion of a hierarchy of laws in which the will of merely human legislators might on occasion be required to assume a subordinate place. Lastly, by the same token, it made rational the notion of judges pitting knowledge against sheer legislative self-assertion." Corwin, "The Progress of Constitutional Theory Between the Declaration of Independence and the Meeting of

his position was known to the framers of the federal constitution [50] and to such state supporters of that document as James Iredell and John Marshall. Varnum furnished his contemporaries and posterity with a full statement of his views by publishing them in pamphlet form together with an account of the trials of both Weeden and the judges. This work was widely disseminated and was even advertised for sale in the Philadelphia press during April and May 1787 as the delegates were entering that city to participate in the Grand Convention.[51] Rhode Island's paper money embroglio had an impact far beyond the confines of the butcher shop of John Weeden, for it provided James Varnum with the opportunity to make a significant contribution to the development of American constitutional thought.[52]

III

The Assembly's dominant paper money faction was undaunted and unawed by its bout with the judiciary. In October 1786 the legislature drafted another harsh penal measure "to stimulate and

---

the Philadelphia Convention," *American Historical Review,* XXX (April, 1925), 523. A good general discussion of the historiography of judicial review is Alan F. Westin, "Charles Beard and the American Debate over Judicial Review, 1790–1961," which is the "Introduction" to Westin's edition of Charles A. Beard, *The Supreme Court and the Constitution* (Englewood Cliffs, N.J., 1962), pp. 1–34.

[50] Raoul Berger, *Congress v. The Supreme Court* (Cambridge, Mass., 1969), pp. 39–40, 45–46 claims that several state cases between 1776 and 1787 (including *Trevett v. Weeden*) "were thought to exemplify judicial review" by the Founding Fathers and in this "rationalistic" sense these cases were "precedents" in the development of that doctrine.

[51] *Pennsylvania Packet* (Philadelphia), April 25, May 2, 9, 16, 23, 1787. See also Varnum to George Washington, June 18, 1787 in Max Farrand, ed., *The Records of the Federal Convention of 1787,* rev. ed. (New Haven, 1937), III, 47–48; and James Madison's remarks on the Rhode Island judiciary on July 17, 1787 during a debate on "judicial negative" of state laws. *Ibid.,* III, 27–28.

[52] Shortly after the Assembly terminated his membership in the confederation Congress, Varnum, a director of the newly formed Ohio Company, was appointed United States judge for the Northwest Territory. He assumed his duties at Marietta, Ohio in June 1788 and gave important assistance in the framing of a code of territorial laws. Although he

give efficacy to the paper bills" and sent it before the town meetings "in order that their sense respecting said bill may be com-
municated" to the General Assembly at the next session. This
move was another example of the Country party's practice of
government by plebiscite.[53]

This proposed force act was as onerous as the statute which
precipitated the *Trevett v. Weeden* clash. The act's preamble,
in a blast aimed at the merchant-speculators, declared that
"whereas certain persons had accumulated great wealth by de-
preciating continental securities and buying them at a reduced
price and were now attempting to depreciate the paper" [54] all
citizens "should be required to take an oath to make every
endeavor to maintain paper currency at par value with specie,
and to sell no article for which the vendor would not take payment in either paper or specie at the same rate." Every person
taking the oath was to be enrolled at the town clerk's office and
certified as having complied with the law. All incumbent officials, future officeholders, practicing lawyers, and all persons entering or clearing vessels at any port were specifically directed
to comply. No person was to be eligible for office until the oath
was taken, and violators of the pledge were to be tried as
perjurers.[55]

---

was of powerful build and a physical culturist, his health failed in the
frontier environment. He did not survive the first winter. On January 10,
1789, Varnum's death at the age of forty cut short his highly promising
career. See James M. Varnum, *A Sketch of the Life and Public Services
of James Mitchell Varnum of Rhode Island* . . . (Boston, 1906), pp.
31–41.

[53] RIGA, Records, XIII, 308; *RICR*, X, 217. This practice of submitting important or controversial bills to the people in town meeting
assembled, so that the freemen could instruct their deputies how to vote
thereon, was a fairly common and democratic feature of Rhode Island's
legislative process. It tended to keep the Assembly somewhat closely in
accord with the wishes of the majority of freemen.

[54] McDonald believes that several large Providence merchants, principally John I. Clark and Joseph Nightingale, were manipulating the paper
and attempting to drive down its market value. McDonald, *E Pluribus
Unum,* pp. 125–26.

[55] Acts and Resolves of the General Assembly, RISA, XXV (1786–
87), 70. This manuscript collection should be distinguished from the pub-

The Providence town meeting drafted a five-point condemnation of the proposed test act and declared it "unconstitutional, unjust and impolitic." Newport's freemen concurred. But opposition to this bold measure extended far beyond the mercantile centers. East Greenwich, Cumberland, and even radical Glocester urged their deputies to reject the test bill. Of the state's thirty towns, only Scituate, Foster, and North Kingstown declared themselves in favor of the harsh measure, and it was soundly rejected by the Assembly in early November 1786.[56]

While the controversy over the ill-conceived penal and test acts was raging, the members of the paper money faction took other punitive action against their hard money opponents. One such reprisal was the revocation of the Newport city charter.

In 1784, just prior to the eruption of the currency controversy, Newport's merchant leaders had secured for their community a municipal charter which incorporated Newport as Rhode Island's first city and brought a termination to its town meeting form of government. Soon after, the city fathers became involved in litigation with influential Nicholas Easton over a certain parcel of seaside land which he claimed. Easton lost the suit and then threw his weight behind efforts to have the new charter revoked.[57]

When the merchant-led city administration opposed the paper issue, the Country party supported the attack upon the municipal charter and the governmental structure it upheld. The paperites hoped thereby to chastize, harass, and weaken their Newport antagonists. In late 1786 the small but active paper money faction within the city petitioned the General Assembly to vacate the

---

lished *Schedules of the General Assembly*. *United States Chronicle* (Providence), October 12, 1786; *Providence Gazette*, October 14, 1786.

56 PAC, pp. 40–44; Providence Town Meeting Records, No. 7 (1783–1804), pp. 74–79. The Providence rejection is printed in William R. Staples, comp., *Annals of the Town of Providence* . . . (Providence, 1843), pp. 306–11, hereafter cited as *Annals of Providence*. For Scituate's approval, see PAC, p. 65.

57 George Champlin Mason, "Nicholas Easton vs. the City of Newport," *Rhode Island Historical Society Collections*, VII (1885), 327–49; *RICR*, X, 30–33 contains a copy of the charter.

charter. This petition, endorsed by 104 freemen, was opposed by a counter document signed by upwards of 400 Newport citizens.[58]

According to partisan Peter Edes, the pro-paper petitioners against the city "did not form a fourth part of the freemen, nor had [they] property to be assessed for more than one seventeenth part of the city tax." Further, "no evidence was adduced to support a single fact in the petition." Nevertheless, this determined and disgruntled Newport minority had the support of the powerful Country party in the state legislature and this was the only majority that counted — the Newport city charter was rescinded in March 1787, as a stern rebuke to that community's hard money leadership.[59]

Another manifestation of the Country party's wrath was their attempt to reduce further the power of the mercantile minority in the General Assembly by an equalization of town representation. The six-four-two apportionment ratio established by the charter gave the vigorous anti-paper forces in Newport and Providence ten votes against the Country party in the lower house. Although this figure represented only fifteen percent of the total vote in that chamber, the intolerant paperites were not content. The more irascible among them revived the equal representation demands of the war years and introduced a bill in March 1787 designed to limit each town to two deputies. Because of the controversial nature of this proposal, it was referred to the freemen in town meeting assembled for an expression of support.[60]

The bill was in direct violation of the charter's apportionment

[58] RIGA, Records, XIII, 306, 351; Petitions to the Rhode Island General Assembly, RISA, XXIII, 83–91. For a memorial to the General Assembly from the Newport merchants opposing the paper emission, see RIHS, Mss., III, 110–12 (#653–55).

[59] RICR, X, 217, 233–34; RIGA, Records, XIII, 351–52; Newport Herald, March 22, 1787.

[60] RIGA, Records, XIII, 366; RICR, X, 238. Smithfield, as early as April 1786, in complaining of the mercantile-controlled Assembly's payment in specie of the interest due on merchant-owned loan office certificates, instructed her delegates to move for a "more equitable" apportionment of the Assembly. PAC, p. 54. Hopkinton made a similar request in August 1786. Ibid., p. 57.

provision. The letter of the charter had, on occasion, been contravened as in the case of proxy voting, and the intent had probably been ignored or misconstrued in such procedures as the filling of vacancies in the general offices by the Assembly, but these diversions were prompted by expediency and a desire to facilitate the governing of the state. The 1787 maneuver, however, was a partisan attempt by the majority faction to emasculate the opposition. This injudicious tampering with the sacrosanct charter gave the moderate paperites misgivings, and it appalled the hard money men in those Bay towns threatened with reduction.

The freemen of Providence referred the proposal to a five-man committee that included David Howell and Nicholas Brown. Quite predictably, their report constituted a vigorous and compelling denunciation of the apportionment bill. It correctly contended that the charter, which was the constitution of the state, could not be altered at the whim of its creature, the General Assembly. "If ever any alterations should be made in the constitution of this state, they ought to originate in a state convention, appointed for that special object and not otherwise," asserted the committee.

The report advanced several arguments against the reduction of representation. It stated that "the true reason for allowing the several towns to be represented, even at that time [1663], by six, four and two deputies, appears to your committee to have been, in order to give the towns weight in the representative body, as nearly as might be proportioned, to their numbers and wealth; *and this reason, instead of losing, has gained strength from that period to the present time.*" After this recitation of objections the committee and the Providence freemen urged the repudiation of the proposed measure.[61]

The bill was so bold in its provisions and the charter still so inviolate to most Rhode Islanders, regardless of their views on the currency question, that the apportionment scheme of the radical paperites failed. The margin of its rejection, however, was

---

[61] Providence Town Meeting Records, No. 7 (1783–1804), pp. 92 ff.; *Annals of Providence*, pp. 312–19. Italics mine.

slight. It was considered by the deputies on November 3, 1787, February 28, 1788, and again in early April 1788. Each time it was referred to the succeeding session, on close votes, after considerable debate. One contemporary newspaper, the *United States Chronicle* (Providence) reported in March 1788 that fifteen country towns with thirty votes had instructed their deputies to support equal apportionment, while nine towns with twenty-eight votes had issued instructions to oppose. Six communities with twelve ballots were uncommitted, and these saved the day for the "Big Four." [62]

After the crisis had passed, the General Assembly helped prevent a revival of this explosive controversy by disclaiming the power to alter the charter by statute. This surprising modification of their omnipotence came in September 1789.[63]

The final significant by-product of the paper money dispute was its impact on Rhode Island's ratification of the Federal Constitution. Unquestionably the currency controversy contributed to the state's reluctance to accept the creation of the Philadelphia convention.

---

[62] *Newport Herald,* November 8, 1787, March 6 and April 10, 1788; *U. S. Chronicle,* March 6, 1788; Journal of the House (October 1786–March 1788), March 16, 1787, November 3, 1787, February 28, 1788. There is no entry for the April 1788 vote; *Schedules,* March 1787, p. 18. The instructions from several towns to their deputies on this question have been preserved in PAC, pp. 40–65. They indicate that the following communities supported equal representation: Smithfield, Charlestown, Hopkinton, East Greenwich, Westerly, Scituate, Foster, Richmond, North Providence, Exeter, Coventry, and Glocester. In opposition were Newport, Portsmouth, New Shoreham, Warwick, Middletown, and Barrington.

[63] *Schedules,* September session 1789, p. 3. This self-limitation was contained in the preamble of an act authorizing the freemen in town meeting to instruct their state representatives on the question of calling a convention to ratify the federal Constitution. The Legislature declared as follows: "This Assembly, on the most careful Examination of the Powers vested in them by the Freemen of this State, are of Opinion, that the same are limited to the Administration of the existing Constitution of the State, and do not extend to devising or adopting alterations therein." For the contemporary legal construction of this legislative dictum, see Elisha R. Potter, Jr., *Considerations on the Questions of the Adoption of A Constitution and Extension of Suffrage in Rhode Island* (Boston, 1842), p. 7.

One leading student of Antifederalism believes the "superior organization" of the Constitution's proponents played an important role in their victory, while the Antifederalists' failure to unite was a significant factor in their defeat.[64] Although this observation is generally valid, Rhode Island is once again the exception to the rule. In this state the dominant Country party was available as an effective vehicle for opposition to the Federal Constitution. The pro-paper country faction firmly held political power from May 1786 until well after the grudging ratification of the Federal document by Rhode Island in mid-1790. Had this group not been called into existence by the paper money plan of 1786, Rhode Island's road to ratification would have been shorter and less hazardous.

---

[64] Jackson Turner Main, *The Antifederalists: Critics of the Constitution, 1781–1788* (Chapel Hill, North Carolina, 1961), pp. 252–53.

CHAPTER FIVE

Rhode Island and Disunion

I

That Rhode Island was the last of the original thirteen states to ratify the Federal Constitution is well known. The state was re-calcitrant from the outset of the constitutional movement, with the exception of its response to the Annapolis convention. Just prior to that Maryland gathering, Rhode Island had expressed a desire to secure uniform and centralized regulation of commerce to protect its re-export trade from the tariffs of her neighboring states.[1] Because that important but limited action was the only topic on the proposed agenda, Rhode Island — its government then under mercantile control — dispatched two delegates to Annapolis. Commissioners Jabez Bowen and Samuel Ward had journeyed as far as Philadelphia when they received news that the abortive conclave had adjourned.[2]

In the following year, when a more broadly empowered convention met to discuss all matters necessary "to render the constitution of the Federal Government adequate to the exigencies

---

[1] *RICR*, X, 180; Bates, pp. 99–105.

[2] RIGA, Reports, IV, 111, contains the commissioners' report dated October 14, 1786; Staples, *RICC*, pp. 561–62.

of the Union," the Country party had seized power. Conse-
quently, the state failed to vote on the February 1787 resolution
of the confederation Congress to hold the Philadelphia convention, and when that momentous assembly convened, Rhode
Island was the only state to boycott its proceedings. Three times
an attempt to dispatch delegates was rejected by the suspicious
General Assembly. Rhode Island's absence was protested by
deputies from Providence and Newport and also by James M.
Varnum and Peleg Arnold, the state's delegates in Congress, but
to no avail.[3]

On September 15, 1787, just prior to the completion of the
federal convention, Governor John Collins offered to the president of the confederation Congress Rhode Island's feeble excuse
for non-attendance at the Philadelphia sessions. Collins (who
was not opposed to the new Constitution as were his country
cohorts) declared that since the freemen at large had the power
of electing delegates to represent them in Congress, the legislature could not consistently *appoint* delegates to a convention
that might be the means of dissolving that Congress. In view of
the broad power which the Assembly was accustomed to exercise,
Collins's remarks seemed evasive indeed. A spirited rejoinder
signed by the Newport and Providence deputies reminded
the governor that the Assembly had dispatched delegates to
the Continental Congress, ratified the Declaration of Independence, and accepted the Articles of Confederation with-

---

[3] James M. Varnum and Peleg Arnold to Governor John Collins,
April 24, 1787, *RICR,* X, 246–47; Staples, *RICC,* pp. 576–78; James M.
Varnum to Governor John Collins, April 4, 1787, *Ibid.,* pp. 578–79;
James M. Varnum to the President of the Federal Convention, June 18,
1787, Updike Papers, RIHS. The Country party seemed somewhat divided, hesitant, and uncertain regarding Rhode Island's attendance at
the Philadelphia convention. For example, in May 1787 the deputies in
the lower house of the General Assembly approved a resolution to dispatch delegates by a narrow two-vote margin only to have the measure
killed by the assistants in the upper house. Then, in June, the assistants
reconsidered and reversed themselves, but their resolution was rejected
by the deputies by a solid margin of seventeen votes. Journal of the
House, May and June sessions, 1787; Journal of the Senate, May and
June sessions, 1787, RISA.

out a popular referendum. Their arguments, though sound, were fruitless.[4]

When the federal convention completed its labors on Septemtember 17, 1787, it transmitted the Constitution to Congress with the recommendation that the document be submitted to the states for ratification by popularly elected conventions. Congress (with Rhode Island absent) complied with this suggestion, and gave the several states official notice of its action. The Assembly took the new Constitution under advisement at its October 1787 session. Thereupon, it voted for the distribution of 1,000 copies of the proposed document to allow the freemen "an opportunity of forming their sentiments" upon it.[5]

With most of the freemen thus apprised of the federal charter's contents, the February 1788 session assembled. Then, to the consternation of Federalists within the state and without, the Assembly authorized a popular referendum on the Constitution and scheduled it for the fourth Monday in March. This ratification procedure was highly irregular and contrary to the recommendations of the Philadelphia delegates, but the legislature was not deterred by this departure from the norm — an action that prompted Federalist James Manning, president of Rhode Island College, to lament that "our rulers are deliberately wicked." In fact, this February session specifically rejected a motion to call a ratifying convention. Over the course of the next twenty-three months a total of eleven such efforts would be spurned.[6]

---

[4] The documents relating to Rhode Island's reaction to the federal convention are published in Staples, *RICC*, pp. 569–585. Rhode Island's abstention from the convention was protested by a group of the state's merchants. Their memorial to the convention is printed in Max Farrand, ed., *The Records of the Federal Convention of 1787* (New Haven, 1937), III, 18–19. The original of Collins's letter and the dissent of the merchants can be found in Letters from the Governor of Rhode Island, RISA, IV (1780–1800), 74–75.

[5] RIGA, Records, XIII, 429; Staples, *RICC*, pp. 584–85.

[6] RIGA, Records, XIII, 446–48. Most historians contend that the Assembly rejected motions to call a ratifying convention seven times (*e.g.*, McDonald, *We The People*, p. 322 and Bishop, p. 33). Irwin Polishook, however, has listed eleven such attempts. "Rhode Island and the Union, 1774–1790: A Study in State History During the Confedera-

The popular election on the Constitution was held according to schedule. The result was predictable — 237 for and 2,708 against — but the margin of defeat is deceptive. The federal port towns of Providence and Newport boycotted the referendum; just one vote was cast in the former and only eleven were registered in Newport. These ballots, with one exception (in Newport) were cast by Antifederalists. The only towns in the Federalist column were the Bay settlements of Bristol (26-23) and Little Compton (63-57). Critics of the Constitution registered lopsided victories in many rural communities: Glocester (228-9), Coventry (180-0), Foster (177-0), and Scituate (156-0).[7]

The total vote in this referendum was 2,945, compared with the 4,287 who had voted in the well-contested gubernatorial election of 1787. Newport and Providence accounted for most of the abstainers, for together these towns had between 825 and 900 freemen in 1788, according to fairly reliable estimates. Yet it is obvious that even if these communities turned out *en masse* for the Constitution, it would have been rejected by an impressive plurality.[8] Eight weeks after this resounding repudiation New Hampshire became the ninth state to ratify the federal document but, despite the rejoicing over this event in Providence, the chances that Rhode Island would follow the lead of her more amenable brethren seemed extremely remote.

The crucial states of Virginia and New York soon fell in line, but Rhode Island was unrelenting. In March 1789, as the new federal government prepared to convene, the Assembly for a fifth time rejected a motion to call a ratifying convention. In May the issue was sidestepped, and in the June and October

---

tion Era" (unpublished doctoral dissertation, Northwestern University 1961), p. 280. Manning to Rev. Hezekiah Smith, June 10, 1788 in Reuben A. Guild, ed., *Early History of Brown University Including the Life, Times, and Correspondence of President Manning, 1756–1791* (Providence, 1897), p. 456.

[7] PAC, pp. 17–36; Staples, *RICC,* pp. 589–606. For a petition from Providence protesting the referendum see Rhode Island Historical Society Manuscripts, III, 119–21 (#664), hereafter cited RIHS Mss.

[8] Staples, *RICC,* p. 606.

sessions it was rejected again.[9] The only other holdout at this late date was North Carolina, a state which, like Rhode Island, was settled by outcasts and was noted for its individualism and separatist tendencies. On November 21, 1789, however, the Carolinians capitulated and left Rhode Island alone beyond the pale.[10]

As 1790 dawned, the pressures on the Antifederalists increased, and prospects for at least a convention grew brighter. Opponents of the Constitution had shown signs of wavering in the early October session when they voted to print and distribute among the towns 150 copies of the twelve amendments to the Constitution that had been recommended by the new Congress of the United States.[11]

In the January session the Federalist minority was further encouraged when the legislature after two unsuccessful efforts narrowly passed a bill introduced by Henry Marchant, authorizing a ratification convention to meet on March 1, 1790 at South Kingstown. Four-term Governor John Collins, always cool towards Antifederalism, courageously incurred the wrath of his country party (of which he was little more than the figurehead) when he cast the deciding vote on Marchant's measure and broke a four-four Senate deadlock. His political associates made him their sacrificial lamb and denied him renomination for governor.[12]

Election of delegates for this convention went unfavorably in the view of Marchant, a Newport Federalist. Two weeks before

---

[9] *Ibid.*, pp. 608–626. As late as May 1789 the Browns observed that "about two thirds of the Freemen of this state are opposed to the new Constitution — our general assembly are by the same majority against it." Nicholas and John Brown to Richard Henry Lee, May 1, 1789, John Brown Papers, RIHS.

[10] Jackson Turner Main, *The Antifederalists,* pp. 242–48.

[11] Records of the Rhode Island General Assembly, RISA, XIII, 667, hereafter cited Records, RIGA; *RICR,* X, 358.

[12] RIGA, Records, XIII, 723–24; *Newport Herald,* January 21, 1790; *U. S. Chronicle,* January 21, 1790; *Providence Gazette,* January 16, 23, 1790. On Collins's conversion to Federalism see Collins to George Washington, May 24, 1790 in Gaillard Hunt, "Office Seeking in Washington's Administration," *American Historical Review,* I (Jan. 1896), 279–80. John P. Kaminski, "Political Sacrifice and Demise — John Collins and

the session he prophesied its outcome: "The Antie's are about ten majority. I have hopes however they will not totally reject the Constitution, but I think they may adjourn it over our Genl. Election." [13]

Marchant's intuition was correct. The convention considered both the Constitution and the twelve amendments thereto proposed by Congress. In addition it adopted a "declaration of rights" and advanced eighteen other amendments to the federal document. These were sent to the freemen for consideration.

The major points of discussion during the six-day March session were the allocation of representatives, direct taxation, the slave-trade, the method of adopting future amendments, the ratification of the congressionally proposed Bill of Rights, and the power of the convention to adopt the Constitution. Although some Antifederalists had mellowed, a majority were resolved to resist the Constitution to the bitter end. Merchant-prince John Innes Clark, one of four Federalist delegates from Providence, observed that "we have as determined a set of men to oppose it as ever were combined together." On Saturday March 6, over protests of the Federalists, the gathering adjourned until May 24 by a vote of 41–28, a margin which was a fairly accurate indication of the relative strength of the anti- and pro-Constitution factions.[14]

Jonathan J. Hazard, 1786–1790," *Rhode Island History,* **XXXV** (Aug., 1976), 91–93.

[13] Henry Marchant to William Marchant, February 15, 1790, quoted in Robert C. Cotner, ed., *Theodore Foster's Minutes of the Convention Held at South Kingstown, Rhode Island in March, 1790 which failed to adopt the Constitution of the United States* (Providence, 1929), p. 20, hereafter cited as Cotner, ed., *Foster's Minutes.* The introduction to this volume contains a good summary by Cotner of the events of 1790, pp. 19–27. The "Genl. Election" to which Marchant referred was held annually on the third Wednesday in April.

[14] John Innes Clark to Lydia Clark, Feb. [March], 5, 1790, John Innes Clark Collection, RIHS (Clark misdated the letter); Cotner, ed., *Foster's Minutes, passim.* For the partisan maneuvering over adjournment and reconvening see *Ibid.,* pp. 81–90. The official minutes of the South Kingstown Convention, kept by Secretary Daniel Updike, are useful but fragmented and incomplete. The original is found in PAC, pp. 1–2. It is printed in Staples, *RICC,* pp. 644–49. PAC, p. 8, also

Between sessions spring elections were conducted and the Country party (minus Governor Collins) scored its fifth consecutive victory. Heading their ticket was Arthur Fenner of the distinguished Providence clan. So formidable and prominent was Fenner, and so potent was his party, that the Federalists endorsed him rather than arouse the ire of the country majority on the eve of the ratification convention.[15]

Despite this success and the Antifederal majority of approximately a dozen or more in the seventy-member convention, several critics of the Constitution were beginning to find their position no longer tenable in the face of increasing pressure from within and from without the state.

When the ratifying body reconvened, the Constitution's adherents — led by the eloquent Marchant, Benjamin Bourne of Providence, and William Bradford from the port town of Bristol — pushed vigorously for its acceptance. Finally, after five days of political jousting Mr. Bourne, in the phrase of convention secretary Daniel Updike, "moved for the grand question of adopting or rejecting the federal government." At 5:20 p.m. on Saturday May 29, the motion squeaked through by a vote of 34–32, though some contemporaries claimed the actual margin of victory was only one.

So close was the contest that a full convention might have reversed the decision. Three absent delegates — Edward Hull and Ray Sands representing remote New Shoreham (Block Island) and Job Durfee of Portsmouth — appear to have been Antifederal, while Country party chieftain Daniel Owen of Glocester

---

contains a draft of the eighteen-article declaration of rights adopted by the March convention. See also William Ellery to Benjamin Huntington, March 8, 1790, Ellery-Huntington Correspondence, RISA.

[15] William Ellery to Benjamin Huntington, March 28 and April 5, 1790, Ellery-Huntington Correspondence. With Fenner at the top of their prox, the Federalists hoped to secure victory for a few of their at-large candidates for the upper house. They did not succeed. The Federalists had originally sought a coalition ticket with Fenner at the head and some of their men in the assistants' spots, but they were in a poor bargaining position and Fenner declined. See *Providence Gazette*, March 27 and April 3, 1790 and *U.S. Chronicle*, April 1, 1790 for the coalition proposal and Fenner's reply.

as convention chairman was prevented from voting, except to
break a tie.[16] Recalcitrant Rhode Island's margin of acceptance
was narrower than that of any other state, and it was one of only
three states in which the delegates voting for ratification represented fewer people than those voting against the federal charter.
But an inch was as good as a mile.[17]

Soon after this momentous action, the formal bill ratifying and
adopting the Constitution was approved by the convention. This
measure also gave assent to eleven of the twelve amendments

---

[16] Staples, *RICC,* pp. 659–673. I have reached my conclusion regarding the sympathies of Hull, Sands, and Durfee for the following reasons:
Hull was from the Antifederal island of New Shoreham and voted with
the Antifederalists for adjournment of the March session. Sands was
actually a resident of the Antifederal stronghold, South Kingstown.
However, he had relatives on New Shoreham and owned land there.
Thus, he was allowed to represent that remote island town. In the 1788
referendum on the Constitution he voted for rejection, and in the
March 1790 convention he voted with the Antifederalists to adjourn. Job
Durfee was from Portsmouth, a town which gradually espoused Federalism, but he disregarded the specific instructions of his town by his March
vote for adjournment. Quite possibly he absented himself on May 29
rather than again defy the written instructions given by the freemen of
Portsmouth to their delegates on the day of the decisive vote. See Cotner,
ed., *Foster's Minutes,* p. 60; Staples, *RICC,* pp. 593, 595, 659, 670–73.
RIHS Mss., III, 130 (#675) is a list of the delegates with their votes on
ratification (probably in Theodore Foster's hand). Alleged irregularities
either in the vote or in the recording of it are discussed in Sidney S.
Rider, "The History of the Hazard Family in Rhode Island," *Book Notes,*
XIII (1896), 182–183. Rider notes that the original papers of Daniel
Updike, secretary of the convention, were in the custody of his younger
brother, Wilkins Updike, before the latter deposited them with the state
in 1863. The vote tabulation on ratification was not among the papers
donated though Wilkins professedly had this sheet when he wrote his
History of the Narragansett Church in 1847. At that time Wilkins
asserted that "the constitution was adopted by a bare majority of one
(some say two) but the original paper upon which the yeas and nays
were minuted gives only the majority of one," p. 329.

[17] Charles W. Roll, Jr., "We, Some of the People: Apportionment in
the Thirteen State Conventions Ratifying the Constitution," *Journal of
American History,* LVI (June, 1969), 33–34. Roll contends that those
48.6 percent of the delegates voting for ratification represented 44.1 percent of Rhode Island's population; that those 45.7 percent of the delegates voting against ratification represented 51.4 percent of the people;
and that the 5.4 percent of the delegates not voting represented 4.5 per-

proposed by Congress and offered twenty-one additional amendments to the federal document.[18]

At the June session the General Assembly gave its necessary approval to the Bill of Rights, established procedures for the election of its congressional delegation, and chose Theodore Foster, a moderate Providence Federalist, and Joseph Stanton, Jr., a die-hard Antifederalist deputy from Charlestown, as Rhode Island's first United States Senators. Foster was the brother-in-law of Governor Fenner, a fact which helped him gain the approbation of the Country party. When Benjamin Bourne, a champion of the Constitution, won the August contest for the state's lone seat in the House of Representatives, Rhode Island at last became a full participant in the new federal Union.

Conspicuously absent from the state's first congressional contingent was Jonathan Hazard, the foremost member of the Country party. Like John Collins before him, "Beau Jonathan" became a scapegoat in the bitter contest. Anticipating ratification, Hazard modified his opposition to the Constitution in the hope of gaining Federalist support for the United States Senate. Ac-

---

cent of the population. My figures on the percentages of the population represented are 44.2, 53.6 and 2.2, respectively; but my adjustments do not alter the validity of Roll's findings. Rhode Island's convention, however, was the third most equally districted of the thirteen with a ratio of 1:6.2 from the smallest to the largest district in the state. *Ibid.*, p. 22.

[18] Staples, *RICC*, pp. 668–69, 672. Of the twelve amendments proposed by Congress, those numbered III through XII were eventually ratified by the requisite number of states and became the Bill of Rights. Numbers I and II failed to secure adoption. The convention and the session of the Assembly sitting pursuant to the action of that convention, gave approval to every proposed amendment except II, which dealt with the compensation of the members of Congress. Rhode Island's twenty-one amendments consisted of those which were drafted by the March convention (*Ibid.*, pp. 653–55) except for #18 dealing with the manner of ratifying the federal Bill of Rights, and four additional amendments drafted in the May convention session (*Ibid.*, pp. 668–69). Sixteen of the twenty-one amendments finally advanced by Rhode Island were also put forward by at least one other state, while five were unique to Rhode Island. A good discussion of these amendments is found in Bates, pp. 201–16. Polishook, *Rhode Island and the Union*, pp. 218–21, errs in stating that the March convention approved twenty-one amendments. See PAC, p. 6.

cording to William Ellery, he "became a trimmer." The move
backfired. Federalists unleashed their hatred for Hazard, the
apostle of paper money; the Country party resented his opportunism and blamed him for their failure to block the Constitution; and powerful Arthur Fenner moved to displace him as
party leader. These forces sealed Hazard's political demise. Years
later, Hazard confided to a relative his political fate: "The people that I have taken the most pains to serve have sacrificed me
. . . in the year 1790. . . . I have not only the men's names,
but the rooms in the houses where it was agreed upon . . . when
they think there is a prospect of selling an old friend for a new
one [Arthur Fenner], they embrace the opportunity." Hazard, the
most influential figure in the constitutional history of Confederation Rhode Island, left the state in 1805 and settled with his
family in Verona, New York where he died two decades later
carrying his resentment with him to the grave.[19]

II

Although the principal events of this turbulent period are fairly
discernible, the motives behind Rhode Island's long-term opposition and then grudging acceptance of the Constitution are multiple and complex. Certainly the paper money controversy contributed to the state's rejection of the new federal instrument.
The Country party came to power on a pro-paper platform in
1786 and this agrarian faction led by Jonathan Hazard, Joseph
Stanton, Jr., John Collins, Job Comstock, and Daniel Owen
firmly held political power from May 1786 until well after the
reluctant ratification of the national document in mid-1790.
Although not monolithic, the party was dominant and cohesive,
and the major opposition to the Constitution emanated from its

---

[19] RIGA, Records, XIII, 753–55; *RICR*, X, 380–88. On Hazard's
political fall see Kaminski, pp. 93–96; Updike, pp. 328–29; and Caroline E. Robinson, *The Hazard Family of Rhode Island, 1635–1894*
(Boston, 1895), pp. 48–49. Jonathan Hazard's letter to Thomas B.
Hazard, June 25, 1801 is printed on pp. 49–50.

ranks. In Rhode Island it served as an effective and organized vehicle of Antifederalism.[20]

When the ratification process began, Rhode Island was too deeply enmeshed in the paper program to back out, and Article I, Section 10 of the federal document would have forced the state to do so. The financial chaos that would have resulted from the abandonment [21] of the paper program before it had run its course would have made the existing financial situation seem peaceful and orderly by comparison.[22]

William Ellery, continental loan officer in Newport, speculating on the possibilities of ratification, several times expressed the view that the Country party would "wait till they shall have completely extinguished the State debt" before accepting the Constitution. Ellery contended that ratification would not take place before the "accursed paper money system" had run its course.[23]

---

[20] Jackson Turner Main, one of the leading students of Antifederalism believes the "superior organization" of the Constitution's proponents played an important role in their victory, while the Antifederalists' failure to unite was a significant factor in their defeat. Main, pp. 252–53. See also Gordon S. Wood, *The Creation of the American Republic, 1776–1787* (Chapel Hill, N.C., 1969), pp. 485–86. Although this observation is generally valid, the Country party made Rhode Island the exception to the rule. While on the subject of exceptions, it should again be noted that Country party Governor John Collins was a moderate supporter of the Constitution. See footnote 17, *supra*.

[21] This abandonment would have been necessitated by the federal constitutional provision which forbade the states to emit bills of credit or to make anything but gold and silver coin a tender in payment of debts. (Article I, Sec. 10). The third amendment to the Constitution offered by the Rhode Island ratifying convention sought to bar Congress and the federal judiciary from interfering "in the redemption of paper money already emitted, and not in circulation, or in liquidating or discharging the public securities of any one state." Staples, *RICC*, p. 678.

[22] McDonald, *We The People*, p. 338.

[23] William Ellery to Benjamin Huntington, March 10, 1787, June 15, 1789, July 13, 1789, Ellery-Huntington Correspondence; Ellery to Ebenezer Hazard, October 16, 1787, William Ellery Letters, Misc. Mss., Newport Historical Society. James Madison observed of the Antifederalists in general that "the real object of their zeal" in opposing the Constitution was to maintain "the supremacy of State Legislatures," in order that they could engage in the printing of paper money and violate con-

There is a definite correlation between the pro-paper towns and those which espoused Antifederalism. Jackson Turner Main, after analyzing the ratification struggle on a nation-wide basis, concludes "that paper money sentiment was in some degree a factor in the existence of Antifederalism is scarcely to be doubted — the Antifederalists drew more heavily by far than their opponents from the ranks of paper money advocates; however the correlation is by no means complete." [24] This statement, applied to Rhode Island, is valid.

Here Antifederalism and advocacy of paper money, though closely related, were not synonymous. Such an equation admits of too many exceptions and incongruities: (1) in numerous local articles on the Constitution no one urged defeat of the document on the specific ground that it would put a stop to paper money; (2) substantial modification of the legal tender features of the paper money act in October 1789 did not dramatically diminish opposition to the Constitution [25]; (3) of the delegates to the ratifying convention of May 1790, sixty-two percent of those supporting the Constitution borrowed paper in 1786 (although at least one of these, merchant John Innes Clark, did so to manipulate and depreciate it) while sixty-three percent of those delegates who voted to reject participated in the emission of 1786; (4) only one of the thirty-two Antifederal delegates had taken advantage of provisions of the currency act to force the settlement of a private debt with paper [26]; (5) although the same towns

---

tracts under cover of law. See Robert R. Rutland, *The Ordeal of the Constitution: The Antifederalists and the Ratification Struggle of 1787–1788* (Norman, Okla., 1966), p. 172.

[24] Main, pp. 269–70. Conversely, Forrest McDonald asserts that those towns constituting the bloc opposed to paper money or, more precisely, the leaders in those towns who induced their communities to reject the paper scheme, formed the hard core of the group which endorsed the Constitution. *We the People,* p. 338. Charles Carroll, in an able general history of the state, asserts that "the alignment in Rhode Island . . . was . . . town-specie-federalist vs. country-paper-antifederalist." Charles Carroll, *Rhode Island: Three Centuries of Democracy* (New York, 1932), I, 397.

[25] Bishop, pp. 26–28.

[26] *Ibid.,* p. 33; McDonald, *We The People,* pp. 343–44. Bishop com-

and the same individuals who favored paper money also opposed the Constitution, a comparison of the vote on the Constitutional referendum with the votes for the Country party candidates in 1786 and 1787 "seems to indicate that the sentiment against the Constitution was noticeably greater than the normal strength of the Country Party." [27]

In the light of these considerations other factors must be identified in addition to the currency controversy to adequately understand the intensity of Rhode Island's Antifederalism. Further economic motives for the state's resistance were strongly in evidence. The most important of these was fear that exorbitant taxes on land and polls would be levied by the new national government to pay the public debt and the "high" salaries of federal officials. Unprecedented and burdensome state taxes on land were in large measure responsible for the paper money emission, and the landholders' dread of similar federal taxes was to a considerable extent responsible for Rhode Island's opposition to the new federal union.

This apprehension was evidenced by the serious attention the question of direct taxes on land and polls received in the March 1790 ratifying convention. It was further exhibited in three amendments (VII, VIII, and IX) proposed and approved by that convention. In suggested Amendment VII, Rhode Island joined New York in urging that "no capitation or poll tax shall ever be laid by Congress"; in Amendment VIII Rhode Island joined six sister states by requesting a prohibition on the laying of direct taxes except after the failure of a federal requisition

---

pares the lodge money notices in the press with the names of those who voted in the constitutional referendum of March 1788. His analysis reveals that "only 70 or approximately 3% of the 2236 freemen voting against the Constitution had discharged even one debt in paper money, while 21 or 1% of the opponents of the Constitution were victims of the same paper money tenders." Bishop, p. 33. The number 2,236 is based upon the vote in twenty-four of the thirty towns; in the other six communities the names of the voters were not recorded. Staples, *RICC*, p. 591.

[27] Bishop, pp. 29–32. Conversely, Country party Governor John Collins was a mild Federalist. Polishook, pp. 186–87.

upon the states; and in proposed Amendment IX (one of five unique to Rhode Island) the state, as an insurance measure, recommended that "Congress shall lay no direct taxes, without the assent of the legislatures of three-fourths of the states in the Union." [28]

Hillman Bishop concludes that of the economic reasons for Rhode Island's reluctance to adopt the Constitution "it would appear that a fear of heavy taxes on land and polls probably influenced more voters than any other single economic factor." [29] This contention seems accurate.

---

[28] Staples, *RICC*, p. 679. Bates, p. 204 erroneously states that the required assent for amendment IX was two-thirds. The aversion of Rhode Island's Antifederalists to direct taxation was well-known to contemporaries. On the eve of the March 1790 convention Massachusetts Senator Fisher Ames urged Welcome Arnold to assure the "Anti's" that they had no cause "to fear direct assessments by the U.S. for it cannot be expected that the landed interest, which predominates in Congress, will abuse this source of taxation." Ames to Arnold, Feb. 20, 1790, W. Easton Louttit Collection, John Hay Library, Brown University.

[29] Bishop, pp. 35–36. Forrest McDonald, *We The People*, p. 339, asserts that "the economic possibilities of independent status were enormous. The most important of such potentials was smuggling to circumvent payment of United States import duties." In support of this contention McDonald cites an article by "Charlestoniensis" in the *Newport Herald* of November 20, 1788, which suggested that an independent Rhode Island might become another St. Eustatius (a Dutch island in the West Indies that served as a base for smuggling into the Briitsh and French West Indies). Although Rhode Islanders were not above such a practice and certain national leaders feared this development, this consideration played a minor role at best in Rhode Island's Antifederalism. One finds it difficult to imagine that residents of non-mercantile, agrarian Charlestown or any other country town would have become genuinely enthused over the state's potential for smuggling. Those who would reap the greatest benefits from this practice were the port towns, and they supported ratification. Furthermore, these seaports indicated in numerous public declarations their fear of being treated commercially as a foreign nation. See for example, Providence Town Meeting Records, City Clerk's Office, No. 7 (1783–1804), pp. 140–43, 146–48, 158–60. Country Party leader Jonathan Hazard while electioneering against the Constitution was one who predicted that the state would benefit economically from an independent status. Polishook summarizes Hazard's contentions as follows: "Free from the yoke of inhibiting tariffs, Rhode Island would sell foreign articles 'for a song' and become the entrepot of commerce in North America. If the United States attempted to interdict this

Perhaps Jabez Bowen, a leading Federalist and former deputy governor, summed up the situation as well as any contemporary in the following letter to George Washington:

> The Towns of Newport, Providence, Bristol etc. with the whole Mercantile interest in the other Towns in the State are Federal, while the Farmers in general are against it. Their opposition arises principally from their being much in Debt, from the Insinuations of wicked and designing Men that they will loose their Liberty in adopting it; that the Sallerys of the National Officers are so very high that it will take the whole of the Money Collected by the Impost to pay them, that the Interest & principle of the General Debt must be raised by Dry Taxation on Real Estates, etc.[30]

As Bowen observed, there were ingredients in Rhode Island's Antifederalism in addition to those of an economic nature. Bowen spoke of the loss of "liberty," which seemed to many a necessary consequence of ratification. A consideration of this pervasive belief suggests political, philosophic, or ideological motivations for Rhode Island's estrangement from the proposed federal union, and these motives were of great and perhaps transcendent importance.

Rhode Island had a long tradition of individualism, separatism, democracy, and liberty both civil and religious. It possessed a long-standing distrust of government too far removed from the people. Its cherished political values were allegedly threatened by the new Constitution. Ironically its concern for those values had been awakened, invigorated, and heightened by the recent, mercantile-inspired campaign against the impost. The specter of an omnipotent national government raised by the merchants in the early 1780s to defeat the impost bill still haunted the imagination of many freemen.[31]

---

trade . . . Rhode Islanders were adept at the ancient art of smuggling." *Rhode Island and the Union*, pp. 193–94. Hazard's arguments seem farfetched and probably had little impact.

[30] Jabez Bowen to George Washington, December 15, 1789 in Department of State, Bureau of Rolls and Library, *Documentary History of the Constitution of the United States* (Washington, D.C., 1894–1905), V, 226, hereafter cited *DHC*.

[31] A by-product of the merchant-led campaign (1781–85) against the

Rhode Island had an attachment to popular control of government and to what one historian has termed "democratic localism." [32] These principles were not endangered by the Articles of Confederation to which the state readily assented. The Articles gave the people of a state, or, more precisely, their legislature, close control over delegates to Congress. Under the Confederation members of Congress were annually appointed in a manner prescribed by the state legislature, they were subject to recall and were paid by their respective states. Under the Articles, as in Rhode Island, the executive was weak and the legislature supreme.

In addition to these features, the Articles, of course, exalted state sovereignty. In all important civil matters Congress was dependent upon the voluntary compliance of state legislatures to carry out its recommendations, and the approval of all states was necessary to amend our inflexible first frame of government.

This system was altered by the Constitution in ways too familiar to enumerate, and Rhode Island disapproved of the change. Some of her specific objections were contained in twenty-one amendments offered by the Rhode Island ratifying convention. They revealed a deep suspicion of the new central establishment — a suspicion that had been increased by the failure of the proposed constitution to contain a bill of rights.

Rhode Island's first suggested amendment requested a guarantee to each state of its sovereignty and of every power not expressly delegated to the United States by the Constitution; amendment II attempted to limit federal interference in a state's conduct of congressional elections; amendment XII prohibited as "dangerous to liberty" standing armies in time of peace; amendments XIII and XIV called for a two-thirds vote of those present in each house to borrow money on the credit of the United States or to declare war, while amendment XVIII sub-

---

continental impost was the persistence of a public opinion hostile to or at least suspicious of every attempt to increase the powers of the central government (see Chapter 4).

[32] Polishook, *Rhode Island and the Union,* pp. 27–28.

jected senators to recall and replacement by their state legislature.

So fearful was Rhode Island that the newly-created federal
system would develop beyond control that it offered a unique
amendment (IV) which would have required all changes in the
Constitution after 1793 to receive the consent of eleven of the
thirteen original states. Rhode Island, of course, supported those
Congressional amendments that eventually became the Bill of
Rights.[33]

The General Assembly in an official communication to Congress on September 19, 1789 quite adequately and accurately expressed the ideological basis of the state's antifederalism:

> The people of this State from its first settlement, have been
> accustomed and strongly attached to a democratic form of gov-
> ernment. They have viewed in the new Constitution an ap-
> proach, though perhaps but small, toward that form of govern-
> ment from which we have lately dissolved our connection at so
> much hazard and expense of life and treasure. . . . We are
> sensible of the extremes to which democratic governments are
> sometimes liable, something of which we have lately experi-
> enced, but we esteem them temporary and partial evils com-
> pared with the loss of liberty and the rights of a free people.[34]

This was not mere rhetoric. Just as Rhode Islanders were
quick to protest an alleged abridgement by England of their individual and collective freedom, so also did they resist an anticipated curtailment of their "liberty" and autonomy by the founding fathers. Self-determination in late eighteenth-century Rhode

---

[33] Staples, *RICC*, pp. 678–80. Amendment I was proposed by five
other states; Amendment II by six; Amendment IV by Rhode Island
alone; Amendment XII by four additional states; Amendments XIII,
XIV, and XVIII by one other *viz.*, New York. Bates, pp. 202–03. Two
proposed amendments were defeated in the March convention. One
would have prohibited the central government from choosing any officials
formerly appointed by the state; the other called for the use of wealth
rather than population as a base for direct taxation. *Providence Gazette,*
March 13, 1790.

[34] General Assembly to the President of the Senate and the House of
Representatives of the eleven United States of America in Congress
assembled, September 19, 1789, Letters from the Governor of Rhode
Island, RISA, IV (1780–1800), 77; Staples, *RICC*, pp. 621–23.

Island was a way of life, and no portion of it would be easily surrendered, as the contest over ratification dramatically revealed.

Another formidable factor contributing to the strength of the state's Antifederalism was strong hostility toward slavery that pervaded the state. Intense among Rhode Island's sizable Quaker community, this attitude was shared by others as well, perhaps to atone for past sins.

Those opposed to slavery realized that the Philadelphia convention had compromised on the question, and they were aware that the Constitution thrice gave implied assent to the institution through clauses on representation, fugitives, and the slave trade. In particular, the twenty-year prohibition on federal legislation banning the foreign slave traffic was a concession too great for many Rhode Islanders to accept.

Only five weeks following the adjournment of the Philadelphia conclave, the General Assembly passed an act, initiated by influential and irrepressible Quakers, prohibiting any Rhode Island citizen from engaging in the slave trade. In vigorous language this statute termed the nefarious traffic "inconsistent with justice, and the principles of humanity, as well as the laws of nature, and that more enlightened and civilized sense of freedom which has of late prevailed." [35] A constitution which gave temporary protection to this trade was not an instrument to be warmly embraced.

Thus, the state's antislavery contingent took refuge in Antifederalism, and, during the critical year 1790, this connection nearly thwarted ratification. Fortunately some abolitionist leaders began to see the difficulties inherent in Rhode Island's continued rejection of the Constitution. Among those was the influential Quaker Moses Brown of the famous mercantile family. Despite some initial misgivings, he embraced the Federalist cause by 1790. Early in that fateful year Brown toured the state talking

---

[35] RIGA, Records, XIII, 419–21; *RICR*, X, 262. See Elizabeth Donnan, "Agitation Against the Slave Trade in Rhode Island, 1784–1790," in *Persecution and Liberty: Essays in Honor of George Lincoln Burr* (New York, 1931). See also *Providence Gazette,* October 6, 13, and Nov. 24, 1787.

with Friends at various monthly meetings in an attempt to overcome their opposition. His campaign seems to have met with limited success, but antislavery objections to the Constitution, enunciated by such zealots as Samuel Hopkins of Newport, were by no means dispelled when the March session of the convention assembled.[36]

At this South Kingstown meeting, slavery engendered much discussion and debate. The slave trade provision of the Constitution provoked such opposition that an amendment (XVII) was specifically proposed and approved that exhorted Congress to ban the traffic immediately. Rhode Island was the only state to suggest such an amendment during the ratification struggle.[37]

---

[36] Mack Thompson, *Moses Brown: Reluctant Reformer* (Chapel Hill, North Carolina, 1962), pp. 239–43; Moses Brown to Isaac Lawton, Jacob Mott, Sampson Sherman or any other Friends to whom they may think proper to communicate, February 4, 1790, Austin Collection, Moses Brown Papers, Box 12, RIHS Library. A reaction to the Constitution which was perhaps typical of local Quaker sentiment was expressed by William Rotch of Nantucket, Massachusetts in a letter to co-religionist Moses Brown, November 8, 1787: "Thou queries how friends can be active in establishing the new form of government which so much favors slavery . . . as to my own part, my heart has been often pained since the publication of the doings of the Convention; and much disappointed I am, as I had entertained some hope that so many wise men would have formed some system of government founded on equity and justice . . . whatever high encomiums are given to it (the Constitution), it is evident to me that it is founded on *slavery* and that is on blood." *Ibid.*, Box 3. See also Dr. Samuel Hopkins to Moses Brown, Oct. 22, 1787, Moses Brown Papers, RIHS; Elizabeth Donnan, ed., *Documents Illustrative of the History of the Slave Trade to America* (Washington, D.C., 1930–35), III, 335–52; and Samuel Hopkins, *Works,* ed., E. A. Park (Philadelphia, 1853), I, 119–127. Two recent studies of Hopkins which reveal the vehement anti-slave sentiments of this outspoken Congregationalist clergyman are David S. Lovejoy, "Samuel Hopkins: Religion, Slavery, and the Revolution," *New England Quarterly,* XL (June, 1967), 227–43 and David E. Swift, "Samuel Hopkins: Calvinist Social Concern in Eighteenth Century New England," *Journal of Presbyterian History,* XLVII (Spring, 1969), 31–54.

[37] Cotner, ed., *Foster's Minutes,* pp. 73–76; Staples, *RICC,* pp. 645–48. Joseph Stanton of Charlestown informed the convention that there is "a material objection to the Constitution with the people where he lives" because it countenances the slave trade. Cotner, ed., *Foster's Minutes,* p. 75.

Some local opponents of slavery doggedly maintained their Antifederalism until the end. When the Providence Abolition Society — founded in February 1789 — received its charter from the state in June 1790, the list of incorporators revealed that ten of its signers were members of the May ratifying convention. Included were president Daniel Owen and Antifederal floor leaders Joseph Stanton, Jr. and Job Comstock. Only three of these ten abolitionist delegates voted to accept the federal document on May 29.[38]

Finally, Rhode Island's hostility toward the United States was conditioned in part by the Union's hostility to Rhode Island. Since the days of Roger Williams — when Rhode Island was dubbed a moral sewer by her haughty Puritan neighbors — the state had been subjected to the abuse of outraged foreigners. In the 1780s attacks from without reached unprecedented proportions. Beginning with Rhode Island's initial rejection of the impost and continuing through the paper money era, the state and its citizens were subjected to an endless stream of invective. Rhode Island newspapers of the day were replete with verbal barbs reprinted from distant presses. Harsh actions and words of condescending foreign critics were most distressing to Rhode Islanders.

The confederation Congress attempted to unseat Rhode Island delegate David Howell for his strenuous opposition to the impost. After the paper money issue the state was caricatured as the "quintessence of villainy" and the Trevett-Weeden affair brought further opprobrium.

---

[38] RIGA, Records, XIII, 755–61; *RICR*, X, 382–85. Cotner (*Foster's Minutes*, p. 50, footnote 48) and McDonald (*We The People*, p. 345) incorrectly say eight convention delegates were charter members of the Providence Abolition Society. Actually delegates Daniel Owen, James Sheldon, Joseph Stanton, Jr., John Sayles, John Williams, Noah Mathewson, Job Comstock, John S. Dexter, Levi Ballou, and Benjamin Arnold signed the charter. Only the last three, however, voted to accept the Constitution. A recent work which emphasizes the importance of slavery in the Constitution-making process is Staughton Lynd, *Class Conflict, Slavery, and The United States Constitution* (Indianapolis, 1967), pp. 153–213. On the Providence Abolition Society see James F. Reilly, "The

During the constitution-making process Federalists took Rhode Island to task. From the outset, when the *Massachusetts Sentinel* described Rhode Island's absence from the Grand Convention as a "joyous rather than a grievous" circumstance, to the end of the ratification struggle, when some proposed her dismemberment and absorption by the surrounding states, Rhode Island endured repeated insult. Even temperate James Madison exclaimed in exasperation, "Nothing can exceed the wickedness and folly which continue to rule there. All sense of character as well as of right have been obliterated."

The most eloquent censure of all came from Connecticut, via the pens of a foursome who later joined a group of literati known as the "Connecticut Wits." Their contribution to Rhode Island's litany of shame was a long poetical satire entitled the "Anarchiad, 1786–1787."

> Hail! realm of rogues, renown'd for fraud and guile,
> All hail; ye knav'ries of yon little isle.
> There prowls the rascal, cloth'd with legal pow'r,
> To snare the orphan, and the poor devour;
> The crafty knave his creditor besets,
> And advertising paper pays his debts;
> Bankrupts their creditors with rage pursue,
> No stop, no mercy from the debtor crew.
> Arm'd with new tests, the licens'd villain bold,
> Presents his bills, and robs them of their gold;
> Their ears, though rogues and counterfeiters lose,
> No legal robber fears the gallows noose.
> . . . .
> Each weekly print new lists of cheats proclaims,
> Proud to enroll their knav'ries and their names;
> The wiser race, the snares of law to shun,
> Like Lot from Sodom, from Rhode Island run.[39]

Providence Abolition Society," *Rhode Island History*, XXI (April 1962), 33–48.

[39] For the controversy surrounding the attempt to expel Howell, see Staples, *RICC*, pp. 375–428. On Rhode Island's reaction to New York editor Francis Child's article, the "Quintessence of Villainy," see *Ibid.*, pp. 579–82, especially James M. Varnum and Peleg Arnold to Governor George Clinton, April 7, 1787. The *Massachusetts Sentinel's* remarks are quoted in Clinton Rossiter, *1787: The Grand Convention* (New York, 1966), pp. 88–9. Madison's statement from a letter of April 2, 1787

Such derisive epithets caused anger and resentment in Rhode Island. They produced a banding together of the citizenry, especially in the country towns, against outside agitators. The Federalists won few friends in Rhode Island with their abusive tirades.[40]

III

Rhode Island's opposition to the Constitution stemmed primarily from an adherence to the paper money program, aversion to direct taxation, attachment to "liberty" and the principles of direct democracy, a detestation of slavery, and adverse reaction to "foreign" criticism. For a time these obstacles seemed insuperable, but countervailing forces eventually produced a tenuous triumph for the cause of Federalism.

Several of these forces worked from the inception of the controversy, others developed gradually as tides of change left Rhode Island high and dry outside the Union. From the outset, the existence within the state of continental loan office certificates in the face amount of $524,000 provided an important source of support for the new, prospectively more stable and fiscally responsible government. Major repositories for these securities and for Federalism were Providence and Newport.[41]

Ratification would benefit not only those private creditors of the national government who held these certificates, but a number of coastal towns as well. Exposed communities such as Newport, Middletown, Portsmouth, Jamestown, Tiverton, Little Compton, Bristol, and Warren held substantial claims against the

---

appears in Clarence Brigham, *History of the State of Rhode Island and Providence Plantations* (Providence, 1902), p. 261. On the "Anarchiad" see Abe C. Ravitz, "Anarch in Rhode Island," *Rhode Island History,* XI (October 1952), 117–24. The poem appeared in the *Providence Gazette,* March 31, 1787.

[40] McDonald, *We The People,* p. 338 also believes that outside criticism strengthened Rhode Island's antifederalism. A similar reaction to foreign agitators occurred in the ante-bellum South.

[41] *Ibid.,* p. 326; E. James Ferguson, *The Power of the Purse: A History of American Public Finance, 1776–1790* (Chapel Hill, N.C., 1961), pp. 280–82. Seventy-one percent of the total federal debt held in Rhode Island was owned by citizens in these two communities.

United States for war damages. Newport, Middletown, and Portsmouth, in fact, had audited claims amounting to $719,280 out of a state total of $899,100. Establishment of a government with effective taxing power would enhance their chances for compensation, but it appears from the slow conversion of these communities — Newport and Bristol excepted — that the claims were a peripheral rather than a decisive consideration.[42]

The mercantile community had also come to realize the importance of unified national control over interstate and foreign commerce. Proliferation of interstate tariffs and the failure of confederation diplomats to secure commercial treaties with such important nations as England and Spain because of the "imbecility" of the Articles in the area of commercial regulation would be remedied by the new Constitution. Effective central direction and encouragement of commerce, merchants felt, would enhance the state's economy and their personal fortunes as well.[43]

Finally, ratification presented the prospect of a protective tariff to the small but growing and influential class of mechanics and incipient industrialists concentrated mainly in Providence. In spring 1789 the newly-created Providence Association of Mechanics and Manufacturers appointed a committee of correspondence to dispatch circular letters to similar groups in other states lamenting Rhode Island's obstructionism and expressing an "anxious desire and fervent prayer that this State may speedily take measures to be reunited under the Federal Head and thereby enjoy the benefits of that Government." [44] The principal

---

[42] McDonald, *We The People*, pp. 326, 337–38. In an Assembly-authorized town referendum conducted in October 1789, the Bay communities of Portsmouth, Middletown and Jamestown were still opposed to the calling of a ratifying convention. For example Jamestown's freemen voted "against choosing a Convention for adopting the new federal government." Book of Town Records, Town Clerk's Office, No. 3 (1744–96), p. 333.

[43] On the importance to the Federalists of uniform regulation of commerce see the May 1789 petition to the General Assembly signed by over 500 Providence residents and printed in Staples, *RICC,* pp. 618–20.

[44] Records of the Providence Association of Mechanics and Manufacturers, I (Feb. 27, 1789 to April 10, 1794), pp. 21–32, RIHS. For a similar stance taken by New York City's mechanics see Lynd, pp. 121–32.

"benefit" that they sought was a protective tariff to encourage the state's infant industries.

As of March 1788, these economic factors notwithstanding, the only Federalist communities were Providence, Newport, and Bristol, the state's principal seaports, plus the coastal town of Little Compton.[45] Certain developments in 1789 and 1790, gradually swung the Bay towns of Portsmouth, Middletown, Tiverton, Jamestown, Warren, and Barrington into the federal camp. They were joined by Westerly, a minor port and shipbuilding town on the southwestern coast.

Surprisingly Hopkinton, Westerly's adjacent but interior neighbor to the north, made a last minute switch to federalism as did inland, but shipbuilding, Cumberland in the state's northeastern corner.[46] Warwick, a four-vote town on the upper Bay had its delegation evenly split on the question of ratification in the May 1790 convention.[47]

---

[45] Bristol and Little Compton supported the Constitution in the March 1788 referendum, the former by a margin of twenty-six to twenty-three and the latter by a count of sixty-three to fifty-seven. Staples, *RICC*, p. 590. See also Little Compton's instructions to her deputies in January 1788. PAC, p. 56. Nicholas and John Brown correctly observed that "the seaport towns are truly desirous of joining the General Government." Nicholas and John Brown to Richard Henry Lee, May 1, 1789, John Brown Papers, RIHS.

[46] Cumberland's important shipbuilding industry was inaugurated in early 1790. Prior to that time the town had produced naval stores, especially pitch. Richard M. Bayles, ed., *History of Providence County, Rhode Island* (New York, 1891), II, 236, 242. Sidney S. Rider, "The Development of Constitutional Government in Rhode Island," unpublished manuscript, RIHS, XVI-2-64-14, hereafter cited as Rider, "Constitutional Government," has contended that convention delegate John Brown of Hopkinton was a relative of the prominent Providence merchants. Rider is also of the belief that the division in Rhode Island was between "maritime" and "agricultural" towns. *Ibid.* The Hopkinton and Cumberland town meeting records give us no indication of why these communities defected to the Federalist camp. On Westerly see Frederic Denison, *Westerly and its Witnesses* (Providence, 1878), pp. 141, 180.

[47] Staples, *RICC,* pp. 672–73. Besides Warwick, the only split delegation in the May convention was that of Portsmouth. The vote from this community was two for adoption, one for rejection, and one absent. Portsmouth's position on ratification is perplexing. In the 1788 referendum the Antifederalists had a margin of sixty to twelve. The town con-

Among the factors accounting for the slow attrition in the Antifederal ranks included the incessant labors of the Federalist press that dramatized the need for union. Notable propagandists were Bennett Wheeler's *United States Chronicle* (Providence), John Carter's *Providence Gazette,* and Peter Edes's *Newport Herald.*[48] Rhode Island felt increasingly isolated as the inexorable ratification movement toppled opposition in state after state. George Washington's snub of Rhode Island during his triumphal New England tour in the fall of 1789 emphasized its ostracism. Isolation was further accentuated — and Rhode Island wavered markedly — after North Carolina capitulated in November 1789.[49] Further, the proposal by Congress of a Bill of Rights coupled with the state's submission of its own amendments gave the Federalist cause a perceptible lift and deprived the "Antis" of a formidable objection.[50] The prestige and integrity of new federal

---

tained a relatively large number of Quakers, and their anti-slave sentiment perhaps explains the Constitution's slow headway there, despite the town's $136,530 claim against the United States for war damages. In 1790, Moses Brown concentrated his pro-Constitution campaign in Portsmouth, and he seems to have had some success, because the town meeting instructed the four-man Portsmouth delegation to ratify. Despite these instructions Job Durfee declined to attend on the day of decision and Giles Slocum cast a negative vote. Staples, *RICC,* pp. 590, 670–72; Thompson, pp. 241–43; McDonald, *We The People,* pp. 337, 343. In divided Warwick 97 freemen had voted against the calling of the ratification convention and 108 had supported the convening of such an assemblage. Warwick Town Meeting Records (1776–1795), RIHS, January 9 and 12, 1790.

[48] These journals, although biased, are the fullest source for the ratification struggle.

[49] On Washington's autumn tour and his by-pass of Rhode Island see John C. Fitzpatrick, ed., *The Diaries of George Washington, 1748–1799* (New York, 1925), IV, 20–51. William Ellery to Benjamin Huntington, December 12, 1789, Ellery-Huntington Correspondence, mentions the impact of North Carolina's ratification as does Peter Edes in the *Newport Herald,* Jan. 21, 1790, and Jabez Bowen, DHC, V, 226.

[50] William Ellery to Benjamin Huntington, May 10, June 15, July 13 and September 8, 1789; *Newport Mercury,* January 28, 1788. After the Constitution was ratified by the requisite number of states, Rhode Island's Antifederalists embraced the amendment device to rectify the document's alleged shortcomings. They did not generally support the movement for a second constitution convention which was pressed by their

officials, especially President Washington, lessened the fears and suspicions about the new governmental system. Moses Brown persuasively argued that the nature of the government would depend more upon the caliber of the men sent to administer it than on the Constitution itself.[51]

A severe jolt was delivered to Antifederalists when Providence threatened to secede from the state unless Rhode Island joined the Union. This drastic but well-considered step — proposed in the Providence Town Meeting on May 24 — was embodied in instructions to that town's convention delegates. If the Constitution was rejected or a decision unduly delayed, Providence delegates were empowered to meet with those from Newport and other interested towns to discuss means by which pro-Constitution communities could apply to Congress "for the same privileges and protection which are afforded to the towns under their jurisdiction." [52]

Proposed assumption of state debts apparently induced a few Rhode Islanders to advocate adoption. Some citizens could and did benefit from such a federal program. It was argued by several shrewd Rhode Islanders that assumption would enable them to receive payment for their state securities a second time. This

---

counterparts in New York, Virginia, and Pennsylvania. Linda Grant De Pauw, "The Anticlimax of Antifederalism: The Abortive Second Convention Movement, 1788–89," *Prologue,* II (Fall, 1970), 105–06.

[51] Thompson, p. 242. The election of Washington as Chief Executive did much to quiet Rhode Island's fears. Conversely, his snub of the state during his national tour of 1789 was a source of embarrassment to Rhode Islanders. On Washington's influence see also John Brown, *et al.* to George Washington, June 10, 1790, Olney Papers, RIHS, I, 43.

[52] Providence Town Meeting Records, No. 7 (1783–1804), pp. 169-70. This move had been in the making for some time prior to May 24. See William Ellery to Benjamin Huntington, Ellery-Huntington Correspondence, April 25, May 14, 1789, March 8, April 17, May 3, May 11, 1790 and Huntington to Ellery, May 8, 1790. On April 17 Ellery asked Huntington if any seceding towns would be protected and admitted to the Union by Congress; Huntington replied that "I have no doubt" that Congress would aid them. Other anticipations of Providence's secession move are Benjamin Bourne to Silas Talbot, Jan. 9, 1790, Peck Collection, RIHS, Box VIII, #31, and Jabez Bowen to George Washington, Dec. 15, 1789, *DHC,* V, 226. McDonald, *We The People,* pp. 323, 345, erroneously asserts that Providence had actually seceded.

could be accomplished if the Assembly would enact a law setting up a scale of depreciation on the paper money, declaring that because of this depreciation only a part of the debt had been paid, and returning the "unredeemed" portion of the state certificates to those who had originally submitted them. A consolidation statute to implement this scheme was actually passed in June 1791, making it possible for a number of state creditors to receive a modest second payment, this time from the government of the United States. Those hard money merchants who had withheld their state securities, and had chosen to forfeit payment rather than submit them to the state for redemption in paper, were also included under the assumption plan by the act of 1791.

Enticing as this scheme appears the assumption program was not an important factor influencing Rhode Island's ratification, Forrest McDonald's assertion notwithstanding.[53] In mid-1790, the mercantile community was leery of assumption because its costs might necessitate an exorbitant impost; many farmers rejected it because they sensed the power and influence such a plan would bestow upon the central government. Existing evidence clearly shows that both the Country party and the merchants were cool to the assumption project.[54] In fact, the state's new

---

[53] McDonald (*We The People,* pp. 345–46) feels that this ingenious plan was one of "two principal economic reasons" which caused a shift in antifederal votes between the March and May conventions and made ratification possible. McDonald erroneously asserts that the depreciation law was passed during the interim between the March and May conventions. Actually, it was not passed until June 1791, over a year after Rhode Island had entered the Union and nearly eleven months after the assumption plan had been enacted over the opposition of Rhode Island's senators. *RICR,* X, 447–50. Stanton and Foster voted against the inclusion of assumption with the funding bill and when they were unsuccessful they voted against the funding bill itself.

[54] The foregoing analysis of the assumption program is derived from *Annals of the Congress of the United States, 1789–1824,* eds. J. Gales and W. W. Seaton (Washington, 1834–56), 1 Cong., 2 Sess., pp. 1012, 1016, hereafter cited *Annals;* William Ellery to Benjamin Huntington, February 2, March 8, and June 12, 1790, Ellery-Huntington Correspondence; Arthur Fenner to Theodore Foster, July 17, and July 31, 1790; Ebenezer Thompson to Foster, July 26, 1790, Foster Papers, RIHS,

senators, Theodore Foster (a moderate Federalist), and Joseph
Stanton, Jr. (an Antifederal stalwart) both opposed it. That
Rhode Island *itself* would likely prove to be a creditor of the
central government, however, may have strengthened the Federalist cause within its borders.[55]

The principal proximate cause for Rhode Island ratification
was economic coercion exerted upon the state by the new federal
government. Within weeks after the first Congress set to work,
William Ellery of Newport began his campaign to persuade the
national legislature to lower the economic boom upon Rhode
Island. Ellery — a signer of the Declaration of Independence, a
commissioner of the loan office, and a staunch Federalist — was
in frequent contact with Congressman Benjamin Huntington and
Senator Oliver Ellsworth, both of Connecticut, urging them to
abandon "a policy of leniency" toward Rhode Island. Repeatedly he advised them that the Antifederalists "must be made
to feel before they will ever consent to call a convention," and

---

Vol. I; [J. Franklin Jameson, ed.], "The Adjustment of Rhode Island
Into the Union in 1790," *Publications of the Rhode Island Historical
Society,* VIII (July 1900), 104–135. Rhode Island was awarded a paltry
$200,000 out of a total of $21,500,000 assumed. A very interesting analysis of the state's June 1791 depreciation act and the complexities of its
implementation is John W. Richmond, *Rhode Island Repudiation, or
the History of the Revolutionary Debt of Rhode Island,* 2nd ed. (Providence, 1855). Richmond believed that the measure was "wise and emi-
nently just," because it repealed the forfeiture provisions of the acts of
1787–89 and because it allowed those who had received depreciated
paper from the state for their securities to get "just compensation," pp.
1–33. An informative up-to-date analysis is contained in Polishook,
Rhode Island and the Union, pp. 235–41.

[55] As Fisher Ames observed just prior to the March ratifying convention: "The plan of the Secretary [Hamilton] affords an argument more
upon a level with their [the Antifederalists] views. The scheme of adjusting accounts between the U.S. and individual states presents to your
people a solid and very alluring advantage. It is equally beneficial to
creditor states who will now get their due and to debtor states who will
get their debts paid for them by the U.S. Rhode Island I suppose will
prove a creditor, and may expect that this will provide an annual sum
from the public treasury sufficient to pay the expenses of civil government." Ames to Welcome Arnold, Feb. 20, 1790, W. Easton Louttit
Collection, JHL.

they can be made "to feel . . . by subjecting the goods, wares, and manufactures of this state" to the same high duties "as foreign States not in alliance with the United States." [56]

'Although such duties would hurt Federalists in the port towns, the result would be worth the sacrifice, claimed Ellery. As time went on he suggested ways to hit the Antifederalists more directly. Place duties on the produce of the country folk, he advised, stop their "lime, flaxseed, and barley" from entering the neighboring states duty free, and "the Antis will . . . be compelled by a sense of interest to adopt the Constitution." Further, "Congress should require an immediate payment of a sum of money from the State with an assurance that if not collected an equivalent will be distrained." [57] The sum to which Ellery referred was Rhode Island's share of the Revolutionary debt. Call for immediate payment would necessitate a re-institution of high taxes on land.

Prodded by Ellery's shrewd observations, Congress began to move. In July 1789 it enacted a tariff program that subjected "all goods, wares, and merchandise" which Rhode Island exported to other states to foreign duties if such merchandise were not of Rhode Island "growth or manufacture." The state immediately petitioned for suspension of these duties and Congress, to Ellery's dismay, relented. In mid-September an act was passed holding the discriminatory levies in abeyance until January 15, 1790. [58]

Just as this period of grace expired, the General Assembly approved, not by coincidence, the act calling a ratifying convention. Immediately Governor Collins informed the President and Congress and requested a further suspension. The patient Congress again complied. On February 8, Rhode Island's privi-

---

[56] William Ellery to Benjamin Huntington, May 14 and June 15, 1789, Ellery-Huntington Correspondence.

[57] *Ibid.,* December 12, 1789, March 28, 1790.

[58] *Annals,* 1 Cong., 1 Sess., 78–9, 887, 889–90, 892, 2132, 2133–58, 2178–79. See the August 27, 1789 petition to Congress from the Newport town meeting requesting that Rhode Island be "relieved of Foreign Tonnage." Henry Marchant Papers, RIHS.

lege was extended "until the first day of April next, and no longer." [59]

Vice President John Adams, the Senate's presiding officer, began to show signs of exasperation. Just prior to the South Kingstown convention he confided to Providence merchants John Brown and John Francis that he was "really much affected at the obstinate infatuation of so great a part of the People of Rhode Island." Then he admonished, "if the Convention should reject the Constitution or adjourn without adopting it, Congress will probably find it necessary to treat them as they are, as Foreigners, and extend all the laws to them as such. . . . If the lime, the barley and other articles, whether of foreign or domestic growth or manufacture, should be subjected to a Duty, it would soon show your People that their interests are in the power of their neighbors." [60]

When the March convention adjourned without issue and the Country party swept the April elections, more drastic pressures, such as those of which Adams warned, appeared necessary. On April 28, 1790 a five-man Senate committe was created "to consider what provisions will be proper for Congress to make in the present session, respecting the State of Rhode Island." Among the membership of this group were Ellsworth and Caleb Strong of Massachusetts. Ellery now reiterated his bold plans to coerce the antifederal majority. He urged prompt action. "It is my opinion," he stated, "that the Convention will adjourn again unless you do something which will touch the interest of the Antis before the Convention meets." [61]

The committee, with Senator Ellsworth in the lead, heeded Ellery's admonition. On May 11, it reported a two-point program imposing a prohibition on all commercial intercourse between the United States and Rhode Island, effective July 1, and demanding an immediate payment, eventually set at $25,000, on

---

[59] *Annals*, 1 Cong., 2 Sess., pp. 941–43, 1106, 2202.

[60] John Adams to [John] Brown and [John] Francis, February 28, 1790, Misc. Mss., RIHS, A 214bf.

[61] *Annals*, 1 Cong., 2 Sess., pp. 966–67; Ellery to Huntington, April 17 and May 3, 1790, Ellery-Huntington Correspondence.

the state's Revolutionary debt. A bill encompassing those recommendations was drawn. On May 18, after long debate, it passed 13 to 8.[62] Noncompliance with the requisition couid, perhaps, offer sufficient pretext for a resort to military force by the United States.

According to Senator William Maclay of Pennsylvania, a vigorous opponent of the measure, some were induced to support it "to get two Senators more into the House on whose votes they can reckon on the question of residence." He was referring, of course, to the controversy over the permanent location of the national capital. This consideration, however, was of secondary importance. As the bill headed for the House, Maclay observed: "It was meant to be used in the same way that a robber does a dagger or a highwayman a pistol, and to obtain the end desired by putting the party in fear." [63]

Merchant John Francis reported from Philadelphia that the bill would "put an entire stoppage to all connection whatever by land or water. This very severe remedy," he said with mixed emotions, "will sorely operate on the Feds, who must bear it with fortitude as the only remaining means [to secure Rhode Island's ratification]." [64]

---

[62] *Annals,* 1 Cong., 2 Sess., 972–76; Senate Journal, 1 Cong., 2 Sess., pp. 63, 75–76; Edgar S. Maclay, ed., *The Journal of William Maclay* (New York, 1965), pp. 257, 260, hereafter cited as *Maclay's Journal.* Ellery's specific recommendation to impose duties on Rhode Island's agricultural staples was not enacted, but the Senate bill was even more far-reaching.

[63] *Maclay's Journal.,* p. 260. In late February Senator Strong, a member of the committee which proposed the coercive measure, wrote to Theodore Foster that "if the Convention adjourns without acceptance" which is "only a delicate mode of rejection, the Government then will be justified even to the discerning People in Rhode Island in pursuing measures that in other circumstances might be thought severe." Caleb Strong to Foster, Feb. 29, 1790, Foster Papers, I, 23. Soon after ratification, Strong congratulated Foster and expressed the hope that Rhode Island would soon be represented in the Senate so that her solons could vote on the upcoming bill providing for the permanent location of the capital. Strong to Foster, June 3, 1790, Foster Papers, I, 24. Ellsworth's leadership in the coercive movement is indicated by his following remarks: "Rhode Island is at length brought into the Union, and by a pretty bold measure in Congress, which would have exposed me to some censure had it not produced the effect which I expected it would." Ells-

Rumors regarding the measure appeared in the Providence press just prior to the convention. This community had long been apprehensive that the federal duty act would become operative for Rhode Island. Now, in view of the Senate's even more drastic action, Providence decided to employ that long-contemplated resort — secession — if ratification were not forthcoming.[65]

Unquestionably some of the reluctant Bay towns, such as Portsmouth, were also moved by the sustained politico-economic pressure of the federal government. No doubt it was a decisive factor in ratification on May 29.[66] Ellery, animated by a not uncommon blend of principle and patronage, was later rewarded by the new central government for his efforts on its behalf when he received the prized appointment of collector of customs for Newport.

IV

Long-held theories that use notions of class struggle, debtor-creditor antagonism, and real versus personal property interests to explain the division over ratification are too simplistic, too cut and dried, for the variegated Rhode Island experience.[67]

---

worth to "a friend," June 7, 1790, quoted in William Garrott Brown, *The Life of Oliver Ellsworth* (New York, 1905), p. 200.

[64] John Francis to James Brown, May 10, 1790, James Brown Papers, RIHS.

[65] *U.S. Chronicle,* May 20 and 27, 1790; *Providence Gazette,* May 15, 22, 27, 29, 1790. For that community's concern for the Federal trade measures see Town Meeting Records, No. 7 (1783–1804), pp. 140–43, 146–48, 169–70, and William R. Staples, *Annals of the Town of Providence* (Providence, 1843), pp. 341–42 (Petition to Congress, August 27, 1789).

[66] At the time of ratification the bill was pending in the House, where it had drawn sharp criticism from Congressman John Page of Virginia. *Annals,* 1 Cong., 2 Sess., pp. 1616–19. On Portsmouth's reaction to commercial pressure see Staples, *RICC,* pp. 636–39, 670–72 (Instructions of town meeting to convention delegates, February 27 and May 29, 1790). Bates, pp. 170–79, 185–93 ascribes considerable importance to the federal government's policy of coercion, Bishop and Polishook slight it, while McDonald ignores it. For a contemporary view of the effect of the commercial pressure see Edwin M. Stone, ed., *The Life and Recollections of John Howland* (Providence, 1857), pp. 160–64.

[67] These theories, of course, are associated with Charles Beard, *An*

One recently advanced theory that seems to have greater validity for Rhode Island — though it also admits of exceptions — is that advanced by Jackson Turner Main. He contends that in all parts of the country "the commercial interest with its ramifications, including those who depended primarily and directly upon commerce, were Federal, and 'non-navigating' folk were Antifederal."

Main cautions that the commercial interest was not just urban. Commercial centers were supported by nearby rural areas that depended upon towns as markets and as agencies through which their produce was exported overseas. The commercial interest embraced large numbers of farmers, and the influence of each town radiated, perhaps in a degree relative to its size or commercial significance. There was a difference between the exporting agricultural sections and the more isolated and self-sufficient farming areas.

---

*Economic Interpretation of the Constitution of the United State*s (New York, 1913). In fairness to Beard, however, it must be said that he only treats briefly of Rhode Island, he uses Bates as a reference, and he correctly emphasizes federal economic coercion and Providence's threatened secession as factors forcing the issue of ratification. *Ibid.,* p. 237. Robert E. Brown, *Charles Beard and the Constitution* (Princeton, N.J., 1956) is a work which casts grave doubts on Beard's general hypothesis but sheds little light on Rhode Island ratification. McDonald's analysis of the *delegates* to the ratifying convention shows that neither party *in the convention* could reasonably be described as an "agrarian" party or a "debtors' faction." Also, the *delegates,* regardless of their stand, "held approximately the same amounts of the same kinds of securities, and it would appear that there was no line of cleavage between public creditors and non creditors." Finally, nearly equal percentages of both parties *in the convention* borrowed paper in 1786. McDonald, *We The People,* pp. 339–44. I have emphasized that McDonald analyzed the economic interests of the delegates only, because I feel that much sharper differences would be apparent if the rank and file of both factions were compared. While a simple class interpretation cannot be sustained, there is no doubt that most merchants, professional men, mechanics, artisans, and other urban dwellers supported the Constitution, and most of the farmers in the remote rural towns opposed it. James Varnum's observation that "the wealth and resources of this state are chiefly in the possession of the well-affected" (*i.e.,* the Federalists), was not far from the mark. Quoted in Wilkins Updike, *Memoirs of the Rhode Island Bar* (Boston, 1842), p. 301.

Rhode Island does no violence to this thesis. The significant and only intelligible generic division in this recalcitrant state was that of commercial interest versus agrarian; "the Federal tide in Rhode Island rose slowly from Providence and Newport to engulf the other bay towns." [68]

Unfortunately, Main does not list the reasons for this cleavage. He could have mentioned the greater fervor for paper money in the interior towns and the farmer's stronger fear of direct taxes on land. Additional considerations included the relatively large amount of continental securities held in mercantile towns, the war damage claims of the Bay communities, and the commercial coercion of Congress.

A final factor, attitudinal in nature, was the more provincial, localistic, democratic, and politically radical beliefs that prevailed among denizens of those isolated country towns. This outlook rendered them slow in grasping or accepting the full significance of the momentous events transpiring on the national stage. Most of the inhabitants of these communities were — to use Lee Benson's concept — "agrarian-minded." Their remote environment and often inferior social status had shaped their ideology, and that ideology predisposed them to distrust the power of government, especially one far removed from local and popular supervision and control. They were pessimistic, parochial men of little faith.[69]

The mercantile interests, on the other hand, were more cosmopolitan and politically sophisticated. Their mode of life brought them into contact with people of other states, making them less suspicious, broader in outlook, more inclined to realize the necessity of change, and less disposed to fear it. Their ideology, which

---

[68] Main, pp. 213, 248, 256, 270–72, 274, 280.

[69] Lee Benson, *Turner and Beard: American Historical Writing Reconsidered* (New York, 1960), pp. 215–17; Cecelia M. Kenyon, ed., *The Antifederalists* (Indianapolis, 1966), pp. xxi–cxvi and "Men. of Little Faith: The Anti-Federalists on the Nature of Representative Government," *William and Mary Quarterly*, 3rd. ser., XII (Jan. 1955), 3–46; Alpheus Thomas Mason, *The States Rights Debate: Antifederalism and the Constitution* (Englewood Cliffs, N.J., 1964), pp. 66–97; Wood, pp. 519–21.

Benson calls "commercialism," was positive and optimistic. "Commercial-minded" Federalists believed that government must be strong and centralized if it were to function creatively, advance the general welfare, and dispense justice. Moreover, they felt it must have both positive powers to enlarge opportunities and coercive powers to prevent groups or sections from indulging their own interests, passions, and errors at the expense of the commonwealth. Theirs was the idea of "nationalism" that found ever-increasing expression under the Constitution of 1787.[70]

---

[70] The above statement of "agrarian-minded" and "commercial-minded" types is derived from the imaginative "social interpretation" of the Constitution developed by Lee Benson, pp. 214–228. Benson's thesis is adaptable to the Rhode Island experience. A useful concept that appears to reinforce a "social interpretation" of the Constitution is the *Gemeinschaft vs. Gesellschaft* hypothesis of German sociologist Ferdinand Tönnies. Applying this theory to the Rhode Island of 1790, it could be maintained that the area in which Antifederalism predominated was essentially a *Gemeinschaft* or community-oriented society; that is one which maintained a rural outlook, possessed homogeneous structure and values, functioned through traditional status arrangements, and was characterized by low mobility, attachment to the soil, unity, close personal relationships, and a home or household economy; whereas the Federalist commercial towns constituted a predominantly *Gesellschaft* or association-oriented society; that is one with a cosmopolitan or urban attitude; one exhibiting a preference for ordering social and economic relations through contract; and one characterized by higher mobility, greater heterogeneity, impersonal relationships, and advanced forms of economic organization and activity. These fundamental societal differences were reflected in the antithetical attitudes of these sections towards the proposed basic law. See Ferdinand Tönnies, *Community and Society (Gemeinschaft und Gesellschaft)*, translated and edited by Charles P. Loomis (East Lansing, Mich., 1957), especially pp. 1–3, 33–35, 64–67, 248–59, 268–69. Other recent works which also view the Constitution as at least a partial consequence of opposing ideologies rooted in differing social circumstances are Rutland, *passim,* and Wood, pp. 471–564. Wood in his brilliant *tour de force* on the development of American constitutionalism during this formative period suggests that "both the proponents and opponents of the Constitution focused throughout the debates on an essential point of political sociology that ultimately must be used to distinguish a Federalist from an Antifederalist. The quarrel was fundamentally one between aristocracy and democracy." Wood, pp. 484–85. This particular ideological dichotomy does not stand in sharp relief in atypical Rhode Island, the least aristocratic of the original thirteen states. Wood generalizes, perhaps correctly, that the Federalists

When members of the commercial community of merchants, bankers, artisans, mechanics, and exporting farmers saw their enterprises deprived of the protection of the United States and shorn of the benefits of her commercial treaties, and when their commerce was faced with heavy duties laid upon it not only by Europe but by the United States as well, they grew more determined in their Federalism.

These Federalists — men like William Ellery, John, Nicholas, and Moses Brown, Henry Marchant, Jabez Bowen, and Benjamin Bourne — worked both for private gain and public good. They regarded their advancement and endeavors as essential to their nation's prosperity and growth. Time and even fate were on their side. Thanks to their exertions Rhode Island rejoined the Union that had left it behind, and embarked upon a new era of political and economic development.

---

were usually aristocratic proponents of deferential politics who devised the Constitution as a check upon democratic elements from the lower socio-economic strata who had seized control of state legislatures in the wake of the Revolutionary upheaval, but there is no compelling evidence in the local literature of the times to prove that Rhode Island's Federalists were primarily animated by such political elitism. See Wood, pp. 471–518.

III. Reapportionment

LONSDALE MILLS.

The mills of Lonsdale (*ca.* 1830) in the expanding Blackstone Valley town of Cumberland were typical of those factories that attracted landless and voteless workers and swelled the population of the towns in Rhode Island's northeastern quadrant creating a demand for political reapportionment (insert from an 1851 Walling map of Providence County, Rhode Island Historical Society).

CHAPTER SIX

Economic Transformation and
Political Polarization

I

The year 1790 marked the state's grudging acceptance of the new federal constitution and also saw an event that served as a catalyst in Rhode Island's transition from a mercantile and agrarian economy to one based principally upon industry. That event, which some have lavishly termed "the beginning of Rhode Island's industrial revolution," was the reconstruction of a cotton spinning frame similar to Arkwright's, and its employment in a mill at Pawtucket Falls, the last plunge of the Blackstone River on its course to the Seekonk and thence to Narragansett Bay.[1]

---

[1] The following economic survey rests heavily on Peter J. Coleman, *The Transformation of Rhode Island, 1790–1860* (Providence, 1963), pp. 71–107, 108–160, 161–62, 216–17. Also useful were [Louis McLane, comp.], *Documents Relative to the Manufacturers in the United States . . .* , 22 Cong., 1 Sess., House Executive Document, no. 308 (Washington, 1833), I, 970–76; George S. White, *Memoir of Samuel Slater* (Philadelphia, 1836), pp. 29–42, 71–112, 183–282; Caroline F. Ware, *Early New England Cotton Manufacture* (New York, 1931), *passim*; Joseph Brennan, *Social Conditions in Industrial Rhode Island: 1820–1860* (Washington, D. C., 1940), pp. 1–28; Mack Thompson, *Moses Brown: Reluctant Reformer* (Chapel Hill, N. C., 1962), pp. 207–08, 221–32; James B. Hedges, *The Browns of Providence Planta-*

145

The men chiefly responsible for this promising venture were Providence merchant Moses Brown, who was seeking to diversify his business interests, and Samuel Slater. The latter was a young Englishman with technical knowledge and managerial experience acquired in the Derbyshire cotton industry, hired by the enterprising Brown for this industrial experiment.

This combination of capital and craftsmanship was successful — in December 1790 cotton yarn was spun by water power for the first time in America. From this event, gradually, almost imperceptibly at first, Rhode Island began a metamorphosis that would alter not only its economic but its political, constitutional, and social complexion as well.

The Rhode Island cotton industry, begun by Brown and Slater, developed slowly with Providence entrepreneurs contributing to its expansion by supplying most of the funds, managers, and technical knowledge. The significant shift of commercial capital into cotton manufacturing began in Rhode Island in 1804, well in advance of the Jeffersonian embargo and the War of 1812, and even before maritime operations had reached their peak. Stimulated by high profits as well as the further transfer of capital from the dormant maritime business, cotton production expanded rapidly during the conflict with England.

In early post-war years the cotton industry suffered several moderate reverses culminating in the panic of 1819. Recovery began in 1820, and production rapidly gained momentum.

tions: The Nineteenth Century (Providence, 1968), pp. 159–185; Margaret Dickie Uroff, Becoming a City: From Fishing Village to Manufacturing Center [Providence, Rhode Island] (New York, 1968); Richard M. Bayles, ed., History of Providence County, Rhode Island (New York, 1891), I, 264–85, 581–650; Noah J. Arnold, "The Valley of the Pawtuxet: Its History and Development," The Narragansett Historical Register, VI (July 1888), 222–59; J. R. Cole, History of Washington and Kent Counties, Rhode Island (New York, 1889), passim; Victor S. Clark, History of Manufactures in the United States (Washington, D. C., 1929), I, passim, especially pp. 529–75; Compendium of the Enumeration of the Inhabitants and Statistics of the United States . . . from the Returns of the Sixth Census (Washington, D. C., 1841), pp. 12–15, 102–13; and John C. Pease and John M. Niles, A Gazeteer of the States of Connecticut and Rhode Island (Hartford, 1819), 305–87.

Throughout the decade of the 1820s the industry flourished. The processing of cotton displaced maritime activity as the backbone of the Rhode Island economy.

Cotton was indeed "king" of the state's burgeoning industrial enterprises, but resourceful Rhode Island entrepreneurs and merchant capitalists experimented with a variety of manufacturing endeavors. The woolen industry, which eventually became second in importance to cotton, was an early example of this pattern of diversification. It achieved a secure basis by the end of the 1820s.

Because of the state's pioneering role in cottons and woolens, it naturally turned to manufacture of textile machinery and equipment. By 1830 this enterprise formed a major, though highly specialized, segment of Rhode Island's rapidly expanding base metal industry. In 1832 this industry boasted ten foundries, thirty machine shops, and several hundred minor operations. A final early and lucrative line of endeavor was manufacture of precious metals, especially gold and silver jewelry. By 1832 twenty-seven firms employing over 280 workers were engaged in this business.

Peter J. Coleman, in a pioneering monograph, traces the remarkable economic transformation of Rhode Island. Its transition began in 1790 with Slater and was well on the way to completion by the end of the third decade of the nineteenth century. This period (1790–1830) Coleman accurately calls "the era of experimentation." When it drew to a close, the economic statistics indicated that Rhode Island's industrial "experiment" was a stunning success. Manufacturing had replaced maritime activity as the dynamic element in the economy, and industry had become the principal outlet for venture capital and the primary source of wealth. After 1830, having a firm economic base on which to build, Rhode Island industry optimistically embarked upon its "era of expansion." Cottons, woolens, base and precious metals all enjoyed unprecedented rates of growth.

This prodigious expansion was aided and accelerated by the introduction of steam power. Once again Samuel Slater was the pioneer. In 1827 he introduced this promising source of energy into Rhode Island's cotton industry by installing a steam engine at his newly-constructed Providence mill.

Steam power soon began to exert an important impact on Rhode Island manufacturing. When utilized in the textile industry it increased production, improved the quality of the product, and often reduced operating expenses. It also made coastal areas, with cheap access to coal, potential manufacturing sites. After its introduction, Rhode Island cotton manufacturers began to locate mills in port towns where they either contributed to the community's further expansion, as in the case of Providence, or afforded a municipality the opportunity to maintain its growth rate which was jeopardized because of the decline in maritime activity as in the cases of Bristol and Warren, or rescued a declining town from oblivion as in the case of East Greenwich.

With steam power playing a major role, the cotton industry developed more rapidly during the 1830s than in any previous decade, overcoming marketing problems and the panic of '37 in the process. In fact, when the depression lifted a minor boom ensued. Secretary of the Treasury Louis McLane's manufacturing survey of 1832 listed 119 cotton mills, most of them in the state's central sector on the Pawtuxet River or in northern Rhode Island on the Blackstone and its tributaries. By 1840 the number of mills had increased to 209, spindlage had more than doubled, and both capital and work force had expanded by approximately forty percent. Of the ninety additional factories nearly eighty percent had been constructed in the Blackstone or Pawtuxet valleys or in Providence, and these areas accounted for over eighty percent of Rhode Island's cotton production.

Providence had the greatest increase in cotton manufacturing during this eight-year span. The number of such mills rose from four to thirty, capital invested quadrupled, yarn production expanded sevenfold, and the labor force showed a rise of more than 600 percent. This boom temporarily placed Providence in second place behind Smithfield among Rhode Island's cotton-producing centers. The city's expansion in this area was due in large measure to the use of steam power.

One adjunct of cotton manufacturing, the finishing industry, grew at an especially impressive rate during this decade. Large amounts of capital did not enter this business until after 1829, but by 1840 seventeen dyeing, printing, or bleaching firms were in operation. The United States census of 1840 lists 12,086 Rhode Islanders employed in the various phases of cotton manufacture, and this figure is equivalent to eleven percent of the total population of the state.

In other areas of industrial endeavor, the 1830s were also years of remarkable progress. By the end of this decade the woolen industry was more than twice as large than at the time of McLane's report of 1832. The one unusual aspect of this business was its geographical distribution. It was based principally in depressed and declining Washington County, and particularly in South Kingstown, which accounted for two-fifths of the state's woolen capital, nearly a third of its workers, and a quarter of its factories by 1840. The atypical dominance of this region, even in one line of industrial enterprise, was not destined to endure, because the woolen center moved northward to Providence, Burrillville, and the valley of the Blackstone in the two succeeding decades.

The 1830s was also a period of notable growth for the base metal industry, with Providence far outstripping her principal rivals, the Blackstone Valley towns. One new aspect of this industry enjoyed an enormous boom, namely, the manufacture of steam engines. The rise of this enterprise accelerated during the 1830s when many Rhode Island factories turned to steam to meet their power needs.

Not to be outdone by other major lines of industrial endeavor, the precious metals industry also enjoyed a relatively rapid advancement at the outset of Rhode Island's era of industrial expansion. To an even greater extent than base metals, this business enterprise was concentrated in Providence.

Thus, by 1840, Providence was the industrial leader in a rapidly industrializing state and possessor of the best balanced and most diversified manufacturing economy. It owed this primacy to its superior financial resources and banking facilities, development of steam power, its position as the center of the base metal industry, and its emergence as the hub of Rhode Island's transportation network being a railroad terminal and the outlet for the Blackstone Canal. As the 1830s drew to a close, Providence (then only one-third its present geographical size) was well on the way to becoming the metropolitan center of southern New England.

Less spectacular but also significant was the economic growth of other northern towns. This expansion was especially pronounced in the Blackstone Valley cotton towns of Smithfield, Cumberland, and North Providence (which included the village of Pawtucket), and the Pawtuxet River community of Warwick, especially its western sector that later became the town of West Warwick. Providence and these nearby municipalities furnished the dynamism in Rhode Island economic life during the second quarter of the nineteenth century.

II

The transition and expansion of Rhode Island's economy had a profound impact upon the demography and political culture of the state. Industrialization effected significant changes not only in the distribution of wealth[2] but also in the distribution of population and the rate of population growth.[3] These changes in turn precipitated demands for constitutional reform, especially in the

---

[2] See Table 6, listing estimates of rateable (i.e., taxable) real and personal property in the various towns after the periodic assessments taken in 1796, 1823 and 1849.

[3] See Tables 3 and 4. These tables and the demographic analysis based thereon are derived from the following sources: Edwin M. Snow, *Report Upon the Census of Rhode Island, 1865,* (Providence, 1867). This compendium of the first state-authorized census since 1782 contains much useful data on the period 1790–1840; it is hereafter cited as Snow, *RI Census.* Also useful are C. W. Parsons, *Notice of the History of Population in the State of Rhode Island* (Providence, 1859); Edwin M. Snow, *Census of the City of Providence Taken in July,* 1855 . . . *Giving an Account of Previous Enumerations of the Population of Providence,* 2nd ed., rev. (Providence, 1856), hereafter cited as Snow, *Providence Census;* Kurt B. Mayer, *Economic Development and Population Growth in*

area of legislative apportionment, because the charter's allocation of representatives was not only rigid but, as successive census reports revealed, increasingly inequitable.[4]

Also, population and immigration trends pointed to the rise of a landless class of artisans and factory workers in crowded mill villages. In Rhode Island the statutory freehold qualification disfranchised this group. As industrialization progressed, the number of these second-class citizens multiplied. Their demands for suffrage reform, first advanced in the early 1820s, grew more incessant and reached an ominous crescendo after the presidential election of 1840.

To understand the growing concern over apportionment and suffrage in the period 1790–1840, one must analyze Rhode Island's demographic data for that eventful era.[5] A useful frame of reference is the classification of towns into three categories: (1) Expanding — those which had a much higher rate of population increase than the state as a whole; (2) Static — those whose population had either remained stationary or increased at a rate below the state average; (3) Declining — those that showed a rate of population loss. Expanding towns were industrialized, and this was the basic factor in their growth; whereas static and declining towns, with Newport a notable exception, were basically rural and agrarian.[6]

Employing these criteria it is possible to designate Providence, North Providence, Smithfield, Warwick, Cumberland, Bristol, Warren, Johnston, and Scituate as expanding towns during the

---

Rhode Island (Providence, 1953), pp. 22–42. I am indebted to Coleman and Clifford Chesley Hubbard, "Constitutional Development in Rhode Island," (unpublished doctoral dissertation, Brown University, 1926) for suggesting the tabular approach as a guide to understanding Rhode Island constitutional agitation prior to the Dorr Rebellion.

[4] See Table 5, depicting the ratio of representatives to population.

[5] The following summation is based on data provided in Tables 3–6.

[6] This concept of "expanding," "static," and "declining" towns was derived from Coleman, pp. 218–19, who in turn was influenced by Snow, *RI Census.* I have made certain adjustments. Coleman, in determining the category into which a town would fall uses population figures for 1790–1860, whereas this study employs figures for 1790–1840. The latter methodological approach is more valid for analyzing the coming of the

Key

	Expanding towns	Political Preference:
		(J) Jackson
	Static towns	(W) Whig
		(S) Split
	Declining towns	

Key to Mill Villages

1 — Slatersville	9 — Olneyville
2 — Woonsocket Falls	10 — Knightsville
3 — Manville	11 — Phenix
4 — Lonsdale	12 — Natick
5 — Central Falls	13 — Arctic
6 — Pawtucket	14 — Crompton
7 — Georgiaville	15 — Chepachet
8 — Centredale	

NOTE TO THE MAP

Source for the political affiliation of the towns for the period 1828-38 is Colasanto pp. 59–72, 90, 121–79. For 1840 consult the *Providence Journal,* April 16, 17, and November 3, 1840. I interpret Colasanto's data for Cumberland differently. Although he lists the town as split, it consistently voted Whig at all levels during this era except for occasional support of Governor John Brown Francis (J). Most of the "split" towns contained either mill river villages or port facilities in one sector which were Whig-oriented and a rural hinterland which was Democratic (e.g., Smithfield, Coventry and Warwick had industrial centers and Bristol, East Greenwich and Westerly were minor ports). The boundaries of the expanding towns of Smithfield, Cumberland, North Providence, Johnston, Providence, and Warwick were dramatically altered in the period 1867–1919 enlarging the city of Providence from approximately 6 to 18.91 square miles and creating by political cell-division the new municipalities of Woonsocket, North Smithfield, Lincoln, Central Falls, Pawtucket (with an annexation from Massachusetts in 1862), and West Warwick. Cady, *Rhode Island Boundaries 1636–1939,* pp. 21–27.

Map of Rhode Island in 1840

showing expanding, declining, and static communities,
selected mill villages, and political preference of the towns

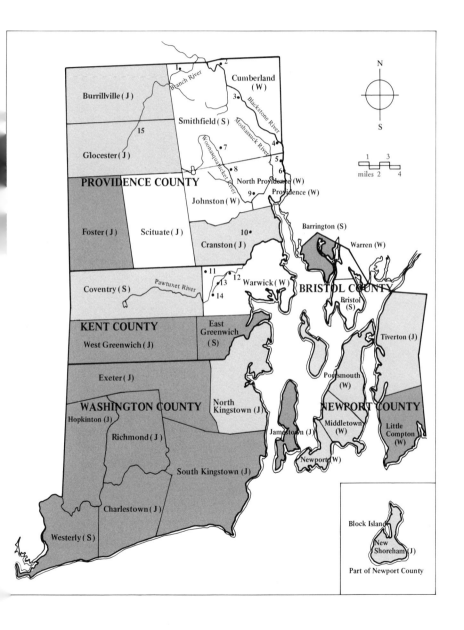

N

S

1   3
miles 2   4

Burrillville (J)

Smithfield (S)

Cumberland (W)

Glocester (J)

15

PROVIDENCE COUNTY

North Providence (W)

Providence (W)

Johnston (W)

Foster (J)

Scituate (J)

Cranston (J)

Barrington (S)

Warren (W)

Coventry (S)

Pawtuxet River

Warwick (W)

BRISTOL COUNTY

Bristol (S)

KENT COUNTY

East Greenwich (S)

West Greenwich (J)

Tiverton (J)

Exeter (J)

Portsmouth (W)

WASHINGTON COUNTY

North Kingstown (J)

NEWPORT COUNTY

Hopkinton (J)

Middletown (W)

Little Compton (W)

Richmond (J)

Jamestown (J)

Newport (W)

South Kingstown (J)

Charlestown (J)

Westerly (S)

Block Island

New Shoreham (J)

Part of Newport County

period under analysis. The striking fact about these communities is their location. All of them are situated in northern and eastern portions of the state; they are either on the upper reaches of Narragansett Bay or on the Pawtuxet or Blackstone rivers. With the exception of Scituate, these communities lay north and east of an imaginary line extending from the Fall River section of Tiverton westward across the Bay to the mill villages of western Warwick (Lippitt, Phenix and Crompton) and thence northward along the Old Seven Miles' Line to Smithfield's manufacturing settlements of Slatersville and the villages at Woonsocket Falls.

The remainder of Rhode Island's towns can be described as static or declining, located in the southern and western portions from the lower Bay to the Connecticut line. In the era 1790–1840 the Bay county of Newport was generally static while Washington County and the towns on the western border experienced a marked decline.

Declining communities included Foster, West Greenwich, East Greenwich, and South County towns of Exeter, Richmond, South Kingstown, Hopkinton, Charlestown, and Westerly. All lost population between 1790 and 1840 as their farms were abandoned and their inhabitants departed to more promising places.

Dorr Rebellion of 1841–42. For example, in 1840 there were twelve declining towns; whereas the development of steam power and other factors had effected a resurgence in six of these communities and raised them to the static level by 1860. Also, Burrillville went from a static growth of 0.27 in 1840 to an expanding rate of 2.5 by 1860, while Scituate suffered a reversal in the 1850s and fell from the expanding to the static category. If such factors as a town's economy, size, and growth rate influenced its attitude on apportionment, suffrage extension, and general constitutional reform, it seems only logical to ascertain the community's status on the eve of the constitutional upheaval rather than its position eighteen years after the crisis.

TABLE 2

[a] In 1806 Glocester was divided, and Burrillville was created from its northern half.

SOURCE: Edwin M. Snow (comp.). *Report Upon the Census of Rhode Island, 1865* (Providence, 1867), pp. xxiv–xxxv. This was the first state-conducted census since 1782.

TABLE 2
The Population of Rhode Island 1790–1840

Towns	1790	1800	1810	1820	1830	1840
Providence	6,380	7,614	10,071	11,767	16,836	23,171
North Providence	1,071	1,067	1,758	2,420	3,503	4,207
Smithfield	3,171	3,120	3,828	4,678	6,857	9,534
Warwick	2,493	2,532	3,757	3,643	5,529	6,726
Cumberland	1,964	2,056	2,110	2,653	3,675	5,225
Bristol	1,406	1,678	2,693	3,197	3,034	3,490
Warren	1,122	1,473	1,775	1,806	1,800	2,437
Johnston	1,320	1,364	1,516	1,542	2,115	2,477
Scituate	2,315	2,523	2,568	2,834	3,993	4,090
EXPANDING TOWNS	21,242	23,427	30,076	34,540	47,342	b1,350
New Shoreham	682	714	722	955	1,185	1,069
Cranston	1,877	1,644	2,161	2,274	2,652	2,902
Coventry	2,477	2,423	2,928	3,139	3,851	3,433
Tiverton	2,453	2,717	2,837	2,875	2,905	3,183
Newport	6,716	6,739	7,907	7,319	8,010	8,333
Portsmouth	1,560	1,684	1,795	1,645	1,727	1,706
Burrillville[a]			1,834	2,164	2,196	1,982
Middletown	840	913	976	949	915	891
North Kingstown	2,907	2,794	2,957	3,007	3,036	2,909
Glocester[a]	4,025	4,009	2,310	2,504	2,521	2,304
STATIC TOWNS	23,537	23,637	26,427	26,831	28,998	28,719
Foster	2,268	2,457	2,613	2,900	2,672	2,181
South Kingstown	4,131	3,438	3,560	3,723	3,663	3,717
Little Compton	1,542	1,577	1,553	1,580	1,378	1,327
Westerly	2,298	2,329	1,911	1,972	1,915	1,912
East Greenwich	1,824	1,775	1,530	1,519	1,591	1,509
Barrington	683	650	604	634	612	549
Richmond	1,760	1,368	1,330	1,423	1,363	1,361
Jamestown	507	501	504	448	415	365
Exeter	2,495	2,476	2,256	2,581	2,383	1,776
Hopkinton	2,462	2,276	1,774	1,821	1,777	1,726
West Greenwich	2,054	1,757	1,619	1,927	1,817	1,415
Charlestown	2,022	1,454	1,174	1,160	1,284	923
DECLINING TOWNS	24,046	22,058	20,428	21,688	20,870	18,761
RHODE ISLAND	68,825	69,122	76,931	83,059	97,210	108,830

TABLE 3

Rate of Population Growth 1790–1840

Towns	1790–1800 %	1800–1810 %	1810–1820 %	1820–1830 %	1830–1840 %	1790–1840 %	Rate per Annum
Providence	19.3	32.3	16.8	43.1	37.6	295	5.90
North Providence	—0.4	64.8	37.6	44.8	20.1	293	5.86
Smithfield	—1.6	22.7	22.2	46.6	39.0	201	4.02
Warwick	—1.6	48.4	—3.0	51.8	21.6	170	3.40
Cumberland	4.7	7.5	20.4	38.5	42.2	166	3.32
Bristol	19.3	60.5	18.7	—5.1	15.0	148	2.96
Warren	31.2	20.5	1.7	—0.3	35.4	117	2.34
Johnston	3.3	11.1	1.7	37.2	17.1	88	1.76
Scituate	9.0	1.8	10.4	40.9	2.4	77	1.54
EXPANDING TOWNS						189	3.78
New Shoreham	4.7	1.1	32.3	24.1	—9.8	57	1.14
Cranston	—12.4	31.4	5.2	16.6	9.4	55	1.10
Coventry	—2.2	20.8	7.2	22.7	—10.8	39	0.78
Tiverton	10.7	4.4	1.3	1.0	9.6	30	0.60
Newport	0.3	17.3	—7.4	9.4	4.0	24	0.48
Portsmouth	8.0	6.6	—8.3	5.0	—1.2	9	0.18
Burrillville [a]			18.0	1.5	—9.7	8	0.27
Middletown	8.7	6.9	—2.8	—3.6	—2.6	6	0.12
North Kingstown	—3.9	5.8	1.7	1.0	—4.2	0	0.00
Glocester [a]	—0.4		8.4	0.7	—8.6	0	0.00
STATIC TOWNS						22	0.44
Foster	8.3	6.3	11.0	—7.9	—18.4	—4	—0.08
South Kingstown	—16.8	3.5	4.6	—1.6	1.5	—11	—0.22
Little Compton	2.3	—1.5	1.7	—12.8	—3.7	—14	—0.28
Westerly	1.3	—17.9	3.2	—2.9	—0.1	—17	—0.34
East Greenwich	—2.6	—13.8	—0.7	4.7	—5.1	—17	—0.34
Barrington	—4.8	—7.1	5.0	—3.5	—10.3	—20	—0.40
Richmond	—22.3	—2.8	7.0	—4.2	—0.1	—23	—0.46
Jamestown	—1.2	0.6	—11.1	—7.4	—12.0	—28	—0.56
Exeter	—0.8	—8.9	14.4	—7.7	—25.5	—29	—0.58
Hopkinton	—7.5	—22.1	2.6	—2.4	—2.9	—30	—0.60
West Greenwich	—1.4	—7.8	19.0	—5.7	—22.1	—31	—0.62
Charlestown	—28.1	—19.3	—1.2	10.7	—28.1	—54	—1.08
DECLINING TOWNS						—22	—0.44
RHODE ISLAND	0.4	11.4	7.8	17.0	12.0	58	1.16

Rhode Island's knowledgeable nineteenth-century demographer, Edwin Snow, spoke of their condition and plight. These towns, observed Snow, "have almost exclusively, a farming population, without any large villages. The population is almost entirely native American." Their families were small. "There is nothing in these towns especially calculated to induce immigration to them; and not sufficient inducements in them to keep their young people at home." Thus, "the young people emigrate, many dwellings are left for many years without children in them, a larger proportion than natural of the population is composed of persons not in the child-bearing period of life, very few children are born, and the population remains stationary, or declines." Snow concluded nostalgically that "a community, or town, which depends exclusively for its progress upon agriculture, cannot be expected, as a general rule, to sustain itself as to numbers, or at least, cannot increase to any great extent." [7] Dr. C. W. Parsons, another statistician, observed in 1859 that "the general tendency of the population has been to centralize itself into villages and large towns, and leave the purely agricultural regions to dwindle and decay." [8]

The woods of southern Rhode Island today harbor tangible evidence of the decline and exodus which Snow and Parsons recorded. They are dotted with gaping cellar holes and interlaced by miles of stone walls that enclose neither pasture nor field, but rather stands of second-growth oak, red cedar, and pine.

---

[7] Snow, *RI Census*, pp. xl–xli.
[8] Parsons, p. 6.

TABLE 3

[a] In 1806 Glocester was divided, and Burrillville was created from its northern half. The growth rates for these two towns have been computed for the period 1810–1840 only.

SOURCE: Edwin M. Snow, *Report Upon the Census of Rhode Island, 1865* (Providence, 1867), pp. xxxvi–xxxvii. The growth rate for Rhode Island in the period 1790–1840 was well below the growth rate for the United States as a whole. George Tucker, *Progress of the United States in Population and Wealth in Fifty Years, As Exhibited by the Decennial Census* (New York, 1843).

The Rhode Island farmer had grown weary of working his stubborn, rocky soil. When cheap and expansive western lands beckoned with their promise of a better life, the South County rustic responded and began his westward trek. Into northern New England, upstate New York, and northern Pennsylvania he traveled in the 1780s and 90s; then out onto the fertile, level lands beyond the Alleghenies. To Ohio, to Indiana and Illinois after the War of 1812, he ventured, and then to Michigan, Wisconsin and beyond.[9]

Others from South County and the western hill towns lacked the inclination to make the westward haul but were disenchanted with their difficult, monotonous, and unprofitable rural existence. Many of these, especially the restless younger generation, made the shorter journey to bustling manufacturing centers like Providence, Pawtucket, Central Falls, and Woonsocket to try their luck in an urban society.

Those hardy, persistent, or complacent farmers who remained behind attempted, often successfully, to make the difficult adjustment from self-sufficient to commercial agriculture and to meet the increasing challenge of western competition. Politi-

---

[9] For the status of agriculture and the effect of this outmigration see Snow, *RI Census,* lii-liv; Lois Kimball Matthews, *The Expansion of New England* (New York, 1909), pp. 139 ff.; Stewart H. Holbrook, *The Yankee Exodus* (New York, 1950); Mayer, pp. 22–36; Charles T. Jackson, *Report on the Geological and Agricultural Survey of the State of Rhode Island* (Providence, 1840); Percy Wells Bidwell, "The Agricultural Revolution in New England," *American Historical Review,* XXVI (July 1921), 683–702; Bidwell, "Rural Economy in New England at the Beginning of the Nineteenth Century," *Transactions of the Connecticut Academy of Arts and Sciences,* XX (1916), 241–399; Bidwell, "Population Growth in Southern New England, 1810–1860," *American Statistical Association Quarterly Publications,* n.s., XV (1916–17), 813–39; Bidwell and John I. Falconer, *History of Agriculture in the Northern United States, 1620–1860* (Washington, 1925), pp. 76, 147–56, 181–82, 259–60; Betty Flanders Thomson, *The Changing Face of New England* (New York, 1958) especially pp. 23–25, 157–58; and Herbert Whitney Allen, "The Narragansett Region Concentrations of Population, 1635–1885," (unpublished doctoral dissertation, University of Michigan, 1962), *passim.* The most recent general analysis is Howard S. Russell, *A Long, Deep Furrow: Three Centuries of Farming in New England* (Hanover, N.H., 1976).

TABLE 4
Ratio of Representatives to Population 1790–1840

Towns	No. of Reps.	Number of Residents per Representative					
		1790	1800	1810	1820	1830	1840
Providence	4	1,595	1,903	2,518	2,942	4,209	5,793
North Providence	2	535	532	879	1,210	1,851	2,103
Smithfield	2	1,585	1,560	1,914	2,339	3,428	4,767
Warwick	4	623	633	939	911	1,382	1,681
Cumberland	2	982	1,028	1,055	1,326	1,837	2,612
Bristol	2	703	839	1,347	1,598	1,517	1,745
Warren	2	561	736	887	903	900	1,218
Johnston	2	660	682	758	776	1,057	1,238
Scituate	2	1,157	1,261	1,284	1,417	1,996	2,045
EXPANDING TOWNS	22	933	1,019	1,287	1,491	2,142	2,578
New Shoreham	2	342	357	361	477	592	534
Cranston	2	938	822	1,080	1,137	1,326	1,451
Coventry	2	1,238	1,211	1,464	1,569	1,925	1,716
Tiverton	2	1,226	1,358	1,418	1,437	1,452	1,591
Newport	6	1,119	1,123	1,318	1,220	1,335	1,388
Portsmouth	4	390	421	449	411	432	426
Burrillville	2			917	1,082	1,098	991
Middletown	2	420	456	488	474	457	445
North Kingstown	2	1,453	1,397	1,478	1,503	1,518	1,454
Glocester	2	2,012	2,004	1,155	1,252	1,260	1,152
STATIC TOWNS	26	1,015	1,017	1,013	1,056	1,140	1,115
Foster	2	1,134	1,228	1,306	1,450	1,336	1,090
South Kingstown	2	2,065	1,719	1,780	1,866	1,831	1,858
Little Compton	2	771	788	776	790	689	663
Westerly	2	1,149	1,664	955	986	957	956
East Greenwich	2	912	887	765	759	795	754
Barrington	2	341	325	302	317	306	274
Richmond	2	880	684	665	711	681	680
Jamestown	2	253	250	252	224	207	182
Exeter	2	1,247	1,238	1,128	1,290	1,291	888
Hopkinton	2	1,231	1,138	887	910	888	863
West Greenwich	2	1,027	878	809	963	908	707
Charlestown	2	1,011	727	587	580	642	461
DECLINING TOWNS	24	1,002	961	851	904	878	781
RHODE ISLAND	72	983	987	1,070	1,154	1,350	1,512

cally, they jealously guarded the prerogatives of their community and watched the rise of the northern towns with awe and apprehension. They were estranged economically and socially from the native-born factory operatives of the mill villages and worlds apart from the immigrant Irish laborers who began to add to the burgeoning industrial population in the decade of the 1830s. The outnumbered rural folk regarded reapportionment and "free suffrage" as their political death knell. Their position on these issues strengthened and stiffened with each passing year and reached unparalleled intensity by 1840, as it became clear that the mounting though landless industrial population would increasingly be composed of such "undesirables" as Irish-Catholic immigrants. The stand of these agrarians was diametrically opposed to majoritarian principles and the powerful national trends toward suffrage extension and equal representation.[10]

By 1840 the battle-lines were drawn. Although the categories were far from rigid, generally the expanding towns were arrayed against the static and declining, the industrial sectors against the agrarian. North and east opposed the south and west. A dynamic and irresistible force struggled against a reactionary and seemingly immovable object with political ascendancy the prize.

---

[10] According to Robert B. McKay, *Reapportionment: The Law and Politics of Equal Representation* (New York, 1965), pp. 23–25, "so widespread had been the original acceptance of the equality principle that no fewer than 36 of the original state constitutions provided that representation in both houses of state legislatures would be based completely, or predominantly, on population."

TABLE 5

SOURCE: *Schedules of the General Assembly*, June session, 1796, pp. 16–17; January session, 1824, pp. 15–16; June session, 1849, pp. 18–22.

TABLE 5
State Estimates of Rateable Property

Towns	1796	1823	1849
Providence	2,950,000	9,500,000	28,407,000
North Providence	380,000	1,250,000	2,974,000
Smithfield	758,523	1,800,000	4,601,000
Warwick	605,000	1,300,000	2,924,000
Cumberland	350,000	870,000	2,833,000
Bristol	600,000	1,500,000	2,368,000
Warren	311,793	620,000	1,280,000
Johnston	330,000	640,000	1,011,000
Scituate	479,543	950,000	1,674,000
EXPANDING TOWNS	$6,764,859	$18,430,000	$48,072,000
New Shoreham	130,000	190,000	177,000
Cranston	490,000	1,000,000	2,016,000
Coventry	330,000	900,000	1,383,000
Tiverton	520,000	790,000	1,776,000
Newport	1,450,000	2,000,000	4,247,000
Portsmouth	450,000	800,000	1,092,000
Burrillville	——	650,000	1,117,000
Middletown	324,000	450,000	783,000
North Kingstown	490,000	870,000	1,196,000
Glocester	721,657	680,000	937,000
STATIC TOWNS	$4,905,651	$8,330,000	$14,724,000
Foster	320,000	630,000	583,000
South Kingstown	720,000	1,100,000	1,414,000
Little Compton	325,000	500,000	863,000
Westerly	370,000	470,000	779,000
East Greenwich	280,000	460,000	738,000
Barrington	110,000	190,000	345,000
Richmond	210,000	300,000	572,000
Jamestown	224,484	350,000	286,000
Exeter	360,000	600,000	574,000
Hopkinton	350,000	470,000	614,000
West Greenwich	280,000	460,000	455,000
Charlestown	280,000	350,000	271,000
DECLINING TOWNS	$3,829,484	$5,880,000	$7,494,000
RHODE ISLAND	$15,500,000	$32,120,000	$70,290,000

CHAPTER SEVEN

George Burrill: Federalist Reformer

I

In the years immediately following the storm over the federal Constitution several sporadic and abortive attempts were made to change or replace Rhode Island's basic law. In March 1792 a Providence deputy made a motion in the House calling for "appointment" of a constitutional convention. Federalist Bennett Wheeler, editor of the *United States Chronicle* (Providence), describing the incident to senator Theodore Foster, observed that "it is now a very proper time to attend to this Business — when the two Parties which have so long distracted the State are so nearly equal."

These sentiments were not shared by the Assembly and Wheeler in his next letter ruefully reported that the measure had been killed. It was "opposed by the Gentlemen from the Southwards, especially the Newport Deputies . . . they suggested that the State was now at Peace and that the measure proposed would throw it again into convulsions." [1] Wheeler might have added

---

[1] Bennett Wheeler to Theodore Foster, March 1 and 8, 1792, Foster Correspondence, RIHS, II, 52–53. See also Wheeler's *United States Chronicle* (Providence), March 8, 1792. On the impact of reapportionment see Table 3. The state was apparently "at peace" also with the na-

that a convention meant reapportionment, which in turn meant a lessening of Newport's influence in the Assembly. This consideration — the maintenance of power — was no doubt as important in explaining the opposition of Newport's deputies as their concern for the maintenance of peace.

In March of the following year another obscure and desultory attempt to secure a convention was made. A petition was laid before the Assembly requesting a constitutional convention. The *Schedules* of the Assembly, the Acts and Resolves, and the Senate and House Journals for the February-March 1793 session disclose no action on the matter, but a line in the *Providence Gazette* tells of the petition's disposition: "consideration postponed." [2]

There may have been similar memorials offered to the Assembly during the early 1790s but, if so, they made little impact and had no success. In 1796, however, a more significant movement for constitutional change began. Its catalyst was the reassessment of the state's taxable property. This revaluation was the result of an Assembly decree that "an Estimate of the Value of Rateable Property in the several towns" be taken. The act's prime mover was Elisha R. Potter, Sr. of South Kingstown, the community most burdened by the prevailing estimate of 1782.[3]

---

tional government which it had so resolutely resisted two years before, because in June 1792 the legislature acquiesced in a decision by the Federal Circuit Court for the District of Rhode Island declaring a stay law of the Assembly unconstitutional. The law involved was a resolve passed in February 1791, in response to a petition of a debtor giving him an extension period of three years to settle his accounts during which time he would be exempt from all arrests and attachments. This case, *Alexander Champion and Thomas Dickason v. Silas Casey* (1792), may be the first in which a United States court declared a state law unconstitutional if the newspaper accounts of the decision are correct. *Providence Gazette,* June 16, 1792; *United States Chronicle* (Providence), June 14, 1792; Charles Warren, "Earliest Cases of Judicial Review of State Legislation By Federal Courts," *Yale Law Journal,* XXXII (Nov. 1922), 15–28.

[2] *Providence Gazette,* March 9, 1793. See also *United States Chronicle,* March 7, 1793. The House Journals for 1792–93 are missing.

[3] J. R. Cole, *History of Washington and Kent Counties, Rhode Island* (New York, 1889), pp. 169–70.

The statute directed each town to appoint a committee to assess the property within its borders while the state legislature selected a supervisory commission to visit every municipality and make any adjustments in the local figures which it deemed necessary and equitable.[4] The work of the state committee caused a furor in Providence and Bristol counties similar to that precipitated a decade and a half earlier in Washington County by the estimate of 1782. This new assessment produced a similar response as well, namely, a convention of aggrieved towns and a demand for reapportionment.

Under the estimate of 1796 Providence replaced South Kingstown as the most heavily taxed and therefore the most disgruntled and reform-minded town. The value of the rateable property in the expanding community was set at $2,950,000, a figure more than double that of second-place Newport and quadruple that of South Kingstown, the leader under the old estimate. This meant that Providence had to pay approximately nineteen percent or $3,806 of the $20,000 tax levied in June 1796 by the Assembly for the upcoming fiscal year. When the taxpayers of Providence paused to consider that their community had a population nearly equal to Newport but a representation in the Assembly inferior to that town, and when they realized that Newport, with more land area was accorded half the valuation, and hence half the tax load of Providence, resentment began to build.[5]

On June 18, 1796, fifteen representatives from the northern towns registered a vigorous written dissent in the Assembly. Providence then formally condemned the new assessment at a town meeting on June 23, and voted not to collect the tax because its apportionment was "unconstitutional."

In addition, two other resolutions were passed at this assemblage. One appointed a committee to write circular letters to the towns of Providence County and "such others as are particularly

4 *Schedules*, June session, 1795, pp. 24–26. RIGA, Reports, V, 79, 89. Some documents relating to this estimate can be found in RISA and others in the Potter Collection, RIHS.

5 *Schedules*, June, 1796, pp. 16–17. For the complete figures on the estimate see Table 6.

aggrieved by the late estimate" inviting them to dispatch delegates to a state convention called "for the purpose of considering their peculiar situation, and of advising such measures as circumstances may dictate." The second resolve instructed the same committee to write circular letters to all towns in the state indicating "the necessity of a reform in our government, and requesting their concurrence by instructions to their respective representatives." [6]

On June 29, the citizens of Providence approved the convention invitation drafted by the committee and elected delegates to the proposed gathering. That conclave convened, according to schedule, in Providence on July 26. Attending were emissaries from eight towns — Smithfield, Scituate, Glocester, Johnston, North Providence, Bristol, Warren, and the host community. All of these towns were either in the northern or eastern sections of the state and located in Providence or Bristol counties.

After electing Daniel Mowry moderator and James Burrill, Jr. secretary, the delegates deliberated for two days, closely analyzed the methods used in computing the valuation, and reached the unsurprising but well-documented and convincing conclusion that the estimate was inequitable. Then the *ad hoc* assemblage adjourned to August 15. This initial session provided for a second circular letter to be dispatched to the other towns urging them to send representatives to the August gathering. Only Cranston responded to this invitation. The August session issued an address to the freemen of Rhode Island which complained of the unsound manner in which the estimates were made and detailed the reasons for their alleged injustice. It then disbanded.[7]

---

[6] Providence Town Meeting Records, No. 7 (1783–1804), pp. 377–78. *Providence Gazette,* June 25, July 2, 1796.

[7] Original Documents Relating to a Movement in Providence and Adjoining Towns in Opposition to the Operation of the New Estimate Law . . . 1796. Rider Collection, John Hay Library, Brown University, hereafter cited as Documents Relating to Estimate of 1796; At a Convention of Delegates from Eight Towns in the Counties of Providence and Bristol . . . Fifteenth Day of August, 1796 . . . Broadside, Rider Collection, hereafter cited as Broadside, Convention August 15, 1796;

Despite the protest of the nine towns, the primary goal of this controversy, a revision of the estimate, was not achieved. In 1798 the Assembly did appoint a committee of review, but it found the estimate just and equitable. Providence did not adhere to its resolution to resist the tax, but it defiantly dragged its feet in the collection of those state levies based upon the new valuation.[8]

The estimates controversy of 1796 is a noteworthy episode in Rhode Island constitutional history because the demand for a more equitable assessment was accompanied, as in the 1780s, by a demand for constitutional revision. As early as April 20, 1796 the Providence Town Meeting had instructed the town's deputies to attempt to obtain the passage of an act by the May session of the Assembly calling a constitutional convention. Delegates were to be chosen on the basis of population "for the purpose of framing a Constitution for the State and equalizing the Representation of the people thereof in the Legislature." [9]

The circular letter of June reiterated this call for a constitutional convention and contended that "those who are imposing the burdens [of taxation] cannot refuse to hear the oppressed — and will not, while they are equalizing the inequality of taxation, object to equalizing the inequality of Representation. If a stand should be made at this juncture, it may have the happy tendency of producing a Constitution of civil Government, by which the property and rights of the Citizens may hereafter be secured from legislative infringement." [10]

The July 26 convention had as its secondary concern constitutional change, and it authorized the drafting of a letter "to the freemen of the State on the expediency and necessity of framing a Constitution of Government therefor." The letter was read and approved at the August 15 session, and was then appended to

Providence Gazette, June 25, July 9 and 30, 1796; _United States Chronicle,_ August 4, 1796.

[8] Stokes, pp. 137–38; Town Meeting Records, No. 7 (1783–1804), p. 384; RIGA, Reports, V, 96.

[9] Providence Town Meeting Records, No. 7 (1783–1804), p. 363.

[10] Documents Relating to the Estimate of 1796, #2.

the printed address issued by the convention. This document, in an obvious reference to the agitation of the 1780s, declared that the question of constitutional revision had "engaged the attention of the people of the State for many years past." It also contrasted the Rhode Island experience with the example set by the federal government and the other states. Then, in a pathbreaking addition to the central theme of reapportionment, the letter criticized the omnipotence of the legislature.

It contended that in a written constitution "the various branches of government are particularly described — their powers limited, and thereby, all interference with one another prevented, and the rights of the people safely preserved. In this state we have no such security," it stated. "Our lives, liberties, rights and privileges, are in the hands of the Legislature, and even in this [body] there is great inequality," because "the Representatives bear no proportion either to numbers or property." Finally the public missive urged a reform of the judiciary. It recommended fewer judges but supported higher salaries and tenure during good behavior for those who were retained.[11]

Reacting to these ancillary demands of the estimates convention and to a formal petition from the freemen of Providence, the Assembly took up the question of constitutional reform in its October session. At that meeting an act was passed requesting the freemen of the several towns to instruct their representatives during the recess regarding the desirability of calling a constitutional convention.[12]

Shortly thereafter, prominent Providence merchant John Brown, who had served on his town's circular letter committee in June, wrote to South Kingstown's emerging political leader, Elisha Reynolds Potter, Sr., to suggest that Washington County join with the northern communities in supporting a state convention. Brown presented a carefully constructed plan whereby delegates to such a conclave would be chosen "in due proportion to the

[11] Ibid., #4; Broadside, Convention of August 15, 1796.
[12] Schedules, October 1796, p. 13; The Providence petition is in Documents Relating to the Estimate of 1796, #6.

number of the white male inhabitants in the respective towns."
Brown, on the basis of his calculations, envisioned a gathering of
seventy-eight delegates; he felt that Newport should "have no
just fault to find nor reason to complain" about his proposed distribution of delegates.[13] Brown's suggestions, if they were publicly
circulated, could not have received a favorable reception in
South County. The cause of the unrest which led this area to
back constitutional change in the 1780s was fast disappearing.
The new estimate had relieved the tax burden on the Washington County towns and shifted it northward.

Typical of this section's reaction to the assessment controversy
was Charlestown's attack upon Providence for opposing the new
tax estimate. Charlestown, which had joined with South Kingstown in spearheading the equal representation, anti-assessment
movement of the preceding decade, approved a resolution on
August 9, declaring that "the late insidious resolutions of the
town of Providence of the 23rd of June, 1796 relative to a law
of the State of Rhode Island establishing an estimate, is a daring and unprovoked insult upon the authority of the State and
deserves the highest censure of all good men, it being subversive
of good order and threatens the destruction of everything that
appertains to American Liberty and the tranquility of the
State." [14] A decade had passed, positions had reversed, but one
thing remained constant — Providence and South County were
still poles apart. The move for a convention could make no headway in the face of such determined opposition.

In the following year, before this tax-inspired constitutional
agitation subsided, a prominent Providence Federalist emerged
to become the state's first full-fledged constitutional reformer —
attorney George R. Burrill, who at various times during his
career served as state representative, captain of the Independent
Company of Cadets, and public notary for Providence County.
He was the brother of state attorney general, chief justice, and

---

[13] John Brown to Elisha R. Potter, Sr., November 2, 1796, Potter
Collection, RIHS.

[14] Charlestown Town Meeting, August 9, 1796, Town Council and
Probate Record, Book 5 (1793–1800).

United States Senator (1817–1820) James Burrill, Jr., and the great-granduncle of United States Senator Theodore Francis Green (1937–1961).

On July 4, 1797, in the traditional Independence Day oration before the townspeople of Providence, Burrill impressed upon a receptive audience the need for alteration of Rhode Island's basic frame of government. At the outset of his talk he condemned in familiar terms the increasingly inequitable apportionment of the Assembly contending that "a hundred inhabitants in one place cannot be represented by one man, while an equal number in another place are represented by ten men. Either, in the first instance, there are ninety who are not represented; or there are, in the second instance, nine persons in the legislature who represent nobody. Such a disproportion always constitutes a tyranny, active or dormant, and severe or not, according as the disproportion is great or small." The speaker then chided those who claimed that the state's basic law was unchangeable because it contained no specific mode of amendment. "It is absurd to maintain," thundered Burrill, "that the government may be so constructed as that it never can alter or improve, and that its errors and abuses must be perpetual."

The remainder of the eloquent address consisted in a radical and revolutionary appeal to the natural law — "the constitution paramount," which Burrill described as "the principles and immutable maxims of free government." For Burrill "equal representation" was an essential provision of this constitution paramount, and therefore the royal charter which contravened this principle, was void and could be legally and morally resisted. Burrill's drastic conclusion was that "rebellion . . . is not to be imputed to those who maintain this supreme authority [the natural law], although they act in opposition to a written constitution; because, wherever the two authorities interfere, the subordinate is void, and must give place to the supreme authority. Still less can the charge be alleged, where there is no written constitution, or where it was never ratified by the people, but imposed on them by an authority which they have in the most solemn manner renounced."

These utterances must have startled many of his listeners, but Burrill was not through. Before he descended from the rostrum he denied that the legislature could "create a constitution," since the legislature itself is the creature of the written constitution, is posterior and subordinate to it. "Neither can the legislature judge of the necessity of forming a constitution, or dictate when or how it shall be formed," he alleged, "for these are the prerogatives of the people." The people have "exclusive jurisdiction" in all questions relating to a constitution, the convention which forms that document is but a "committee of the people," the legislature in constitutional matters is an "incompetent tribunal." With these extreme conclusions Burrill ended his address.[15]

During the next decade this outspoken attorney remained the leading exponent of constitutional change. The citizens of Providence, apparently not offended by Burrill's views, invited him for an encore on July 4, 1805. On that occasion the reformer included in his message a call for an independent judiciary as a check upon the legislature, and he observed that a "government . . . where the Judiciary is not independent cannot be constitutionally free." [16]

Burrill's exhortations deserve more than passing notice, for in 1797 he attempted to legitimize the radical path reluctantly traveled by Thomas Wilson Dorr and his associates in 1841–42 — namely, by-passing the legislature with a direct appeal to the people to secure a written constitution for Rhode Island. Burrill did not crusade for suffrage reform, because his definition of "the people" was much narrower than Dorr's, and understandably so, but in his appeal to the ultimate authority of "the people" in constitutional matters Burrill's influence upon Dorr is apparent. Dorr recommended the inclusion of Burrill's oration of 1797 in

---

[15] This notable address is published in [Edmund Burke, comp.], *Interference of the Executive in the Affairs of Rhode Island,* 28 Cong., 1 Sess., House Report No. 546, pp. 271–74, hereafter cited as *Burke's Report.* This volume is a valuable compendium of source materials prepared by a congressional investigating committee after the Dorr rebellion.

[16] George R. Burrill, Oration delivered before the Citizens of Providence, July 4, 1805, manuscript, RIHS.

Burke's Report, a congressional defense of the Dorr rebellion compiled in 1844 with Dorr's advice and guidance.[17] Unfortunately Burrill was not able to inspire his contemporaries to action. Although there were several public meetings held during 1797 in Providence and the northern towns to promote a constitutional convention, the legislature soundly defeated a proposition to call such a conclave in its October session of 1797. Then in June 1799 a resolution presented by Providence representative John Smith requesting a convention with the delegates elected from the towns according to population (one delegate for each thousand inhabitants) received its death blow in the House on a rising vote by the adoption of the previous question.[18]

The unsuccessful constitutional agitation of the 1790s was, with Burrill a notable exception, reactive in its origin and narrow in its aims. The principal demand, reapportionment, was sought by Providence and other northern towns because they believed that a reconstructed legislature, based upon population, would give them more control over future assessments and would allow those communities with greater wealth and more inhabitants a stronger voice in state affairs.

Providence was the most aggrieved town. It had 5.7 percent of the representation in the lower house and 9.3 percent of the state's population; yet it was called upon to bear nineteen percent of the state tax in 1796. The other protesting towns, although far less burdened, joined with Providence, because of the drastic increase in the assessed valuation of their rateable property over the estimate of 1782.[19]

---

[17] *Burke's Report,* pp. 271–74. For Dorr's assistance in the preparation of the *Report* see Dorr to Edmund Burke, February 26, 1844, Edmund Burke Papers, Library of Congress, I, 203–06. This letter was written from prison.

[18] *Providence Gazette,* November 4, 1797; June 22, 1799. In June 1799, forty-four representatives voted for the previous question. The House Journal for these sessions is missing. See also Clarence S. Brigham, *History of the State of Rhode Island and Providence Plantations* (Providence, 1902), p. 286.

[19] Compare Tables 1, 3, 5 and 6.

The opponents of change had equally obvious motives for their adherence to the status quo. The Washington County communities [20] benefited as much from the 1796 estimate as they had suffered from its predecessor, and thus were not at all disposed to challenge it; whereas most Newport County towns stood to lose political power from a reapportionment based on population. Newport would sacrifice her premier position in the House, and every other town in the county (Tiverton excepted) would experience a proportionate diminution of its representation. As George Burrill observed in his July 1797 address: to demand equitable representation "is to require the majority to surrender their power — a requisition which it is not in human nature to grant." Burrill was correct; the eighteenth century closed with the charter intact and with a sectional clash developing over whether or not that increasingly controversial document would remain inviolate.

II

Despite the failure to change the charter during the so-called Federalist era, there were some accretions to the statute law of the state that had constitutional significance during the decade of the 1790s. These additions were embodied in the *Digest of 1798,* the first compilation and revision of the general laws since 1767.

Since preparation of these digests consisted not only in gathering and arranging Rhode Island's laws but also in amending and enlarging them when "proper," this digest contained a notable,

---

[20] Some caution should be exercised when considering the extreme decline of South Kingstown, Richmond, and Charlestown during the decade of the 1790s (Tables 3 and 4). There is no doubt that outmigration caused them to experience a population loss. However, it has been suggested by demographers that the 1790 figures for these towns were excessive. Further, Indians were not enumerated in 1800, and there were about 500 of them in the state, most of whom resided in Charlestown and vicinity. Mayer, pp. 24–26. Even if the figures for these towns were exaggerated in 1790, their rate of decline over the period 1790–1840 would still be substantial.

new feature — a statutory bill of rights. These "political axioms or truths," which were declared "to be of paramount obligation in all legislative, judicial and executive proceedings," were contained in ten provisions. They included the right of all to a legal remedy for injuries or wrongs to property and character, protection against unreasonable search and seizure, immunity from double jeopardy, protection from excessive bail and cruel and unusual punishment, the privilege of *habeas corpus,* a guarantee of procedural due process, the termination of imprisonment for debt once the debtor's estate had been delivered up for the benefit of his creditors, a ban on *ex post facto* laws, freedom from involuntary self-incrimination, and a presumption of innocence until guilt was proven.[21]

Following this "Act Declaratory of Certain Rights of the People of this State" was another "Relative to Religious Freedom and the Maintenance of Ministers." This remarkable statute was as advanced as any drafted or conceived during this era of liberal religious declarations, but it was no more than an explicit rendering of the principles upon which Roger Williams founded his Providence plantation. The act itself declared that "no man shall be compelled to frequent or support any religious worship, place or ministry whatsoever; nor shall be enforced, restrained, molested, or bothered in his body or goods, nor shall otherwise suffer on account of his religious opinion or belief; but that all men shall be free to profess, and by argument to maintain, their opinions in matters of religion, and that the same shall in no wise diminish, enlarge or affect their civil capacities."

The act's preamble was even more emphatic. It condemned laws compelling a man to contribute money to support opinions in which he disbelieved as "sinful and tyrannical," and called forced contributions to support particular teachers of one's own religion a deprivation of liberty. It also claimed that civil rights had no dependence on religious opinions, so therefore, "the prescribing any citizen as unworthy the public confidence, by laying

---

[21] *The Public Laws of the State of Rhode Island and Providence Plantations* . . . (Providence, 1798), pp. 79–81, hereafter cited *Digest of 1798.*

upon him an incapacity of being called to offices of trust and emolument, unless he profess or renounce this or that religious opinion, is depriving him injuriously of those privileges and advantages to which, in common with his fellow citizens, he has a natural right." Such a proscription, the act concluded, tended "only to corrupt the principles of that religion it is meant to encourage, by bribing, with a monopoly of worldly honours and emoluments, those who will externally profess and conform to it." [22]

This enlightened measure was a vigorous reaffirmation of Rhode Island's long-standing commitment to the principles of religious liberty and church-state separation. Roger Williams would have rejoiced at the enduring nature of his "lively experiment."

As the eighteenth century drew to a close Rhode Island's government, her basic law, and the statutes which implemented that document still compared favorably with those of the other states. The retention of her charter was unusual, but few people were disturbed by its continued operation, except at assessment time. Religious liberty continued to be as broad as anywhere, the freehold statute was not unduly restrictive, nor was a landed qualification uncommon at the turn of the century.[23] In fact, there were no serious complaints except those occasioned by the charter's inequitable apportionment. But times and conditions were destined to change, the inflexible charter could not.

III

For several years after the assessment controversy, Rhode Island's constitutional waters were placid. This period of calm was broken in 1805 by the death of long-time governor Arthur Fenner. This wily and politically indestructible product of one of Rhode Island's first families had ascended to the governorship in May 1790 as the Antifederal replacement for John Collins. He had

---

[22] *Ibid.*, pp. 81–84.

[23] In the *Digest of 1798* the £40 qualification was transposed to an approximate dollar equivalent, *viz.*, $134, pp. 114–15.

been elected with the acquiescence of the pro-Constitution party. This group was not strong enough to block Fenner, and they were reluctant to provoke the Antifederal majority on the eve of the May ratification convention by contesting his candidacy.[24]

Once elected, however, Fenner appeared to stand above partisan strife. His position was unaffected by the development of the two-party system, and he apparently stayed on cordial terms with members of both political camps, except in 1802 when he was unsuccessfully opposed by former governor William Greene, a Federalist.

When death removed the ailing Fenner from the executive chair on October 15, 1805, the campaign began to elect his successor. A power struggle developed among the Democratic Republicans for that party's nomination. This intraparty feud was not resolved and two Republican gubernatorial candidates, Henry Smith and Peleg Arnold, contented with one another and with Federalist Richard Jackson, Jr. for the post of chief executive in the April 1806 election. Balloting in this three-cornered race produced the following result: Jackson, 1,662; Arnold, 1,094; Smith, 1,097.[25] Then the trouble started. Although Jackson had a wide plurality over his Republican opponents he failed by 268 votes to receive a majority of the total ballots cast.

In the other contests Republican Issac Wilbour won the lieutenant governorship, the Federalists achieved a narrow edge in the House, and the Republicans dominated the Senate and thereby captured control of the Grand Committee (Senate and House sitting jointly). As a result of this control, the Grand Committee

---

[24] William Ellery to Benjamin Huntington, March 28 and April 5, 1790, Ellery-Huntington Correspondence, RISA.

[25] *Providence Phenix*, April 12 and 26, 1806; Rhode Island Secretary of State, comp., *Manual With Rules and Orders for the Use of the General Assembly of the State of Rhode Island* (Providence, published biennially), 1965–66, p. 211, hereafter cited as *Rhode Island Manual*. I have used the 1965–66 edition for statistics on gubernatorial elections. However, I used the 1937–38 edition for congressional elections, because it is the last issue to reprint the statistics of nineteenth-century congressional contests. In the 1806 gubernatorial battle, six votes are listed "Scattering."

declared the office of governor vacant because of the inability of any candidate to receive the votes of a "greater part of the freemen." [26] The Assembly interpreted this provision of the charter to mean that a person must receive a majority of the votes cast for governor to be elected to that position, although a law of October 1664 specified that a mere plurality was sufficient.

Since no candidate met the Grand Committee's arbitrarily imposed requirement, a statute was enacted on May 9, 1806 empowering the lieutenant governor to "perform and execute all the functions and duties which are by law to be done, performed and executed by the Governor," if the office of chief executive should become vacant either by death, resignation or "by reason of no election being made by the freemen." It was by virtue of the last mentioned contingency that Republican Isaac Wilbour became acting governor in 1806.[27]

This development brought a protest from some Federalist communities and from several Federalist leaders as well. Most notable among the latter was George Burrill, who at that time was a representative from Providence. Burrill made a futile attempt to persuade the Grand Committee that a mere plurality was sufficient to elect a governor, and offered a resolution to that effect. Even many of his Federalist associates were not convinced, however, for Burrill's motion was soundly rejected by a majority of forty-six votes.[28]

---

[26] *Providence Phenix,* June 14 and 21, 1806; Hubbard, pp. 35–37; Brigham, p. 292; Marcus W. Jernigan, "The Tammany Societies of Rhode Island," in J. Franklin Jameson, ed. *Papers from the Historical Seminary of Brown University,* VII (1897), 7–10.

[27] *A Supplement to the Digest of the Laws . . . 1798* (Providence, 1810), pp. 86–87. For the 1664 measure see *RICR,* II, 83–4. A succession law was passed on June 11, 1805, perhaps in anticipation of Fenner's death from a lingering illness, but this statute did not cover the contingency of "no election." *Supplement to the Digest of the Laws . . . 1798,* p. 75.

[28] Journal of the House (1805–07), May session, 1806; Journal of the Senate (1805–14), May session, 1806; *Providence Phenix,* May 17, 1806; *Providence Gazette,* May 17, 1806. The *Phenix* was the Democratic Republican organ; the *Gazette* was Federalist; see Maude O. Brown, "The *Providence Patriot and Columbian Phenix,* 1802–1835" (unpublished research paper, RIHS, 1975).

Although most Federalists could not agree with Burrill's interpretation of the charter, they did agree with his long-standing contention that it should be replaced. Thus, they acceded to a May 9 motion, offered by Amos Collins of Hopkinton with Burrill's backing, "to recommend to the people" the selection of members to a constitutional convention. The Republican Senate refused to concur.

Then, just before adjournment, the exasperated House Federalists resubmitted their convention resolves in modified fashion asking the towns "to give their votes upon the question of whether a Convention ought to be called for the purpose of framing a Constitution for the State." The question, however, was postponed until the June meeting.[29] In the interim between sessions several northern towns including Cranston, Smithfield, and Cumberland specifically instructed their representatives to support a convention call. The communities to the southwards, however, opposed this move.[30]

When the legislature reassembled in June, the deferred convention resolves were taken up. After first reading, James De-Wolf, a prominent Bristol Republican, moved that they be postponed to the next session. His motion carried and the controversial question was temporarily quashed.[31] While this succession-inspired controversy was raging, Smithfield representative Enos Mowry offered a plan for a convention composed of one delegate from every town plus an additional delegate for every 1,500 people which a town possessed. Such an allocation would have resulted in the following distribution: Providence, five;

---

[29] Journal of the House (1805–07), May session, 1806; Journal of the Senate (1805–14), May session, 1806. A copy of the postponed resolution is in the Dorr Manuscripts, John Hay Library, Brown University, III, #1, hereafter cited as D. Mss.

[30] Copies of the instructions to the representatives of Cranston (June 2), Smithfield (June 2), and Cumberland (June 2) to support a convention and that to the representatives of North Kingstown (June 3) to oppose such a measure are in D. Mss., III, #2–5.

[31] Journal of the House (1805–07), June session, 1806. On June 13, David Bartlett of Cumberland introduced a resolution for the framing of a constitution. On the following day he was given leave to withdraw it. *Ibid.* See also *Providence Phenix*, June 14 and 21, 1806.

Newport, four; South Kingstown, two; Smithfield, two; and all other communities one each. The plea from Smithfield, however, fell upon deaf ears; no action was taken by the adamant Assembly.[32]

Undaunted by the legislature's repeated failure to act, George Burrill in 1807 published *A Few Observations on the Government of the State of Rhode Island*. This pamphlet was the most extensive attack upon the charter that had appeared to that time. Burrill questioned the very validity of the basic law because it had failed to receive the ratification of a popular convention after independence was declared. He then repeated his criticism of the charter's apportionment and lamented the document's failure to conform to the recently espoused theory of separated powers.

The thoughtful Burrill, himself a legislator, also complained of the omnipotence of the Assembly and the dominance of that body over the governor and the judiciary. Finally, he alleged that the government as presently organized failed to provide properly either for education or for the militia (Burrill was Captain of the Independent Company of Cadets). The proposed remedy for these deplorable conditions, he urged, was a written constitution, framed by a convention and ratified by the people with the uncooperative Assembly by-passed in the process.[33]

Burrill's suggestions were ignored, however, as the impasse that gave rise to the constitutional agitation was removed by the April 1807 election. In this contest the magic name of Fenner was invoked. James, United States senator and son of the recently deceased governor, got the support of one wing of the divided Democratic Republican Party and received Federalist backing as well. This combination, the "Union Prox," enabled young

---

[32] D. Mss., III, 8. The Mowry recommendation is undated, but the internal evidence suggests that it was a product of the 1806 controversy.

[33] [George R. Burrill], *A Few Observations on the Government of the State of Rhode Island* (Providence, 1807). Sidney Smith Rider, learned Rhode Island antiquarian and bibliographer, identifies Burrill as the author of this anonymous pamphlet. Rider, "Constitutional Government," XVII/3/1/7.

Fenner to overwhelm Republican Seth Wheaton (father of Henry, the famed expert on international law)[34] by a two-to-one margin. Fenner was thrice reelected in 1808, 1809, and 1810. In the latter year he headed both the Union and the Republican prox.[35]

In 1811, however, William Jones, a full-fledged Federalist, defeated Fenner 3,885 to 3,651. The well-intentioned but unsuccessful foreign and commercial policies of Thomas Jefferson and James Madison had made most New England Democratic Republicans (even a Fenner) politically undesirable.[36]

When William Jones ascended to the governorship in May 1811 he became the first (and last) Federalist governor of Rhode Island. His victory was the culmination of a Federal advance that had begun in the Congressional elections of 1810 with the victories of Richard Jackson and Elisha R. Potter, Sr. For discouraged Democratic Republicans (or "Anti-Federalists" as they often styled themselves) there was one bothersome aspect of this Federal resurgence, namely the remarkable increase of voters in the Federalist stronghold of Providence. The leading Republican newspaper, the *Columbian Phenix* (Providence) charged, with considerable foundation, that Federalists had resorted to "manufacturing voters."

---

[34] On the occasion of the elder Fenner's death, Henry Wheaton had written to his father expressing the hope that the "little, mean, insulating, and vicious policy which has so long depressed and brutalized" Rhode Island would end, and that "the present opportunity for giving her a thorough reform and constitutional government will not be lost." Henry Wheaton to Seth Wheaton, March 2, 1806, George Dexter, ed., "Letters of Henry Wheaton," in *Proceedings of the Massachusetts Historical Society,* XIX (1881–82), 374–76.

[35] Jernigan, pp. 8–9, 19; *Rhode Island Manual,* 1965–66, p. 211. Isaac Wilbour, anticipating the scramble for the governorship in 1806, had urged James Fenner to come forward at that time to succeed his father. Wilbour to James Fenner, Dec. 30, 1805, Misc. Mss. RIHS, Wi 641.

[36] Fenner helped to undermine his own position in November 1810 by casting the tie-breaking vote in Grand Committee for Republican Jeremiah B. Howell, thus making Howell United States senator. The indignant House Federalists thereupon passed a resolution censuring Fenner. Brigham, p. 294.

The *Phenix* was referring to a practice whereby freeholders subdivided their land and gave ostensible life leases on certain parcels to landless individuals thus qualifying them and their eldest son to vote. A lease of this kind was granted subject to the condition that it would be forfeited at the end of a year if the exorbitant rent on the land "conveyed" went upaid. Needless to say most of the land transferred in this manner reverted to the grantor once the political purpose for the transfer had been fulfilled.[37]

When Providence Federalists brought forth 124 new deeds in the January 1811 town meeting, alarmed and aggrieved Democratic Republicans assumed the status of reformers. They circulated a petition and introduced a bill into the February session of the Assembly which in effect abolished the freehold qualification for voting. This measure provided for free white adult male suffrage, the only requirements being payment of property or poll taxes or service in the militia. The measure passed the Republican-controlled senate by a margin of six to two but the Federalist House postponed its consideration after an acrimonious debate by a vote of thirty-nine to twenty-five, despite efforts of Bristol's James DeWolf to secure its enactment. In the June session it was finally taken up by the House and rejected, thirty-eight to twenty-eight.[38]

This bill is the first recorded attempt to remove Rhode Island's freehold suffrage qualification [39] but the motives of its sponsors

---

[37] *Columbian Phenix,* March 23 and April 20, 1811; *Burke's Report,* pp. 208–09.

[38] Journal of the House (1811–12), February session, 1811; Journal of the Senate (1805–14), February and June sessions, 1811; *Columbian Phenix,* March 16 and 23, 1811; *Burke's Report,* pp. 208–09. The bill is reprinted in Jacob Frieze, *A Concise History of the Efforts to Obtain an Extension of Suffrage in Rhode Island from the Year 1811 to 1842* (Providence, 1842), p. 161.

[39] During this period at least two other bills were introduced to prevent voting abuses. One, in March 1803, was designed to eliminate bribery and corruption; another, of June 1811, was intended to prohibit the use of money, liquor, or property to influence elections. Both failed to pass. Miscellaneous Papers of the General Assembly, folder 8 (1800–1820), RISA.

differed markedly from those of suffrage reformers in a later era.
Republicans of 1811 were merely trying to eliminate a fraudulent
source of Federalist strength. Elisha R. Potter, Jr., a keen student of Rhode Island politics, has observed (perhaps on the
basis of his father's recollections) that "the exasperation produced" by the devious actions of the Federalists caused their opponents, "to pass the suffrage bill as a mere maneuver," for
"many of the senators were zealously opposed to free suffrage."

Potter implies that Republicans approved the measure for
propaganda purposes because they anticipated its defeat in the
House. This suggestion is reinforced by the fact that all thirty-
nine House Federalists voted for the bill's postponement whereas
several Republicans abstained on this controversial roll call.
Curious also is the fact that John Pitman, the bill's senate sponsor, was a leader of the anti-suffrage forces in 1842,[40] and James
DeWolf, its advocate in the House, was cool towards "free suffrage" in the 1830s.

While this controversial measure was pending, William Jones
dethroned James Fenner by 234 votes. In Providence alone the
total vote increased by 185 over the 1810 figure and the Federalist vote was up by 190.[41] Republicans had good reason to protest,
but free suffrage as a solution merely put their agrarian-based
party on the horns of a dilemma.

In November 1811, when the horse (and the election) had

---

[40] Potter's observations are expressed in marginal notes written upon
the private copy of his 1842 pamphlet, *Considerations on the Questions
of the Adoption of a Constitution and Extension of Suffrage in Rhode*
Island (Providence, 1842), opposite p. 14. Potter Collection. One Republican senator sincerely interested in free suffrage was William Peckham. In a letter to Thomas W. Dorr in 1837, Peckham recalled the
events of 1811. He voted for the early suffrage measure "to supersede the
great number of sham deeds and leases, which qualified the very dregs
of society to vote, and a conscientious belief that all the male citizens of
this State over the age of 21 years who performed military duty or paid
taxes ought in republican justice to have a right of suffrage." Peckham
to Dorr, February 3, 1837, Dorr Correspondence, Rider Collection, John
Hay Library, Brown University, hereafter cited as DC. Other interesting observations on the 1811 effort are contained in William I. Tillinghast, "Free Suffrage Address," [1833], D. Mss., VII.

[41] Jernigan, pp. 30–32.

been stolen, Federalists, after first rejecting a suffrage petition,[42] passed a mild reform measure declaring that "no tenant for life, where there is a rent reserved, is entitled to vote, or act as a freeman, in any town meeting in this State, unless the yearly value of such life estate shall exceed the amount of the rent reserved, by the sum of seven dollars." [43] By the time of the next election the tide had so turned against the party of Jefferson and Madison that this reform was not sufficient to reinstate the Republicans. In fact, they remained on the "outs" until Governor Jones was vanquished in April 1817 by Nehemiah Knight.[44]

By the second decade of the nineteenth-century, the form and style of Rhode Island politics had changed but little from pre-Revolutionary days. The General Assembly still conducted two regular annual sessions, one commencing on the first Wednesday in May and the other on the last Monday in October. Those state representatives elected at their town meetings in April sat for the May conclave in Newport and its June adjournment in East Greenwich, while those chosen in August legislated for the October meeting of the Assembly conducted alternately in Providence and South Kingstown with adjourned sessions held during January in Bristol.[45] The senators, ten in number, were selected annually on the third Wednesday in April by statewide referendum.

The five general officers continued to be elected with the members of the upper house. Their names appeared at the head of

---

[42] This petition to the General Assembly, dated October 1811, is signed by 118 persons including such Republican leaders as William Pabodie, Peleg Arnold, and William Sprague. D. Mss., III, 10.

[43] *Digest of 1822*, p. 90; *Columbian Phenix*, November 9, 1811; Journal of the House (1811–12), October session, 1811.

[44] *Rhode Island Manual*, 1965–66, p. 212. A reasonably accurate but non-documented account of the Federalist rise to power is Samuel H. Williams, "The Federal Ascendancy of 1812," *The Narragansett Historical Register*, VII (October, 1889), 381–94. Very useful biographical sketches of Rhode Island's Federalist leaders are contained in David Hackett Fischer, *The Revolution of American Conservatism: The Federalist Party in the Era of Jeffersonian Democracy* (New York, 1965), pp. 277–84.

[45] *Digest of 1798*, p. 128; *Digest of 1822*, pp. 100–01.

the same prox or ballot on which the senatorial slate was listed. The positions of governor and deputy governor were generally and sometimes bitterly contested, but the posts of secretary, attorney general and general treasurer were not usually the objects of partisan rivalry, perhaps, because these officers were not members of the powerful legislature like the chief executive and his deputy.

The federal constitution had created a new layer of elected officials. United States senators were chosen by vote of the Grand Committee of the General Assembly,[46] while congressmen were elected to the House on an at-large basis by the freemen in August of the odd-numbered years. After 1793 the state was allocated two members of the House of Representatives giving Rhode Island a total of four presidential electors chosen by the freemen. An extremely important requirement was that a *majority* of the votes cast for the positions of general officer, state senator, and United States Representative was necessary for election. A mere plurality required another race for the contested office.[47]

Some important features of Rhode Island politics had changed, however, since colonial times, especially the ratio of qualified voters to the whole number of free white adult males and the ratio of an expanding town's population to its representation in the lower house. In fact, disfranchisement and malapportionment were fast becoming the rules rather than the exceptions, and thus the need for reform became more urgent and more conspicuous as nineteenth-century urbanization and industrialization progressed.

---

[46] The Grand Committee consisted of the House and the Senate sitting jointly.

[47] This majority requirement necessitated five elections for governor in 1832 and resulted in a six-man state senate in 1835.

CHAPTER EIGHT

The First Convention

I

Because Rhode Island was preoccupied with the War of 1812 (more as an unpredictable spectator than as a combatant), no significant alterations in the state's government were advanced during the conflict or in the months of readjustment that followed. By 1817, however, a ripple of reform sentiment began to stir Rhode Island's placid constitutional waters and set in motion a small wave of agitation that culminated in the constitutional convention of 1824.

The movement that began in 1817 was inspired not only by an increasing dissatisfaction with Rhode Island's governmental structure but also by the example of its sister states. The years 1816–1821 marked one of the most significant periods of constitution-making in American history. In that brief span the new states of Indiana (1816), Mississippi (1817), Illinois (1818), Alabama (1819), Maine (1819), Missouri (1820), and the states of Connecticut (1818), Massachusetts (1820–21), and New York (1821) framed new basic laws or (in the case of Massachusetts) liberalized their existing document.[1]

---

[1] Shirley S. Abrahamson, ed., *Constitutions of the United States:*

A close student of this development has described how "the mere process of growth made manifest the errors and defects of the Revolutionary state constitutions [nearly all of which had been drafted by state legislatures rather than by popularly elected conventions]. Where they obstructed progress or blocked the aspirations of newly ascendant groups in the community, there were demands for constitutional reform; and backed by the force of Revolutionary ideas of freedom and equality, these demands became irrepressible." [2] The intensity of reformist zeal that was predicated of other states during this great wave of constitutionalism did not reach the "irrepressible" stage in Rhode Island until 1841, but the nation-wide movement of 1816 to 1821 did generate enough concern in the land of Roger Williams to produce a sustained and successful effort to secure a constitutional convention.[3]

Agitation for constitutional reform began in the Providence press as early as 1818. In the vanguard of that town's crusading journalists was James Davis Knowles, who is remembered chiefly for his laudatory *Memoir of Roger Williams* (1834), the first extended biography of Rhode Island's founder. In 1818, Knowles, a brilliant lad of twenty, joined the staff of the *Rhode Island American* as foreman of the printing office. His labors with this Federalist sheet were not merely confined to those of a manual nature, for the gifted youth was soon filling the pages of the *American* with his articles and poems. Among Knowles's

---

National and State (Dobbs Ferry, N. Y., 1962), unpaginated introductory notes to the constitutions of the several states. The years listed are those in which the conventions were held.

[2] Merrill D. Peterson, ed., *Democracy, Liberty, and Property: The State Constitutional Conventions of the 1820's* (Indianapolis, 1966), pp. xiv–xvii; see also George Dangerfield, *The Awakening of American Nationalism, 1815–1828* (New York, 1965), pp. 215–16.

[3] The imminence of a new tax estimate or revaluation which would bear heavily on the expanding northern towns also contributed to the sentiment for constitutional apportionment. An estimate bill was continuously before the Assembly from 1817 through 1824. The *Manufacturers' and Farmers' Journal,* June 17, 1822 sheds light upon the constitutional implications of a new estimate; see also Journal of the House (1817–19), June session, 1818.

essays the most notable were those authored under the the pseudonym "Algernon Sidney," which urged a modernization and improvement of Rhode Island's basic law.

In these cogently written articles the youthful reformer advocated not only an equalization of representation, but also an independent judiciary, the enlargement of the suffrage, and a general diminution of the powers of the Assembly. These desirable goals could only be achieved, he admonished, if "sectional fears" could be allayed and the "state managers on both sides" (*i.e.,* party bosses) could be reconciled to reform.[4]

In the most striking of his passages the young Federalist concurred with Burrill that the "people" could by-pass the legislature in the constitution-making process. His account of the method by which this could be effected is a perfect description of the course taken by Thomas Dorr and his fellow reformers in 1841–42:

> The people of this state are sovereign and independent; and should the Legislature, as heretofore, disappoint their wishes, can in their sovereign and corporate capacity, delegate members to a Convention, draw up, approve, and establish a Constitution of government, proceed to elect magistrates and a new Legislature under that Constitution, organize their government, and relieve the present holders of power from their burthens and responsibilities. This is their undoubted right, but a right which I am persuaded they will exercise only in the last extremity.[5]

Knowles so impressed his employer, William G. Goddard (who ironically was among Dorr's most inveterate foes in 1842), that he was elevated to the position of co-editor in July 1819 upon attaining his majority. Before the young editor could establish himself as the reformist successor to George R. Burrill (who died in 1818), however, his interests turned toward the Baptist ministry. In the autumn of 1820 Knowles left the *American* for Philadelphia and the Baptist Theological School. He spent the remainder of his relatively short life as a clergyman. In 1838

---

[4] *Rhode Island American,* February 17, November 17, November 27, December 3, December 11, 1818 and April 23, 1819.

[5] *Ibid.,* December 11, 1818.

while a professor in the Baptist Theological Institute (Newton, Massachusetts) he contracted smallpox and died.[6]

At approximately the time that Knowles relinquished his role as constitutional advocate, a newspaper was founded in Providence called the *Manufacturers' and Farmers' Journal*. This new publication, dedicated to the promotion of manufacturing and the maintenance of the so-called American System, was edited by William E. Richmond and published by John Miller and John Hutchens. This urban-oriented paper took a reformist tack on the issue of legislative apportionment and filled the void created by Knowles's departure.[7]

In late 1820 it began a series of articles, admittedly inspired by constitutional developments in neighboring Connecticut and Massachusetts, which were designed to dispel the complacency of Rhode Island freemen concerning the adequacy of their basic law. The *Journal's* candid premise was that "the glaring defects of our miserable system, and its utter inconsistency in principle with all our received notions of republican government" should be "fully laid before the people" so that Rhode Islanders would apply themselves "to the work of regeneration."

In waging its campaign of enlightenment the paper emphasized the excessive power enjoyed by the General Assembly. In somewhat extreme language the fervent journalists contended

---

[6] The information on Knowles was obtained principally from an obituary written by his one-time employer William G. Goddard and printed in Francis W. Goddard, ed., *The Political and Miscellaneous Writings of William G. Goddard* (Providence, 1870), I, 303–15. Sidney Rider identifies Knowles as the author of the reform articles; Rider, "Constitutional Government," XVII/3/1/16. Useful information on the Providence newspapers of the early 19th century is found in Staples, *Annals of Providence*, pp. 538–61, 642–44; H. Glenn Brown and Maude O. Brown, *A Directory of Printing, Publishing, Bookselling and Allied Trades in Rhode Island to 1865* (New York, 1958); and [William Carroll, *et al.*], *Printers and Printing in Providence, 1762–1907* (Providence, 1907), pp. 21–38.

[7] On the formation and aims of the *Manufacturers' and Farmers' Journal,* the forerunner of the *Providence* (Daily) *Journal,* see William E. Richmond, "Some Notes on the Early History of the Journal," in *Semi-Centennial of the Providence Journal* (Providence, 1870).

(not without some basis in fact) that Rhode Island's government "was not established by the people of this State, nor is it amenable to them; it acknowledges no superior or creating power, and claims to exist and act by its own omnipotence; it answers to our ideas of a pure despotism, because the General Assembly engrosses and exercises, in person or by substitution, all the powers of sovereignty."

In a follow-up article the *Journal* indelicately warned the legislature of the possible consequences of intransigence on the issue of constitutional change: "That omnipotent body should consider that the people are competent to form a convention for themselves, without the authority of their *high mightinesses;* and that a longer delay of duty on the part of those who now set up the title of *legitimacy,* may produce such a result." [8] Two other Providence papers which mounted the reform bandwagon during this era of agitation were the *Patriot,* a Republican publication, and the *Gazette,* which had followed the Federalist line. As early as the spring of 1819, the publishers of the *Patriot,* Josiah Jones and Bennett Wheeler, began to give prime space to articles by "Publius Junior" urging constitutional change similar to that which had been effected in Connecticut. The *Providence Gazette* cast its lot with the reformers in 1820 when Walter R. Danforth (a staunch Dorrite in 1842) became its editor.[9]

II

Reform demands voiced during the years 1818 to 1820 by the Providence press and the example of other states, combined to induce a cautious and skeptical Assembly to yield on the question of a convention, but not before several moves were rebuffed.

---

[8] *Manufacturers' and Farmers' Journal,* November 27, December 11, 18 and 25, 1820 and January 11 and 25, 1821. Excerpts from several of these articles are reprinted in *Burke's Report,* pp. 274–76.

[9] *Providence Patriot,* March 6, 13 and 27, April 10 and 17, May 1, 8 and 15, 1819; *Providence Gazette,* January 10, 24 and 31, February 10 and 24, 1821.

The first such effort was made on October 29, 1817 when a motion was advanced in the House for the appointment of a committee to draft resolutions providing for the call of a constitutional convention. The Speaker selected a committee which soon submitted several resolves. These called for the freemen to assemble in town meeting that December to decide upon the "expediency" of a January convention. If the freemen approved they were to elect delegates according to the charter ratio. Fifty delegates selected in this manner would form a quorum for the convention to become operative. Unfortunately, the House postponed consideration of these resolves until the February session and then failed to act upon the committee's ambitious recommendations.[10]

Next, in the June 1818 meeting of the Assembly a proposition "to extend the right of suffrage to citizens who are not freeholders, provided they pay taxes or do militia duty," was first "agitated" and then deferred.[11] Later in the year, the House created a special six-man committee to make a report on the subject of free suffrage. At this October session "a proposition was made respecting a Constitution for the state, but no order was taken thereon." [12]

In 1819 reform demands to the Assembly became more vigorous. When the legislature convened in February, it was greeted by a memorial from a number of prominent Newporters seeking an enlargement of the franchise. Among the 150 petitioners were Justice Daniel Denham of the Newport County Court of Common Pleas, Henry Y. Cranston, clerk of that court, Robert B. Cranston, the county sheriff, and Daniel Shenton, David Melville, Jonathan Almy and Dutee J. Pearce, justices of the peace. The durable Pearce eventually became attorney general, con-

---

[10] Journal of the House (1817–19), October session, 1817; *Rhode Island American,* November 7 and 11, 1817.

[11] *Providence Patriot,* June 20, 1818. This was not a motion, for there is no record of it in the Journal of the House or Senate.

[12] Journal of the House (1817–19), October session, 1818. The Constitution "proposition" was not made in the form of a motion for there is no record of it in the Journal. See also *Providence Patriot,* November 7, 1818; *Rhode Island American,* November 3 and 10, 1818.

gressman, and finally a Dorr supporter in 1842. These prestigious islanders labeled the existing suffrage statute "partial and defective" because it deprived "a large and valuable portion of our fellow citizens of the privilege of suffrage." [13]

While the legislature was considering this petition, a resolution was introduced by Representative Joseph Hines of Coventry calling for the freemen of the several towns to express their views on the desirability of extending the elective franchise. At this juncture reactionary Benjamin Hazard of Newport and Hartford Convention fame moved to postpone. He suggested instead that a committee be appointed "to inquire into what alterations may be made upon the election laws to prevent frauds." His motion carried forty-three to eighteen, and for good measure his landed colleagues rejected the Newport memorial as well.[14]

In 1820, despite these setbacks, the reform tempo quickened. On June 23 a bill passed the Senate to extend the vote to citizens who equipped themselves and served in the militia, but on the following day the House used the postponement device to kill the measure.[15] The most noteworthy event of the political season, however, was the holding of a popular convention in Providence to promote the cause of a written constitution.[16]

This sustained agitation in the press and in the Assembly coupled with the example furnished by Connecticut, Massachusetts, and a host of other states finally caused the legislature to relent. On February 23, 1821, it passed the resolution of Representative Samuel Dexter of Providence authorizing the freemen

---

[13] Petitions to the General Assembly, Not Granted, RISA, February 15, 1819, hereafter cited Petitions Not Granted. Information on the positions of the prominent signatories as of 1819 can be found in Joseph Jencks Smith, comp., *Civil and Military List of Rhode Island, 1800–1850* (Providence, 1901), pp. 276–78.

[14] Journal of the House (1817–19), February session, 1819; *Rhode Island American,* February 23, 1819; *Providence Patriot,* February 24, 1819; Miscellaneous Papers of the General Assembly, folder 8 (1800–1820).

[15] Journal of the Senate (1814–1820), June session, 1820; Journal of the House (1819–22), June session, 1820.

[16] Brigham, p. 304.

at their April town meeting to decide upon the desirability of convening a constitutional convention.[17]

The referendum was voted upon according to schedule, but it was overshadowed by a hard-fought gubernatorial contest with sectional overtones between Republican William C. Gibbs of Newport and Samuel W. Bridgham of Providence who headed a "Union" (Federalist-Republican) prox. Because some members of the Union ticket were amenable to constitutional reform they polled especially well in the expanding towns. Downstate, however, this slate fared poorly. Out of 6,602 ballots cast for governor, Gibbs obtained a 1,000 vote majority. The convention question attracted the interest of only 3,524 freemen, and the call was defeated by a margin of 1,619 to 1,905.[18]

A close look at the convention referendum reveals two facts: the sectional nature of the vote, and the lack of a burning interest by the freemen in constitutional change. The convention call won by lopsided majorities in the northern and eastern areas of the state. It carried the three towns of Bristol County and the seven towns of Providence County within the expanding-industrial perimeter. In Providence the question triumphed 598 to 2. Downstate and on the western border, however, the decision was reversed. Three western country towns of Providence County, all of Kent (except East Greenwich), all of Newport County and all of Washington County (Hopkinton excepted) rejected the call. The most promising attempt yet made to secure a written constitution was thus foiled by a sectional coalition of static or declining towns, many of which would be adversely affected by the reapportionment that such a document might bring.

Providence's leading reform organ, the *Manufacturers' and*

---

[17] Journal of the House (1819–22), February session, 1821; *Rhode Island American,* February 27, 1821; *Schedules,* February, 1821, pp. 32.

[18] RIGA, Reports, VIII, pp. 39–40; *Providence Gazette,* May 9, 1821; *Manufacturers' and Farmers' Journal,* April 23, 1821. On the reform sentiments of the "Union" prox see *Rhode Island American,* February 16, 1821 and *Providence Gazette,* March 17 and 31, 1821. Edward F. Sweet, "The Origin of the Democratic Party in Rhode Island, 1824–1836," (unpublished doctoral dissertation, Fordham University, 1971), pp. 28–30, contends that the combination of southern and western votes which

Farmers' Journal attributed the defeat to "the obstinacy with which some demogogues in the remote towns have opposed" the project, and "the apathy with which the people of those towns treated the convention question." [19] Despite this discouraging reversal, the issue stayed alive. The *Journal* continued its advocacy of a convention through the remainder of the year and received an unexpected assist from a contributor to Newport's *Rhode Island Republican*. During September 1821 an able but anonymous "freeman" submitted a draft constitution to the Newport paper. This proposed basic law contained a detailed bill of rights and a suffrage clause bestowing the vote upon free white male citizens of one year's residence who paid a tax or performed militia service. It also embodied provisions for a lower house with a maximum of fifty and minimum of forty members apportioned after each decennial census on the basis of population, with each town entitled to at least one representative; and it created a senate of twelve members, four elected at large from each of three districts. One of these districts comprised Providence County, another Kent and Washington and the third, the counties of Newport and Bristol.[20] One student of Rhode Island constitutional development has called this suggested basic law "the first complete constitution for Rhode Island ever put together." [21] Unfortunately, the painstaking labors of the unknown draftsman were largely in vain.

Continued interest in constitutional change did have one salutary result. It persuaded the assembly in January 1822 to send a second convention referendum before the freemen at their April town meeting elections.[22] But this referendum fared more

---

elected Gibbs and defeated the convention call represented the same interests that later formed the Jackson party.

[19] *Manufacturers' and Farmers' Journal,* April 23, 1821. See also *Providence Gazette,* April 18, 1821.

[20] *Rhode Island Republican,* September 12, 19 and 26, 1821.

[21] Hubbard, pp. 60–61. My intuitive and unsupported guess is that Dutee J. Pearce was its author.

[22] *Schedules,* January session, 1822, p. 18; *Supplement to the Digest of 1822* (Providence, 1838), pp. 529–30; *Rhode Island American,* January 29, 1822.

poorly than the first. The convention call was denied by a vote of 1,804 to 843.[23] The total number of those taking a position on this issue was down 877 from the preceding year. This decline was produced not only by indifference but also by the fact that Governor Gibbs had only token opposition in the 1822 election.

The apathy and the general state of affairs that prevailed prior to the vote were described by contemporary Christopher Robbins, a Newport County politician, who correctly forecast the fate of the convention question to Congressmen Job Durfee. "I have no hope, myself," confided Robbins, "that for years to come, we shall obtain any solid improvement, either legislative or judicial. Not a word is said by any one on the subject of a Constitution, tho' the resolution passed both Houses nearly unanimously. I presume therefore, it will again be rejected." [24] Robbins was a prophet indeed.

As in 1821, defeat of the referendum could be traced to sectional antagonism. In addition, proponents of change seem to have been discouraged by their previous reversal. Further, they were somewhat skeptical concerning the reform inclinations of a convention that was a replica of the General Assembly. Both the referenda of 1821 and 1822 provided for a constitutional conclave apportioned in the same manner as the legislature. For this reason the reform-minded *Journal* opposed the 1822 convention call. We are "as much in favor of a new constitution as ever," it asserted, "but it is most doubtful that a worthwhile document could emanate from a convention composed of delegates distributed in the same manner as the lower house." [25] Evidently many of the *Journal's* townsmen shared these misgivings because Providence's vote for the convention was an unenthusiastic 110 to 26.[26]

---

[23] *Supplement to Digest of 1822,* p. 537.

[24] Christopher E. Robbins to Job Durfee, March 27, 1822, Durfee Papers, RIHS.

[25] *Manufacturers' and Farmers' Journal,* April 8, 1822. The *Providence Gazette,* in commenting upon the election, referred to the antagonisms between town and country, merchant and farmer, north and south. April 13 and 17, 1822.

[26] *Manufacturers' and Farmers' Journal,* April 18, 1822. *The Rhode*

The desire of the small or declining towns to preserve their charter-granted political prerogatives was an obvious element in their opposition to the referenda of 1821–22. Less obvious and less compelling but also significant was their economic stake in the status quo. Quite simply, a legislature dominated by rural and agricultural interests would be both able and inclined to place the tax burden on the urban and industrial sector or, at the very least, to prevent that burden from bearing too heavily upon the landed interest. In 1822 this attitude was especially apparent, for just prior to the constitutional balloting, the Assembly enacted a law imposing a substantial annual license fee upon brokers, a tax on the capital stock of banks, and another on insurance dividends.[27]

Most of those who voted on the constitutional referenda in 1821 and 1822 realized that the group that controlled the Assembly controlled the mode of taxation. Thus the farmers were wary indeed lest reapportionment wrest that control from them and place it in the hands of inimical industrial interests. The best way to prevent this occurrence, of course, was either to stop a convention from being convened or, failing that, to control any such body that might be called into existence. In 1821–22 both bases were covered.

Island American on April 23, 1822 remarked that "in the present state of political affairs," the defeat of the 1822 referendum was "a source of congratulation rather than regret to many of the warmest friends of a well-balanced constitution."

[27] *Supplement to Digest of 1822*, pp. 532–34. See the strong opposition to this revenue bill voiced by the business-oriented *Manufacturers' and Farmers' Journal*. On March 7, 1822 they charged that the tax was "partial and oppressive" and a discrimination against Providence enacted by "several leaders of what is now called the Country Party." Later (April 15) they stated their view on the logic of the tax, *viz.*, if the expenses of government can be "levied on the money corporations, the farms of the landholders will escape taxation." Finally, (April 22), the *Journal* contended that the tax bill, according to the intention of its sponsors, would furnish the small country towns "with new motives for opposing an equitable apportionment of representatives." A court challenge to the license act by the Providence Bank was unsuccessful. In the bank's argument before the United States Supreme Court the burden on the state's business and financial interests was well documented. 7 L. Ed. 514 (1830).

III

The year that saw the convention call defeated for a second time also witnessed another setback for the cause of governmental reform. This reversal was embodied in the *Digest of 1822*. At the very time when requests were being made for an extension of the franchise and serious consideration was being given to the abolition of the primogeniture provision of the suffrage law,[28] the revised election statute of 1822 produced a new exclusion — it denied the vote to Negroes. This regressive measure was enacted even though some blacks were exercising the suffrage by virtue of their status as freemen. This racial disqualification has escaped the notice of many historians, but it deeply disturbed the leaders of the Providence Negro community and became a source of considerable controversy a generation later during the Dorr Rebellion.[29]

In the wake of the rejection of the convention call and the publication of the new *Digest* with its ban on Negro suffrage, a reapportionment proposal emanated from a most unlikely source. During the June 1822 legislative session, state representative Elisha R. Potter, Sr., of South Kingstown introduced a bill to alter slightly Rhode Island's system of apportionment.[30] Potter,

---

[28] See for example William E. Richmond's editorial suggesting that the revision committee broaden the franchise to include those who paid a personal property tax or served in the militia. *Manufacturers' and Farmers' Journal,* January 21, 1822. On the anticipated abolition of the primogeniture provision see *Providence Gazette,* January 19, 1822; and John Howe to Job Durfee, Jan. 23, 1822, Durfee Papers.

[29] *Digest of 1822,* pp. 89–90; James Truslow Adams, "Disfranchisement of Negroes in New England," *American Historical Review,* XXX (April, 1925), 543–47. For the status of the Negro generally see Irving H. Bartlett, *From Slave to Citizen; the Story of the Negro in Rhode Island* (Providence, 1954); Julian Rammelkamp, "The Providence Negro Community, 1820–1842," *Rhode Island History,* VII (January, 1948), 20–43, and William J. Brown, *The Life of William J. Brown of Providence, R. I. with Personal Recollections of Incidents in Rhode Island* (Providence, 1883). On the Negro community's attempts to remove this disability see Petitions Not Granted, January 1831, January 1838, and June 1841; and Acts and Resolves of the General Assembly, RISA, XLIII (1841–42), 36–7.

[30] *Manufacturers' and Farmers' Journal,* June 17, 1822; *Providence*

it will be recalled, vaulted into prominence as the prime mover behind the estimate or revaluation of 1796. Since that time he had served as a Federalist congressman and as a state representative from his native South Kingstown.[31] Potter was a man of great presence and enormous size — he paid for two seats when he travelled by coach. Contemporary Josiah Quincy observed of Potter that he "seemed to carry about with him a certain homespun certificate of authority, which made it natural for lesser men to accept his conclusions." [32]

In 1818 Potter ran unsuccessfully for governor against Nehemiah Knight. At that time an opposition newspaper printed and circulated a most controversial statement which it attributed to Potter. The gubernatorial aspirant was accused by the *Providence Patriot* of having made the following declaration during the February 1818 session of the Assembly when the question arose as to the extent which the legislature was limited by the charter:

> I am not afraid of exercising the powers of this House: I am not afraid to declare my views in the General Assembly. The powers of this House are unlimited: they being without a written Constitution, are omnipotent: they have as much right to govern the affairs of this State and the citizens, as the Supreme Ruler of the Universe has to manage his own affairs.[33]

Certainly this was not the statement of a reformer, but in fairness to Potter, it is possible that the partisan press on the eve of a crucial election distorted or detached from context its opponent's remarks.

It seems that by 1822, however, this able and influential South County spokesman for the landed interest had come to accept the

---

Gazette, June 15 and 19, 1822; Miscellaneous Papers of the General Assembly, folder 9, (1821–25).

[31] A useful though superficial account of Potter's career, but very weak on the 1822–24 period, is Kenneth Thomas Langer, "Elisha Reynolds Potter, Sr.: Politician," (unpublished master's thesis, University of Rhode Island, 1957).

[32] Quoted in Fischer, *The Federalist Party*, p. 284.

[33] *Providence Patriot*, April 14, 1818. A clipping of this article is in the Potter Collection.

inevitability of political reform. Potter's acquiescence in limited change placed him in a middle ground between activists of Providence and reactionaries of Newport such as Asher Robbins and Benjamin Hazard, but he always remained much closer to the latter. It is most unfortunate that personal correspondence and manuscripts relating to the constitutional movement of 1817 to 1824 are lacking. Potter bequeathed to posterity a sizeable collection of letters; but none sheds light on constitutional reform during this period, despite Potter's prominent involvement in the movement from 1822 through his tenure as chairman of the convention of 1824.

Thus we can only speculate from fragmentary notices in the press on the motives for Potter's perplexing course of action. His 1822 reapportionment proposal, for example, was probably introduced as a palliative to appease Providence and other expanding towns. The reason for his mollification of the northern communities is evident from the other major action taken by the General Assembly in June 1822. The action consisted of the creation of a ten-man committee to make a new estimate of all rateable property in the state.[34]

The estimate bill, the first to secure passage since 1796, had been before the legislature for nearly five years. It was obvious to Potter and his fellow representatives that the industrial growth of the northern towns would be reflected dramatically in this new valuation, and that these towns would be called upon to pay an increased portion of the state tax load. It was also obvious to all concerned that any attempt to collect taxes from the northern towns based upon the new estimate would engender a furor that would dwarf the assessment controversy of 1796, *unless* some attempt was made to increase the representation of those communities.

Convinced of the necessity for compromise, Potter introduced his reapportionment bill. According to its provisions Providence would be allowed seven representatives and Smithfield, Bristol, Coventry, Foster, North Kingstown, and South Kingstown

---

[34] *Supplement to Digest of 1822,* pp. 539–41.

three each, with the other municipalities unchanged. The first three towns were rapidly expanding communities; the last four were large towns considerably underrepresented at the time of the first federal census and, although their growth had leveled off, their population per representative was still well in excess of the state average.[35]

According to the *Manufacturers' and Farmers' Journal*, Potter's measure was "connected with the subject of valuation and taxation." It was read, and "by general consent, postponed to the next session" when the new estimate was scheduled for submission. "Both measures (according to the understanding of the members) are to proceed, *pari passu*," observed the paper.[36] The reapportionment bill raised several issues. First was the question of whether a simple law could change the charter. During the equal representation movement of the 1770s and 1780s many believed that it could, but, as we have seen, the Assembly denied to itself this power in September 1789.

As a result of the circumstances in 1822, the possibility of the Assembly reversing its earlier position loomed large. A second call for a convention had just been soundly defeated; a new estimate was necessary; Providence and its expanding neighbors might not permit or abide by this new valuation unless apportionment concessions were made; if Providence should strenuously resist the estimate, civil disorder might ensue. Hence, it was easy to rationalize, as did the *Journal*, that "a reform of the Representative Power would be just and politick, and would not transcend the power of the General Assembly." [37] "If a great addition is to be made to the taxes of the northern section of the state," argued lawyer-editor William Richmond, "its power in the house of representatives should also be increased." [38]

---

[35] See Tables 3, 4 and 5. *Manufacturers' and Farmers' Journal*, June 17, 1822. The bill also gave one-year terms to representatives.

[36] *Manufacturers' and Farmers' Journal*, June 17, 1822.

[37] *Ibid.*, December 12, 1822. In this issue Richmond published a most revealing table of the "Population, Representative Power and Direct Taxes, of the Towns and Counties of Rhode Island." See also *Providence Gazette*, Dec. 15, 1822.

[38] *Manufacturers' and Farmers' Journal*, October 28, 1822.

Elisha Potter was ideally suited to advance a compromise proposal. He was a powerful man of considerable ability whose interests and ambitions transcended the confines of South Kingstown. In 1822 he had his sights set on the United States senatorial seat held by his old political adversary Nehemiah Knight. His chances for northern support would be hurt by his sectional attachment and by his chairmanship of the estimates committee. His reapportionment bill might offset these liabilities and gain him important northern backing.

Potter's measure, however, did not go as far as some would have wished. The *Journal,* for example, pointed out that it would give "full representation" to Bristol, Coventry, Foster, North Kingstown, and Potter's own community of South Kingstown, whereas Providence would still have four and Smithfield one less representative than that to which they were entitled. "Nevertheless," the Providence paper added, "this offer should be accepted," for "it is an evidence of a more liberal spirit than has heretofore prevailed in certain parts of the state: It justifies the hope that unwarrantable sectional jealousies will not, much longer, operate against . . . political reform." [39]

In the light of these remarks it appears that Potter's move was just and politically wise, and it nearly carried him into the United States Senate. In October 1822 the scheduled senatorial election was deferred, and when the showdown came in January 1823 the reluctant reformer from South County came within one vote (forty to thirty-nine) of ousting the favored incumbent, Senator Knight.[40] Unfortunately for Potter's candidacy, his re-

---

[39] *Ibid.,* June 17 and 24, 1822.

[40] *Ibid.,* January 20, 1823. John R. Waterman in describing the senate contest to Knight observed that he had "no doubt Mr. Potter has made more promises to secure his election than he can readily perform." Waterman to Knight, Jan. 20, 1823, Warwick Mss., Box 10, Misc. Mss. RIHS. Other "inside" information on Potter's senatorial quest can be found in an anonymous pamphlet at the RIHS entitled *Address to the Freemen of Rhode Island on the Annual Election of State Officers . . . 1828* (n.p., n.d.), pp. 12–14. In 1823 John R. Waterman was a state senator. It seems from his remarks to Knight that he double-crossed Potter and, in the secrecy of the balloting, cast the vote that returned Knight to the United States Senate.

apportionment bill was still pending in January, because the estimates committee, struggling with its formidable task, had failed to meet its schedule. In fact, the valuation was not ready for submission until the January 1824 session of the Assembly.[41]

Meanwhile Potter, his aspirations and reform inclinations undiminished, turned to more orthodox methods of constitutional change. In June 1823 he advanced a resolution proposing that the towns choose, at their August election meetings, delegates equal in number to their representatives, to meet for "the purpose of forming a written Constitution of government." The bill after desultory discussion was tabled.[42]

In the October session, with the prodding of Potter, its consideration was resumed. A five-man committee was appointed, failed to agree on the arrangements for a convention, and was discharged. Thereupon, a ten-member group was created and instructed to report its plans for the drafting of a convention proposal at the January session. Potter was a member of this select body that also included the able Samuel Bridgham of Providence.[43]

As this latest reform effort got underway the *Manufacturers' and Farmers' Journal* cautioned the Assembly that the new estimate was nearing completion. "The very great alteration which will shortly be made in the new apportionment of taxes upon the different towns of the State, will undoubtedly, arouse the people," admonished the Providence paper.[44] Events were reaching a critical stage.

---

[41] RIGA, Reports, VIII, 47; *Supplement to the Digest of 1822,* pp. 576–77. Scattered committee papers relating to the estimate of 1823 are contained in the Potter Collection. Potter's reapportionment bill remained before the Assembly until June 1827 when it was finally dismissed. Misc. Papers of the General Assembly, folder 10 (1826–30).

[42] *Manufacturers' and Farmers' Journal,* June 16, 1823. Potter later contended that he desired a convention to create an independent judiciary which would be ultimately responsible to the people, to divide the state into senatorial districts and to provide for the election of representatives but once a year. *Manufacturers' and Farmers' Journal,* July 15, 1824.

[43] *Ibid.,* November 8, 1823; *Rhode Island American,* November 4, 1823.

[44] *Manufacturers' and Farmers' Journal,* October 27, 1823.

In the January session of 1824 decisive action was taken. Potter's committee submitted its revised valuations, the expanding towns groaned;[45] the constitution committee advanced its convention plan; an air of expectation developed. Both measures secured the approval of the apprehensive Assembly after "animated" debate, but with no substantive alteration.

The convention bill drew the fire of diehard reactionary Asher Robbins of Newport. He made a long and determined effort on the House floor to block its passage. Among the most annoying and ludicrous of Robbins's contentions (in the eyes of his northern colleagues) was that he could see no evil in the government that needed remedy. Thus he moved for postponement and then for amendment; his motions failed and the bill passed on a voice vote.[46]

The convention authorized by the January session was apportioned, of course, according to the charter formula. The date for convening was set at June 21, 1824. The Assembly did not require a popular referendum to bring this gathering into existence; all that was necessary was for the freemen of the towns to elect the number of delegates allocated to their respective communities. There was one way by which the convention could be cancelled, namely the refusal of the towns to select and dispatch delegates. Such a procedure, however, was risky and self-defeating, because only a majority of delegates (thirty-seven) was necessary to begin formal deliberations.[47] In the April town meetings twenty-two towns chose delegates; eight others performed this function later in the spring. Three communities — North Kingstown, Burrillville, and West Greenwich — staged a boycott and refused to participate.[48]

---

[45] See Table 6 for the 1823 valuations. *Schedules*, January session, 1824, pp. 15–16.

[46] *Schedules*, January session, 1824, p. 2; *Rhode Island American*, January 20, 1824, contains an account of Robbins's remarks. *Supplement to the Digest of 1822*, pp. 573–77.

[47] *Supplement to the Digest of 1822*, pp. 573–75.

[48] *Manufacturers' and Farmers' Journal*, April 26, June 14 and 21, 1824. In the April elections there was no formidable opposition to Governor James Fenner, hence the turnout was light. *Ibid.*, April 26, 1824.

IV

On Monday, June 21, the long-awaited convention assembled and began its appointed task.[49] Of the sixty-four delegates who eventually attended many had distinguished or would distinguish themselves in the politics of the state. The Newport contingent included the able reactionaries Christopher Fowler, Asher Robbins — a future United States Senator — and former House Speaker Benjamin Hazard. Also from Newport was the more progressive but enigmatic Attorney General Dutee J. Pearce and the eminent journalist Henry Bull. Providence sent prominent China merchant Edward Carrington, former Lieutenant Governor Caleb Earle, lawyer William E. Richmond — one-time reform editor of the *Manufacturers' and Farmers' Journal* — and John Pitman, who became federal district court judge and a legal nemesis of the Dorrites in 1842.

Other local luminaries were Elisha Potter; House Speaker Albert C. Greene of East Greenwich, a future attorney general and United States Senator; Congressman Job Durfee of Tiverton, who was destined to preside as chief justice over the trial of Thomas Wilson Dorr; affluent North Providence industrialist Abraham Wilkinson; the articulate historian-politician Wilkins Updike from South Kingstown; future United States Senator Nathan F. Dixon of Westerly; former federal senator and Rhode Island House Speaker Elisha Mathewson of Scituate; William DeWolf of the famous Bristol dynasty; and Warwick's astute and politically durable John R. Waterman, a spokesman for the landed interest.

This formidable assemblage unanimously chose Potter as its

---

[49] The sources for the Convention of 1824 are the Journal of the Convention . . . 1824, RISA, and the record of debates and proceedings reported by young journalist-politician Benjamin F. Hallett for the *Rhode Island American* and the *Manufacturers' and Farmers' Journal*. The latter paper announced tentative plans for the publication of the debates and proceedings of the convention in a volume which would sell for $1.25. The cost of publication was to be defrayed by subscription. This project was never carried through, owing perhaps to a lack of popular interest.

president in recognition of his ability and his instrumentality in securing the convention call. Two non-delegates, Christopher Robbins and Welcome Burgess, were then named secretaries. After fixing the members' compensation and appointing a rules committee, the body adjourned until the following morning.[50]

On Tuesday five committees were created to examine the major issues before the convention. The committees and the areas delineated for their consideration were: (1) bill of rights, (2) the legislative and executive departments, apportionment, suffrage, and qualifications of electors, (3) the judiciary, (4) local government, and (5) education. Later, a sixth committee on amendments and "general provisions" was established. The president appointed the membership of these important bodies, and it was their function to submit proposals to the convention dealing with their respective areas of concern.[51]

In an incredibly short time these committees began to report. On Thursday, June 24 a draft bill of rights, a judicial article, and a statement on education had been completed. On Friday the delegates resolved themselves into a committee of the whole, and debate on the declaration of rights began. For the next seven working days the process of report, debate, and amendment was repeated. Finally, in the late afternoon of Saturday, July 3, after a compromise document had been hammered out, a final vote was taken. The proposed constitution was passed by the wide margin of fifty-two to nine and sent to the freemen for approval at an October 11 referendum.[52]

Of the nine dissidents, two came from Richmond, one from

---

[50] Journal of the Convention . . . 1824, pp. 5–6.

[51] The chairmen of these committees were as follows: bill of rights — Joshua Bicknell (Barrington); legislative and executive etc. — Christopher Fowler (Newport); judiciary — John Pitman (Providence); local government — Abraham Wilkinson (North Providence); education — Caleb Earle (Providence); amendments — William Richmond (Providence). There were also two major procedural committees: rules — Dutee Pearce (Newport) and business — Job Durfee (Tiverton). See the list of committees in Potter's hand, Potter Collection; and Journal of the Convention . . . 1824, pp. 7–12.

[52] Journal of Convention . . . 1824, pp. 1–12, 44–47.

Portsmouth and six from Newport. The delegates from the island communities opposed the document principally because it cut their representation in the lower house. However, three Portsmouth delegates surprisingly supported the convention's product.[53]

The new document — which had attracted such unexpected and encouraging delegate support — was fairly progressive in its provisions with the exception of the clause relating to suffrage.[54] It contained nine articles.[55] The first distributed the powers of government into "three distinct departments," thus in effect curbing the prerogative of the legislature. Article II established a bicameral assembly composed of a ten-member senate elected at-large and a house selected by the qualified voters of the several towns according to the following ratio:

> Each town, having three thousand inhabitants, and under five thousand, shall be entitled to elect three Representatives; each town having five thousand inhabitants, and under eight thousand shall be entitled to elect four Representatives; each town having eight thousand inhabitants, and under twelve thousand, shall be entitled to elect five Representatives; each town having twelve thousand inhabitants, and under seventeen thousand, shall be entitled to elect six Representatives; and each town having seventeen thousand inhabitants, shall be entitled to elect seven Representatives; but no town shall be entitled to elect more than seven Representatives; nor shall any town be entitled to less than two.

The legislative article also extended to one year the term for House members, established a veto process that conferred upon the governor a negative that could be overridden by a simple majority of each chamber, and provided for impeachments.

Article III created an executive department headed by a governor elected for a term of one year. To be eligible for the

---

[53] *Ibid.,* 45–47.

[54] A letter to the editor of the *Providence Patriot,* September 25, 1824 urged the adoption of the constitution because it incorporated the freehold in the basic law "beyond the caprice of legislation." See also *Providence Beacon,* September 25, 1824.

[55] The following summary is from a printed copy of the constitution of 1824, Broadside File (1824), RIHS. The document was published in the *Manufacturers' and Farmers' Journal,* July 12, 1824.

governorship one had to be an elector, thirty years of age, a native-born citizen of the United States, and a five-year resident of Rhode Island. The chief executive was empowered to grant reprieves and pardons, preside in joint (*i.e.*, "grand") committee of the senate and house when assembled for the election of officers, convene special sessions of the Assembly, adjourn that body in case of dispute, sign all commissions, and serve as commander-in-chief of the militia.

The lieutenant governor was to have the same term and qualifications as the governor, be first in the line of succession, and serve as president of the senate. The other elective state officers given constitutional status were the secretary, the general treasurer, and the attorney general.

The judicial branch of government was embraced by Article IV. It was to consist of the Supreme Judicial Court, a Circuit Court of Common Pleas and General Sessions of the Peace, and such other courts as the legislature chose to establish. Supreme Court justices were to be three in number and appointed by the Grand Committee for six-year terms. The Circuit Court was to consist of five members, one from each county. Its members were to be appointed for a term of one year. Any justice could be removed by impeachment or by a joint resolution passed by two-thirds of the whole membership of each house.

Article V concerning elections and suffrage was the least progressive portion of the new document. In effect it made constitutional the existing suffrage statute. That is, it gave the vote to *white* adult male citizens who were freeholders. The only significant deviation was the elimination of a lingering vestige of primogeniture by the deletion of the provision that had enabled non-landholding eldest sons of freemen to vote. According to the draft constitution no person was to be eligible for *state* office unless he possessed the $134 freehold necessary to qualify him in his own right as an elector.

Article VI was a "declaration of certain constitutional rights and principles" that closely resembled the 1798 statutory bill of rights and the accompanying "act relative to religious freedom." Added to these previously proclaimed rights, as a result of successful motions from the floor of the convention,[56] were sections dealing with freedom of the press, the right of assembly and petition, eminent domain, trial by jury, the subordination of the military to the civil power, and the quartering of soldiers.

Article VII on education contained an enlightened provision creating a perpetual Free School Fund;[57] while Article VIII provided for amending the basic law by a vote of two-thirds of the whole membership of each house in two consecutive sessions, a general election intervening, followed by the approval of two-thirds of the electors voting thereon at a special town meeting. This cumbersome procedure and the two-thirds requirement made the document somewhat inflexible. A final article dealt with general provisions such as the continuity of government, contractual obligations, and the operative date of the new basic law.

During the twelve-day convention the provision of the proposed constitution that engendered the most intense controversy was the allocation of representatives to the respective towns. This issue was within the purview of the important fifteen-member committee on the legislative and executive departments. This group, under the chairmanship of Newport's Christopher Fowler, submitted its draft to the convention on the afternoon of Friday, June 25. Five days later heated discussions began in the committee of the whole over that part of the Fowler committee's handiwork that dealt with the touchy topic of apportionment.[58]

Fowler's group, a majority of which came from the static and declining towns, recommended a bicameral assembly. Their proposed senate was to be chosen from districts whose boundaries would correspond to the five counties. Providence County was allocated five senators, Washington and Newport three each,

---

[56] *Manufacturers' and Farmers' Journal,* June 28 and July 1, 1824.

[57] This provision was a forerunner of the Free School Act of 1828. Charles Carroll, *Public Education in Rhode Island* (Providence, 1918), pp. 333–35.

[58] *Manufacturers' and Farmers' Journal,* June 28, 1824. A copy of the committee draft is contained in the Potter Collection with a committee draft of the declaration of rights, the manuscript rules of the convention, a list of committees, and a printed copy of the constitution of 1824.

Kent two, and Bristol one. In the lower house each municipality received a guarantee of two representatives; thereafter a scale of representation was established ranging from 3,000 to 13,000, the former figure entitling a community to three representatives and the latter to six. In no event, however, was any town to be allowed more than six members in the lower house.

Debates in the convention and the amendments introduced pursuant thereto [59] had the cumulative effect of accomplishing a slight liberalization of the committee's plan for the lower house, but the ratio finally adopted was still a concession to the smaller towns. The pro-business *Manufacturers' and Farmers' Journal* reported that these small communities "were apprehensive of the growing population of the north and bent on the adoption of an increasing ratio," that is, one which discriminated against the larger, expanding towns by progressively increasing the population requirements for gaining additional representatives.[60]

The convention also altered the Fowler group's recommendations regarding the composition of the senate. The originally advanced district plan was opposed by Providence County delegates because they "were unwilling to surrender the advantage which the population of the county gives it in a general [*i.e.* at-large] vote." Under the proposed district system, Providence and Bristol Counties, with a combined population of 41,343, and growing, would have elected only six senators, whereas the other three counties, with a total population of 41,686, would have been granted eight senators and control of the upper house. After considerable discussion, districting was abandoned, and the prevailing system of ten senators elected at-large was preserved.[61]

Throughout the apportionment hassle, despite the diversity of plans for the allocation of representatives, one theme was often

[59] *Manufacturers' and Farmers' Journal,* June 28, July 1 and 5, 1824.

[60] Committee draft, Potter Collection; *Manufacturers' and Farmers' Journal,* June 28 and September 30, 1824.

[61] *Manufacturers' and Farmers' Journal,* September 30, 1824. One of the drawbacks of at-large elections was that a senate chosen in this manner would usually be "entirely composed of men of the prevailing political sect," whereas districting would produce more diversity and balance in the upper chamber. *Ibid.*

repeated by the delegates from the south, namely: "The necessity of preserving to the *agricultural* interest an undoubted pre-
ponderance over the *manufacturing* and *mercantile* interests." [62]
In this endeavor the farmers enjoyed considerable but not complete success.

The only other issue that produced both extended debate and
sharp controversy related to the judiciary and arose on June 26,
when delegate Nathan Dixon of Westerly moved to give a life
tenure to judges of the Supreme Judicial Court. Dixon, in an
able defense of his proposal, claimed that it would produce a
more independent judiciary that could not "be removed from
office at the whim or caprice of any party or any body of men."
Further, he argued, tenure of office coupled with an adequate
salary would induce men of "talents and learning" to accept the
position of judge and thereby upgrade the state's court system.
John Pitman, Edward Carrington, and William Richmond of
Providence agreed, as did Newport's Henry Bull and Asher
Robbins.

The opposition, however, was equally formidable. Elisha Potter, Wilkins Updike, Job Durfee, and Dutee Pearce rejected life
tenure not only in principle, but for practical reasons as well.
They argued that such a provision would render the proposed
constitution impossible to ratify. In this vein, delegate Updike
posed a rhetorical question that is timeless in its application:
"Did we come here," he said in exasperation, "to speculate and
try experiments on paper and make a perfect Constitution which
we know the people will never sanction?"

Updike believed the convention must propose the possible and
the palatable. Dutee Pearce concurred. "We must wait the gradual process of opinion," he observed, "before anything so totally
adverse to the habits and views of a people can be introduced
among them with any chance of success." Pearce then boldly suggested that his reactionary fellow-townsman, Asher Robbins,
supported judicial tenure because "it would defeat the whole
constitution." The transition from annual appointment to life

---

[62] *Ibid.*, September 30, 1824.

tenure was too drastic for either the delegates or the electorate to accept. After three days of lively discussion the measure went down to defeat.[63]

Another amendment, also too progressive for this convention, shared a fate similar to that accorded the Dixon proposal. This was Pearce's motion to extend the suffrage to all white males, twenty-one years of age, who had one year's residency in the state, provided they paid their taxes, performed military duty, or possessed at least $100 worth of real or personal property.

The attorney general's long argument in support of his amendment was liberal and enlightened. After prefacing his speech with the dubious contention that suffrage was a natural right, Pearce perceptively described those conditions in Rhode Island which made the freehold restriction anachronistic. He acknowledged that land as a basis for suffrage was appropriate during the early colonial era, but times, he warned, had changed. "Real estate now," Pearce observed, "bears but a small proportion to other more active capital, and but a small proportion of our citizens have an inducement to invest their funds in that species of property. We have become a trading, a commercial, and a manufacturing community."

"The plan which I propose," he continued, "is intended to introduce to the privileges of freemen the man who pays his tax or does military service or who possesses his hundred dollars in bank stock, in a river boat, in his implements of industry, or stock in trade." Before concluding, the controversial Newport delegate addressed himself to several objections which had been raised by adherents of the freehold requirement. To those who claimed an extension would encourage corruption, he pointed to the current practice of fraudulent franchisement by temporary transfers of land; to those who feared the increased political power of the commercial towns he observed that fraudulent voting already occurred in these communities due to the large con-

---

[63] *Ibid.*, June 28, July 1, 15, 19, 26 and 29. A petition for court reform from Scituate bearing 52 signatures was presented to the General Assembly in October 1824. Petitions Not Granted, RISA. The document called for an enlargement of the powers of the justices of the peace.

centration within them of men who could be temporarily enfranchised; and to those who contended that the landless laborer
was lacking in community ties and likely to emigrate, Pearce re-
torted that this argument applied with more force to the small
farmer, especially "while the farming interest is as unproductive
as it now is."

Ironically, Pearce's most outspoken opponent was court-re-
former Nathan Dixon. This Westerly delegate eulogized the yeoman farmer and asserted that any man who cannot acquire $134
worth of real estate "is too improvident to have any concern in
the management of the government." But Dixon was not the only
foe of "free suffrage," for when the tally was taken the Pearce
proposal received a scant three votes from the landholding delegates.[64]

Throughout the late summer and the fall of 1824 public reaction to the convention's handiwork oscillated between apathy
and mild discussion. The four-cornered presidential race, especially the candidacies of William Crawford and John Quincy
Adams, seemed to be uppermost in the minds of most politically
oriented Rhode Islanders, if the local press was an adequate
mirror of public concern.

In Newport, the Rhode Island *Republican* attempted to trans-
form the passive attitude regarding the new basic law to one of

---

[64] *Rhode Island American,* August 17, 20 and 24; *Burke's Report,*
p. 722. The *Manufacturers' and Farmers' Journal,* cool on suffrage extension, did not give space to Pearce's speech, but merely noted the
Newporter's amendment (July 1, 1824). Gadfly journalist William S.
Spear was the most outspoken proponent of free suffrage, and he
plumped for it repeatedly in the pages of his *Providence Beacon,* July 3,
10 and 24, September 25, October 2 and 9, 1824.

TABLE 6

SOURCE: RIGA, Reports, VIII, 53. Those towns which were designated at the outset of this chapter as "expanding" voted 2½ to 1 for
ratification (1,280–527); the "static" communities 6½ to 1 against (226–
1,477); and the "declining" 8½ to 1 in opposition (132–1,130). Warwick voted against the document because it had not as yet grown sufficiently to merit the four representatives that it possessed under the
charter.

TABLE 6

Vote on the Proposed Constitution of 1824

Towns	Approve	Reject
Providence	653	26
North Providence	64	10
Smithfield	128	18
Warwick	67	160
Cumberland	140	14
Bristol	100	24
Warren	57	28
Johnston	58	13
Scituate	13	234
EXPANDING TOWNS	1,280	527
New Shoreham	2	49
Cranston	36	52
Coventry	71	195
Tiverton	13	96
Newport	5	531
Portsmouth	0	183
Burrillville	27	37
Middletown	1	96
North Kingstown	6	207
Glocester	65	31
STATIC TOWNS	226	1,477
Foster	4	242
South Kingstown	47	100
Little Compton	6	91
Westerly	12	68
East Greenwich	30	80
Barrington	21	12
Richmond	0	90
Jamestown	6	16
Exeter	0	114
Hopkinton	5	69
West Greenwich	1	173
Charlestown	0	75
DECLINING TOWNS	132	1,130
RHODE ISLAND	1,668	3,206

active hostility. As early as July 15, it began a series of articles addressed "To the Freemen of Rhode Island" on the issue of constitutional change. These articles were misleading, distorted, and demagogic, but they appear to have had an appreciable impact on the electorate in the lower Bay communities.[65] In Providence, on the other hand, the *Manufacturers' and Farmers' Journal* and the *American* tried to generate support for the proposed document. The former sheet published a series of articles by "Roger Williams & Co." explaining and extolling the provisions of the proposed frame of government, while the latter stressed the disproportionate political influence enjoyed by the southern communities under the prevailing system.[66]

As the October 11 referendum date drew near the townspeople of Providence began to campaign actively for ratification. On the evenings of October 8 and 9 they organized large bipartisan demonstrations at the Town House to agitate for adoption.[67] Unfortunately for the cause of reform these expressions of support were not infectious.

On the following Monday, 4,874 ballots were cast state-wide; and the constitution succumbed by a two to one margin. (By the act of January 1824 it needed three-fifths of the total vote to become operative).[68] Only nine towns, led by Providence (653–26), voted to approve; the others, led by Newport (5–531), turned thumbs down. Extensive analysis of the referendum is not required; all the returns, with the exception of those from Scituate, Barrington, and enigmatic Glocester, were predictable. As the voting tabulation (Table 7) reveals, support came principally from the expanding northern and eastern towns and opposition stemmed mainly from the static and declining communities of the south and west.[69]

---

65 Hubbard, pp. 127–38 summarizes these articles. See *Providence Patriot*, November 3, 1824.

66 *Manufacturers' and Farmers' Journal*, September 16, 20, 23 and 30, October 4 and 11, 1824. *Rhode Island American*, September 24 and October 5, 1824.

67 *Manufacturers' and Farmers' Journal*, October 11, 1824.

68 *Supplement to the Digest of 1822*, p. 575.

69 RIGA, Reports, VIII, 53. At this point we might recall Ferdinand

Tönnies hypothesis to illuminate a possible source of this rural vs. urban antagonism (see chapter V, note 70). Southern and western Rhode Island constituted a predominantly *Gemeinschaft* or community-oriented society; that is one which maintained a rural outlook, possessed homogeneous structure and values, functioned through traditional status arrangements, and was characterized by low mobility, attachment to the soil, unity, close personal relationships, and a home or household economy; whereas the expanding industrial towns constituted a predominately *Gesellschaft* or association-oriented society; that is one with a cosmopolitan or urban attitude; one exhibiting a preference for ordering social and economic relations through contract; and one characterized by higher mobility, greater ethnic heterogeneity, impersonal relationships, and advanced forms of economic organization and activity. These fundamental societal differences appear to have magnified and exacerbated political conflicts over suffrage and reapportionment because reforms in these strategic areas would produce alterations in the orientation of government from rural to urban. The *Gemeinschaft-Gesellschaft* concepts are, of course, ideal types that seldom exist in pure, unmixed form. See Tönnies, *Community and Society (Gemeinschaft und Gesellschaft)*, pp. 1–3, 33–35, 64–67, 248–59, 268–69; and Robin M. Williams, Jr., *American Society: A Sociological Interpretation* (2nd rev. ed., New York, 1960), 482–83. Paul L. Murphy, "Sources and Nature of Intolerance in the 1920s," *Journal of American History*, LI (June, 1964), 60–61, 68–69, 75 is an effort to understand the rural-urban conflict of that decade in the light of Tönnies's hypothesis; whereas Lee Benson's attempt to explain the ratification of the federal Constitution in terms of "agrarian" and "commercial" types (*Turner and Beard*, pp. 214–28) also bears some similarity to this approach.

IV. Equal Rights

Thomas Wilson Dorr, patrician reformer and the leader of the fight for Equal Rights and free suffrage in Rhode Island that culminated in the Dorr Rebellion (from a daguerreotype in the possession of Frank Mauran III, Providence).

CHAPTER NINE
Free Suffrage

I

In the immediate wake of the constitutional debacle of 1824, reform interest diminished and few voices were raised against the status quo. In January 1825 a House committee expressed support for reapportionment but could not devise a suitable plan.[1] "General suffrage" was urged, but to no avail, by eccentric and outspoken William Spear in the pages of his *Providence Beacon* until that uninfluential weekly expired in February 1826.[2]

Then in late 1826 a movement for court reform gained momentum in the General Assembly. Prodded by the local press and influenced by spirited judicial debate in the 1824 convention, the legislators enacted a statute in January 1827 session that upgraded the state Supreme Court in both personnel and procedure. The provisions of this restructuring act reduced the size of the court from five to three and more than doubled the salaries of the justices. The intention of the act's sponsors was that

---

[1] Miscellaneous Papers of the General Assembly, folder 9 (1821–25).
[2] Hubbard, p. 156; *Annals of Providence,* p. 552.

the Assembly would henceforth appoint distinguished men with legal training and experience and refrain from the common practice of elevating non-lawyers to such an exalted judicial post.

In anticipation of qualified appointees, the reconstituted high court was commissioned "to instruct the Grand Juries in the law relating to crimes and offenses cognizable" by the Supreme Court and "to instruct the Petit Jury in the law that may be applicable to each case by them tried, by giving them publicly in charge, before they retire to consider their verdict, the opinion of the Court upon the law." Prior to this change the jury could decide both law and fact.

The court reform statute became effective in May 1827 over strong objections of those incumbent justices who were replaced and the able Samuel Eddy, distinguished advocate and former congressman, was chosen chief justice. Eddy, who succeeded Isaac Wilbour, a farmer-politician with no formal legal training, has been called by one student of Rhode Island judicial development "the first of the new regime." Although the Assembly retained the power to appoint Supreme Court justices annually, the caliber of the new tribunal henceforth discouraged interference with the judiciary.[3]

With limited court reform achieved, certain Rhode Islanders began to espouse more controversial alterations in their state's system of government; specifically, they demanded suffrage reform. Beginning in 1828, a series of hard-fought, interest-inspiring presidential campaigns were waged that quickened the political pulse of Rhode Island's citizenry and made many who were disfranchised by the freehold qualification resentfully aware of their disability.

Historian Richard P. McCormick persuasively shows that the election of 1828 did not, as was once thought, produce a "mighty

[3] On the court reform of 1827 see *Manufacturers' and Farmers' Journal*, January 8, 1827; *Digest of 1822*, pp. 107–12; *Supplement to the Digest of 1822*, pp. 644–45; Edward C. Stiness, "The Struggle for Judicial Supremacy," in Edward Field, ed., *State of Rhode Island and Providence Plantations* . . . (Boston, 1902), III, 163–4.

democratic uprising." [4] It did, however, mark the beginning of a new period of political concern in Rhode Island which contrasted with the relatively placid decade that followed the Nehemiah Knight-Elisha R. Potter gubernatorial struggle of 1818 and the demise of the Federalists.[5] And it did provide an occasion for a new alignment of political parties.[6]

The Rhode Island turnout of 3,575 in the Adams-Jackson mud-bath of 1828 represented 18 percent of the state's *total* white adult male population, a significant increase over the 12.4 percent which had voted in the intraparty feud of 1824. In Jackson's re-election attempt of 1832 the proportion of adult white males participating was 22.4 percent; in 1836 it reached 24.1 percent; and in the free-wheeling "log cabin and hard cider" campaign of 1840 it climbed to 33.2 percent.

Despite these increases in the four presidential contests from 1828 to 1840, Rhode Island's percentage of adult white males voting was far lower than that of any other state. In 1840 the state's 33.2 percent contrasted markedly with an incredible national average of 78 percent. McCormick, in his study of Jacksonian voting behavior, shows that Rhode Island's adult white males balloting during the so-called "Age of the Common Man" did not approach the percentage turn-out registered immediately preceding the War of 1812. Rhode Island's early nineteenth-century high-point of 49.4 percent had been reached in the nip-and-

---

[4] Richard P. McCormick, "New Perspectives on Jacksonian Politics," *American Historical Review*, LXV (Jan., 1960), 288–301. McCormick does not view the participation in the presidential elections of 1828, 1832, and 1836 as impressive and contends that the key to the relatively low vote was "the extreme political imbalance that existed in most states as between the Jacksonians and their opponents" coupled with "the immature development of national political parties." Florence Weston, however, refers to the contest of 1828 as "the first modern election." Florence Weston, *The Presidential Election of 1828* (Washington, D.C., 1938), p. 191.

[5] The only hotly-contested gubernatorial election in 1819–29 inclusive was the Gibbs-Bridgham race of 1821. *Rhode Island Manual*, 1965–66, pp. 212–13. Of the five congressional races 1818–1827 inclusive, three were not contested. *Ibid.*, 1937–38, pp. 202–03.

[6] Richard P. McCormick, *The Second American Party System* (Chapel Hill, N. C., 1966), p. 86.

tuck William Jones-James Fenner gubernatorial battle of 1812 (with the help of fraudulent deeds).[7]

These figures, if read superficially, would suggest that political apathy prevailed in the state from 1828 to 1840; viewed in proper perspective, however, they point to quite different conclusions. During the period 1828 to 1840, the proportion of the total adult white males voting in presidential elections increased nearly 70 percent despite the fact that the percentage of *eligible* voters in this group steadily diminished as the ranks of the urban landless swelled. The election that generated the peak percentage in voter turnout — that of 1812 — came before the onset of widespread industrialization at a time when the ratio of eligible electors to the whole number of white adult males was much higher than in the Jacksonian era. Rhode Island's comparatively small percentages of adult white males voting during the period 1828 to 1840 were mainly attributable to the enormously repressive effect of the real estate qualification.

After Virginia abandoned the freehold requirement in her constitution of 1830, only Rhode Island gave general adherence to this relic of a bygone age. Although the Old Dominion's franchise provisions remained illiberal even after 1830 — because personal property requirements were imposed — nowhere in the nation by this time was there a suffrage law as restrictive as that in reactionary Rhode Island, due not only to the provisions of the statute itself but also to the type of society in which it operated. By the 1830s Rhode Island was among the most urbanized and industrialized states in the nation — precisely the kind of state in which a freehold requirement produced severe disfranchisement.[8]

---

[7] McCormick, "New Perspectives," p. 292; Robert Remini, *The Election of Andrew Jackson* (Philadelphia, 1963), p. 187. The highest actual turnout prior to 1840 occurred in the 1818 gubernatorial contest be-between Potter and Knight (*viz.*, 8,402).

[8] North Carolina demanded a freehold requirement for state senatorial elections and Louisiana had a sizeable tax-paying requirement. Neither matched Rhode Island in restrictiveness. Chilton Williamson, *American Suffrage from Property to Democracy* (Princeton, N. J., 1960), pp. 223–41; McCormick, "New Perspectives," pp. 290–91; Fletcher M.

As political interest revived during the campaign of 1828 and intensified in subsequent state and national elections owing to development of the second American party system, the unparalleled restrictiveness of Rhode Island's suffrage law was brought into sharp focus and became an increasing source of discontent. Suffrage extension replaced reapportionment as the most urgent reform demand.

II

Shortly after the campaign of 1828 drew to a close, the state's first significant and concerted suffrage agitation began with a major rally on March 14, 1829 in Pawtucket, then a densely populated mill village in the town of North Providence. Attended by 300 demonstrators, this gathering had as its prime purpose "to propose and adopt a memorial to the General Assembly" for the extension of suffrage. This task completed, the group — chaired by Barney Merry, a freeholder — approved two recommendations: that other towns hold similar meetings, and that a suffrage convention meet in Newport to coincide with the next June session of the legislature.

These Pawtucket protestors argued that under existing laws a large and respectable body of free citizens paid taxes on substantial personal estates but were denied the name and privileges of free men. After citing appropriate passages from the Declaration of Independence, the memorialists next questioned the justice of a government that denied the vote to those taxed to support it. Having attacked the automatic enfranchisement of a freeholder's eldest son, they urged the General Assembly to extend the vote to all free white male inhabitants of twenty-one who possessed property that was taxed or who were personally liable to perform military duty in defense of the state or the United States. They prophetically warned that revolution would

Green, *Constitutional Development in the South Atlantic States, 1776–1860* (Chapel Hill, N. C., 1930), pp. 210–24; Peterson, *State Constitutional Conventions,* pp. 279–81.

ensue unless the franchise was extended before further population growth made the state's small area actually incapable of conferring suffrage on even a majority of adult males.[9]

Similarly disfranchised residents of other expanding towns began to register their protest. In Providence on March 28 a giant
suffrage rally of "not less than 1500 persons" elected Samuel
Brown its chairman, and proceeded to draft a lengthy memorial
for the legislature's perusal.[10] The Providence petition correctly
declared that "the civil laws recognize no class of citizens but
those owning lands, and extends to all others no privileges that
are not equally enjoyed by the stranger or foreigner, the moment
he treads on our soil." [11]

The complainants referred to the fact that a non-freeholder
could bring no civil action in any Rhode Island court, except
with the consent of a freeman, and to the fact that a non-freeholder had no right to serve as a juror and had no standing as a
plaintiff in any suit, except those involving divorce or bank-
ruptcy. Further, no person who was not a freeholder could obtain from a town clerk "any writ of arrest or original summons,
against any person . . . unless some sufficient freeholder" en-

---

[9] Free Suffrage Petitions, 1829, Petitions Not Granted, RISA, Outsize
petitions, Box #1. *Microcosm* (Providence), March 17, 1829. This paper
contains the fullest account of the free suffrage movement of 1829. Its
editor, Benjamin F. Hallett, was a leader in this agitation. An unflattering and unfair portrait of Hallett the politician is found in Arthur M.
Schlesinger, *The Age of Jackson* (Boston, 1945), pp. 173–74. A more
favorable estimate is Joseph L. Blau, ed., *Social Theories of Jacksonian
Democracy* (Indianapolis, 1954), p. xviii.

[10] *Microcosm,* March 31, 1829. *The Manufacturers' and Farmers'
Journal,* March 30, 1829 estimated the crowd at between 1,200 and
1,500.

[11] Free Suffrage Petitions, 1829, Petitions Not Granted, RISA, Outsize petitions, Box #1. The Providence memorial is printed in *Microcosm,*
March 31, 1829 and in Seth Luther, *An Address on the Right of Free
Suffrage* (Providence, 1833). Luther in a lavish estimate said that it was
signed by "nearly 2000 petitioners, including 700 freeholders." The correct figure was 998. Apparently the Providence demonstration irritated
the town fathers, for an ordinance was passed in 1829 authorizing the
moderator of the town meeting to employ five constables to keep all non-
freeholders off the floor of the town house. Public indignation soon
caused the act's repeal. *Ibid.,* p. 19.

dorsed the writ and guaranteed legal costs.[12] The protestors were painfully aware that the freehold was not only the prerequisite for suffrage and officeholding, but the ticket of admittance into civil society as well.

The Providence memorial next brought to light another startling condition. It asserted that there were only 8,400 freeholders in the state against 12,365 non-freeholders. If these figures were reasonably reliable — and there is no reason to doubt their accuracy — then as of 1829 close to sixty percent of Rhode Island's free white adult males were relegated to the status of second-class citizens by the freehold qualification. If the General Assembly insisted upon retaining a property qualification, the petitioners concluded, it should be extended to personalty, including agricultural implements and mechanical tools, and those who performed their military requirements should also be enfranchised.[13]

One noteworthy aspect of the Providence agitation was the attempt of suffragists to gain the power to vote in local elections. At this time a proposed city charter was in the drafting stage. The reformers met and decided to seek its amendment by the insertion of a clause extending the *local* franchise to white adult males with three years' municipal residence if they were taxed on real or personal property in the amount of $150 or if they had served three years as firemen. At the April town meeting this proposal was advanced and secured approval of those freemen in attendance by a margin of eighty-seven to eighty. After its passage some town fathers had second thoughts. The objec-

---

[12] *Digest of 1822,* especially pp. 89–98, 112–15, 136–41.

[13] Benjamin F. Hallett, suffrage leader and *Microcosm* editor, after a careful study of the Providence Tax Lists for 1828, asserted that in this year there were 1,384 adult males taxed. Of this number 903 were freeholders and 481 were non-freeholders. The latter were taxed on personal property in the value of $690,000 and paid an aggregate tax of $2,139. *Microcosm,* April 7, 1829. The leading student of Providence's financial history, examining the years 1790–1832, states that "at no time in this early period was there more than two-thirds, and most of the time a little over one-half of the town's income raised by a tax upon real estate." Stokes, pp. 135–36.

tion was quite validly raised that such a provision would ensure the rejection of the proposed charter by the Assembly. Once reconsidered, the suffrage amendment was deleted by general consent.

According to Benjamin Hallett, who figured prominently in this proceeding, reconsideration was agreed to by non-freeholders under the express understanding that the Providence representatives should be instructed to request that the Assembly insert a local suffrage clause in the charter when it came before that body for approval. Some of the freemen reneged, for a formal motion to this effect made at a subsequent town meeting failed to pass.[14]

During the restless year of 1829, demonstrations were also held in Bristol and Warren. Memorials drafted by committees in these expanding towns set forth similar though more limited grievances and demands than those expressed in Providence. Basically they urged not universal, "indiscriminate" suffrage and enfranchisement of "the rabble," but rather the granting of suffrage to those who paid taxes of any sort or to those who performed militia duty. "We are not advocates of universal indiscriminate rules of suffrage," contended the Warren reformers, we only ask you "to allow those who share the burden of government to share likewise in the election of its officers." [15] The modest requests embodied in these 1829 petitions suggest that these early suffrage agitators were respectable citizens possessed of a moderate amount of personal property. Restraint rather than radicalism characterized their appeal.

The 1829 suffrage movement had repercussions in places as far distant as Virginia where a final and successful onslaught was being launched against that state's freehold law. The *Richmond Enquirer* alluded to suffrage reform meetings in Rhode Island as an example of the course that Virginian reformers should pursue.[16] Rhode Island's General Assembly was neither moved

---

[14] *Microcosm*, April 17 and 24, May 1, 1829.

[15] Free Suffrage Petitions, Petitions Not Granted, May, 1829. These are printed in the *Microcosm*, April 17, 1829 (Bristol) and April 24, 1829 (Warren).

[16] *Richmond Enquirer*, February 14, 1829, cited in Williamson, p. 225.

nor impressed by the suffragists' demands. The four memorials presented to that insensitive body in May 1829 were accorded not merely a cool but a hostile reception — representative Elisha Potter, staunch defender of the agrarian interests, even objected to their being read and his position was honored.

Reactionary Benjamin Hazard, a Newport merchant and manufacturer who nonetheless subscribed to the agrarian myth, recommended the creation of a committee to consider the memorials and "put the subject at rest." Five representatives were selected with Hazard as chairman. Their report — over the signature of Hazard and exclusively the product of his pen — was presented to the legislature at its June session.[17] The document was rambling and discursive, sprinkled with sophistry and non-sequiturs, and saturated with a fear of change. For his authorship of this panegyric to the past, what has been said of archconservatives in general might be observed of former Federalist Benjamin Hazard: "His pigmy hope that life would some day become somewhat better, punily shivered by the side of his gigantic conviction that it might be infinitely worse."[18]

Hazard's *Report* began with the discouraging assertion that the committee found "nothing in those memorials, either of facts or reasoning, which requires the attention of the house." Therefore, "without troubling the house with any further mention of these memorials, the committee recommend that the memorialists have leave to withdraw them." Following this defiant introduction was a 14,000 word lecture on sound, honest, and stable government and the safeguards required for such a government

---

The observations of the Virginia paper show that even minor demonstrations held prior to the Pawtucket rally of March 14 attracted notice outside the state.

[17] *Microcosm,* May 15, 1829; Journal of the House (1829–31), May and June sessions, 1829. The Assembly did allow the reading of written instructions to the representatives from Glocester, Burrillville, and North Kingstown in opposition to free suffrage.

[18] Morley's *Voltaire,* quoted in Dixon Ryan Fox, *The Decline of the Aristocracy in the Politics of New York, 1801–1840* (New York, 1919), p. 243. For a biographical sketch of Hazard see Caroline E. Robinson, *The Hazard Family of Rhode Island, 1635–1894* (Boston, 1895), pp. 83–86.

to endure. Foremost among these safeguards, of course, was the freehold — the shield against rule by floating "emigrants" from other states and foreign nations and by those who through their "improvidence, extravagance, or vices . . . are . . . unfit to be intrusted with any control over the property rights of others." Equally incredible was Hazard's further assertion that the Assembly was morally powerless to alter the suffrage.[19]

The majority of legislators agreed with this preservative pronouncement and the House disdainfully rejected the demands of the reformers. On the motion of Wilkins Updike, the protestors were allowed to withdraw their petitions, a gracious gesture which prompted a contemporary journalist to lament — "Thus died without a struggle, a subject which has created so much excitement in our state." [20]

The attitude of the Assembly, which completely controlled the suffrage — despite Hazard's rationalizations to the contrary — stemmed from the overriding influence, especially in the lower house, exerted by representatives of the agrarian towns. By the end of the third decade of the nineteenth century these rural lawmakers and their rustic constituents had come to regard as inviolate the freehold qualification upon which the franchise was based. For them, industrialization and urbanization had become clear and present dangers. Landless capitalists, shopkeepers, artisans, mechanics, and factory workers in the mill villages were a source of political power that must not be unleashed. The farmers' fears of this "rootless" class, this anonymous democracy divorced from the soil, were not partisan and were only accidentally sectional. Essentially, political and economic preservation of what they termed the "agricultural interest" was at stake.[21]

The animus against suffrage extension, strongest in static and

---

[19] Benjamin Hazard, *Report on the Subject of an Extension of Suffrage to the General Assembly of Rhode Island* (Providence, 1829). This tract is printed in *Burke's Report,* pp. 377–401.

[20] *Manufacturers' and Farmers' Journal,* June 29, 1829; Frieze, pp. 17–18. The proposed Newport suffrage convention never assembled.

[21] See for example [John R. Waterman?], A Farmer to the Farmers and Landholders of Rhode Island, March, 1828, Warwick Papers, Box 10, RIHS, which defended the freehold by claiming that those who

declining towns of the south and west, drew influential allies
from expanding or urban areas as well. Growing Warwick split
on the issue with support for extension centered in the mill villages of the Pawtuxet Valley and opposition based in the rural
easterly sector; in Providence and Newport opposition to enlargement of the franchise was prevalent among the old mercantile elite. This entrenched group realized that suffrage reform
would tend to weaken their dominance in local political affairs.

Many of the urban upper-class establishment had ideological
roots in the Federalist Party. They derived religious and philosophical justification for their political conservatism from such
local apologists as the Reverend Francis Wayland, a Baptist intellectual who had assumed the presidency of Brown University
in 1827. This prolific professor of moral theology issued a host of
sermons, pamphlets, and book-length studies emphasizing the
natural depravity of man, defending the sanctity of private property, exalting stability, and reprobating the tyranny of the
majority.

Wayland's philosophical utterances were to many a Rhode
Island patrician what Hazard's politically-oriented diatribes were
to the yeoman farmer. Each served to steel the freeholder, urban
or rural, against the "dangerous tendencies" of "levelling democracy." Remnants of the urban Federalist aristocracy and the
old Jeffersonian yeomanry joined in an incongruous alliance to
prevent the enfranchisement of the new breed of men which
the changing economy of early nineteenth-century Rhode Island
had spawned.[22]

---

owned the country ought to govern it, and warned the yeoman that the
state was filling up with commercial towns, banks, and chartered companies run by those "varient in political interests" from the farmer. Also
of interest is the anonymous pamphlet *Address to the Freemen of Rhode
Island on the Annual Election of State Officers . . . 1828* (n.p.), pp.
4–6, RIHS.

[22] Francis Wayland and H. L. Wayland, *Memoir of Life and Labors
of Francis Wayland* (New York, 1867). Wayland's role in the development of higher education has been treated, but there is need for a study
of his political and economic thought. Of Wayland's early works those
most revelatory of his political conservatism are: *The Duties of An
American Citizen* (Boston, 1825); *Occasional Discourses* (Boston, 1833);

III

Most arguments against liberalization of the state's ancient suffrage law espoused the familiar — and by 1829 — outdated
"stake in society" theory. Spokesmen for the farming interest
understandably asserted that the franchise should be restricted to
owners of the soil. They expressed fears of landless urban dwellers and claimed — as did *young* Jefferson — that "the mobs of
great cities add just so much to the support of pure government,
as sores do to the strength of the human body." [23]

But the eclectic Jefferson these farmers cited in support of their
position had wisely altered his views. By 1816, the aging sage
of Monticello had condemned the fact that in his own Virginia
"one half of our brethren who fight and pay taxes, are excluded,
like Helots, from the rights of representation, as if society were
instituted for the soil, and not for the men inhabiting it." [24]

Latter-day Rhode Island agrarians unfortunately did not display such adaptability; the early Jefferson conveniently remained
their infallible guide. By their intransigence in the face of a
changing society, they perverted the Jeffersonian ideal of a freeholders' republic so that it became a shield of aristocracy rather
than a sword of democracy. Theirs were no longer the utterances
of Jefferson, but rather the desperate exhortations of such defenders of status quo as Chancellor James Kent and Chief Justice
Ambrose Spencer of New York, and Virginia's inflexible John
Randolph and Benjamin Watkins Leigh.[25]

The Affairs of Rhode Island (Providence, 1842); and *The Duty of Obedience to the Civil Magistrate* (Boston, 1847). Useful material is also
contained in "Pamphlet Publications of Francis Wayland" and Wayland
Mss., John Hay Library, Brown University. From the latter see Wayland
to his uncle, August 22, 1842, for his political pessimism and his reaction to the Dorr Rebellion.

[23] Dumas Malone, *Jefferson the Virginian* (Boston, 1948), p. 238,
384. This work is volume one of Malone's multivolume biography *Jefferson and His Time*.

[24] Jefferson to DuPont de Nemours, April 24, 1816, Charles M. Wiltse,
The Jeffersonian Tradition in American Democracy (New York, 1960),
p. 104.

[25] For the attitudes and arguments of New York conservatives see

During the twenties Rhode Island's agriculturalists reacted fearfully to the threat of suffrage reform with the manufacturer and his workers generally on the side of extension as the battle lines between Arcadia and Enterprise were drawn. A removal of the freehold, one rustic claimed in 1824, contained "within itself a necessary and dangerous tendency to aristocracy," because the rich could bring their adherents to the polls, the merchant his sailors, and the manufacturer his workingmen. This apprehension was not unfounded for the secret ballot was an election device unknown in Rhode Island. The present suffrage law, this farmer continued, placed "small but independent landowners, the middling interest of the community, between the very rich and the very poor, guarding the one against the influence of the other. Once break down this barrier and allow the power of wealth to be exercised on the dependence of poverty, and instead of a government of agriculturalists you will have a government of capitalists. It may be well for the hardy yeomanry of the state to pause before they surrender to four or five individuals an influence which they and their fathers have enjoyed." [26]

Fox, pp. 229–70 and Marvin Myers, *The Jacksonian Persuasion: Politics and Belief* (Stanford, California, 1960), pp. 234–53. On Virginia see Peterson, *State Constitutional Conventions,* pp. 279–81, 337, 395. The sentiments of Rhode Island's defenders of the status quo on suffrage were remarkably similar to those of their more illustrious counterparts in New York and Virginia. Enlightening on the attitudes of the Southern agrarians during the decade of the 1820s is Norman K. Risjord, *The Old Republicans: Southern Conservatism in the Age of Jefferson* (New York, 1965), pp. 256–281.

[26] Letter from "A Native of Rhode Island," *Providence Patriot,* September 25, 1824. A recent researcher has suggested an economic motive for the deepening estrangement between the rural and urban sectors during the 1820s. Until the beginning of that decade Providence merchants had as one of their prime concerns the exportation of agricultural produce grown by local farmers. By 1820 the need for flour (not a Rhode Island commodity) by Latin America caused merchants to "restructure their trade." In addition, merchants began to concentrate more on the exportation of the products of Rhode Island's expanding industries. "As a result, the old trading alliance between the merchant and farmer was brought to a close," and the two groups moved further apart. James L. Marsis, "Political and Economic Change in Rhode Island as Reflected in the Population Growth of Washington County, 1790–1820," (unpub-

Again, these were sentiments once expressed by Jefferson. As a young statesman he had predicted that intense industrialization would endanger the republican experiment because it would produce a situation wherein the mass of workers were dependent upon the will of the privileged few for their sustenance.[27] The Virginian later discarded these myopic apprehensions; the isolated and deprived Rhode Island farmer still clung to them tenaciously.

The 1829 suffrage excitement, the first concerted movement against the freehold — quite naturally evoked strong reaction from most freemen, especially those with bucolic attachments. Hazard's *Report* was one example, but a tract much more revealing of rural attitudes on political and constitutional questions is an anonymous pamphlet, *Address to the Freemen of the Agricultural and Manufacturing Interests of Rhode Island* (1829), printed at the office of the *Republican Herald,* a Providence Democratic newspaper, which was rabidly pro-Jackson. A copy of the *Address* is among the Elisha Potter papers (RIHS) and this — coupled with the style and sentiment — indicates that Potter may have been its author.[28]

The immediate occasion for the production of this tract was

---

lished doctoral research paper, New York University, 1970), pp. 10–15; and "Agrarian Politics in Rhode Island 1800–1860," *Rhode Island History,* XXXIV (Feb., 1975), 13–21.

[27] Adrienne Koch, *Jefferson and Madison: The Great Collaboration* (New York, 1950), pp. 131–34.

[28] Potter at this time remarked to an associate that "if I had served my God with half the zeal that I have [served] the Landed Interests of this State, I should now almost be prepared to go to Heaven in the Flesh." Potter to John R. Waterman, April 7, 1828, Warwick Mss., Box 10, RIHS. The person who cataloged the copy in RIHS surmises that the author was Job Durfee. Another interesting pamphlet of 1829 vintage is Wilkins Updike's *Hints to the Farmers of Rhode Island* — also a *Republican Herald* imprint — intended to create antagonism between the farmers and the state legislature by criticizing the alleged extravagance of the Assembly. Updike also warned that suffrage extension would prostrate landholders because even a restricted extension would give votes to 12,000 new men, twice the number of existing freemen. Such an enlargement of the franchise would give manufacturers, bankers, merchants, and large capitalists control of the state which they would use to tax the land.

to secure the defeat of Republican Congressmen Tristam Burges
and Dutee Pearce in the August election of 1829 because they
allegedly had "no common feeling . . . with the landholders,"
the former being a "mere rhetorician" and the latter a "shuffling
advocate of the manufacturing interest." Of far greater import
than the issues of this specific election was the enlightening —
if somewhat exaggerated — analysis of recent Rhode Island political and constitutional development as perceived by the em-
bittered and embattled farmer who penned this pamphlet.[29]

The twenty-four page *Address* began with the premise that
"there has been adopted, by certain individuals, a system for the
eventual destruction of the landed interest of this State." This
conspiracy reached the virulent stage with the attempt to establish a constitution in the early 1820s. According to the anonymous pamphleteer, "The projectors of this measure saw that our
country towns were each, under the existing form of government, entitled to two representatives, and some of them to more;
and they felt that so long as this was the case, it would be impossible for the manufacturing and monied interests of the State to
obtain a complete ascendancy in our General Assembly."

These conspirators, so this unbalanced survey reads, were "not
satisfied with the political advantages which great wealth always
gives to its possessors," nor "with having the press, which is the
medium through which all political information and deception
pass to the farmers, immediately within their control, and acting
in subserviency to their purposes." Neither were they "satisfied
with their superior advantages, in being able at any moment to
concentrate and form their plans." They would only be satisfied,
contended this rural polemicist, when "the number of their immediate representatives were such as to give them a majority, on
all questions, over those of the landholders."

For this end, goes the story, the manufacturing interests sought

---

[29] Potter was one of six candidates in this congressional contest. Burges
and Pearce won; Potter finished a dismal fifth. *Rhode Island Manual,*
1937–38, p. 203. *Address to the Freemen of the Agricultural and Manufacturing Interests of Rhode Island* (Providence, 1829), pp. 5, 24, hereafter cited *Address of 1829.*

a constitution, but fortunately the General Assembly "wisely provided" that the towns should send a number of delegates to the convention equal to their representation in the House. Because of such provident foresight "the scheme of stripping the landed interest of all political power, was . . . partially defeated, and was finally completely overthrown when the constitution proposed was submitted to the people." [30]

After this slightly jaundiced account of the convention of 1824, the campaign to submerge the "landed interest" was traced by the *Address* through the remainder of the decade. The story told of such hostile maneuvers as the successful exclusion of this faction from the Congress of the United States by the selection of representatives Burges and Pearce and senators Asher Robbins and Nehemiah Knight,[31] and the attempt to eliminate agrarian legislators from the state senate, especially those such as John R. Waterman who was instrumental in the passage of the bank tax.[32]

The *Address* then alluded to a contemporary plot potentially more pernicious than those that had gone before — a "bold measure" that would "effectually put down the rebellious landed interest, and leave it nothing further to hope for." This measure was "the introduction to the polls of 12,000 non-freeholders — men without any qualification other than that of doing military duty, or paying a trifling town tax, and, with these 12,000 non-freeholders, to vote down and annihilate the political power of the landed interest in this State."

The "ultimate object" of this nefarious scheme, according to the *Address,* "was to introduce an entire new order of things; to place the political power of this State in the hands of the aristocracy of wealth; to give a single manufacturer . . . the power of putting into the ballot-boxes from 20 to 300 votes besides his own." [33]

---

[30] *Address of 1829,* pp. 1–5.

[31] In 1823 Knight edged Potter by one vote (40–39); in 1825 Robbins beat him by a margin of 43–36. *Rhode Island Manual,* 1937–38, p. 178.

[32] *Address of 1829,* pp. 5–7.

[33] *Ibid.,* pp. 7–8. The possibility of a manufacturer influencing the

This revealing pamphlet must have been published in July of that pivotal year 1829, on the eve of the congressional election and on the heels of the Assembly's rejection of suffrage petitions, for it speaks of the "special interposition of Divine Providence" (presumably in the form of Benjamin Hazard) which snatched the farmer from the "anticipated dominion" of his enemies.

The relatvely restrained and respectable "free suffrage" movement of early 1829 was viewed from the farm in a much different light. The *Address's* description of the suffrage campaign is as follows:

> The project was, indeed, urged forward previous to the April town-meeting, with a spirit bordering on fanaticism. Meetings were held in most of the manufacturing districts, some of them claiming to consist of from a thousand to fifteen hundred persons. Memorials were adopted, and committees appointed in every part of the State to procure subscribers. Sums of money were to be advanced for a nameless purpose, and delegates were to be appointed to meet at Newport, at the June session of the General Assembly, for the purpose of controlling or overawing the deliberations of your Legislature. Such was the note of preparation; and to those who are acquainted with the effect which incessant clamor, and continued appeals to the fears, the feelings, and the corruptions of the human heart, produce upon it, it was of fearful import. It left them every thing to apprehend, and little to hope for.[34]

Although the eruption was quelled, the hopes and prospects of those "political adventurers" who precipitated the crisis still lived and would be revived. The "cabal" responsible for the suffrage disturbances was headed by the congressional delegation and "the Lilliputian, renegade Editors who control the *American,* the *Microcosm* and the [*Manufacturers' and Farmers'*] *Journal.*"[35]

The principal congressional villains were Burges, a National Republican soon to become a leading Whig, and Pearce, who

---

vote of his employees or others financially dependent upon him was great because of the absence of a secret ballot. See Benjamin Knight, *History of the Sprague Families of Rhode Island* (Santa Cruz, Calif., 1881), p. 15, regarding the practices of banker-industrialist William Sprague.

[34] *Address of 1829,* p. 9.

[35] *Ibid.,* pp. 8–9, 15–16, 22–24.

had urged suffrage extension in his 1819 memorial and in the 1824 convention. The gentlemen of the press so disparagingly alluded to were presumably John Miller of the *Manufacturers' and Farmers' Journal* and Francis Y. Carlile and Benjamin F. Hallett, who produced both the *Rhode Island American* and the *Microcosm*.[36] Pearce and Hallett were destined to play prominent roles in the constitutional controversy of the 1840s, but 1829 was not their year to achieve reform. By the end of summer things had returned to normal. Farmers, large and small, and the old aristocracy had weathered the initial storm. The congressional elections in 1829 brought victory to National Republican Congressmen Burges and Pearce primarily because of their support for a protective tariff, but the governorship continued to be held by Democratic Republican James Fenner, a substantial Providence landholder who supported the agrarian interest and strongly opposed the extension of suffrage.[37]

Future Democratic Governor John Brown Francis of Warwick — member of the gentry and violent foe of electoral reform — wrote one of his frequent letters to fellow-agrarian Elisha Potter in a spirit of guarded optimism. "The old party lines are now entirely demolished," he observed. "But who is to rule the roost? Will the manufacturers take the power entirely into their hands and give us free suffrage — or are we to expect a more elevated state of politics — the latter . . . I trust will happen." [38] The lord of "Spring Green" was not disappointed; "free suffrage" for a time ceased to vex those who "ruled the roost." [39]

---

[36] Staples, *Annals of Providence*, pp. 545–46, 550–52.

[37] Sweet, pp. 158–179.

[38] John Brown Francis to Elisha R. Potter, Sr., August 28, 1829, Potter Collection.

[39] Worthy of extensive citation for the light it sheds on the free suffrage agitation of 1829 is the following letter from Francis to Potter: "I am anxious to learn how your pulse beats on this free suffrage question, and what policy you think best in regard to it. For your friends in Providence (and you have a few very warm and powerful friends there) trust to your management in stopping the floodgate. Is it not the only safe way to put the project down in the first instance by an overwhelming vote? . . . and to secure such a vote those who have anything at stake should be extremely critical as to who represents them in the next Assem-

bly. We have already taken that precaution in this town [Warwick] having held a caucus before which the old deputies pledged themselves in favor of the freehold system. . . . The free suffrage party in this town form an extremely small party. They are confined to the factory meridian and do not include the Rhodes's or Sprague. If all the towns will sift their Reps. as we have ours, we are in no danger. Altho the intention is avowed by these people of subscribing a fund for carrying on this war against the landed interest, for stripped of all its disguises it is nothing more or less than this. . . . The idea has presented itself to me that our freehold system might be strengthened and no great mischief done by giving the right of suffrage to *all* the sons of a freeholder. . . . The class of men admitted might perhaps, as a general rule, be presumed to be on the side of their sires, who, as a matter of course, would be attached to the freehold qualification. This system would embrace the great mass of the country population, but would continue to operate as our present system does, to the exclusion of a certain portion of our factory village and city population. . . . Pass this suffrage bill and the power of the landed interest in this State is utterly and irretrievably annihilated! ! ! ! A combination between a few manufacturers in the County of Prov. and of this County [Kent], would effect any purpose. . . . The manufacturers in the County of Prov. (generally) either secretly, or openly are in favor of free suffrage. . . . In fact a free suffrage man once declared to me that with free suffrage they (the manufacturers) could pull the strings in every town in the State!!!!!!!" Francis to Elisha R. Potter, Sr., April 7, 1829, John Brown Francis Collection, RIHS.

CHAPTER TEN

Workingmen, Constitutionalists and the Convention of 1834

I

The Jackson-Clay presidential campaign of 1832 and the protracted but indecisive gubernatorial struggle of that year between Lemuel Arnold (National Republican), James Fenner (Democrat), and William Sprague (Antimason) resuscitated the enfeebled suffrage cause, to the dismay of those who thought it safely buried. The freemen's participation in this election showed an increase over the more colorful 1828 contest in both absolute and relative terms.[1] We may safely assume that the non-freeholders also experienced a heightened sense of interest, but their concern served mainly to make their frustration more acute and their inferior status more intolerable.

An 1832 list of Providence freemen, one of the few documents of its kind that have survived, enumerates 1,216 eligible voters. In view of the approximately 3,823 white adult males the town

---

[1] McCormick, "New Perspectives," p. 292; *Rhode Island Manual*, 1965–66, pp. 213–14. There were five gubernatorial elections in 1832, none of which resulted in a decision because of the majority vote requirement for election.

possessed at the time of the 1830 census, a rough projection indicates that sixty-eight percent were disfranchised by the prevailing suffrage requirements at the time of the 1832 campaign.[2]

Shortly after Jackson had won re-election, therefore, suffrage excitement began anew, with Providence — quite naturally — its center. As early as January 1833, an anonymous newsletter entitled the "Voice of the People" was being published and quietly circulated in that community "to promote a constitution and free suffrage." [3]

The first overt manifestation of non-freeholder discontent, however, came on April 1, the date designated for the militia's spring drill. It has been estimated by contemporaries that approximately three-quarters of the state's militiamen were landless and therefore voteless in 1833. To protest this condition Rhode Island's second-class citizen-soldiers donned "fantastical" costumes for their April Fool's Day maneuvers. This demonstration was a catalyst for further expressions of discontent and before the month was through, militiamen were meeting at the Old Town House on College Hill to devise means of elevating their political status.[4]

The first important gathering of these artisans, shopkeepers, mechanics, and machinists, who doubled as militiamen and fire-

---

[2] List of Freemen . . . (Providence, 1832). This rare pamphlet is document #8 in a bound volume labeled "Providence City Charters, Etc." RIHS. Figures on the free white adult males were derived from National Archives, Record Group 29, Records of the Bureau of the Census; Fifth Census (1830), Population Schedules, Rhode Island, Vol. II, sheets 58 and 118 (microcopy #19, roll #168). In 1832 Providence was incorporated as a city and control over the qualifications and admission of freemen passed to the newly created Board of Aldermen and the Common Council. See *The Charter and Ordinances of the City of Providence; With the Acts of the General Assembly Relating to the City* (Providence, 1845), especially pp. 8–12.

[3] J. W. Cory to William I. Tillinghast January 29, 1833 in "Papers of William I. Tillinghast, letters from distinguished men, etc., 1833," D. Mss., XVII, #38. This volume contains numerous important documents relating to the hitherto unnoticed suffrage movement of 1833; it is hereafter cited Tillinghast Papers.

[4] Tillinghast Papers, #8 (Providence Suffrage Committee to Nehemiah Knight), #25, #28, #31.

fighters, occurred on the evening of April 19. This assemblage was treated to a long and inspiring lecture by "working-class rebel" Seth Luther, a widely-traveled Rhode Island native, who had been instrumental in organizing the recently created (1832) New England Association of Farmers and Mechanics.[5]

Luther's initial speech was repeated before another Town House gathering on April 26, and was eventually printed as *An Address on the Right of Free Suffrage*. This production was tainted by sarcasm, bombast, ridicule, and irreverence, but its attack on Rhode Island's freehold was surprisingly learned and basically accurate. Luther, as he loved to remind his audiences, was "merely a poor journeyman carpenter," but he was self-educated and very widely read. His address was a blast against the "small potato aristocrats" (Lords of the Soil?) who were responsible for the perpetuation of a freehold system that was "contrary to the Declaration of Independence, the Constitution of the United States, the Bill of Rights of the State of Rhode Island, and the dictates of common sense."

Luther's fulminations against the suffrage statute reinforced those criticisms that had been voiced in 1829, but his proposed method of securing relief was more drastic. To exert pressure on the legislature, he recommended that non-freemen refuse to pay taxes and decline to perform military duty. "No law . . . assessing a tax on non-voters, can with justice be collected; for they have never given their assent to the tax, directly or indirectly, by themselves or their representatives," he argued. "Resist tyranny," Luther exhorted, "if need be, sword in hand."

Although he recommended "passive resistance" at the outset, the speaker's use of the aphorism "peaceably if we can, forcibly

---

[5] Brennan, pp. 53–55; Louis Hartz, "Seth Luther, Working Class Rebel," *New England Quarterly*, XIII (Sept. 1940), 401–18; Marvin E. Gettleman, *The Dorr Rebellion: A Study in American Radicalism*, 1833–1849 (New York, 1973), pp. 18–22; and Carl Gersuny, "Seth Luther — The Road from Chepachet," *Rhode Island History*, XXXIII (May, 1974), 47–55. According to Gettleman, "Luther's philosophy was a radical Jeffersonian communitarianism, which accepted economic inequalities in society but insisted upon political equality, social civility and mutual respect," p. 19.

if we must," no doubt shook the complacency of the landed establishment. So also did Luther's assertion, reminiscent of George Burrill and James Knowles and anticipatory of Thomas Dorr, that the "people" possess "a right to assemble in primary meetings, and appoint Delegates to a Convention" that has "a right to form a Constitution, and submit it" for ratification and adoption as "the law of the land." [6] This bold course of by-passing the General Assembly was the one eventually pursued, but in 1833 hope for less impetuous change still existed and more moderate alternatives temporarily prevailed.

The Providence gathering to which Luther appealed on April 19, when he first delivered his *Address,* was designated the "meeting of the citizens of Rhode Island, favorable to the adoption of the Massachusetts mode of suffrage." This *ad hoc* association comprised mainly of "workingmen," appointed a committee that evening to correspond with "friends in different parts of the State, for the purpose of fixing a time and place, for holding a State [Suffrage] Convention." This committee, headed by William I. Tillinghast, a Providence barber, was composed of three freemen and three non-freemen. The other members, who proudly listed their occupations on all reports and correspondence, were "Lawrence Richards, blacksmith; William Mitchell, shoemaker; Seth Luther, housewright; William Miller, currier; and David Brown, watch and clock maker."

This energetic committee reported at a subsequent meeting on May 10 "that the public mind has not yet been sufficiently awakened to call a Convention." At this same gathering they announced that arrangements had been made for the printing of 1,000 copies of Luther's speech and its deliverance at Warren on May 14. Further, the group informed their cohorts that they had corresponded with former Congressman Francis Baylies of nearby Taunton regarding the desirability of the Massachusetts mode of suffrage, *viz.,* that system which conferred the franchise

---

[6] Seth Luther, *An Address on the Right of Free Suffrage* (Providence, 1833), especially pp. 3–5, 9, 21–24. The *Address* was repeated in Warren in mid-May 1833. *Ibid.,* p. vi.

upon those citizens with one year's residency in the state if they paid any kind of tax.[7]

Baylies was contacted because of his familiarity with the Rhode Island situation and because of his stand for the extension of suffrage in the Massachusetts Convention of 1820–21. His observations were most encouraging to the reformers. Rhode Island's freehold qualification, he wrote, "might have been expedient once — the population being entirely agricultural . . . but circumstances have changed, society has assumed a new aspect, other interests have sprung into life and activity which would seem to render it expedient that other classes besides agriculturalists should have some voice in the election of their rulers and some influence on legislation." [8]

The views of another Massachusetts man of standing were solicited by Tillinghast and his colleagues at the same time they wrote to Baylies. This statesman was John Quincy Adams. The former president was asked if the Massachusetts suffrage law was operating effectively. On May 10, the date of Tillinghast's report, Adams replied curtly that he knew of no dissatisfaction with the system. He added that he was "not competent to give an opinion deserving to be considered of any authority" on the question of "whether it would be expedient for the People of Rhode Island to adopt it." [9] Tillinghast later observed that Mr. Adams's letter "was exceedingly *civil*, but . . . cold as an icicle." [10]

During the course of 1833, Tillinghast's correspondence committee contacted several other notables to ascertain their views on the suffrage issue. Those who were recipients of inquiries included Andrew Jackson's protégé, Martin Van Buren of New York; Rhode Island's United States Senator, Nehemiah Knight;

---

[7] The report of May 10 is in Tillinghast Papers, #51. It was printed as an appendix to Luther's *Address*.

[8] Francis Baylies to William I. Tillinghast, *et al.*, April 29, 1833, Tillinghast Papers, #12, #13.

[9] John Quincy Adams to William I. Tillinghast, *et al.*, May 10, 1833, Tillinghast Papers, #10.

[10] Draft of an Address by Tillinghast [mid-1834], Tillinghast Papers, #45.

Richard Rush of Pennsylvania, a skillful diplomat and former United States attorney-general; James DeWolf, prominent Bristol politician; James L. Hodges, a one-time champion of suffrage extension in the Massachusetts constitutional convention; Whig chieftain Daniel Webster; and Rhode Island Democratic potentate John Brown Francis, a grandson of Providence merchant John Brown, and the owner of seven hundred acres of farmland at Spring Green in the eastern portion of the town of Warwick.[11]

The most enthusiastic response came from Rush, who vigorously espoused "universal suffrage" including the extension of the franchise to naturalized foreigners. Van Buren acknowledged that his earlier preference for a personal property qualification (which he had expressed in the New York convention of 1821) had been abandoned. "It has given me the highest gratification to be convinced that my fears [of universal suffrage] were without adequate justification," the "Little Magician" announced.

Also on the side of the suffragists were James L. Hodges, who expressed firm support for the Massachusetts mode, and James DeWolf who was more cautious in his reply. The latter, a member of the famous merchant family of Bristol, was approached because he had participated in the first move for suffrage extension in 1811 while a Democratic Republican representative. DeWolf said he was in favor of a constitutional convention, and he supported a liberalization of the franchise. He felt, however, that the "stake in government" principle required that some property qualifications for voting be retained.[12] National Republican

---

[11] *Ibid.* Copies of the committee's letters and the replies thereto are preserved in the Tillinghast Papers. They have recently been edited by Marvin E. Gettleman and Noel P. Conlon, "Responses to the Rhode Island Workingmen's Reform Agitation of 1833," *Rhode Island History,* XXVIII (August, 1969), 75–94. Biographical sketches of most of Tillinghast's addressees can be found in the *Dictionary of American Biography* or *The Biographical Directory of the American Congress.* On Governor Francis consult [Abby Isabel Bulkley], *The Chad Brown Memorial* (Brooklyn, 1888), pp. 82–83.

[12] Richard Rush to Tillinghast, Dec. 23, 1833; Martin Van Buren to Tillinghast, July 9, 1833; James R. Hodges to Tillinghast, Dec. 25,

Senator Nehemiah Knight, on the other hand, informed the committee that "to abolish the real estate qualification of a freeman would not at this time be judicious, were it practical, nor would it conduce to the interest and welfare of the State." [13] Political conservatives Daniel Webster and John Brown Francis, Rhode Island's Democratic governor, did not even honor the reformers with a reply.[14]

The suffragists of 1833 became increasingly active as the year progressed. At their June 17 meeting they approved a declaration of rights and passed a resolution which, in final form, urged militiamen who were non-freeholders to appear for regimental training in September dressed in a "fantastical manner" — a repeat of their April Fool's Day performance.[15]

At this June gathering and at those that followed during the summer of 1833, barber William Tillinghast gave folksy, anecdotal, yet impressive addresses to encourage his associates. His remarks at these meetings cast light upon the nature of the movement, its supporters, and its opponents. Tillinghast's utterances make it clear that the agitation stemmed mainly from the ranks of the disfranchised militia and firemen and that the opposition came primarily from the "country." On one occasion he blasted "Sir" John Whipple and Elisha Potter, "the Duke of Kingston," for their statements against free suffrage in the May 1833 session of the General Assembly. The Duke, grumbled Tillinghast, has "about 100 freemen (so called) under his influence by means of mortgages," and yet talks about the danger of the manufacturer controlling votes.[16]

1833; James DeWolf to Tillinghast, Dec. 11, 1833, Tillinghast Papers, #1–7.

[13] Nehemiah Knight to Tillinghast, Sept. 2, 1833, Tillinghast Papers, #8, #9.

[14] Draft of an Address by Tillinghast [mid-1834], Tillinghast Papers, #45.

[15] Tillinghast Papers, #18, #25, #28, #43.

[16] William Tillinghast, Free Suffrage Address [1833], D. Mss., VI. Tillinghast was not far from the mark. The Potter Collection contains numerous lists of "made" voters. See also the anonymous pamphlet *What a Ploughman Said* (Kingston, 1829), pp. 4–5, for Potter's notorious elec-

Another striking fact about the 1833 movement was its non-partisan character. Although those few freemen associated with the cause were drawn from the ranks of the three major parties, the political organizations themselves took a stance that fluctuated between indifference and hostility. Tillinghast lamented that the National Republican, the Antimason and the Democratic parties "have all forfeited their claim to Republicanism (so far as they are opposed to F. Suffrage)." I propose, said Tillinghast, "that we call our party '*Militia Republicans.*' This would signify no more nor less than '*Citizen Soldiers,*' and it implies," warned the disgruntled barber, "not only that the *duty* of training and the *privilege* of voting are of right inseparable, but also that we have the physical power to make them so." [17]

Of the three established parties in 1833, the one which did the most to discredit and discourage free suffrage was the rural-based and agrarian-oriented Democratic organization.[18] Its leaders, Governor John Brown Francis, Elisha Potter, Sr., Wilkins Updike, and Jeffrey Hazzard of Exeter, were inveterate opponents of extension. As Tillinghast observed: "the Jackson Party which is truly Democratic in other states do not know what a set of

---

tioneering tactics. This work, at the RIHS, is ascribed by its cataloger to Tristam Burges.

[17] William Tillinghast, Free Suffrage Address [1833], D. Mss., VI. On the non-partisan nature of the movement see also Nehemiah Knight to Tillinghast *et al.,* Sept. 2, 1833, Tillinghast Papers, #9.

[18] The *Democratic Review* in 1839 made an observation on the source of party allegiance which coincided with the Rhode Island situation when it contended that it was on the rural elements "that the main reliance of our party has always rested"; that in the towns and cities not only the mercantile and professional classes, but a "large proportion" of the laboring classes were Whig from the time of Jackson's first election. *Democratic Review,* VI (Dec. 1839), 500–02. For the persistence of early Jeffersonian agrarianism within the party of Jackson see Merrill D. Peterson, *The Jeffersonian Image in the American Mind* (New York, 1960), pp. 69–111. On the rural base of the Rhode Island Jackson party see Sweet, *passim;* and Robert M. Colasanto, "All the King's Men: The Jackson Party in Rhode Island, 1828–1838" (unpublished honors essay, Rhode Island College, 1971), a very useful and competent study which provides a detailed listing of all Jackson and anti-Jackson members of the Assembly elected during this era.

landed aristocrats their brethren in R. I. are;" but, he added,
"I'm determined to expose them." [19]

Rhode Island's illiberal country Democrats evidently failed
to espouse the myth accepted by some later historians that the
urban workingmen marched en masse under the banner of Jackson. The Democratic farmers of Rhode Island no doubt realized
that a sizeable proportion of newly enfranchised artisans, shopkeepers, mechanics and other workingmen would harbor anti-
administration views, especially on the tariff question. This rural
Democracy feared also, in the absence of a secret ballot, that the
workingmen's vote could be controlled by anti-Jackson urban industrialists.[20] An anonymous 1835 election pamphlet "To the
Farmers of Rhode Island" reflects this rural Democratic apprehension. Free suffrage would strengthen the "city party" — a
Whig faction "not only in favor of increasing the expenditures
of the State, by every means in their power," but one that is con-
stantly "endeavoring to throw the whole burden of taxes upon
the land" by repealing the tax on banks. Recalling the tribula-
tions of the Confederation era, the pro-Francis pamphleteer admonished his readers that "when the landholders look back and
consider the hardships they were obliged to undergo, while the
system of land taxes was in operation, and the oppressions which
many of the country towns were subjected to, by means of a disproportionate valuation, it will make them careful how they run
the risk of getting into the same difficulties again." [21] Thus, the

---

[19] Draft of an Address by Tillinghast [mid-1834], Tillinghast Papers,
#45.

[20] Schlesinger, especially pp. 132–43, 251–305 is the classic exposition
of the "workingmen's" thesis. However, Richard P. McCormick, "Suffrage Classes and Party Alignment: A Study in Voting Behavior," *The
Mississippi Valley Historical Review*, XLVI (Dec., 1959), 397–410, has
shown that suffrage liberalization in New York and North Carolina during this era did not produce "any measurable change in party alignments." Newly admitted voters in the lower socio-economic strata, including urban workingmen, "divided fairly evenly in party preferences." Lee
Benson, *The Concept of Jacksonian Democracy* (Princeton, N. J., 1961),
also contends that in New York the working-class, "lower-class Democratic relationship is a spurious one" (pp. 123–64).

[21] [Anon.], *To the Farmers of Rhode Island* (n.p., 1835), pp. 1–3.

Potter-Francis clique steadfastly clung to the *status quo* for philosophical and practical reasons. Free suffrage for these Democrats was not a promising program to be embraced, but rather, one of dubious and perhaps disastrous consequences, and therefore, a program to be shunned.

In fairness to the administration forces, however, it should be stated that the urban Democratic minority was less reactionary on the question of suffrage than their powerful country colleagues. In the industrial and mercantile towns it was the controlling anti-administration men, soon to coalesce into the Whig Party, who provided the major opposition to suffrage extension. Benjamin Hazard was a conspicuous example. As long as they remained dominant in Providence, Newport and the other large towns, they were adverse to supporting a reform whose consequences were unpredictable. Their "bird in the hand" approach further dimmed the prospects for change. Toward the other persistent reform demand, namely reapportionment, the urban Whigs (except in Newport) were amenable, whereas the country Democrats were inveterately opposed for reasons of political survival. Equal representation would favor Providence, which was

---

The Providence Bank had challenged the constitutionality of the agrarian sponsored act of 1822 "imposing a duty upon licensed persons and others, and bodies corporate within the state," the so-called "bank tax," that the plaintiffs alleged to be "a violation of the contract contained in the charter of the bank." When the Supreme Judicial Court of Rhode Island upheld the tax, the Providence Bank appealed to the United States Supreme Court which reaffirmed the judgment of the state judiciary. The bank's argument contains an interesting discussion of the economic impact of the 1822 tax: "With the exception of one tax of $15,000, ordered by an act of May 1824, the whole expenses of the state have been paid under the Act of 1822. The whole amount collected under the License Act of 1822, from its commencement to the end of the year 1827 is $35,921.12. Of that amount $26,380.86 was paid by the town of Providence, and $12,818 by the banks. The largest proportion of bank capital is in that town, and the effect of the License Act has been to burden it with more than two-thirds of the taxes of the State. . . . The proportion has been increasing against the town from 1822 to the present time. . . . The whole real estate, and all other property in the state, is exempted from taxation; and the paying part of the business of government thrown principally upon one town." *The Providence Bank v. Alpheus Billings and Thomas G. Pittman* 7 L. Ed. 514 (1830).

overwhelmingly Whig, and other expanding industrial towns where the Whigs were strong.[22]

The state's third major political organization, the Antimasonic party, did not address itself directly to the question of constitutional reform. It was a one-issue faction. Despite the Whiggish principles of many of its leaders on programs like the American System, the Antimasons formed an incongruous alliance with the Democrats. According to its most careful historian, this party was "a union of men and not of principles." Individual Antimasons were on both sides of the suffrage question with Aaron White, Jr., Benjamin Hallett, Jonah Titus and John S. Harris (all leading Dorrites in 1842) among those prominent Antimasons strongly supportive of reform.[23]

By late summer, despite formidable opposition, the suffrage movement spread to other parts of the state and gained momentum as it grew. Committees of correspondence similar to the one headed by Tillinghast in Providence came into existence in Warren, where journalist Charles Randall gained 109 signatures on a free suffrage petition, and also in Tiverton, Smithfield (Slatersville), and Cumberland (Woonsocket Falls).[24] The cause even attracted attention outside the state, for in October a Boston convention of the New England Association of Farmers and Mechanics endorsed a resolution demanding the establishment of manhood suffrage in Rhode Island.[25]

As the movement expanded so did the aims of the reformers.

---

[22] Colasanto, pp. 59–73 and p. 90 gives a detailed account of partisan voting in the state's thirty-one towns from 1828 through 1838.

[23] Susan Porter Benson, " 'A Union of Men and Not of Principles': The Rhode Island Antimasonic Party" (unpublished master's thesis, Brown University, 1971), pp. 10–13, 40, 165–73; *Proceedings of the Antimasonic State Convention Held January 16, 1835* . . . (Providence, 1835).

[24] Tillinghast Papers, #32–37, #42; Petitions Not Granted, RISA, May, 1833.

[25] John R. Commons, et al., *History of Labour in the United States* (New York, 1918–35), I, 319; Brennan, pp. 53–55. The initiator of the resolution may have been Seth Luther, a founder of this association. A similar plea for an extension of suffrage in Rhode Island had been made at the organization's first convention in September 1832.

At the Providence free suffrage meeting on August 16, 1833, the city's correspondence committee was instructed to contact the several towns in the state concerning "a general convention on the subject of Free Suffrage." This convention proposal was well-received. By December, the Woonsocket Falls and Slatersville reformers urged a February 1834 conclave in Providence. David Daniels, Ariel Ballou, and Christopher Robinson of the former village and Metcalf Marsh of the latter recommended a broadening of reform goals as well. The Woonsocket enthusiasts advocated a general state prox in the April elections and a constitutional convention, while Marsh, on behalf of the Slatersville group advised Tillinghast that equal representation must be achieved if free suffrage was to be meaningful.[26]

On January 13, 1834, the Providence City Council added its voice to those of the *ad hoc* suffrage committees by formally memorializing the Assembly to devise a more equal mode of apportionment.[27] Three weeks later, the reformers of Smithfield and Cumberland took a decisive step. They held a joint meeting at Lonsdale, a mill village in the latter community. At this gathering, chaired by Larned Scott, an important resolution passed — namely, "that it is expedient that a State Convention favorable to the adoption of a Constitution, the equalization of Representation, the extension of the Suffrage, and the amendment of our

---

[26] Tillinghast Papers, #33, 34, and 44. As early as November 11, 1833, Marsh had expressed his support for a convention when he wrote to Tillinghast on behalf of the Smithfield suffragists. Ibid., #42. Marsh's personal papers have been recently acquired by the Rhode Island Historical Society.

[27] *Manufacturers' and Farmers' Journal*, January 16, 1834. Providence claimed that it possessed one-sixth of the state's population, one-seventh of those who voted in the last election, and over one-fourth the rateable property under the now conservative estimate of 1823. Yet, it had only one-eighteenth of the representatives in the lower house. It is important to note that Providence then embraced about six square miles. It did not include the present-day sections of Wanskuck, Elmhurst, Mount Pleasant, Manton, Olneyville, Silver Lake, Elmwood, South Providence or Washington Park. These areas, some of which were industrialized, were parts of the surrounding towns of North Providence, Johnston and Cranston which were later added to the capital city (1868–1919) to bring its present size to 18.91 sq. miles.

Penal Code, should be called for devising the best means of
effecting the above objects, and that the 22nd of February, the
birthday of the Father of His Country, be designated as a suitable one for such a Convention to assemble in Providence." [28]

This resolve met with an immediate response in the northern
towns, and meetings were hastily convened for the selection of
delegates.[29] While this process was in progress, the "Workingmen
of the City of Providence" gave an additional impetus to reform.
At their quarterly meeting on February 12, they too approved a
set of ambitious resolves. One called for the creation of a munici-
pal-level workingman's political party, because the existing organizations were not responsive to reform. Another declared that
"the true interests of the Workingmen consists in an extension
of the right of suffrage,[30] the adoption of a State Constitution,
equalizing representation and defining the powers of our General
Assembly, a system of general education, a revision of the penal
code, an effectual lien law for mechanics, a reform in the judiciary system, the abolishment of imprisonment for debt, and
the abolition of the present system of chartered monopolies"
through which a privileged few exploited the many.[31] After issu-
ing this remarkable recommendation, unsurpassed in its compre-

---

[28] *Ibid.*, February 6, 1834.

[29] *Ibid.*, February 13, 17 and 20. See also "Papers Relating to the
Labors of the Constitutional Party, 1834–1837," D. Mss., XXVI, #4
(Providence delegates), #14 (Johnston delegates), hereafter cited as
Constitutional Party Papers. The minutes of the meeting to select the
four Johnston delegates were signed by "secretary" Samuel Ward King,
who became the anti-reform, "law and order" governor in 1842.

[30] Most Rhode Island reformers of this era believed that the suffrage
was a *right* and referred to it as such. Technically, however, American
legal authorities have considered it merely a privilege to be granted by
the state as it deems fit. See *Black's Law Dictionary*, 4th ed. (1957),
p. 1602.

[31] *Manufacturers' and Farmers' Journal*, February 17, 1834. On
working men's parties in general Edward Pessen has remarked that they
were motivated "precisely by the failure of the Democrats — not to mention the National Republicans — to work toward goals that were regarded as of the highest importance." This situation existed in Rhode
Island. Pessen, "The Working Men's Party Revisited," *Labor History*,
IV, (Fall, 1963), 203–26.

hensiveness, these workingmen (many of whom had been active with Tillinghast in 1833) joined other interested Providence citizens to select delegates to the reform convention.

The Providence meeting for delegate election was held on February 19 at the Old Town House, where a variegated twenty-four man contingent was chosen. This body contained a number of individuals drawn from the ranks of the Providence Workingmen's Association, including its new chairman David Brown. William I. Tillinghast, of course, was designated along with several members of his correspondence committee. Chosen from the other end of the social scale were two able attorneys, Joseph K. Angell and Thomas Wilson Dorr.[32]

II

The appointment of young Thomas Dorr, by this *ad hoc* group was, in retrospect, a momentous event. It marked Dorr's debut as a constitutional reformer and launched him on a career unparalleled in Rhode Island political history. Almost from this moment of his initial involvement, until his tragic and untimely death twenty-one years later, his name was synonymous with the cause of political, economic, and social reform.

The youthful Dorr lent not only energy, leadership, and zeal to the movement; he gave it an aura of respectability as well. Thomas was a member of one of the state's first families. His grandfather was Ebenezer Dorr, a Boston mechanic who rode with Paul Revere in that fateful April of '75. His father, Sullivan Dorr, was a prominent merchant-industrialist who had amassed a modest fortune in the China trade. Sullivan Dorr's only social drawback, other than being a *nouveau riche,* was that his roots were not deeply planted in Rhode Island soil. Thomas's mother, the former Lydia Allen, effectively offset this impediment. She was indirectly descended, through the clans of Crawford, Bernon, and Harris, from the William Harris who accompanied Roger Williams to Providence in the spring of 1636.

---

[32] *Manufacturers' and Farmers' Journal,* February 20, 1834.

Even more impressive than the lineage and the social standing of Thomas Dorr, however, were his accomplishments and his potential. His education was one befitting the eldest son of a merchant prince. It included study at the Providence free school, the Latin Grammar School, Phillips-Exeter Academy in New Hampshire, and Harvard. He entered college in 1819, at the age of fourteen. In 1823, after attaining membership in all of Harvard's literary societies, the studious and diligent youth was graduated with high honors, the second-ranking scholar in his class. Ironically young Thomas was a docile and well-behaved undergraduate despite considerable student unrest during his stay. He was one of a small group (that included George Ripley, founder of Brook Farm) "blacklisted" by dissident classmates for supporting the administration during the "great rebellion in Harvard College."

From Cambridge Dorr went to New York where he studied law under the renowned James Kent. After his sojourn with the Chancellor, Thomas clerked in the office of John Whipple, Rhode Island's foremost legal craftsman of the era. He gained juristic knowledge from these eminent attorneys, but he emphatically rejected their political conservatism.

After admission to the bar in March 1827, the youthful barrister hung his shingle for a time in Providence. Then, to improve his fragile health, he took an excursion through the West and South. Upon the completion of his travels Dorr practiced briefly in the thriving city of New York where he specialized in maritime and commercial law. Here he first made contact with a number of distinguished individuals including John L. O'Sullivan, the Jacksonian exponent of equal rights and expansionism, legal innovator David Dudley Field, and William B. Adams, British inventor, and a leading proponent of the Reform Bill of 1832.[33]

---

[33] This capsule biography is derived mainly from two autobiographical sketches in the Dorr Papers, John Hay Library, Brown University, #A 1154 and #A 1155. This collection is hereafter cited as DP. Also useful were the letters in DC, I(1820–1835); Catherine R. Williams, "Recollections of the Life and Conversation of Thomas W. Dorr . . ." (un-

Dorr's correspondence with Adams, in fact, reveals the Rhode Islander's ardent interest in reform. In his extended letters to the British political pamphleteer, Dorr exulted over the July Revolution of 1830, deplored Russia's suppression of the Poles, and urged parliamentary reform and suffrage extension in England. His remarks on these momentous events of 1830–32 afford a glimpse into the mind of this young liberal on the eve of his entrance into public life.

Dorr viewed the European upheavals as part of a "universal cause" aimed at asserting "the natural rights of our species" and bringing the "greatest happiness to the greatest number." To him they were symptomatic of the growing demand that "all persons competent to do so may take part in the choice of their rulers, lawmakers and judges, either immediately, or mediately thru their chosen representatives; and that all persons not at present competent may be made so as soon as possible by a general system of public education." To Dorr, the contemporary political cataclysms were examples not of "the operation of a leveling system . . . but of an elevating one, that raises men to the feeling of personal worth and independence, and gives them the places designed for them by Nature."

When speaking of the manner in which the lot of man could be ameliorated, Dorr, despite the Federalist tradition in which he was reared, espoused a Jeffersonian view. "Submission to very bad or imperfect government," he observed to Adams, "is enjoined in many cases by expediency, but by nothing else. Mankind are disposed to wait and to suffer long before they attempt

published paper, n.d. in the D. Mss.); Jane Louise Cayford, "The Sullivan Dorr House in Providence, Rhode Island" (unpublished master's thesis, Univ. of Delaware, 1961); Pickering Dodge, "Brief Account of the Class of 1819–23," in Samuel Eliot Morison, "The Great Rebellion in Harvard College and the Resignation of President Kirkland," *Transactions of the Colonial Society of Massachusetts*, XXVII (1927–30), 54–112; Gettleman, pp. 12–18; and American Historical Society, *Sayles and Allied Families: Genealogical and Biographical* (New York, 1925), pp. 101–17. This was prepared for Mary Dorr (Ames) Sayles and has a section on the Dorr line. On Adams see Henry Trueman Wood, "William Bridges Adams," *Dictionary of National Biography*, I, 108–09.

political revolutions; but their delay and acquiescence sanctify
no abuses, confirm no tyrannies; and a recurrence to the popular
sovereignty is always a right and true remedy, tho not usually
resorted to till others have failed." At another point, in a spirit
unburdened by tradition, he asserted that "the actual living majority of the day possess the true sovereignty of the country, and
have a right to investigate, revive and amend its political constitution, and to accommodate it to the just demands and necessi-
ties of the people." [34]

Optimistic, articulate, concerned — these were among the
qualities of Thomas Dorr. Belief in fundamental human good-
ness, the brotherhood of man, and majoritarian rule were basic
articles in his political creed. Liberty and equality were to him,
as much as to any reformer of this remarkable age, the indispensable conditions of human activity.

In 1832 Dorr returned permanently to Providence. Once
home, he familiarized himself with political conditions in his
native state. During 1833 he waited in the wings while Luther
and Tillinghast waged their campaign for free suffrage. This
movement caught his attention and fired his interest. By February 1834, Dorr — at the age of twenty-eight — was ready to
translate his lofty ideals into action.

III

On February 22, 1834, delegates from ten towns, most of them
expanding and industrialized communities, convened at Providence to consolidate their reform efforts.[35] The assemblage included adherents of the state's major political parties — Whigs,

---

[34] TWD to William B. Adams, May 30, 1831, DP, #A 6328; *Idem.*,
November 7, 1831, May 28, 1832, DC, I. George Dennison has said of
Dorr that "he joined the disinterestedness of the Jeffersonian elitist tra-
dition with the majoritarianism of Jacksonian America." *The Dorr War:
Republicanism on Trial, 1831–1861* (Lexington, Ky., 1976), p. 16.

[35] The towns represented were Providence, Smithfield, Bristol, Warren,
Cranston, Johnston, North Providence, Burrillville, Cumberland, and
Newport. *The Constitutionalist,* March 12, 1834.

Democrats, Antimasons, and Workingmen.[36] The Whig members were the most numerous and were to be, in the long run, the most influential.

The reform convention was well-planned and those who attended immediately set to work. The delegates elected Nathan A. Brown as president and then chose a committee chaired by Dorr, to formulate and "report to the Convention subjects proper to be acted upon." This group wasted no time. By early afternoon on the first day its task was completed, and Dorr introduced the committee's recommendations with "a number of pertinent and eloquent remarks." These recommendations, presented in resolution form, were debated, altered slightly, then passed. They were nineteen in number.[37]

These resolutions served as the reformers' blueprint for action during the period 1834 to 1837. The determined delegates resolved that it was "repugnant" to the spirit of American independence to acknowledge the charter of a British king as a constitution of civil government; that the need for political reform was urgent; that the powers of the Legislature and the rights of citizens should be explicitly defined; that there should be an equal distribution of representatives; that an exclusively landed qualification for suffrage was unjust; that all white, male, native-born citizens twenty-one and older with one year's residence in the state should be allowed to vote upon the payment of a property tax, but a freehold should still be required of naturalized citizens; and that inequitable apportionment and the exclusive landed requirement prevented Rhode Island's government from being democratic.

Improvements must be made in the judicial system, the dele-

---

[36] See Dorr's party breakdown of the Providence delegation, DP, A 828. Biographical sketches of several leading Constitutionalists and their antagonists can be found in Abraham Payne, *Reminiscences of the Rhode Island Bar* (Providence, 1885). Included in Payne's *Reminiscences* are accounts of John Whipple, David Daniels, John H. Weeden, Benjamin Hazard, Asher Robbins, Henry Y. Cranston, Tristam Burges, Samuel Ames, Samuel Y. Atwell, Dexter Randall, and Nathan F. Dixon.

[37]*Manufacturers' and Farmers' Journal,* February 24, 1834; *The Constitutionalist,* March 12, 1834.

gates declared, and a great need existed for the adoption of a written constitution. They decided that the group henceforth would be known as the Constitutional party, an organization strictly local in nature and dedicated to the aforementioned goals, and it would enter a ticket of general officers in the ensuing April election to be composed of men friendly to the cause "without distinction of party." Standing committees would be established in each town to provide better party organization and communication. Further, the number of white male citizens over twenty-one who were nonfreeholders would be enumerated, so that it could be ascertained how many in this disfranchised group paid property taxes and in what amount. They called for a constitutional convention to be convened with delegates allocated on the basis of a town's population and elected by all those who would qualify under the proposed suffrage extension. A state committee was to be appointed for the new party and a newspaper would be established to promote the constitutional cause. Another group should be appointed to compose an "Address to the People" on the subject of reform and a nomination committee should be created to draft a slate of general officers for the April election. A printed copy of the resolves would be transmitted to Governor Francis and the legislature and the resolutions would be published in the local press.[38]

The only one of these ambitious proposals which engendered significant debate was the retention of the freehold qualification for naturalized citizens. The discrimination was objected to by Thomas Doyle, father of Providence's famed mid-nineteenth century mayor; attorney (later judge) David Daniels of Cumberland; and Charles C. Harrington, an Irishman from North Providence who was naturalized but a freeholder. Not only was such a restriction unjust, they argued, but it was of doubtful constitutionality.

Dorr, Rivers, and Angell replied to these charges, advocating a double-standard because of "its expediency as a precautionary

---

[38] Constitutional Party papers, #1 is a copy of the resolutions in Dorr's handwriting. The talented Joseph K. Angell was Dorr's collaborator in this drafting effort.

measure, and its peculiar applicability to a manufacturing state."
Dorr also argued that most immigrants "have been subjects of
great oppression in the countries from which they came, where
they were kept in ignorance and imbued with ideas of a mon-
archical system. They are welcome to our shores and to the
greater freedom and security of our laws," he maintained, but
"they ought to become in some measure assimilated to our habits
and feelings, and acquire a knowledge of our institutions and an
attachment to them before being admitted to a perfect equality
of political privileges." [39] In later years Dorr would term his
stand on this issue his "former Whiggish heresy." [40] It became
for him a source of embarrassment and regret. But in 1834 (in
fact, until 1888) this position dominated the suffrage policy of
Rhode Island's political establishment.

Once the debate was concluded those committees created by
the resolutions were appointed, and the gathering adjourned to
March 12.[41] On the day appointed the convention reassembled
with Scituate and North Kingstown now in attendance, and the
business of reform resumed.[42] The committees had performed
their tasks well. First, the nomination committee presented a
fifteen-man slate of general officers headed by United States
Senator Nehemiah Knight of Providence and Joseph Cross [43] of
Charlestown, who were nominees for governor and lieutenant
governor respectively.

Then, the able contingent which had been directed to prepare
a statement of party principles — Dorr, Angell, Rivers, William
Smith, and attorney Christopher Robinson — presented its re-

---

[39] *The Constitutionalist*, March 12, 1834; *Manufacturers' and Farmers'
Journal*, March 6, 1834.

[40] DP, A 1154. Such a position, of course, was inconsistent with the
reformers' claim that suffrage was a natural right.

[41] *The Constitutionalist*, March 12, 1834.

[42] *Ibid.*, April 7, 1834.

[43] Cross, a former senator, was suggested to the committee by Dr. Dan
King of Charlestown, who, in his letter of recommendation, noted that
"people in this county [Washington] are told that free suffrage would
deprive them of all their rights, and give every thing to Providence."
King to William Tillinghast, March 4, 1834, Tillinghast Papers, #19–21.
On Cross see Cole, p. 658.

port — the famous *Address to the People of Rhode Island*. This document, sixty pages in final printed form, was composed principally by Dorr with assistance from Angell and Smith.[44]

The work was divided into six major categories: (1) the nature of a constitution and its need; (2) the defects of the charter; (3) inequality of representation; (4) extension of the suffrage; (5) the qualifications for electors in the several states; and (6) the need for improvements in the judiciary.[45] The document, although impressive in scope and logical in arrangement, was essentially a compilation and explication of the grievances and reform demands which had been accumulating in the half-century since independence. Stated more cogently and more comprehensively than ever before, the *Address* demanded nothing essentially different than those reforms advocated in the nineteen resolves of February 22.

Some of the statistics advanced to support the document's contentions shed light on the need for constitutional adjustment. It was pointed out, for example, that Jamestown sent one representative to the Assembly for every eighteen freemen, whereas the ratio in Smithfield was 206 and in Providence 275 to one. Further, it was shown that certain selected small towns, with less than a third of the state's population, elected a majority of the lower house.[46] Even the use of taxable property as a criterion for representation revealed a glaring inequality. The six wealthiest

---

[44] The original handwritten copy in the D. Mss., Vol. XVIII, has a notation to the effect that sixty-six pages of the manuscript draft were written by Dorr, nine by Angell and five by Smith. The learned Elisha R. Potter, Jr., in an extensive critique of the *Address,* contended that the historical parts of the pamphlet were contributed by Angell, the statistics by Smith, and "the remainder, including all the argumentative part, by Thomas Wilson Dorr, Esq." Potter, *Considerations on the Questions of the Adoption of a Constitution & Extension of Suffrage in Rhode Island* (Boston, 1842), pp. 27 ff. The Constitutional Party Papers, #17, #19–20 indicate that Angell also had a part in compiling the statistics, and that Christopher Robinson furnished some thoughts on suffrage. On the authorship see also DP, A 1154.

[45] [Thomas Wilson Dorr, *et al.*] *Address to the People of Rhode Island* . . . (Providence, 1834), *passim,* hereafter cited as Dorr, *Address.*

[46] Dorr, *Address,* pp. 20–23.

communities in the state had a tax-base equivalent to the total of the remaining twenty-five towns. Yet the former sent only fourteen representatives to the Assembly out of a total of seventy-two.[47]

On the issue of suffrage it was asserted that a majority of the white, adult male citizens of the state were disfranchised by the freehold.[48] Drawing upon information gathered in pursuance of February resolution #12, the *Address* contended that in recent assessments, sixty-six non-freeholders in Smithfield, 361 in Providence, 210 in Cumberland, and seventy-nine in Warren, paid property taxes. In addition, the industrial town of North Providence in 1830 had 779 adult male inhabitants only 200 of whom were entitled to vote.[49] This condition was deplorable, contended the *Address*, because the franchise is "a natural right; which cannot be abridged, nor suspended any farther than the greatest good of the greatest number imperatively requires." [50]

The *Address* eloquently concluded by urging the Assembly to call an equitably apportioned constitutional convention. It further exhorted the legislature to suspend the freehold qualification for native-born citizens in the election of delegates "for the

---

[47] *Ibid.*, p. 24

[48] The *Address,* due to a defect in William Smith's calculations, erroneously states that about 13,000 of the over 23,000 white adult male citizens in the state were disfranchised (p. 26). In the June 1834 debates on the convention bill, Benjamin Hazard correctly contended that the *Address* was inaccurate on this point. Dorr rechecked the figures and acknowledged the mistake. He concluded that there were nearly 10,900 white adult male citizens who were disfranchised out of a state total of approximately 20,000 such persons. The state proportion of white adult male citizens who were denied the suffrage was fifty-four percent; however, that ratio was much higher in the industrialized communities. *Manufacturers' and Farmers' Journal,* Sept. 1 and 8, 1834. DP, A 851, A 854 contain Dorr's computations.

[49] Dorr, *Address,* pp. 38–9. On the gathering of these statistics see Charles Randall and William Wheaton to Joseph K. Angell, March 10, 1834; Daniel Wilkinson to Angell, March 3, 1834; and William H. Cooke to Dorr, March 17, 1834, Constitutional Party Papers, #19–22. The *Pawtucket Chronicle* listed only 180 freemen in North Providence out of 779 adult males. *Manufacturers' and Farmers' Journal,* March 13, 1834.

[50] Dorr, *Address,* p. 26. For a rather feeble justification of the discrimination against naturalized citizens see p. 52.

single purpose of facilitating the exercise by the People of the great, original Right of Sovereignty." [51] Once the *Address* was read, provisions were made for its publication, and the convention adjourned.[52] The next project for the reformers was the April election.

While the Constitutionalists were remonstrating and expressing their grievances, a number of National Republicans and a few disenchanted Democrats began to mobilize for the 1834 state and congressional campaigns. These anti-Administration forces, who complained of "the deranged state of the currency and the general stagnation of business," soon coalesced to form the Whig party.[53] After holding numerous rallies they finally assembled in grand convention on April 2 to nominate general officers under the banner of "Liberty and Union." Chaired by James DeWolf of Bristol, a pro-Bank defector from the Democratic ranks, a former U.S. Senator, and a self-made merchant-industrialist, the gathering selected a full slate of at-large candidates headed by United States Senator Nehemiah Knight and George Irish of Middletown.[54]

There were several similarities between this Whig prox and the final slate [55] endorsed by the Constitutional party. Knight was the choice of both groups for governor. Also identical were the candidates for secretary (Henry Bowen) and attorney general (Albert C. Greene). In addition, three senatorial candidates,

---

[51] Dorr, *Address,* p. 60.

[52] *The Constitutionalist,* April 7, 1834.

[53] *Manufacturers' and Farmers' Journal,* February 6, 10, 1834; March 10, 17, 20, 24, 27 and 31, 1834.

[54] *Ibid.,* March 31 and April 3, 1834. A sketch of the fascinating career of DeWolf, which included command of a slave ship, active involvement in the slave trade, service on privateers, pioneer cotton manufacturing, and a tenure as speaker of the Rhode Island House (1819–21), see Wilfred Harold Munro, *Tales of An Old Sea Port* [Bristol] (Princeton, N.J., 1917), pp. 205–224.

[55] There were five personnel changes made in the senatorial positions between the time that the tenative Constitutionalist prox was presented to the party at its March 12 meeting and the final promulgation of the ticket on April 3. *Manufacturers' and Farmers' Journal,* March 13 and April 3, 1834.

Samuel Ward King of Johnston, Thomas Whipple of Coventry, and William Peckham of South Kingstown, appeared on both ballots. On the other hand, the Constitutional candidate for general treasurer (John Sterne) was the nominee of the Democratic/Antimason coalition.[56]

The presence of the popular and prestigious Senator Knight at the head of the Constitutional prox is perplexing in view of his unenthusiastic response to the Tillinghast committee in 1833 on the question of constitutional reform. He undoubtedly backed reapportionment, but free suffrage and sweeping governmental revision were proposals too rash for him.[57] In fact, when the final Constitutional ticket was being prepared for publication, Knight wrote to the nominating committee asking that his name be scratched from the reformers' slate. Dorr, on behalf of the committee, deftly sidestepped this eleventh hour request.[58]

The April elections were a disappointment to Whigs and Constitutionalists alike. The Democratic/Antimasonic coalition under Governor Francis swept in by a narrow margin over the Whigs, while the Constitutionalists ran a distant third. The eight Constitutional candidates who ran only under the reform banner without major party connections averaged a paltry 448 votes out of the 7,200 cast.[59]

---

[56] *Ibid.*, March 13, April 3 and 7, 1834. A useful but superficial account of the 1834 elections and the successful Democratic/Antimason coalition is Philip Grant, "Party Chaos Embroils Rhode Island," *Rhode Island History*, XXVI (Oct., 1967), 113–125, XXVII (Jan., 1968), 24–33. See also, Knight, *Sprague*, pp. 13–15.

[57] Tillinghast and other workingmen, remembering Knight's 1833 letter, were very cool towards the senator's candidacy. See broadside "To Workingmen" [1834], Rider Collection, JHL.

[58] [TWD] to Nehemiah R. Knight, April 3, 1834, DP, A 869. Knight's opponent, Governor John Brown Francis, thought he could derive an advantage from Knight's predicament. Francis wrote to party chief Elisha Potter, Sr., as follows: Knight, Whipple, and King are "in the free suffrage prox as well as in the National [Whig]. If the National landholders in S[outh] K[ingstown] were told this, it might give our prox a larger majority." Francis to Potter, April 12, 1834, Francis Collection.

[59] *Manufacturers' and Farmers' Journal*, May 12, 1834. Before the results were official in this close contest, it was rumored that the three Whig senatorial candidates (Whipple, Peckham, and King) who were

One of the very few bright spots in the party's first electioneering effort came in Providence where Thomas Dorr, a self-proclaimed Constitutionalist-Whig [60] was chosen one of the city's four representatives.[61] Dorr's election to the Assembly helped to propel him into leadership of the reform cause.

Despite the Constitutionalists' disappointing performance, they showed immediate resiliency. On May 2, the "friends of a Constitution" assembled in Providence for a "pep rally" to prepare them for the upcoming Assembly session. Dorr chaired the meeting, and delivered a long but stirring talk. A significant portion of this oration was devoted to rebutting those critics who claimed the Constitutionalists were a universal suffrage party. Fifteen more resolutions were then adopted. These, drafted by Joseph Angell, a brilliant attorney of high social standing, were similar to the February reform demands, except for the addition of a clause calling for the abolition of imprisonment for debt. On this high note the gathering adjourned.[62]

---

also in the Constitutional prox had been victorious. John Brown Francis attempted to prevent Whipple and Peckham from combining their Whig and Constitutionalist ballots by contending that they had run in different slots on the two slates. For example, Whipple was the Whig nominee for 1st Senator and the Constitutional candidate for 2nd Senator. Francis sought the opinion of the attorney general to support his position that "the votes for Tom W[hipple] . . . as 1st Senator are of no use to him as 2nd Senator, and his being run on two Proxes, therefore, in *two positions*, does not advance him a single step." Francis to Attorney General Albert C. Greene, April 23, 1834, Albert C. and Richard Ward Greene Collection, RIHS. Fortunately for Francis the final tally gave his entire slate a clear-cut victory, thus averting a legal hassle over the senatorial posts.

[60] DP, A 1155. Dorr said he was "elected a Constitutionalist," but acted "in general matters with the Whig or N. R. Party."

[61] *Manufacturers' and Farmers' Journal,* April 17, 1834.

[62] Constitutional Party Papers, #18; *Manufacturers' and Farmers' Journal,* May 1 and 8, 1834. On Angell see Sidney S. Rider, *Bibliographic Memoirs of Three Rhode Island Authors: Joseph K. Angell, Frances H. (Whipple) McDougall and Catherine R. Williams* (Providence, 1880). *Rhode Island Historical Tracts,* 1st Series, No. 11. Angell, prior to his entrance into the Constitutional party, had authored several distinguished legal treatises. His specialties were littoral and riparian rights (*i.e.,* tidewaters and watercourses).

When the General Assembly convened in Newport in May 1834, Dorr, as a freshman legislator from Providence, presented the resolves of the February convention for discussion. They were laid on the table for future consideration over the objection of Benjamin Hazard who wanted them referred to his special committee for mutilation and burial. Hazard, not to be outdone, then introduced a resolution on May 10 providing for the calling of a constitutional convention to consider *amending* the royal charter. On the motion of Elisha Potter, Sr. this measure was referred to the June session for consideration.[63] On June 26, according to schedule, a long and bitter debate commenced on Hazard's bill — a proposal that was considered a thunderstealing, half-loaf by the Constitutionalists. This classic rhetorical confrontation pitted Hazard, a Newport Whig, and Elisha Potter, a South County Democrat, against Dorr, Levi Haile, a Whig from densely populated Warren, and John W. Weeden, another Whig from the manufacturing community of North Providence (a town which then embraced the heavily industrialized villages of Wanskuck and Pawtucket). The latter group received an occasional assist, especially on the topic of reapportionment, from Whig merchant James DeWolf of Bristol.

Dorr sprang quickly to the attack. Hazard's bill, he contended, was just a device to preserve the charter. That document, the Providence representative stated, "had a valid existence as a written instrument until the 4th of July, 1776"; then it "ceased to exist as an instrument binding upon the people of this state." It could not interpose any "obstacle to the adoption by them of such a form of government as they might deem proper," and was now merely "a part of the political common law of this State." "Such institutions of government as ours are unworthy of a free people; they ought to be changed radically and totally," Dorr boldly asserted. Thus, he moved to amend Hazard's bill so that the proposed convention's duty would be to draft a *new*, written constitution for the state.

---

[63] Journal of the House (1833–36), May session, 1834; *Manufacturers' and Farmers' Journal,* May 12, 1834.

Hazard, a veteran of twenty-five consecutive years in the House, was not to be intimidated by this green upstart. He lashed back at Dorr and his colleagues with a torrent of invective and hyperbole. They wish to "revolutionize" the state, he said. "They know that if the charter is once amended, there will be an end to all their revolutionizing projects," he fumed. He drew the act in such a manner, Hazard explained, "that the provisions to be adopted should be in the form of amendments to the charter." He was "perfectly satisfied that the people of this state would not denounce the charter of their ancestors."

When Hazard took his seat Levi Haile remarked in disgust: "No person ever comes in collision with that gentlemen, without receiving the most virulent personal abuse at his hands." With tempers at the boiling point, Elisha Potter offered a compromise amendment authorizing the convention either to amend the present *or* draft a new constitution for the state. This phraseology won the assent of the House.[64]

Then Dorr rekindled the embers by offering a crucial proposal, namely, that the delegates be chosen from the towns on the basis of population (each town having at least one), and that all *native born* white adult male citizens with one year's residency who have paid taxes on at least $134 of real or personal property in the preceding year be eligible to elect delegates and vote on ratification. This measure was designed to overcome twin obstacles, one posed by the rural towns to reapportionment and the other by the freeholders to suffrage extension. If Dorr's ploy failed and the proposed convention became merely a replica of the House (and the Convention of 1824), then all hope for sweeping reform would be extinguished.

Weeden, Haile, and Dorr made a strenuous effort to persuade the Assembly that the amendment was desirable. Potter joined Hazard in defense. The aging South Kingstown politician insisted that the convention contain "the same number of repre-

---

[64] *Manufacturers' and Farmers' Journal,* June 30, Aug. 28 and September 1, 1834. The extensive debates on this bill were not printed until the eve of the 1834 convention.

sentatives that we now have, and elected by the voters of the same qualifications as at present." Hazard agreed, and then heaped more abuse on Dorr and his associates. The irascible Newporter sarcastically surmised that the relatives of these young gentlemen would be "mortified" to find them supporting and leading such people "as the levelling laborers and mechanics of the factory villages." He derisively called his antagonists "children, not out of their primers," and tried to affix upon the Constitutionalists the stigma of free suffrage. Hazard, as always, zealously battled any political Pandora who dared to open the ballot box.

But Dorr was never one to submit to such an onslaught. In a verbal counteroffensive he laid bare the reason for Hazard's obstructionism:

> He clearly forsees the effect of a reformation in this state. He reads a handwriting on the wall; and it announces too clearly to be misinterpreted, the doom of a certain class of politicians, who, when the present unjust and oppressive system of things goes down, go with it, and do not rise agin. It is this dread of personal consequences which makes some men cling with such a desperate grasp, strengthened by the energy of self-preservation, to the decaying remnants of the present fabric. Their influence perishes upon the introduction of justice and equality into the distribution of political power.[65]

Reason may have been on the side of the reformers, but the House was not. Dorr's amendment lost by the lopsided margin of fifty-eight to four. Only Dorr, Weeden, Haile, and Otis Mason, a Cumberland Whig, voted in support of the measure.[66]

With the crucial issue of the convention's composition decided in favor of the reactionaries, the House adjourned. On the following day it put the bill in final form. The gathering would assemble in Providence on September 2, 1834. The delegates would serve without pay.[67]

---

[65] *Ibid.,* September 1 and 3, 1834.

[66] *Ibid.,* June 30, Sept. 8 and 11. James DeWolf abstained. He favored apportioning delegates but not the extension of suffrage.

[67] *Ibid.,* June 30 and Sept. 11, 1834. It was also decided, this time against Hazard's wishes, that the product of the convention would be voted on as a whole rather than separately or article by article.

IV

The Constitutionalists must have been greatly disheartened by the provisions of the convention act, for they were not particularly active during the summer of 1834. William I. Tillinghast, who had been eclipsed by Dorr as the leader of the reform movement, staged one of the few significant public demonstrations of the pre-convention period by arranging a July 4 oration on the right of suffrage. This address was delivered by Nathan C. Rhodes at the Providence Town House before a sizeable gathering of "mechanics and other workingmen." [68]

The Constitutional party itself formed a committee to draft and publish a list of articles that "were deemed indispensable to a Constitution for this State." This select group, composed of Dorr, Angell, Weeden, and William T. Wheaton, completed its manifesto in August and published it in the local press. Their party's principal demands were as follows: a constitutional bill of rights, a clear-cut delineation of powers among the three branches of government, house apportionment based upon population, the establishment of an independent judiciary by giving supreme court justices tenure for good behavior, reorganization of the courts of common pleas, and an enlarged franchise. The Constitutionalists' suffrage proposal called for an extension of the vote to all native born white adult males who paid taxes on real or personal property; a freehold was still to be required of naturalized citizens. Also, they advocated a strict registration of voters, the use of the secret ballot, and the abolition of the voting privilege that was extended to a freeholder's eldest son.[69]

These recommendations were not likely to be fulfilled by the so-called "Freemen's Convention of 1834" that convened in the State House in Providence on Tuesday, September 2. Only fifty-eight delegates were in attendance because seven rural towns decided to boycott the proceedings.[70] The two most influential

---

[68] *Ibid.,* June 30, 1834.

[69] Constitutional Party Papers, #6, 9 and 15; *Manufacturers' and Farmers' Journal,* August 21, 1834.

[70] The seven towns were Scituate, Foster, Barrington, West Green-

participants were Hazard and Potter. Thanks to their success in the June Assembly, they could count on the support of approximately fifty members of this stacked convention. On the weak side were Dorr and Thomas Rivers of Providence, Weeden and Haile. They got an occasional show of support from DeWolf and Equal Rights Democrat Samuel Y. Atwell of Glocester, a man destined to play a leading role in the reform crusade of the 1840s.

From the outset when Ben Hazard's nominee, Judge Joseph Childs, a prosperous Portsmouth Whig, was elected convention president, the tiny coterie of reformers suffered setback after setback. Hazard took personal charge of the committee on the elective franchise and hammered out an article which was even more restrictive than the existing suffrage statute.[71] It not only retained the freehold and the privilege of eldest sons, but it made the acquisition of freemanship more difficult for the foreign born. It required of this group three years' residence after naturalization and then admitted them to the franchise only by a special act of the Assembly. Hazard's pet article had one salutary effect — it made fraudulent election practices more difficult to perpetrate.

When Dorr tried to amend this ironclad article by the insertion of a personal property qualification, he got only seven votes; and Atwell's attack on the primogeniture provision was defeated by a margin of two to one.[72] A journalist covering the convention summed up the situation quite accurately: "They have met and

---

wich, Richmond, New Shoreham, and Charlestown. Six of these communities were strongly Democratic while Barrington was "mixed" in its political allegiance. Colasanto, p. 90.

[71] Hazard's motion creating the committee read as follows: That a committee be formed to frame an article "which shall define, secure, and guard from abuse, the elective franchise or right of suffrage, upon the present basis of a freehold qualification and in conformity to the ancient institutions of this state." *Manufacturers' and Farmers' Journal,* September 8, 1834.

[72] *Ibid.,* September 3, 8, 11, 22 and 25; Proceedings of the Freemen's convention to frame a Constitution, September, 1834, D Mss., VIII, 1–2, 4–9, hereafter cited as Convention Proceedings, 1834. Some of Dorr's notes and draft proposals relating to the convention are contained in DP, A 829–A 854.

rejected every endeavor to essentially vary or change the right of suffrage as it now exists in this state." [73]

In approximately a week-and-a-half Hazard, Potter and others had nearly finished their work and they had done so with little effective obstruction. Only two minor articles remained to deliberate. However, on Saturday, September 13, the day the finishing touches were to be applied, a quorum failed to appear, and the gathering adjourned until November 10.[74] The tentative handiwork of the convention was published in the local newspapers during the interim under the title "Articles of Amendment" to the charter. Hazard's victory was total.[75]

Some of the abortive document's features, in addition to the retention and strengthening of the freehold system, were a mild reapportionment, a lengthening of judicial terms for the supreme court, and a plurality election provision. There was no strengthening of the office of chief executive and no substantial diminution in the power of the legislature. The plurality election clause, which had Hazard's strong support, was designed to prevent "no election" situations such as occurred when there was a three-cornered race for general office. This condition existed in 1806 and — more recently — in 1832, when an incredible five general elections were held without any gubernatorial candidate obtaining a majority, due to the presence of the Antimasons in the field.[76]

The court tenure provision was an improvement, but it was more modest than the Constitutionalists desired. Few were satisfied with annual appointment of supreme court justices, but fewer still espoused Dorr's desideratum of life tenure. In final form, therefore, the judiciary article provided for six-year staggered terms for the three supreme court judges. Contrary to the

---

[73] *Manufacturers' and Farmers' Journal,* Sept. 11, 1834.

[74] Convention Proceedings, 1834, pp. 23–24.

[75] *Manufacturers' and Farmers' Journal,* Sept., 18, 1834.

[76] The candidates in 1832 were James Fenner (Democrat), Lemuel Arnold (National Republican) and William Sprague (Antimason). Arnold, who by 1834 was a Whig, had a sizeable plurality in each contest. *R.I. Manual,* 1965–66, pp. 213–14.

reformers' recommendations, no alterations were made in the courts of common pleas.[77]

The legislative article, in a concession to the static and declining towns, abolished the at-large system of senatorial selection and established a fifteen-member upper chamber elected from areas corresponding to the five counties. Providence County was allocated six senators, Newport and Washington three each, Kent two and Bristol one. The membership of the House was increased to eighty-three and the representation of several towns was altered. Under the proposed ratio Providence was awarded eight members; Newport six; Smithfield five; Warwick four; Portsmouth, Cumberland, Scituate, North Kingstown, South Kingstown, North Providence, Coventry, and Bristol three apiece; all other towns two, with the exception of Barrington and Jamestown which were reduced to one.[78] Again, this allocation, though an improvement, fell far short of the Constitutional party's demand for equal representation according to the "one man, one vote" principle, for Providence's 1830 population of 16,836 entitled her to fourteen representatives in an eighty-three member house. Apportionment was a most divisive issue in this ill-fated convention. Some expanding towns were disenchanted because their representation was not sufficiently increased; while several declining communities vigorously objected to the relative or absolute lessening of their legislative influence.[79]

The embryonic constitution of 1834 pleased neither reactionary nor reformer. Thus, when November 10 arrived, the date of the adjourned session, a quorum failed to appear. Another ad-

---

[77] *Manufacturers' and Farmers' Journal,* September 18, 1834. For the Constitutionalists' recommendations regarding the reorganization of the courts of common pleas see Constitutional Party Papers, #15. In 1838, however, the General Assembly by statute abolished the courts of general sessions of the peace and transferred their "jurisdiction, rights, powers and duties" to the courts of common pleas, *Supplement to the Digest of 1822,* pp. 1012–13.

[78] *Manufacturers' and Farmers' Journal,* Sept. 18, 1834.

[79] See Table #3. Delegate Samuel Y. Atwell later recollected that "It was this inequality of representation that broke up the convention." *Manufacturers' and Farmers' Journal,* February 8, 1841.

journment was called to February 9, 1835, and on that day the
process was repeated with June 29 designated as the new but
elusive target date. Finally, at the scheduled June meeting, the
convention died, with only Dorr and Metcalf Marsh in attendance to "perform the obsequies." [80]

---

[80] *Manufacturers' and Farmers' Journal,* Nov. 13, 1834 and Feb. 12,
1835. For Dorr's remarks on the convention's demise see *Burke's Report,*
p. 734.

CHAPTER ELEVEN

The Constitutional Party in Decline

I

After the disintegration of the convention of 1834, the Constitutional party struggled onward. Tenacious Thomas Dorr, Charles Randall, Metcalf Marsh, Joseph K. Angell, Christopher Robinson, Otis Mason, John H. Weeden, Charles N. Tilley, William Smith, David Daniels, Dr. John A. Brown and a handful of others labored to keep their creation alive, but it was slowly failing.

In 1835, the Constitutionalists refrained from nominating general officers or senators when a special committee composed of Dorr, Weeden, and Marsh informed the party's state committee that it was "inexpedient" to draft a slate for the April election. Dorr, in rendering this decision, mentioned that those at-large legislators to be chosen in 1835 were to elect a United States senator, whereas "all subjects connected with national politics were expressly excluded from the range of" the party's political action.[1]

Dorr felt that the involvement of the Constitutionalists in this

---

[1] *Northern Star and Constitutionalist* (Warren), Jan. 24 and March 28, 1835. The general election of 1835 was so close that "no election"

contest might indirectly influence the senatorial selection. This was of concern to Dorr, because he warmly supported the candidacy of Whig Tristam Burges and felt that the presence of the Constitutionalists in the Assembly race might complicate matters and adversely affect Burges's chances for the senatorial post. But disillusionment engendered by the failure of the recent convention was undoubtedly another factor contributing to the Constitutionalists' abstention from the 1835 political campaign.[2]

The remainder of the year 1835 was a quiet one for the Constitutional party, and before they were able to take the field for the next gubernatorial quest, their cause received another setback. This reversal came in February 1836 when the Assembly redrafted the state suffrage statute in a manner that actually tightened the procedures for voting. This was accomplished by a requirement that all land deeds be recorded at least forty-five days prior to the time of election.[3] Although some grumbled about this additional demand, it must be admitted, in fairness to the Assembly, that its primary purpose was the prevention of fraud. The new act included penalties for bribery and a provision allowing the attachment of land which was conveyed fraudulently to qualify voters.[4] Nonetheless, the Democratic-dominated legislature, with the question of suffrage squarely before it, turned a deaf ear to reform.

In the 1836 Assembly debates over the franchise, Constitutionalist Henry H. Luther of Warren offered a resolution granting the vote to any person who paid a tax on real or personal property (or a combination of the two) valued at $250 or more. It received two votes, one from Dorr and the other from Luther

---

was declared in four of the ten senate races because no candidate received a majority of the vote cast.

[2] On Burges see Thomas John Sullivan, "From Federalist to Whig: The Political Career of Tristam Burges," (unpublished master's thesis, University of Rhode Island, 1964), pp. 86–96; and Henry L. Bowen, ed., *Memoir of Tristam Burges* (Providence, 1835). Dr. John A. Brown felt the constitutionalist effort in 1834–35 had been a "complete failure." Brown to Dorr, November 12, 1835, DC, I.

[3] *Supplement to the Digest of 1822,* pp. 869–85.

[4] *Ibid.*

himself.[5] Dorr thereupon attempted to modify the vestiges of primogeniture in Rhode Island's prevailing suffrage law. He advanced an amendment proposing that "whenever the real estate of such a freeholder and freeman shall exceed in value the sum of $134, it shall qualify so many of his sons to be voters as there are times $134 in the value of said estate above his own qualifications." [6] This curious proposal, like Luther's, attracted only two supporters.

The passage of the new election law without any concession to their cause, greatly dimmed the prospects of the Constitutionalists. On the heels of this reversal their gubernatorial candidate — Charles Collins, nominated in a January party convention [7] — was drubbed in the April balloting. He polled only 135 ballots out of the 7,151 that were cast, a mere two percent of the total vote.[8]

Undaunted, the die-hard Dorr persisted, and, through his urging, another party convention was held on January 4, 1837. At this State House gathering, chaired by Martin Robinson of Providence, sixteen reform resolutions were passed, most of which were identical to those of 1834. In addition, a decision was made to enter the lists in the April election.[9] When this conclave adjourned, Dorr, still a Providence representative in the General

---

[5] Constitutional Party Papers, #62; Journal of the House (1836–38), January session, 1836. The debate on the bill was conducted on February 11.

[6] Constitutional Party Papers, #63; Journal of the House (1836–38), January session, 1836. Dorr had advanced a similar proposal in the 1834 convention. DP, A 847.

[7] DP, A 872.

[8] RI Manual, 1965–66, p. 215. On the eve of this election James Fenner declared that "I consider the success of our [Democratic] prox to be important at this time, as well for the *security* of our *right of suffrage,* as well [as] for great State and National interests." Fenner to [Edward] Wilcox, April 9, 1836, William Davis Miller Collection, RIHS.

[9] Constitutional Party Papers, #3; DP, A 873 contains a list of delegates to the 1837 convention. The Metcalf Marsh Papers at the North Smithfield Heritage Association contain approximately a dozen letters (mostly from Dorr to Marsh) concerning the Constitutional party's efforts to arrange slates in 1835, 1836 and 1837. One letter (TWD to Marsh, April 5, 1836) suggests that one reason the Constitutionalists continued to field slates despite their poor showings was to prevent either

Assembly, formally requested that body to call another constitutional convention. The insensitive House killed his resolve on January 21, 1837 by a vote of thirty-nine to seventeen.[10]

In February 1837 the Constitutionalists, after some searching, nominated William Peckham as their candidate for governor. He was an elderly South Kingstown Whig who had supported suffrage extension as a young state senator in 1811. In the April contest the reluctant Peckham went head-to-head against Governor Francis. The Whigs chose not to run. Their reticence was prompted by the four successive beatings they had absorbed at the hands of the Democratic squire from Warwick.

In an extremely low turnout, indicating the futility of Peckham's candidacy, Francis scored a 2,762 to 946 triumph.[11] The Constitutionalists' vote, however, is deceptive. At first glance, it indicates a doubling of their 1834 strength, but in actuality, Peckham — a Whig on national questions — received the votes of many Whigs. Some of the members of that party, having no candidate of their own, voted the Constitutional ticket as a protest against Francis's candidacy. Others chose Peckham rather than abstain, because they sympathized with some of the reformers' goals, especially reapportionment. The Whig strength was in those large expanding towns like Providence which would benefit from an equitable allocation of representatives. Their help made Peckham's showing respectable; but formidable it was not.

II

Although Antimasons such as William I. Tillinghast, Workingmen such as David Brown and Nathan Rhodes, and Jacksonians such as William Miller, Benjamin Joy, and Lawrence Richards

---

major party from gaining a majority vote. A mere plurality would force a run-off election wherein the Constitutionalists could demand concessions in return for their support.

[10] Journal of the House (1836–38), January session, 1837; Constitutional Party Papers, #61. This resolution "in Relation to Political Reform in Rhode Island" is in Misc. Papers of the General Assembly, folder 12 (1836–40).

[11] RI Manual, 1965–66, p. 215.

were instrumental in forming the Constitutional party,[12] the Dorr Correspondence makes it abundantly clear that by 1837 its managers, its candidates, and nearly all its supporters were drawn from the ranks of the Whigs.[13]

Dorr, Angell, Rivers, Randall, Marsh, Tilley, Weeden, Robinson, Mason, and William Smith had Whig affiliations; so also did Collins and Peckham. The connection was so obvious that Marsh warned Dorr on the eve of the April 1837 election that "we shall at present receive the most aid from the Whigs, but we must be careful that we do not become identified with that party so as to lose our own peculiar character." Because of the difficulty in attracting Democratic support, Marsh added, that, "when due exertions have been made to give the Van Buren party a fair representation on our Ticket, if we do not succeed, the fault is not ours and they will have no grounds for complaint." [14]

These observations, showing that Constitutionalist strength came mainly from *individual* Whigs, should not lead one to the unwarranted conclusion that the Whig party organization supported the Constitutionalists' reform demands. Whig leaders such as James F. Simmons, Lemuel Arnold, Nathan F. Dixon, John Whipple, Robert Cranston, Joseph Tillinghast, Joseph Childs and suspicious, crusty Benjamin Hazard, had little enthusiasm for political reformation, especially if it could lead to universal suffrage. Some merely sought to use or absorb the Constitutionalists to strengthen the Whig cause.[15] Most maintained

---

[12] On the political affiliations of these men see DP, A 838.

[13] For example, Asahel Johnson to TWD, March 24 and June 7, 1837; Charles Tilley and John Clarke to TWD, May 31, 1837; William Peckham to TWD, March 21 and May 31, 1837, DC, II.

[14] Marsh to TWD, *Ibid.*

[15] The absorption of the Constitutionalists by the Whigs is alluded to in William H. Hazard to TWD, June 1, 1837, *Ibid.* A learned Democrat, Elisha Potter, Jr. described the political situation in the mid-thirties: "About this time, the Whigs being out of power, some of them took up the subject of a constitution, and uniting with the friends of extension of suffrage, formed and supported a ticket of State officers, but not getting any votes, and finding it was then rather unpopular, it was dropped." Potter, *Considerations,* p. 15. Prior to the election of 1836

an anomalous position — they wished increased representation
for their area (the northern industrial centers) while simultaneously opposing the granting of political privileges to those
upon whom their claim for reapportionment rested.

By the late 1830s, Whig leaders were becoming increasingly
opposed to tampering with the franchise, because of the influx
of foreigners. The Providence census of 1835 showed that the
burgeoning city had a total population of 19,277 of which 1,005
were classified as "foreigners not naturalized." The number of
these aliens was not as yet substantial, but it represented a dra-
matic increase over the thirty-nine who were recorded in the
census of 1820.[16]

Of even greater concern, this non-native population was
mounting yearly, and it contained a significant percentage of Irish
Catholics. The pastor of the Providence Catholic community, the
Reverend John Corry, estimated the size of his flock at under
two hundred in 1830.[17] By January 1839, however, a census conducted by the Hibernian Orphan Society counted 1,696 souls,
of which all but "8 or 10" were Irish.[18]

Nehemiah Knight asked Whig chieftain James F. Simmons: "Why not
take up the Constitutional ticket with some modifications? Without
Warren we cannot go alone." Knight to Simmons, Feb. 22, 1836,
James F. Simmons Papers, Library of Congress, Box 2 (1830–39), hereafter cited as Simmons Papers. Towards these developments Democratic
governor John Brown Francis took a more hysterical view: "The Whigs
of Providence, Newport, Bristol and Warren will unite with the factory
population in the valley of the Blackstone, and with these allies, having
a majority, they will impose such a constitution upon us as may effectually put down the freehold system! This is no chimera but the honest
conviction of my mind." For Francis this would be "the last fight of the
landed interest." Francis to Benjamin Thurston, March 23, 1836,
Francis Collection, RIHS.

[16] Snow, *Providence Census,* pp. 73–4.

[17] Rev. John Corry to William R. Staples, Jan. 10, 1843, Rhode
Island Manuscripts, RIHS, X, 120. Corry was furnishing material for
Staples's *Annals of Providence.* According to Corry growth of the Providence Catholic community was as follows: 1830 — 150 to 200; 1832 —
300; 1834 — about 1,000; 1842 — Sts. Peter and Paul had from 1,200
to 1,400 in its congregation and St. Patrick's (established in 1841) had
between 800 to 1,000, for a total of 2,000 to 2,400.

[18] Henry J. Duff to TWD, Nov. 11, 1841, DP, A 949. Dorr requested this

These "low Irish" were also beginning to make inroads elsewhere in the state. They established sizeable communities in the Fall River section of Tiverton, in the mill villages of Woonsocket and Pawtucket, and in Newport, where many were employed in the construction of Fort Adams. This island town had an estimated 700 Catholics by 1837. Concrete evidence of the rise of Rhode Island's Irish-Catholic community was the establishment of churches. The first, St. Joseph's (later renamed St. Mary's) Newport (1828), was followed by St. Mary's in the village of Pawtucket (1829), St. John the Baptist in the village of Fall River (1837), Sts. Peter and Paul, Providence (1838), and St. Patrick's, Providence (1841).[19]

---

information at the time the suffrage provisions of the People's and the Landholders' constitutions were being drafted. Duff further informed Dorr that the Catholic population of Providence had increased by "one half at least" between January 1839 and November 1841. The figures Duff gave for the 1839 census are identical to those furnished by pioneer priest James Fitton in his undocumented account of New England Catholic growth, *Sketches of the Establishment of the Church in New England* (Boston, 1872), p. 225. Fitton, however, states that the census was taken in December, 1839.

[19] The best studies of the development of the Catholic Church in Rhode Island prior to 1840 are Robert H. Lord, *et al.*, *History of the Archdiocese of Boston* (Boston, 1944), II, 83–87, 163–66, 282–85, and Conley and Smith, pp. 1–42. Also useful are Thomas F. Cullen, *The Catholic Church in Rhode Island* (North Providence, 1936), pp. 77–112; James W. Smyth, *History of the Catholic Church in Woonsocket and Vicinity* (Woonsocket, 1903), pp. 53–64; Fitton, pp. 188–238; John H. McKenna, *The Centenary Story of Old St. Mary's, Pawtucket, R. I. 1829–1929* (Providence, 1929); John H. Green, "The Story of Early Catholicism in Newport and the History of Saint Joseph's Parish" in *The St. Joseph's Church Reference Book, Golden Jubilee, 1885–1935* (Newport, 1935), pp. 11–30; Brennan, pp. 63–66; Coleman, pp. 242–48; and Francis J. Bradley, *A Brief History of the Diocese of Fall River, Mass.* (Fall River, 1931), pp. 16–21. The Fall River section of Tiverton was ceded to Massachusetts in 1862. St. John's Church was located directly on the *old* boundary line between the two states. On the general aspects of Irish immigration at this time see William F. Adams, *Ireland and Irish Emigration to the New World from 1815 to the Famine* (New Haven, 1932). The only work dealing specifically with the Irish in Rhode Island during this period is Sister Mary Edward Walsh, "The Irish in Rhode Island from 1800 to 1865," (unpublished master's thesis, The Catholic University of America, 1937), a superficial study.

Apart from religious differences, the Whigs of Rhode Island were acutely aware that the newly arriving Irish "Papists" had a strong affinity for the party of Jefferson and Jackson. The political practices and preferences of the Catholic Irish of New York were for many Rhode Island Whigs a source of disgust and apprehension.[20] Thus as early as 1835, the Whig party organ, the *Providence Journal* (a daily, founded in 1829 and affiliated with the bi-weekly *Manufacturers' and Farmers' Journal*), in a reversal of form, began its campaign "for the maintenance" of Rhode Island's "ancient suffrage law in all its purity." [21]

This campaign was moderate and relatively low key [22] until July 1838, when Joseph Knowles and William L. Burroughs bought the sheet and retained young, vituperative, and bigoted Henry Bowen Anthony, secretary of the Whig State Committee, as their editor; then it became a crusade.[23] From the moment of his accession to the day of his death as United States Senator in 1884, Henry Anthony compiled a record perhaps unsurpassed in the annals of American nativism.[24]

---

[20] The well-known attachment of the Irish for the Democratic Party during the ante-bellum era is persuasively discussed in Benson, pp. 171–73, 187–91; George Potter, *To the Golden Door: The Story of the Irish in Ireland and America* (Boston, 1960) pp. 217–41; William V. Shannon, *The American Irish: A Political and Social Portrait* (New York, 1966), pp. 47–54; Oscar Handlin, *Boston's Immigrants* (Cambridge, Mass., 1959), pp. 190–206; Murray S. Stedman, Jr. and Susan W. Stedman, "The Rise of the Democratic Party of Rhode Island," *New England Quarterly*, XXIV (Sept., 1951), 329–41; and Conley and Smith, pp. 20, 42, 45, 46, 51.

[21] *Providence Journal*, July 10, 1835. I have termed this a "reversal in form" because the *Journal* at this time was under the ownership of John Miller who had also published the reform-oriented *Manufacturers' and Farmers' Journal* since 1820. Staples, *Annals of Providence*, pp. 550–51.

[22] See, for example, *Providence Journal*, March 5, 1836, August 30, 1837, April 16, 17 and 19, 1838. From January 1836 to July 1838 the *Journal* was published by George W. Jackson.

[23] Staples, *Annals of Providence*, pp. 550–51. On Anthony's activities as secretary of the Whig State Committee see Simmons Papers, Box 2 (1830–39).

[24] For the persistence of his extreme nativism see Henry Bowen Anthony, "Limited Suffrage in Rhode Island," *North American Review*,

In August 1838 Anthony launched his public vendetta against the enfranchisement of the "foreign vagabond." Frequently he compared the "purity" of Rhode Island's elections to those of the immigrant-infested city of New York. He bitterly assailed the Equal Rights Democrats or Locofocos of the metropolis for their universal suffrage stand, but these attacks prompted a vigorous rebuttal from New York's Democratic press.[25] The boldest retort came from Jared Bell's *New Era,* which condemned Rhode Island's freehold system in September 1839 and urged the "people" to meet in convention and form a new government based upon universal suffrage. This audacious exhortation began a running battle between Anthony and the New York Democratic papers that continued through the crises of 1842.[26]

The germs of intolerance, insularity, and prejudice that the xenophobic Anthony spread in the late 1830s had an appreciable effect upon Whig attitudes as the Irish Catholic influx continued. When Thomas Dorr and his colleagues attempted to enfranchise this "rabble" in 1842, an epidemic of nativism infected Rhode Island.

During the life of the Constitutional party, however, the Democratic organization posed the biggest obstacle to change. Throughout the 1830s the party of Jackson in Rhode Island was rural-based, agrarian-oriented, and thoroughly reactionary on nearly all local questions relating to political and constitutional reform.

CXXXVII (1883), 413–21. See also William Barrie Thornton, "Henry Bowen Anthony: Journalist, Governor, and Senator" (unpublished master's thesis, University of Rhode Island, 1960) and Conley and Smith, pp. 42, 46–47, 63–64, 82, 98–100, 103 and 115.

[25] *Providence Journal,* August 16, 29, October 5, 1838; Jan. 18, March 1, April 16, 30, July 15, 22, 30, August 1, 5, 9, Sept. 3, 6, 10, November 25, 1839.

[26] For the *New Era's* exhortation and Anthony's retort see the *Providence Journal,* September 3, 6 and 10, 1839. On the *New Era* see Schlesinger pp. 220–21, 232, 365; *New Era* (New York City), August 31, September 7 and 10, 1839.

III

Soon after William Peckham's defeat in April 1837, Dorr decided to plunge his hapless party into another electoral fray — the August contest for Congress. Since the Constitutional party was avowedly concerned only with the issue of local political amelioration, the motives that prompted Dorr to seek a national office are somewhat obscure. There is high probability that Dorr's renunciation of Whiggery and his conversion to the Democracy influenced his course of action. Eighteen thirty-seven was Dorr's year of political transition.

The young attorney, since entering the General Assembly, had been a champion of liberal causes. He is popularly identified as a crusader for constitutional change, but his interests, in the spirit of the age, were far more diverse. His projects included an upgrading of the judiciary by increasing both the tenure and the salary of the judges, abolition of imprisonment for debt, civil service reform, the defense of religious liberty, antislavery, improvements in public education (he was a member of the Providence School Committee and later became its president), prison reform, a humanization of the state's harsh penal code, and greater public regulation of banks.[27]

Dorr's banking proposals upset his fellow Whigs. During 1836 he proposed, secured, and participated in an investigation of state banks. This inquiry resulted in a report disclosing usurious practices. Because of such findings, Dorr became the prime mover in the drafting and passage of the Bank Act of 1836, a

---

[27] See D Mss., Vols. XXII, XXV, XXVIII, XXX which contain Dorr's observations on these leading issues of the day. Establishment historians of the late nineteenth and early twentieth centuries neglected Dorr's diversity as a reformer, but writers less hostile to Dorr have hinted at his contributions in general surveys of their respective topics. On Dorr and educational reform see Charles Carroll, *Public Education in Rhode Island* (Providence, 1918), pp. 120–21, 287–88, 353, 363, 371, 401 and 426; on Dorr and anti-slavery consult Arline Ruth Kiven, *Then Why the Negroes: The Nature and Course of the Anti-Slavery Movement in Rhode Island: 1637–1861* (Providence, 1973), pp. 54–55. There is a definite need for a modern biography of Dorr.

measure that has been called "the first comprehensive American banking statute." [28]

This law created a permanent banking commission with extensive supervisory powers; it also put a six percent ceiling on interest rates, detailed numerous malpractices for which a bank might forfeit its charter, mandated the submission by banking institutions of semi-annual reports, and required that banks recover debts in the same manner as individual creditors.[29] This final provision was, in effect, a repeal of the notorious "bank process," a privilege written into the charters of thirty institutions incorporated between 1791 and 1818, which gave them first lien on the real property of insolvent debtors to the virtual exclusion of other creditors. This privilege, according to one report, prompted "banks to extend and multiply loans to many where ruin is the inevitable consequence." [30]

Dorr's statute, a product of his belief that banks tended to exploit the people,[31] made him *persona non grata* with Providence Whig leaders in general, and especially with those bankers who

---

[28] Coleman, pp. 197–99; Dorr claimed that his act was a first, and added that "it was very generally copied in other states abroad without acknowledgement," Dorr Papers, A 1154. The act seems to have been based in part, however, on an unsuccessful bank bill introduced into the General Assembly in 1831. Coleman, p. 198. See also John B. Rae, "Rhode Island Pioneers in Regulation of Banking," *Rhode Island History*, II (Oct., 1943), 105–09.

[29] *Supplement to the Digest of 1822*, pp. 898–906.

[30] For an enlightening discussion of the "bank process" and Dorr's role in its destruction see Sidney S. Rider, "The History of the Rhode Island Bank Process," *Book Notes*, XXII (1905), 74–77, 89–93. Coleman, pp. 196–99 takes a generally favorable view of the banking act, but notes that it left some abuses untouched. See also Hedges, *The Browns: The Nineteenth Century*, pp. 194–97. Dorr's own account is as follows: "This act was the first in any state to establish a thorough visitation of the banks, and to reduce them to their just responsibility. . . . The abolition of the bank process against real estate (a special remedy in favor of banks) was a great benefit to the borrowing community." DP, A 1154.

[31] Dorr later supported Van Buren's independent treasury system. He favored the "keeping of the revenues of the country, by public officers, under proper safeguards, exclusively for the public uses, without being loaned or discounted." DP, A 931.

were deprived of their privileged process by what they believed to be an unconstitutional law. Dorr later recollected that he was "hated for this act, & for the *truths* of the report by the money party [the Whigs]." "By investigating the banks," said Dorr, he was "led to consider the unsound doctrines of Whigs and Federalists on banking"; when he found them unjust, he "announced his change of sentiment." For this, Dorr was, in his own words, "denounced, assailed, voted out as representative." [32]

Dorr had still another grievance against his erstwhile Whig associates. The young reformer was enraged over what he considered the unfair treatment accorded to former Congressman Tristam Burges, one of his respected mentors and a close personal friend. Burges, according to Dorr's testimony, was promised a United States senatorship by the Whig managers in 1835. The Whig leaders reneged, however, and by-passed Burges in favor of two-term incumbent Nehemiah Knight. This breach of faith disturbed Dorr greatly. After his open break with the Whigs, he publicly condemned it by penning, under the pseudonym "Aristides," an intemperate pamphlet entitled *Political Frauds Exposed, or A Narrative of the Proceedings of "the Junto in Providence" Concerning the Senatorial Question from 1833–1838.*[33]

Another very important factor in Dorr's conversion to the Democracy appears to have been the image that party projected as a result of the development within the New York Democratic organization of the Locofoco or Equal Rights faction. The Equal Rights movement, which Dorr strongly supported,[34] arose as a protest against conservative control of the New York State Democratic party, and, according to Edward Pessen, "helped fasten an egalitarian reputation on that party both nationally and in

---

[32] *Ibid.,* A 1154.

[33] Aristides [TWD]. *Political Frauds Exposed* . . . (Providence, 1838). See also Documents relating to the alleged political trade between Nehemiah R. Knight and Tristam Burges . . . 1836, a collection of newspaper clippings and manuscripts, in the Rider Collection.

[34] See his squib, "DeLocofocis," ridiculing the Whigs for their fear of Equal Rights Democrats. DP, A 928. This article was published in the *Providence Courier,* April 19, 1839.

New York." Whether or not the Locofocos were radical prole-
tarians, expectant capitalists, or neo-Jeffersonian "opponents of
industrialism" is much debated by historians, but there is little
doubt regarding the egalitarian façade that they projected.[35]
It was this liberal image that attracted Dorr. The Whigs had no
group to match the Locofocos, so Dorr disregarded such relatively conservative elements within the party of Jackson as the
local South County farmers and the Tammany leaders, and
hitched his wagon to the Democracy.

The Democratic ideology of Equal Rights which Dorr embraced was an amalgam of Lockean theories of freedom, *laissez-
faire* economics, Calvinistic moral scruples, hostility towards
"aristocratic" privilege, and a belief in the negative liberal state.
To one adherent it meant "the equal protection of every citizen
in his rights — the impartial administration of justice, the supremacy of the laws in their power of punishment and protection over all — equal means of wealth, education and advancement to every citizen — the universal diffusion of intelligence
and the promotion of honesty, industry and virtue among every
class — and the subordination of all mere pecuniary and temporary interests to the good of man, in all his moral and immortal
qualities." To the Equal Rights Democrat an "aristocrat" was
someone empowered by law to affect the economic and social
welfare of his contemporaries, or who enjoyed legal privileges

---

[35] Edward Pessen, *Jacksonian America: Society, Personality, Politics*
(Homewood, Illinois, 1969), pp. 293–97. The radical aspects of Locofocoism are presented by William Trimble, "Diverging Tendencies in
New York Democracy in the Period of the Locofocos," *American Historical Review*, XXIV (April, 1919), 396–421 and "The Social Philosophy of the Locofoco Democracy," *The American Journal of Sociology*,
XXVI (May, 1921), 705–15. The "capitalist on the make" interpretation is found in Walter Hugins, *Jacksonian Democracy and the Working
Class* (Stanford, Calif., 1960), pp. 112–28, 132–202; the emphasis on
their agrarian mentality and their opposition to the emerging commer-
cial-industrial order is found in Carl Degler, "The Locofocos: Urban
'Agrarians,'" *Journal of Economic History*, XVI (Sept., 1956), 322–33,
A good contemporary account of Locofocoism is Fitzwilliam Byrdsall,
*History of the Loco-Foco or Equal Rights Party, Its Movements, Conven-
tions and Proceedings, With Short Characteristic Sketches of Its Prominent Men* (New York, 1842).

that gave him an advantage over his fellow citizen. Property
qualifications for voting, corporate charters with monopolistic
grants, and special business concessions like the Rhode Island
"bank process" were examples of privilege and denials of equal
rights.

The ultimate target of the equal rights crusade was not wealth
but privilege. New York editor Levi Slamm, a strong supporter
of Dorr in 1842, proclaimed that he "would remove every obstacle in the road to wealth, every act of legislation conferring
advantages to the *few*, and adding unjustly to the burdens of the
many, and confine legislation to its purely legitimate object, *protection to person and property.*" It was equal *rights* for which
these Democrats contended — not the leveling of all social and
economic distinctions, but the eradication of unwarranted social
distinctions that represented the triumph of privilege over equality. "It is said ours is a leveling system," William S. Balch told
the Rhode Island Suffrage Association in 1841. "I admit it. But,
thank God, we level *up*. . . . We destroy no man's rights; but
contend for the rights of the oppressed, the proscribed, the dis-
enfranchised." [36]

Dorr's political and ideological conversion sheds much light

---

[36] This analysis of Equal Rights ideology is derived mainly from the
perceptive study by Rush Welter, *The Mind of America, 1820–1860*
(New York, 1975), pp. 77–104. Balch's statement is contained in *Popular Liberty and Equal Rights. An Oration, delivered before the Mass
Convention of the R. I. Suffrage Association . . . July Fifth, 1841*
(Providence, 1841), p. 21. On the concept of the "negative liberal state"
see Lee Benson, *The Concept of Jacksonian Democracy: New York as
a Test Case* (Princeton, N. J., 1961), pp. 86–109. It should be noted
that the egalitarian philosophy of equal rights made no provision to
forestall the development of a wealthy class that did not depend on legal
privilege. Perhaps this fact helps explain the conclusion reached by Edward Pessen that "during the age of egalitarianism [1828–1845] wealth
became more unequally distributed with each passing season. Shared
less equally, even at the era's beginnings, than 'it had been a generation
or two earlier, in the aftermath of the Revolution, wealth became concentrated in the hands of an ever smaller percentage of the population. . . . Far from being an age of equality, the antebellum decades
were featured by an inequality that surpasses anything experienced by
the United States in the twentieth century," in "The Egalitarian Myth
and the American Social Reality: Wealth, Mobility and Equality in the

on the Constitutional party's role in the August 1837 congressional election. The Democrats, suffering from the stigma of economic depression, were running scared. The Whigs, who had not even contested the April state election, sensed their opportunity and advanced a slate composed of Robert B. Cranston and Joseph L. Tillinghast. At this juncture Dorr, still a nominal Whig whose political conversion was unannounced,[37] put a Constitutional prox into the field. This ticket, bearing his own name and that of Dr. Dan King, caused many who were Whigs nationally and Constitutionalists locally to react with anger and astonishment. They felt that Dorr's candidacy would draw off votes from the Cranston-Tillinghast ticket and allow Democrats Dutee Pearce and Jesse Howard to emerge victorious. Unbeknown to them, this was Dorr's intention.

William Peckham, the recent Constitutionalist candidate for governor, was first suggested for a congressional spot, but informed Dorr that he could do nothing in the coming election to defeat the Whig candidates.[38] Later, after Dr. Dan King of Charlestown had been selected as Dorr's running mate, Peckham approached the South County physician and urged him to withdraw. King informed Dorr that the Whigs in his area "abominate our measures and censure you and me severely for taking a course that they say will defeat the election of their candidates." They charge, said King, that those who back us in this election are "reprobate Whigs, and they declare that they will never again be caught in our ranks." [39]

Newport Whigs agreed with Peckham. Charles Tilley expressed his "astonishment" to see Dorr's name advanced as a candidate for Congress. Tilley declared himself "decidedly opposed" to the party's participation in this election, and added that he spoke

---

'Era of the Common Man,' " *American Historical Review,* LXXVI (Oct., 1971), 1027.

[37] Dorr waited until late 1837, when the Panic had cost the Democrats their popularity, to divulge his switch to the Jackson party, so that he "could join them without a disreputable imputation of selfish motives." DP, A 1154.

[38] Peckham to TWD, June 14, 1837, DC, II.

[39] Dan King to TWD, July 24, 1837, *ibid.*

"the sentiments of every Constitutionalist in this County." In disgust he resigned his place as one of the Constitutional party's Committee of Nomination, proclaiming that "I shall do all I can to aid the Whig candidates." [40]

Dorr's closer friends, such as John H. Weeden and Charles Randall, did not oppose his candidacy, but they had grave doubts concerning the ability of the Constitutional prox to poll a respectable vote. "I am now of opinion," said Weeden of Pawtucket, "that a great majority of those who would rank themselves as Constitutionalists and vote and act with us upon the abstract question of constitutional reform is against running a ticket at this time." [41] Charles Randall of Warren in Bristol County concurred. "All our friends are Whigs," he observed, "and I have heard many of them say that they shall not vote for us this time." We must accept the fact, he concluded, "that the Constitutionalists in this county are Whigs." [42]

Notwithstanding these admonitions, Dorr persisted. But the predictions of his colleagues were borne out, and the Constitutional slate fared dismally. Dorr's attempt to strike a blow for the Democracy while publicizing his constitutional cause was frustrated. He and King polled seventy-two and twenty-five votes respectively, out of a total turnout of 7,615, and the Whig candidates were both victorious. [43]

The Constitutional party never again contested an election. On the heels of this humiliating defeat even the zealous Charles Randall informed Dorr that "he had pulled down the Constitutional flag." "I have gotten most discouraged," the Warren

---

[40] Charles N. Tilley to TWD, July 15, 1837, *ibid.*

[41] Weeden to TWD, July 31, 1837, *ibid.*

[42] Randall to TWD, July 12, Aug. 15 and 26, 1837, *ibid.*

[43] *RI Manual,* 1937–38, p. 205. The Democratic leaders desperately tried to salvage victory. Their efforts in this contest, as revealed by Governor Francis, were typical of Rhode Island political campaigns: "Pearce sent me a letter from Block Island, this P.M. They want $500 more on the Island. The writer frankly confesses that nearly every vote on the Island can be bought." Francis to E. R. Potter, Jr., Aug. 26, 1837, Potter Collection. In an earlier missive Francis exhorted Potter: "Let our whole strength be brought out and never mind what it costs." Francis to Potter, Aug. 19, 1837, Francis Collection.

editor lamented, "when I find, as I have here, that no one seems to care . . . anything about the party — especially nonfreeholders — that it is almost impossible to get up a meeting, to get delegates or get money." [44]

In October of this disappointing year the downtrodden reformers experienced yet another setback. A memorial from the town of Smithfield protesting the inequality of representation was disdainfully rejected. After a perfunctory examination of Smithfield's plea, the House Judiciary Committee reported that "the General Assembly have no jurisdiction over the subject of this memorial." [45]

Dorr, displaying his characteristic tenacity, tried to secure the convening of another state convention in January 1838 to nominate a slate of general officers for the April election. Few responded to the call; the convention never met; and the Constitutional party died a peaceful death.[46]

IV

There are many reasons for the demise of the Constitutionalists. Inadequate financing was a principal cause. Those party records that survive give ample evidence of its fiscal plight, and nowhere was the paucity of funds more evident than in the organization's futile efforts to publish its own newspaper. The first experiment, the *Constitutionalist*, collapsed in 1834 after two issues. Then Charles Randall came to the rescue. He offered to append to the title of his *Northern Star* the word "Constitutionalist" and to devote several columns each week in publicizing the need for reform.[47] In 1836, the newly-founded *Providence Morning*

---

[44] Randall to TWD, Sept. 10 and Dec. 20, 1837, Constitutional Party Papers, #50–51.

[45] D. Mss., III, memorial dated October, 1837.

[46] Randall to TWD, Dec. 20, 1837, Constitutional Party Papers, #51; Note by Dorr on verso of a letter from Philip B. Stiness to TWD, Nov. 8, 1838, DC, II.

[47] Charles Randall to TWD, June 23, Aug. 11, and Oct. 22, 1834, DC, II.

Courier also espoused the cause. This sheet, published by temperance advocate William G. Larned, was a semi-weekly of small circulation to which Dorr contributed numerous reform articles because of Larned's disposition to "open his columns to all good tempered constitutional communications." [48]

Despite the assistance of Randall and Larned, however, the party wanted its own press. But every attempt to resurrect the *Constitutionalist* failed. The most concerted effort came in December 1835. A plan was devised by Metcalf Marsh to raise the $1,000 a year necessary to sustain a paper by getting fifty subscribers to underwrite the expense of publication through a pledge of twenty dollars each. By February 1836 only twelve had subscribed, and no further funds were offered.[49]

Financial destitution was but one of many reasons for the organization's demise. In addition, the faction labored under the disabilities peculiar to a third party with one limited and local goal. The two major political camps commanded the attention and allegiance of the electorate because of their alignment with the national issues and personalities of this turbulent age — the Constitutionalists paled by comparison. Popular absorption with what one dejected Coventry reformer called "grand national political principles" weakened the Constitutionalists' appeal.[50] Further, several of the party's candidates were at best lukewarm supporters of governmental revision. Included among these tepid reformers were such men as Nehemiah Knight and Samuel Ward King. The later, a Constitutionalist candidate for state senator in 1834, eventually emerged as the Law and Order (anti-Dorr) governor in 1842.[51]

---

[48] *Morning Courier* (Providence), 1836–37, *passim*. TWD to Marsh, June 27, 1836, Marsh Papers. Only scattered issues of the *Courier* have been preserved. *The Pawtucket Chronicle,* the *Woonsocket Patriot,* and the *Manufacturers' and Farmers' Journal* were also sympathetic to reform. See *The Constitutionalist,* April 7, 1834.

[49] Constitutional Party Papers, #25. TWD to Marsh, Nov. 10, 1835, Marsh Papers.

[50] Asahel Johnson to TWD, Jan. 10, 1837, DC, II.

[51] Journalist Jacob Frieze who was active in the formation of the Constitutional Party (Constitutional Party Papers, #13) was also a "Law

The Panic of 1837 also had a debilitating effect on the Constitutionalist movement, for the depression placed economic survival ahead of political rights on the average Rhode Islander's list of priorities. And another factor contributing to the party's disintegration was Dorr's congressional candidacy in August 1837. Many Whigs were so disturbed by this maneuver, and by Dorr's political switch, that they made their temporary defection from the Constitutional ranks permanent.[52]

Further, a majority of the disfranchised failed to give the reform campaign of 1833 to 1837 vigorous and sustained support. This apathy was a frequent complaint of Dorr and Randall.[53] Finally, and most important, the moderate movement of the 1830s failed because the landholding establishment resolutely resisted. Although freemen such as Dorr, Angell, and Tillinghast played leading roles in the formation of the Constitutional party, the vast majority of the freeholders disapproved. As conservative Democrat John R. Waterman correctly observed in 1834 when the party was in its infancy: "The question of a constitution and free suffrage, either connected or alone, are the most unpopular subjects that can be brought before the freemen of this state." [54] This unpopularity was further increased when opponents distorted the party's relatively mild suffrage plank by claiming

---

and Order" man in 1842. His *Concise History of the Efforts to Obtain an Extension of Suffrage in Rhode Island* . . . (1842) was heavily slanted against the Dorrites. Even Dorr's brother-in-law, Samuel Ames (later chief justice of the state Supreme Court), an active Constitutionalist in 1834, became a staunch opponent of the 1842 movement. It seems that the reformers' resort to force and extra-legal procedures account for the defections of Frieze and Ames.

[52] By December 1837 Dorr was an announced Democrat and even on speaking terms with arch-conservative John Brown Francis. The latter breathed a sigh of relief when Dorr "acknowledged that his Constitutional party" was "defunct." Francis to Potter, Dec. 23, 1837, Francis Collection.

[53] See for example Randall to TWD, Sept. 10, 1837, Constitutional Party Papers, #50; and Randall to TWD, Jan. 20, 1836, DC, II.

[54] John R. Waterman to Elisha R. Potter, Sr., March 14, 1834, Potter Collection; See Dexter Randall to Dutee J. Pearce, March 2, 1834, William Davis Miller Collection; and John Brown Francis to John R. Waterman, Jan. 1, 1834, Warwick Mss., Box 10, Misc. Mss., RIHS.

that the reformers sought "universal," and "indiscriminate" suffrage.[55]

Any one of these obstacles was formidable; together they were insuperable. In November 1838, Philip B. Stiness, a Providence businessman and civic leader, wrote to Dorr urging a resurrection of the party and claiming the time was propitious for such a move. Dorr called on Stiness and gave him this terse report: "Marsh, Angell and myself *died* in the last ditch of Constitutionalism in January last. The towns refused to send delegates to a convention. The freemen had decided to act in the Constitutional cause, and the non-freeholders were entirely indifferent as to its success, and seemed quite willing to have the *foot* set down upon their necks. That being the case, they deserved their fate. We owed it to self-respect to make no more vain calls to ears dead to all questions relating to political liberty and equal rights." [56]

In later years Dorr rendered a harsh appraisal on the efforts of the Constitutional party — it "accomplished nothing," he asserted.[57] This judgment, though severe, is almost accurate. Apart from securing the call of the abortive constitutional convention of 1834, the party's only significant achievement was to demonstrate to would-be reformers that moderation and traditional methods of obtaining redress were inadequate remedies

---

[55] The Constitutionalists were very much disturbed by this distortion and its possible effect upon their appeal. See Dorr's remarks to a party gathering on May 2, 1834, *Manufacturers' and Farmers' Journal,* May 8, 1834; and his comments in the 1834 debate over the convention bill. *Ibid.,* Sept. 3, 1834; and Charles Peckham to TWD, March 11, 1836, DC, II.

[56] Philip B. Stiness to TWD, Nov. 8, 1838 and Dorr's notation on the reverse of this letter, DC, II. A decade and a half later, Dorr, in an obituary for Metcalf Marsh, summed up the situation in the 1830s as follows: "Those who controlled the state through a limited suffrage were satisfied with things as they were. It was easier to control a small than a large constituency; and they regarded the attempt [at constitutional reform] as an unwarranted intrusion upon long standing arrangements and vested rights, with the intimation that those who were dissatisfied with the present order of things, and who did not like the state, were at liberty to leave it." Clipping from *Providence Post,* 1852, DP.

[57] DP, A 1154.

for eliminating the political abuses that continued to beset the state.[58] Bolder, more drastic action was necessary, or so it seemed, to persuade the adamant establishment to yield.

---

[58] The cautiousness and moderation of the Rhode Island reform movement prior to mid-1841 is stressed by Robert Wetmore Stoughton, "The Philosophy of Dorrism," (unpublished master's thesis, Brown University, 1936), pp. 105–122; Robert L. Ciaburri, "The Dorr Rebellion in Rhode Island: The Moderate Phase," *Rhode Island History*, XXVI (July, 1967), 73–87; and George Marshel Dennison, "The Constitutional Issues of the Dorr War: A study in the Evolution of American Constitutionalism, 1776–1849," (unpublished doctoral dissertation, University of Washington, 1967). Dennison went so far as to state that "reform in Rhode Island had suffered the long-time ailment of overcautiousness, acquiescing when the freeholders, very clearly a minority, refused to ratify reforms at the polls" (p. 159). Dennison's work is mainly an analysis of the national impact of three basic issues raised by the Dorr Rebellion and its legal offspring, *Luther v. Borden* (1849): (1) the right of the people to draft a constitution without the sanction of existing governmental authorities; (2) the doctrine of political questions; and (3) the use and meaning of martial law. In his extensive study Dennison provides a thirty-seven page survey of Rhode Island constitutional development from 1776 to 1840 (pp. 129–166). It is drawn mainly from secondary accounts and nineteenth century pamphlet material, and thus, it contains several inaccurate statements that are repeated in Dennison's published revision, *The Dorr War: Republicanism on Trial, 1831–1861* (Lexington, Ky., 1976).

CHAPTER TWELVE

The Forceful Effort

I

At the close of the Revolutionary era, America's golden age of constitution-making, Nathaniel Chipman, an eminent Vermont jurist, congratulated America's political practitioners for having included in the new basic laws of the several states "a healing principle," a "plan of reformation," and "means for their own improvement." If the constitutional convention was one of the most distinctive institutional contributions our revolutionaries made to Western politics, then the idea of incorporating in that instrument itself a process of amendment was a special stroke of genius.

Chipman, in a perceptive pamphlet entitled *Sketches of the Principles of Government* (1793), commented on this innovation. He observed that all previous societies had been compelled to suffer with inflexible forms of government despite extensive changes in their nature. "The confining of a people who have arrived at a highly improved state of society, to the forms and principles of a government, which originated in a simple, if not barbarous state of men and manners," was, said Chipman, like Chinese foot-binding, a "perversion of nature," causing an incongruity between the form of the government and the character of the society, *that usually ended in a violent eruption, in a forceful effort to bring the government into accord with the new social temperament of the people.*[1]

Such was the situation in Rhode Island at the end of the fourth decade of the nineteenth century. During the period from 1790 to 1840, manufacturing transformed Rhode Island's economy and helped produce significant alterations in the distribution, concentration, and characteristics of the population. These demographic changes rendered Rhode Island's legal and constitutional structure anachronistic and inadequate to meet the needs of a new society.

When proposals for reform were repeatedly rejected or ignored for sectional or selfish interests by the landholding establishment, storm clouds had gathered and reformers from all sides of the political spectrum, such as George Burrill, James Davis Knowles, William E. Richmond, and Seth Luther, espoused bold, extralegal, and even radical measures to achieve their desired ends.

By 1840 the determination to maintain the status quo and the necessity for reform had reached their greatest intensity. This internal pressure was augmented by strong national currents of change. In the period from 1829 through 1851, twenty-five of the thirty-one states held constitutional conventions. This was an era of "vigorous constitutional activity." [2] It was also an age of reform. In 1841 Ralph Waldo Emerson observed that America was conducting a "general inquisition into abuses. . . . In the history of the world the doctrine of Reform had never such scope as at the present hour." It seemed to Emerson that every human institution was being questioned —"Christianity, the laws, commerce, schools, the farm, the laboratory"— and that there was

---

[1] This paraphrase of Chipman (italics mine) is taken from Gordon S. Wood, *The Creation of the American Republic, 1776–1787* (Chapel Hill, N. C., 1969), pp. 342–43, 613–15. Wood renders a brilliant analysis of the development of constitutional theory during this formative era.

[2] Bayrd Still, "State Constitutional Development in the United States, 1829–1851" (unpublished doctoral dissertation, University of Wisconsin, 1933).

not a "town, statute, rite, calling, man, or woman, but is threatened by the new spirit." Indeed, "the demon of reform" roamed the land — moralistic and comprehensive — seeking the liberation and perfection of the individual in a truly egalitarian society.[3] These broader impulses fueled the fires of discontent in reactionary Rhode Island. A showdown between the immoveable object and the irresistible force appeared imminent. Only a catalyst was needed.[4]

That spark came in 1840. In January the Assembly passed an ill-advised militia reorganization act. This stringent measure imposed a burdensome and elaborate system of fines and penalties on those liable to service if they failed to comply with its directives.[5] Since the overwhelming percentage of militiamen were non-freeholders, this act "bore with disproportionate heaviness" upon them, aroused them from their lethargy, and reawakened sentiments similar to but stronger than those which marked the 1833 suffrage campaign. The measure has been described by one

---

[3] Emerson's statement is contained in his essay "Man the Reformer" printed in Henry Steele Commager (ed.), *The Era of Reform, 1830–1860* (Princeton, N. J., 1960), pp. 20–24. See also Walter Hugins (ed.), *The Reform Impulse, 1825–1850* (New York, 1972); C. S. Griffin, *The Ferment of Reform, 1830–1860* (New York, 1967); John L. Thomas, "Romantic Reform in America, 1815–1865," *American Quarterly*, XXII (1965), 656–81; Alice Felt Tyler, *Freedom's Ferment: Phases of American Social History to 1860* (Minneapolis, 1944); and Arthur M. Schlesinger, *The American As Reformer* (Cambridge, Mass., 1950). On contemporary British reform (which influenced Dorr) consult Geoffrey B. A. M. Finlayson, *Decade of Reform: England in the Eighteen Thirties* (New York, 1970).

[4] Contemporary political scientists have described similar situations: "Political systems have a disagreeable tendency to remain static in the face of sociological change, and it is quite possible for the degree of resistance to political adjustment to manifest itself in direct proportion to the intensity of social change." William C. Havard and Loren P. Beth, *The Politics of Mis-Representation* (Baton Rouge, La., 1962), p. 2. In an analysis of the American constitution-making process, James Willard Hurst contends that the action of Rhode Island's political establishment prior to the Dorr Rebellion affords the prime example of a "fundamental political truth: the peril of unreasonably damming up change." Hurst, *The Growth of American Law: The Law Makers* (Boston, 1950), pp. 206–07.

[5] *Schedules,* January session, 1840, pp. 3–32, especially pp. 24–26.

perceptive contemporary as "the nucleus" of the suffrage agitation during the years 1840 to 1842.[6]

At approximately the time the onerous militia law was enacted, the New York Locofocos decided to export their universal suffrage doctrines to Rhode Island. On August 31, 1839, Jared Bell's *New Era* had urged the Democrats of the state "to commence immediately the agitation of [suffrage] reform." Next, Bell and his associates drafted a memorial to Congress attacking "the unconstitutional charter of Rhode Island" and requesting federal legislation allowing "citizens of the United States" to vote for presidential electors and a constitutional amendment to "admit all free white citizens of the United States, similarly circumstanced as the unenfranchised white people of Rhode Island, to vote for members of Congress from the states wherein they reside, so that the voice of the majority of the inhabitants of Rhode Island, instead of a chartered minority, shall be heard with the rest of their fellow citizens in the councils of the nation." [7]

By January 1840, other Equal Rights Democrats from the Empire State decided to make Rhode Island their missionary field. The "First Social Reform Society of New York" prepared and published *An Address to the Citizens of Rhode Island Who Are Denied the Right of Suffrage* — an eight-page brochure that was widely disseminated in the early months of this turbulent political

---

[6] [Frances H. (Whipple) McDougall], *Might and Right* (Providence, 1844), pp. 70–71. This work is the most useful and reliable of the many contemporary accounts written from the Dorrite viewpoint. Abraham H. Stillwell assisted Mrs. McDougall in its preparation. The most formidable anti-Dorr tracts are Elisha Potter's *Considerations* and Dexter Randall's, *Democracy Vindicated and Dorrism Unveiled* (Providence, 1846).

[7] *New Era*, August 31, September 7, 10 and 14, 1839. The *New Era* began its crusade upon the receipt of news from Rhode Island that Democratic congressional candidates Benjamin B. Thurston and Thomas Wilson Dorr had been narrowly defeated in the August House election. Bell, Levi Slamm, and others associated with the *New Era* urged suffrage extension in part to discredit the Whigs and also because they assumed that an enlarged franchise would benefit the Rhode Island Democracy. The latter was, however, a questionable assumption. *Providence Journal*, September 3, 6 and 10, 1839.

year. This tract detailed procedures for the calling of a constitutional convention, with delegates to be apportioned on the basis of population and elected by all adult male citizens. The regular Assembly was to be bypassed, and the government created under the new document was to elect state and congressional officials. The members of Congress thus chosen were to claim their seats in the national legislature and "the responsibility would then devolve upon Congress of deciding whether members from a majority of the people, elected under a Republican Constitution, framed by the people themselves, shall have seats in the councils of the nation, or [whether] members from an incorporated body of land *Lords,* and their eldest sons," should be so favored.[8]

"Unadulterated locofocoism," responded the Whig *Journal,* which labelled the tract the product of "political Jacobins." The Democratic organ, the *Republican Herald,* in more subdued tones, averred that the Democrats of Rhode Island were "firmly attached to the present laws regulating the elective franchise." Their New York brethren were causing them considerable embarrassment.[9]

On the heels of the militia statute and the bold recommendations of the First Social Reform Society, several small meetings were held in Union Hall by mechanics of Providence for the purpose of obtaining an enlargement of the franchise and an equalization of representation. Each successive gathering attracted additional malcontents until finally, on March 27, 1840, these dissidents formally created the Rhode Island Suffrage Association.[10]

---

[8] First Social Reform Society of New York, *An Address to the Citizens of Rhode Island Who Are Denied the Right of Suffrage* (n.p., 1840), Rider Collection. Gettleman doubts that this pamphlet originated in New York (pp. 31–32), but I see no compelling reason to deny its authenticity in view of previous New York Locofoco interest in Rhode Island.

[9] *Providence Journal,* January 29, February 5 and April 25, 1840; *Republican Herald* (Providence), February 1, 1840.

[10] *Might and Right,* pp. 70–72. Arthur May Mowry, *The Dorr War* (Providence, 1901), the standard study of the Dorr Rebellion, errone-

According to contemporary accounts, this nonpartisan group was formed by workingmen "without wealth, [and] with no pretensions to learning"; by those voteless men "who did military duty and worked the fire engines." [11] Their primary demand was universal suffrage; their subsidiary request was reapportionment. These malcontents also realized that the status of freeman conferred civil as well as political advantages, because a landless citizen could not serve on juries nor could he commence a court suit for the recovery of a debt, or obtain redress for a personal injury (tort) unless a freeholder endorsed his writ. Other reformers were disturbed by abuses in the freehold system whereby bogus voters were qualified. According to the testimony of a land conveyancer, tracts in mill villages "were divided into house lots and these lots were conveyed to individuals who would vote as the grantor desired; the grantor retaining the grantee's note for a sum above the actual worth of the land for his security." This long-standing practice was "extensively used" in 1840.[12] These conditions the suffragists resolved to eliminate.

The Association invited to membership "any American citizen, resident of Rhode Island of the age of twenty-one years." It levied no discrimination against naturalized citizens such as that imposed by the Constitutional party of the 1830s (making the group especially reprehensible to many a Rhode Island nativist), and it was more militant than its predecessor. "The right of suffrage we do not ask as a favor," these exasperated mechanics asserted, "we claim it as our own. We demand it." Their first

---

ously states that the Association was "organized in the autumn of 1840" (p. 50). Mowry's account of the 1840 excitement is further weakened by his failure to recognize the significance of the militia act. The greatest defect in his study, however, is his total neglect of the anti-Irish-Catholic sentiment that served as a serious obstacle to sweeping suffrage reform in the period 1841–42.

[11] Frieze, pp. 28–9; *Providence Journal*, February 17, 1842. See also the remarks of Dorr, *Burke's Report*, pp. 724, 734.

[12] *Preamble and Constitution of the Rhode Island Suffrage Association Adopted Friday Evening, March 27, 1840* (Providence, 1840), pp. 10–11; *Burke's Report*, 12–13 and 276–77 (testimony of Aaron White, Jr.,); *New Age*, Feb. 5, 1841.

appeal, they avowed, was "to heaven," next "to the whole people of Rhode Island," then "to the General Assembly." "These
failing, our final resort shall be to the Congress of the United
States . . . and, if need be, to the Supreme Judicial Power, to
test the force and meaning of that provision in the Constitution,
which guarantees to every State in the Union a republican form
of government." Here was a determination unequalled by earlier
reformers. In conclusion, they vowed "not to shrink from the
task till it shall have been accomplished." "We know our rights,"
they admonished, "and knowing, dare maintain them." [13]

When the Rhode Island Suffrage Association sprang to life
in 1840, it had a large constituency from which to draw recruits.
According to the most reliable figures, there were at that time
25,674 white adult males in the state. The suffragists deducted
3,000 from that total for aliens, criminals, insane, and those
under guardianship, leaving 22,674 potential white male voters.
The reformers further calculated that there were 9,590 freeman
in 1840. These statistics showed that approximately 13,084 or
57.7 percent of the white adult males were disfranchised by the
prevailing suffrage law. In addition, there were close to 700 adult
male Negroes who suffered a similar disqualification and who
were increasingly restive because of it. Such a large body of
second-class citizens, numbering nearly 13,800, could not be ignored with impunity,[14] as the growing ranks of the suffragists
revealed.

The excitement among Rhode Island's non-freeholders produced by the militia act, the "meddling" Locofocos, and the formation of the Suffrage Association was further heightened by the
development of the hectic "Log Cabin and Hard Cider" cam-

---

[13] *Preamble, R. I. Suffrage Association,* pp. 8–9.

[14] *Burke's Report,* pp. 120–22; Snow, *RI Census,* xlv–xlvi. In 1840,
there were 3,243 blacks in Rhode Island and they composed 2.98 percent
of the population. Of these all but five were free. See "table of population," Broadside File (1840), RIHS; J. D. B. DeBow, *Statistical View of
the United States . . . Being A Compendium of the Seventh Census*
(Washington, 1854), pp. 63, 83; J. Stanley Lemons and Michael A.
McKenna, "Re-enfranchisement of Rhode Island Negroes," *Rhode Island
History,* XXX (Winter, 1971), 3–8.

paign of 1840.[15] Although the colorful duel between "Tippecanoe" and "Little Van" tended to obscure and overshadow
local issues, it also rekindled resentments among those many
Rhode Islanders who were denied the right to participate in the
selection of their nation's president.[16] In the aftermath of this
contest, therefore, as was the case subsequent to the elections of
1828 and 1832, the disfranchised of Rhode Island rebelled
against the disabilities to which they were subjected. But now,
they were more exasperated, more impatient, more determined,
more numerous, and better organized than they had been eight
or twelve years before.

Further, the techniques of the "Coonskin Campaign" of 1840
gave the suffragists an infectious *modus operandi*. Parades, mass-
meetings, songs, banners, slogans, torchlight processions, oxen-
roasts, and bonfires helped carry the day for the Whigs, and this
hoopla generated intense enthusiasm and unprecedented popular participation. The suffragists, therefore, reasoned that they
could use such devices to arouse Rhode Island's second-class citizens and incite them to vigorous action. These demonstrations
lacked the logic and decorum of the traditional petitions, but
they indicated a show of strength that could not be so insolently
denied.[17]

---

[15] Another factor contributing to the agitation of 1840 has been suggested. Beryl Lee Crowe, "The Dorr Rebellion: A Study of Revolutionary Behavior," (unpublished master's thesis, University of California,
1961), in a jargon-laden and error-riddled account, vainly attempts to
show that the Dorr Rebellion was "causally related to the Panic of
1837." One of Crowe's mentors, on the basis of this dubious interpretation, likened Dorr's Rebellion to the Russian Revolution of 1917 and the
Egyptian Revolution of 1952 in a study of the causes of civil disturbances. For this far-fetched analogy see James C. Davies, "Toward a
Theory of Revolution," *American Sociological Review*, XXVII (February, 1962), 5–19.

[16] Charles T. Congdon recalled that "the year 1840 was one of great
political activity everywhere, and the contest in Rhode Island was a particularly lively one. People who could not vote, more than ever envied
those who could." Congdon, *Reminiscences of a Journalist* (Boston,
1880), p. 106.

[17] Some cautious Rhode Island Whigs were apprehensive concerning
the consequences of their popularly-oriented campaign: "I fear that the

II

The election of 1840 brought complete victory to Rhode Island's Whigs. In April, Samuel Ward King trounced Equal Rights Democrat Thomas F. Carpenter in the race for governor by a margin of 4,797 to 3,418. This large turnout (second numerically only to the gubernatorial contest of 1818) [18] also gave the Whigs firm control of the General Assembly.

In the fall, Rhode Islanders emphatically rejected Martin Van Buren and awarded their votes to "Tippecanoe" and John Tyler (5,278 to 3,301). Then, in late October, the legislature sent Whig party boss James F. Simmons to the Senate of the United States. These results were especially embarrassing to Thomas Dorr, for he now held the chairmanship of the Democratic State Committee and presided over a party divided between the formerly dominant conservative agrarians led by John Brown Francis and a newly emergent Equal Rights faction whose principal spokesman was Dorr himself.[19]

Log Cabin & hard cider scheme will be carried too far by our friends — there is nothing in that sort of nonsense that is in good keeping with our Rhode Island & Roger Williams character — It is the essence of Locofocoism, and carries with it to most minds the idea of hickory tree days." Henry Y. Cranston to James F. Simmons, Simmons Papers, Box 8 (1840). The Whig tactics in this national campaign are described in Schlesinger, pp. 283–305 and Robert Gray Gunderson, *The Log-Cabin Campaign* (Lexington, Ky., 1957). The impact of techniques such as those employed by the Suffrage Association has been assessed by a leading student of the mob: "despite their peaceful pretensions, these colorful and massive displays alarmed the authorities and propertied classes almost as much as the acts of violence themselves." George Rudé, *The Crowd in History . . . 1730–1848* (New York, 1964), p. 239.

[18] The state's highest *percentage* of free white adult males voting was 49.4. This was registered in the William Jones-James Fenner gubernatorial contest of 1812. McCormick, "New Perspectives," p. 292. Thomas Carpenter was an Equal Rights Democrat who supported Dorr in 1842, defended Irish-born John Gordon in the famous murder trial of 1844, and eventually converted to Roman Catholicism. Conley and Smith, pp. 53–54.

[19] *Rhode Island Manual*, 1965–66, pp. 211–16; Brigham, pp. 332–33. On the agrarian Democrat's fear of Rhode Island "locofocoism" consult Charles Greene to John Brown Francis, March 5, 1838 and Elisha R. Potter, Jr. to Francis, February, 1838, Francis Collection, RIHS. The

Once Rhode Island's privileged minority had completed its electioneering, however, their deprived and aggrieved brethren again took the field. In Providence on November 20, 1840, Dr. John A. Brown, botanical physician, former Constitutionalist and president of the Rhode Island Suffrage Association, began publication of the *New Age and Constitutional Advocate,* a sheet whose primary aims were "to urge upon the attention of all fair and candid men of all parties, sects and classes, the odious and unjust restrictions of our present suffrage laws," and "to strike a blow" for "equal rights." [20] This paper, soon subsidized by the Suffrage Association,[21] was destined to be much more successful than the *Constitutionalist* of 1834. It waged a campaign of education and inspiration during the ensuing months which gave a perceptible lift to the suffrage cause.

As Dr. Brown embarked upon his new venture, the tempo of reform activity quickened, especially in the expanding industrial towns. Local suffrage chapters were created in several villages, and the ranks of the reformers grew as more and more non-freeholders became aroused. The movement also enlisted the support of some altruistic freemen similar to those who had formed the nucleus of the defunct Constitutional party, and it attracted a few opportunistic urban Democratic politicians, recently unburdened from the cares of office by the local Whig landslide.[22] The latter felt, as William Tillinghast once phrased

---

Francis correspondence also includes several 1840 letters from Democratic State Committee Chairman Thomas Wilson Dorr.

[20] *New Age and Constitutional Advocate* (Providence), November 20, 1840. An interesting account of the origins of the *New Age* is found in Congdon, pp. 106–07. Congdon, who became Horace Greeley's principal assistant on the *New York Tribune,* was a nineteen-year-old Brown graduate in 1840 when he was hired by Dr. Brown to edit the *New Age.* Congdon's *Reminiscences* reveal that this New Bedford, Massachusetts native was more interested in a job and experience than in political reform. Congdon stated that he "engaged to convulse Rhode Island (with the Plantations thrown in) for the modest remuneration of five dollars per week." He said in 1880 "that whoever read my long dissertations upon the nature and origin of government, is, at this moment, if living, entitled to my most abject apologies." Congdon, p. 107.

[21] *New Age,* December 4, 1840.

[22] Democratic opportunism was a factor in the agitation of 1841–42

it, that when suffrage was extended, the formerly disfranchised citizens of Rhode Island would "not be so pusillanimous as to choose for their rulers those who have always been their tyrants, or so ungrateful as not to remember their liberators." [23]

Another evidence of activity in December 1840 was the circulation of a petition in the northern towns requesting a written constitution and an extension of suffrage. This document, the so-called Dillingham Petition, contained 581 signatures when it was presented to the General Assembly at its January session 1841.[24]

This meeting of the legislature, like that of the preceding January, was a most important gathering, not so much for what it accomplished as for the blunders it made. Its major mistakes insofar as they related to the prevailing reform demands were threefold. First, it accorded the Dillingham document the fate traditionally reserved for such presumptuous requests by tabling it permanently.[25] A second but lesser tactical error was prompted by a petition from several Providence Negroes. Alfred Niger, a leader of the city's 1,300 member Negro community, George McCarty, and several associates, submitted a remonstrance that argued that the suffrage law's discrimination against blacks, imposed in 1822, was deleterious both to habits of industry and to respect for law among blacks. Though one of the requests, namely, that Negroes be allowed to sell liquor, deprived the plea of some nobility, they asked the legislators, in addition, to confer

---

but its significance has been overstated by contemporary Whig pamphleteers, for example, Frieze, pp. 30–32. That it did exist, however, can be seen in the post-election comments of the Democratic organ, the *Republican Herald,* November 4 and 14, 1840, as this sheet began to reverse gears and consider the desirability of "freer suffrage." Dorr himself thought that the suffrage restrictions had hurt the Democrats in the election of 1840. TWD to Amos Kendall, Septmber 24, 1840, DC, III. Basically the movement stemmed "from the people themselves and not politicians." TWD to Henry Dorr, June 17, 1841, DC, III and *Burke's Report,* p. 734.

23 William Tillinghast, "Free Suffrage Address," [1833], D. Mss. VII.
24 Petitions Not Granted, RISA, January 1841.
25 *Ibid.;* Journal of the House (1839–41), January session, 1841; *Burke's Report,* pp. 402–03; *New Age,* January 29, 1841.

upon them "the same rights of suffrage enjoyed by their more favored white fellow citizens." [26]

The Assembly responded in a curious and unwise manner. It passed a law that retained the color qualification for voting, but exempted men of color from town and state taxes on real and personal property to compensate for their exclusion.[27] This expedient satisfied neither the Negroes nor the host of white nonfreeholders who paid taxes despites their disqualification.[28] The legislature, almost unwittingly, was fanning the embers of discontent.

The Assembly's third *faux pas* was its inadequate response to a memorial from Smithfield asking the legislators to "take the subject of the extreme inequality of the present representation from the several towns under consideration, and in such manner as seems most practicable and just, to correct the evil complained of." [29] Since the ailing Benjamin Hazard had declined reelection the preceding August, ending a string of sixty-two consecutive House victories (his constituents obviously liked his brand of conservatism), this memorial was referred to a select committee chaired by Asher Robbins, the Newport nemesis of the convention of 1824. This group recommended that the *freemen* be allowed to decide in April town meeting whether or not a convention should be convened to effect reapportionment and other changes in the state's basic law. After much discussion and a recommittal of this resolution, the Assembly voted to call a convention without first ascertaining the wishes of the freemen. This was only a slight concession, however, because the convention

---

[26] Acts and Resolves of the General Assembly, 1841–42, RISA, XLIII, 36–37.

[27] *Schedules,* January session, 1841, p. 82. An earlier petition from Niger and other blacks in 1831 had suggested that Negroes either be enfranchised or exempted from taxation. An exemption bill was drafted, but it died in the House. Petitions Not Granted, January 1831.

[28] For evidence of Negro dissatisfaction with this arrangement see their 1841 petition demanding a repeal of the exemption statute. Petitions Not Granted, June 1841. For white resentment see *New Age,* March 5, 1841.

[29] *Burke's Report,* pp. 401–02.

resolves of February 6, 1841, authorized a November assemblage chosen in the same manner and on the same basis as the conventions of 1824 and 1834 and the Assembly itself.[30]

This was the rock upon which all chances of conciliation foundered. The reformers interpreted this maneuver as one of insincerity and diversion. Such a freeholders' convention, they reasoned, was no more intended to be a vehicle of reform than the previous conservative conclaves that had been summoned to appease the aggrieved. Acting upon this interpretation, the Rhode Island Suffrage Association met on the day following the passage of the act and approved resolves affirming the power and the right of the citizens to bypass the Assembly, draft and ratify a written constitution that would become the state's basic law.[31]

In the ensuing months the Association set out to convince a majority of the potential electorate that its position was sound and it retained dynamic speakers such as Orestes A. Brownson and Seth Luther to arouse the masses. On April 17 it conducted a giant parade in which 3,000 participated including prominent Democrats Dutee J. Pearce of Newport and Samuel Y. Atwell of Glocester. This display culminated with "a magnificent collation" of beer, roasted ox, calf, and hog consumed on Jefferson Plain overlooking the city.[32] It was followed by a more sober gathering in Newport on May 5 as the new Assembly convened. This meeting adopted twenty-one resolutions including one creating an eleven member state committee "to call a convention of delegates to draught a constitution at as early a day as possible." The dissidents then adjourned to July 5.[33]

---

[30] *Schedules*, January session, 1841, pp. 85–86; Journal of the House (1839–41), January session, 1841; *Burke's Report*, pp. 401–02; *Providence Journal*, January 23, 1841. Robbins had first attempted to secure an indefinite postponement of the memorial. The final vote in favor of calling a convention was thirty-seven to sixteen.

[31] The resolves are printed in *Burke's Report*, pp. 403–04.

[32] *New Age*, April 23, 1841; Gersuny, p. 49.

[33] For a copy of these resolves see *Burke's Report*, pp. 404–07. Members of the state committee included Charles Collins and William Peckham, gubernatorial candidates of the old Constitutionalist Party, and long-time advocate of suffrage extension, Dutee J. Pearce. *Republican Herald*, May 8, 1841.

Soon after the May demonstration, the General Assembly yielded somewhat to the mounting pressure by amending the convention bill so as to alter slightly the allocation of delegates.[34] This concession fell short of the reformers' demands, which were embodied in a bill introduced on May 7 by Samuel Atwell that not only contained a liberalized apportionment but also extended the vote for delegates and ratification to all adult male citizens with two years' state residency. This bill, which was similar to Dorr's 1834 proposal, suffered a similar fate. It was referred to the Judiciary Committee, chaired by Whig leader Henry Y. Cranston, reported and debated on June 25, with Dorr's brother-in-law, Samuel Ames, its principal opponent, and then defeated by a margin of fifty-two to ten.[35]

This rebuke further incited the suffragists, and when they met on July 5 at the Dexter Training Ground in Providence they made specific reference to the rejection of Atwell's proposal. Because the Assembly "had denied to a majority of the people . . . any participation in the convention to be held November next," a people's convention must be called. Nine members, including former Constitutional party stalwart Metcalf Marsh, were then added to the state suffrage committee. This select group set about the task of drafting specific plans for a convention,[36] urged on by Rev. William Balch who asked rhetorically: "Call it a revolution that we say intelligence, virtue, honor, patriotism makes the man and not dirt and primogeniture? Call it a revolution that we level every false distinction, every grade not based on talent or moral worth, and proclaim liberty and rights to the

---

[34] *Schedules,* May session, 1841, p. 45; *Burke's Report,* p. 409. On the inadequacy of this amendment see the *New Age,* May 14, 1841.

[35] Journal of the House (1839–41), June session, 1841; *Burke's Report,* pp. 439–42; *Providence Journal,* June 26 and 27, 1841. In an unsuccessful attempt to salvage the bill, Atwell replaced the simple residency requirement with a general taxpaying qualification. *Burke's Report,* pp. 732–33.

[36] *Burke's Report,* pp. 407–09. Before the defeat of Atwell's bill the state suffrage committee had been divided on the issue of calling a convention without authorization from existing governmental authority. For example, the committee voted against this bold course of action by the narrow margin of three to two on June 3. *New Age,* June 25, 1841.

people? Then we are revolutionists and glory in it; and we will
rejoice when such a revolution is consummated and its blessings
all revealed! . . . It is said our legislators are omnipotent. The
people are more so!" [37] According to Marvin Gettleman, "this
heady belief in the majesty of popular power signaled a subtle
but important shift in the Association's aims, as the conviction of
the people's right to act independently of constituted authority
began to overshadow the advocacy of specific reforms." [38]

On July 24 the state committee issued its "call to the people
of Rhode Island to assemble in convention." The delegates to the
proposed gathering were to be apportioned according to population and chosen by universal suffrage in town elections on August 28. The convention was to convene on October 4, 1842, a
month prior to the freemen's conclave.[39]

As these events transpired, Thomas Dorr's disillusionment concerning the possibility of reform was gradually dissolving. He
had played no part in the genesis of the 1840 agitation, and he
had demurred when the Suffrage Association attempted to secure his active participation in February 1841. At late as May
of this critical year, Dorr had declined an invitation to address
the Newport mass meeting, though he expressed support for the
cause.[40]

But Dorr's will was always weak before a noble principle, and,
as the determination of the disfranchised intensified, his earlier
frustrations as a Constitutionalist were overridden. Thus it was
Dorr who drafted Atwell's controversial convention bill in May
1841.[41] His hat and heart were in the ring again. In August,

---

[37] Balch, pp. 21–22.

[38] Gettleman, p. 43.

[39] *Burke's Report,* pp. 410–12. The suffragists were anxious to beat
the freeholders to the punch by conducting their business prior to the
November gathering scheduled by the Assembly. *New Age,* July 23, 1841.

[40] Mr. Ames to TWD, January 4, 1841, DC, III; Congdon, p. 109;
TWD to Jesse Calder, May 4, 1841, DC, III.

[41] For Dorr's role in the framing of Atwell's bill see his "Address to
the People of Rhode Island," August, 1843, *Burke's Report,* pp. 732–33.
Rudé makes several interesting observations concerning the leadership
of crowds that shed light on the nature of Dorr's involvement in the

when the citizens of Providence's second ward approached Dorr and inquired if he would serve as a delegate to the People's Convention, the once-apprehensive reformer immediately replied that his services would "be very cheerfully rendered." In response to their query concerning his views, Dorr added that he "subscribed to the resolutions of the mass conventions at Newport and Providence," and that he was "numbered among those who are denominated in politics Democratic Republicans, of the school of States Rights and Equal Rights, including universal suffrage to be exercised by all American citizens." [42]

Dorr was endorsed and elected as a delegate to the People's convention.[43] His organizational experience, his legal expertise, his high moral purpose, and his zealous desire for political reform immediately propelled him into the leadership of this bold and seemingly inexorable movement. Dorr would become the principal draftsman of the People's Constitution and the head of the extralegal government created pursuant to that liberal document — a government he was determined to sustain.

The political establishment, regardless of party, had sown the wind, and, in 1842, they would reap the whirlwind — that "forceful effort" of which Judge Chipman warned, known in Rhode Island as the Dorr Rebellion.

1841 agitation: "Leaders, too, played a part in giving the crowd cohesion and unity in guiding and directing its energies. Yet they probably never enjoyed the lonely eminence nor played the outstanding role ascribed to them in such events. . . . A distinction must be made among leaders operating from outside the crowd, those drawn from within the crowd itself, and those acting (or appearing to act) as intermediaries between the two. The first group of leaders are those that may more properly be called the 'heroes' of the crowd — men in whose name it riots or rebels . . . and whose speeches, manifestoes, or ideas serve as an ideological background or accompaniment to its activities. . . . Occasionally, far from exercising the 'very despotic activity' that LeBon ascribes to them, they were reluctant rather than enthusiastic leaders. . . . Such leaders were almost invariably drawn from social classes other than their followers." Rudé, pp. 247–48.

[42] Parley M. Mathewson to TWD, August 11, 1841, and TWD to Parley M. Mathewson, August 12, 1841, DC, III.

[43] New Age, August 27 and 30, 1841.

V. Epilogue

NATIVE AMERICAN CITIZENS!
READ AND TAKE WARNING!

A SHORT SERMON.

LET EVERY SOUL BE SUBJECT TO THE HIGHER POWERS. *Romans*, 13, 1.

Christians, like all other men, have the right to protect themselves against oppression. They have also the right to aid in the protection of others, but our Savior said, "MY KINGDOM IS NOT OF THIS WORLD," and thus taught his followers that it was inconsistent with their duty to him, and with their respect for his doctrines, to mingle in the strife for power. Paul, in the above quoted text, did not intend to teach his brethren that they should submit, with degrading servility, to tyranny, cruelty, and oppression, when they could remove the evil without producing another equally great. But his frequent exhortations, as well as those of his DIVINE MASTER, fully show that they considered it the indispensable duty of CHRISTIANS to submit to existing governments for the sake of peace, until oppression became too cruel to be borne, or until the evil could be remedied without unnecessary violence; and that, in ALL CASES, for the HONOR of the CHURCH, the SUCCESS of the GOSPEL, and the PEACE of the COMMUNITY, CHRISTIANS should "be subject to the HIGHER POWERS," as *long as forbearance would be a virtue.*

CHRISTIAN PROFESSORS OF RHODE ISLAND, I put to you a plain question—Will you answer it as on the ALTAR of GOD, to HIM AND YOUR OWN CONSCIENCES? Does it appear that the Constitution is to be voted on for adoption or rejection, on the 21st, 22d, and 23d, inst. is of such a character as to threaten danger to your rights and privileges, or those of others? Is it oppressive in its provisions or bearings? Would you be justified in rejecting it, and in adopting another which will place your government, your civil and political institutions, your PUBLIC SCHOOLS, and perhaps your RELIGIOUS PRIVILEGES, under the control of the POPE of ROME, through the medium of THOUSANDS of NATURALIZED FOREIGN CATHOLICS? Does the honor and prosperity of the church require it? Do the peace, welfare, and prosperity, of the State require it? Yet, reject the Constitution now presented to you, and you show your preference for another, which, *should it ever be adopted,* WILL PLACE THE BALLANCE OF POWER IN THE STATE, IN THE HANDS OF THOSE PEOPLE. The event can readily be predicted: Would you defend yourselves and your church against the operations and predominance of such a power, and preserve the State

from anarchy and ruin? Would you preserve peace, and thereby avoid violence and bloodshed? Would you pay that respect to the CONSTITUTED AUTHORITIES WHICH THE GOSPEL DEMANDS? Would you keep a conscience pure and undefiled, by pursuing a course on which you can hereafter look with approbation, and for the correctness of which, you can CONFIDENTLY APPEAL TO HEAVEN IN THE HOUR OF DEATH, AND AT THE DREAD TRIBUNAL HEREAFTER? Then, and I must suppose such to be your wish, array yourselves on the side of the "HIGHER POWERS," in a quiet and peaceable manner, GIVE YOUR VOTES FOR THE CONSTITUTION ON MONDAY NEXT. Show those who act in the opposition only to carry out their will, that you value too highly your CHRISTIAN PROFESSION, your CHRISTIAN CHARACTER, and your CHRISTIAN PRINCIPLE, to countenance sedition, and to endanger the peace of an entire community, only to defeat the benevolent object of the existing government, and to give encouragement and support to a spirit of violence and disorder. Tell those who would allure you to aid them in the work of strife. 'WE HAVE NOT so LEARNED CHRIST.'

REV. WILLIAM S. BALCH.

The above gentleman, late Pastor of the First Universalist Church in this city, and who, while here, did much for the party which have made and voted for the "People's Constitution," was requested by that party to lecture during his visit here this week from New York. He very properly refused to do so; and said he *would not were he now a resident here*; for the reason, that the *party have carried the thing too far,* and are now making a *political affair of it, and he would have nothing to do with it,* This is valuable testimony from one of the *ablest* and *fastest friends of the* suffrage cause.

AN EXAMPLE.

In a "Short Sermon" published in our extra sheet, the writer alluded to the possibility that, should a constitution like that called the "People's Constitution" be adopted, the naturalized foreign Catholics might exercise a pernicious influence on our political, civil, and religious institutions, and on our public schools. We have a case in point. The CATHOLIC BISHOP HUGHES, of New York, at the last election in that city, ARRAYED UNDER HIS CONTROL, some THREE THOUSAND FOREIGN CATHOLIC VOTERS, after an effort of a few days, to sustain at the BALLOT box his own views on the question of public schools, for the purpose of diverting to the use of the CATHOLIC CHURCH, a portion of the common school fund of the State. With a

longer period for the purpose, it is probable a body of foreign naturalized Catholics might have been organized, and will hereafter be organized, in that city and State, under PAPAL ECCLESIASTICAL INFLUENCE, *to carry out their views.* The excitement on the question still continues. The Bishop and his party are determined to succeed in their efforts. The native citizens have become alarmed. And meetings have been held to prevent the abhorred attempt from becoming successful.

On Wednesday last, a meeting was held in the Park, New York city, on the question. And during the proceedings, a band of foreigners broke in upon the assemblage, and by means of violence, broke up the meeting. A New York paper says, "Our cheeks are suffused with shame and indignation as we write about this matter; for so gross an insult to our rights as Americans, we have never seen or heard of before. Bands of filthy wretches, whose every touch was offensive to a decent man, drunken loafers; scoundrels who the police and criminal courts would be ashamed to receive in their walls; coarse, blustering rowdies; blear eyed and bloated officscourings from the stews, blind alleys and rear lanes; disgusting objects bearing the form human, but whom the sow in the mire might almost object to as companions—these were they who broke into the midst of a peaceful body of American citizens—struck and insulted the chosen officers of the assemblage, and with shrieks, loud blasphemy, and howling in their hideous native tongue, prevented the continuance of the customary routine. We saw Irish priests there—sly, false, deceitful villains—looking on and evidently encouraging the gang who created the tumult. We noticed two or three tavern bullies strike on the head a presiding officer—one of the most aged and respectable men of our city. We beheld the whole body of those officers forced, at length, from their seats, and driven, with jibes and blows, from the stage. And these officers were native Americans—men with grey heads—men known for long years among us, as gentlemen of reputation, philanthropy and exalted worth!

And is New York to utter no loud voice of abhorrence towards this transaction? Is this hypocritical scoundrel Hughes, and his minions, to drill ranks of ignorant and vindictive followers—and send them forth to act as those wretches acted—and shall no note be taken of it? It is a blot and an insolent violation of our dearest and most glorious privileges. The whole city—the whole state—ought to rise up as one man, and let these jesuitical knaves, and their apt satellites, know what it is to feel the blast from an injured and outraged country."

RHODE-ISLANDERS—Read this. Ponder seriously on it. Say—are you prepared to witness such scenes enacted in your State, and hitherto peaceful and prosperous State? Are you prepared to see a Catholic Bishop, at the head of a posse of Catholic Priests, and a band of their servile dependents, take the field to subvert your institutions, under the sanction of a State Constitution. If not, vote for the Constitution now presented to you, which is well calculated to protect you from such abuses. ROGER WILLIAMS.

As the reformers and the defenders of the status quo moved toward a showdown, political nativism reared its ugly head. This March 1842 broadside in support of the Landholders' Constitution was an early indication of the significance of ethnic and religious factors in the political and constitutional controversies of mid-nineteenth century Rhode Island (from the Broadside file (1842), Rhode Island Historical Society).

CHAPTER THIRTEEN

The Dorr Rebellion and Its Legacy[1]

I

On October 4, 1841, with all but three rural towns represented, the People's Convention met in Providence to implement long overdue reforms and to test the theory of popular constituent sovereignty. The gathering was a distinguished one in which respectable freeholders and professional men were prominent, among them former Congressman Dutee J. Pearce, Dr. John A. Brown, Ariel Ballou, Samuel Y. Atwell, John R. Waterman, Samuel H. Wales, Benjamin Arnold Jr., John S. Harris, William H. Smith, Wager Weeden, Thomas Dorr and Joseph Joslin, a Newport attorney who was elected convention president. After

---

[1] At the suggestion of Professors Marshall Smelser, Stanley N. Katz and Albert T. Klyberg, I have appended this interpretative overview of the Dorr Rebellion and its aftermath to my study. Several factors prompted this decision: (1) there was a need to round out my narrative for those unfamiliar with the broader aspects of Rhode Island constitutional development; (2) the three full-length published studies of the rebellion by Mowry, Gettleman and Dennison, though admirable in most respects, neglect the role of political nativism; and (3) an effort now seems appropriate to correlate and synthesize the work of the above historians

five days' deliberation, this extralegal assemblage produced the draft of a progressive basic law permeated with the ideology of Equal Rights and responsive to the demands of those who called it into being.[2]

Article I of the People's Constitution — its bill of rights[3] — incorporated the best features of the federal model in areas of free speech, free press, religious liberty and procedural due process, but it went much further than a simple repetition of traditional freedoms. It attacked "privilege" (that was more than mere rhetoric to the locofoco) by its assertion that "no favor or disfavor ought to be shown in legislation toward any man, or party, or society or religious denomination" (I,4); and it emphatically affirmed that "the people have an inalienable and indefensible right in their original, sovereign and unlimited capacity to ordain and institute government and in the same capacity to alter, reform or totally change the same" even without prior legislative authorization (I,4). The draft also contained a "personal liberty clause" that guaranteed the right of trial by jury for fugitive slaves (I,14). Here was evident the hand of Dorr, former Rhode Island delegate to the national convention of the American Anti-Slavery Society.

---

and the interpretations of several other scholars who have done valuable research on the rebellion — *viz.*, Sidney S. Rider, Joseph Brennan, Anne Mary Newton, Chilton Williamson, Peter J. Coleman, Robert L. Ciaburri, C. Peter Magrath, J. Stanley Lemons and Michael A. McKenna, and William M. Wiecek. Although my present study focuses on the period 1776–1841, I have consulted every known source on the Dorr Rebellion and its legacy in conjunction with a forthcoming biography of Thomas Wilson Dorr.

[2] The fullest account of the convention's proceedings is contained in the hostile *Providence Journal,* October 5, 7, 8, 9 and 11, 1841. See also *New Age,* October 8 and 22, 1841.

[3] This analysis of the People's Constitution is based upon the *Proposed Constitution of the State of Rhode Island and Providence Plantations as finally adopted by the People's Convention Assembled at Providence on the 18th Day of November, 1841* (Providence, 1841). That document is compared with the October draft in Gettleman, appendix A. Mowry conveniently reprints the Charter, the People's Constitution, the Landholders' Constitution, and the original version of the present state constitution in the appendices of his study, pp. 307–85. Two conservative features of the

State support of education was deemed so essential that it was mandated not only in a separate article (XII) but also in the bill of rights that decreed it "an imperative duty of the legislature to promote the establishment of free [not merely public] schools" (I,5). Dorr, president of the Providence school committee, was undoubtedly that provision's prime sponsor. These peaceful revolutionaries finally declared that "the military shall always be held in strict subordination to the civil authority" (I,20).

The "People's Constitution" in its other sections remedied many abuses that had persisted under the old regime. The most notable and controversial departure from the charter system occurred in the area of suffrage. The statutory $134 freehold requirement was repudiated by a clause that extended suffrage to adult *white* male citizens with one year's residence in the state (II,1). Insertion of that racial qualification was accomplished over strenuous objections from Dorr and Benjamin Arnold, Jr. of Providence who correctly asserted that this inconsistent restriction violated the principle of equal rights upon which their movement was based.

Many Suffragists, including Atwell and Dutee Pearce, feared that enfranchisement of Negroes would alienate enough voters to prevent ratification of the People's Constitution by a majority of the state's white adult male population. The convention therefore rejected a motion to strike the word "white" by forty-six to eighteen, but it exempted blacks from taxation or militia duty (II,3). When Dorr persisted in his advocacy of blacks, his fellow delegates agreed to insertion of a clause mandating a popular referendum on the defeated motion at the first annual election following the initial session of the People's Legislature (XIV,22). This arrangement and the fugitive slave clause notwithstanding, several abolitionists including Frederick Douglass, Abby Kelley

---

People's Constitution were its denial of the vote on financial questions to an elector "not possessed of, and assessed for, ratable property in his own right, to the amount of one hundred and fifty dollars," and the ineligibility of such an elector for the offices of mayor, alderman or common councilman in any city.

and William Lloyd Garrison came to Rhode Island to demonstrate against the People's Constitution.[4]

Despite discrimination against blacks, no effort was made to
disfranchise their equals on the social scale — the Catholic Irish.
Dorr, member of the convention's suffrage committee, requested
and received statistics that revealed the rapid growth of the local
Irish-Catholic population from Henry J. Duff. This Irish community leader informed Dorr that Catholic adherents in Providence alone totaled nearly 1,700 according to a January 1839
census and had increased by "one half at least" since then. This
trend and its long-range political impact did not cause the People's Convention to yield to the seductions of nativism. On the
Irish question Dorr and his colleagues were faithful to Equal
Rights and their fidelity would cost them dearly.[5]

In the crucial area of reapportionment the reformers devised
an eighty-member House wherein Providence was entitled to
twelve representatives, two from each of its six wards. Smithfield
and Newport were allocated five members each, Warwick retained four, Cumberland, North Providence and Scituate were
raised to three, Jamestown, Middletown and Barrington were
reduced to one and all other towns were allotted their customary
two representatives (V,2–3). This plan gave the nine expanding
towns approximately 46 percent of House representation, a significant increase over the 30 percent they were then allowed under the inflexible charter system. A twelve-member senate elected
from twelve districts gave to the nine expanding towns of Providence and Bristol counties an influence approximately equal to
that of the remaining twenty-two towns (VI,1–2). Perhaps
through oversight, the document contained no provision for mandatory reapportionment.

Other significant features of the People's Constitution diminished the power of the legislature by providing for a clear sepa-

---

[4] Philip S. Foner, *Frederick Douglass,* (New York, 1964), p. 48. Documents relating to the blacks' protest are found in *Burke's Report,* pp.
110–17. See also Lemons and McKenna, pp. 7–9 and the *New Age,* Dec.
17, 1841.

[5] Henry J. Duff to TWD, Nov. 11, 1841, DP, A 949.

ration of powers according to the three branch principle (III), gave the governor a mild veto (IV,12), and barred the Assembly from exercising its traditional judicial functions (IX,4). The document established a one year term for general officers, gave increased tenure to the judiciary, made juries judges of both law and fact, required a secret ballot, and provided for impeachment and trial of public officials. The amendment procedure was not difficult. Change could be accomplished by vote of a majority of the whole membership of each house of two successive Assemblies, a general election intervening, followed by simple majority approval at town or ward meetings especially convened to consider the amendment (XIII). This easy alteration process partially offset the failure of the document to mandate periodic reapportionment.

Among the general provisions of the People's Constitution were several clauses (IX,7–12) which embodied the position of the Equal Rights Democrats on such currently controversial issues as privilege and positive government. The reform oriented draftsmen provided that "the General Assembly shall have no power hereafter to incur state debts to an amount exceeding the sum of fifty thousand dollars, except in time of war, or in case of invasion, without the express consent of the people." They insisted on a local referendum before taxes could be levied to finance capital improvements in any city. They required assent of two-thirds of the whole membership of each house for "creating, continuing, altering, or renewing" any non-banking corporation and — reacting to Justice Story's decision in the Dartmouth College Case — insisted that "all grants of incorporation shall be subject to future acts of the General Assembly in amendment or repeal thereof." The delegates' greatest suspicion however was reserved for banks. Their convention gave constitutional status to the visitorial commission created by Dorr's legislation of 1836, and it required a popular referendum on every bank bill. Dorr lost his effort however to constitutionally abolish imprisonment for debt.

Such "unadulterated locofocoism" was certain to alienate Whig business, industrial and financial interests even more than the white voting clause antagonized blacks and abolitionists. Rural Democrats could take strong issue with reapportionment provisions; nativists with enfranchisement of naturalized citizens, and freeholders with any extension of suffrage whatsoever. And nearly all those who held positions under the Charter opposed the method that the reformers employed, because it threatened to usurp their power and dramatically overturn the ruling establishment.

If and when the reformers lost momentum, a vigorous counterattack would ensue from varied interests adversely affected by the People's Constitution. This eventuality was not sufficiently anticipated by the Suffrage Association in its program of "peaceable revolution" because many of its members were convinced of the justice and propriety of their action as a revival of the principles of 1776.

After the convention's October session, Dorr's younger brother advised him not to take "so leading a part" in the reform movement, but Dorr and his zealous allies were too caught up in their cause.[6] As "father" of the People's Constitution, Dorr issued a public address at the rising of the final session of convention on November 18, 1841. Reaffirming the necessity and validity of the course the reformers had taken, he assured his fellow citizens that "our appeal . . . is not to the cartridge box but to the ballot box." [7] The popular referendum was scheduled for December 27, 28 and 29. Although absentee voting was allowed in event of illness, the Suffragists established detailed election procedures and took numerous precautions to prevent fraud. Those who would be freemen under the proposed document were allowed to vote on its ratification. All ballots were to be signed and moderators were to make registers of all persons voting. The People's Convention was to reassemble on January 12, 1842 to tabulate the results (XIV,1–4). When Dutee Pearce, animated more by opportunism than by principle, suggested privately to Dorr that aliens be allowed to vote in December, Dorr emphat-

---

[6] Henry C. Dorr to TWD, Oct. 25, 1841, DC, Vol. III.

[7] *Burke's Report,* pp. 851–64.

ically refused because it contravened the provisions of the People's Constitution.[8]

Two weeks before the balloting Dorr speculated on its outcome — "we ought to have more than 12,000 votes to place the result beyond all doubt or cavil; 13,000 will do it; 14,000 will make a triumphant majority." [9] To achieve that triumph Dorr, Pearce, David Parmenter and other Suffragists stumped the state explaining the new basic law. Disregard for the landholding requirement in the three-day referendum and allowance of shut-in voting swelled the turnout to nearly 14,000 — largest in Rhode Island history. Because charter adherents boycotted the election only fifty-two votes were cast against the People's Constitution. Dorr and the Suffragists claimed that the constitution had been ratified by an absolute majority of nearly 2,400 because 13,944 of the state's estimated 23,142 white adult males had expressed their approval of the document including a majority of the freemen.[10] There was a possibility of fraudulent voting as for any election in that age and undoubtedly some bogus ballots were cast, but when results were tabulated and certified on January 13, 1842, the reformers insisted that the People's Constitution had supplanted the royal charter as the paramount law of the state.[11]

Supporters of the regular government were temporarily stunned. Elisha R. Potter, Jr. exclaimed to John Brown Francis that "Dorr's plan has succeeded beyond his most sanguine calculations." [12] As 1842 dawned, momentum belonged to the Dorrites because the charter faction tenaciously clung to the status quo. The Landholders' Convention had met in November and adjourned after drafting an incomplete basic law that left issues of suffrage and reapportionment unresolved.[13] Premature ad-

---

[8] TWD to Dutee J. Pearce, Dec. 13, 1841, DC, Vol. III.

[9] *Ibid.*

[10] 4,960 out of a total of 9,590 freemen voted for the People's Constitution according to the tally of the Suffragists. *Burke's Report,* pp. 121, 204–05.

[11] *Ibid.,* pp. 202–06.

[12] Potter to Francis, Jan. 1, 1842, Francis Collection, RIHS.

[13] *Draft of Constitution of the State of Rhode Island and Providence*

journment was an evasive tactic which the freemen had successfully employed during the abortive convention of 1834, but in
1841 reformers gained from such an insincere delay. Samuel
Atwell, one of a handful of reform delegates to the landholders'
conclave, appealed to the convention for liberalization of the
franchise lest the people be forced to choose between "blind submission or open rebellion." By their recalcitrance the freemen
opted for rebellion.[14]

II

Ironically the Suffragists relinquished their momentum in January 1842 at the peak of their campaign. The very orderly and
peaceful nature of their revolution impaired its decisiveness, for
they had decreed in the People's Constitution (XIV,17) that
the charter government "shall exercise all the powers with which
it is now clothed, until the said first Tuesday of May 1842, and
until their successors, under this constitution, shall be duly
elected and qualified." This clause — overlooked by most historians — gave the Charterites nearly four months to devise an
official counteroffensive to prevent the People's Constitution
from taking effect. Seldom have revolutionaries been so obliging
or observant of an existing government.

Too much was at stake for the long entrenched establishment
to acquiesce without a fight, but their forceful counter effort was
not anticipated by most reformers — especially those who naively
believed that the December referendum would be legally and
morally binding on all Rhode Islanders. They were warned of
the impending crisis in January at the height of their success
by Henry Dorr — Thomas's younger but more conservative
brother — who, after challenging the validity of the People's
Convention, predicted that most people would bow before "constituted authority." If the Suffragists persisted, he admonished,

Plantations . . . November, 1841 (Providence, 1841) at JHL. For the
proceedings of the first session of the Landholders' Convention, see
Providence Journal, November 2–13, 1841.

14 *Providence Journal,* November 13, 1842.

they "would be like the Chartists of England with a few leaders, and those not the right men to head such an enterprise — and no people on which you can depend to support you at all risks." The younger Dorr proved a prophet indeed! [15]

Many reasons explain the Charterites' resistance towards the People's Constitution — its radical doctrine of popular constituent sovereignty, its anti-corporate ideology of Equal Rights, its impact on the "agrarian interest" through reapportionment, and its enfranchisement of the "low Irish" — but undoubtedly the never-articulated urge for political self-preservation was the underlying motive animating leaders of the Law and Order coalition; changes proposed by the Dorrites simply made retention of their power more imperative.

Dorr's opposition — mainly politically dominant urban Whigs associated with the commercial-business-industrial complex and rural Democrats from South County and the western hill towns — had every intention of asserting their legal authority, and in January 1842 they launched a determined bid to undermine the revolutionaries' position. Their attack on the Dorrites was multi-faceted. The prestigious judiciary spearheaded one thrust; during winter and early spring 1842, federal district judge John Pitman and Job Durfee, chief justice of the state supreme court, descended from their neutral benches to attack the People's Constitution openly on theoretical and legal grounds. Pitman, a supporter of suffrage extension during the 1811 controversy, penned a January address *To the Members of the General Assembly of Rhode Island* which attacked the extralegal methods of the Suffragists and urged that their criminal, "revolutionary movement" be immediately suppressed. Pitman also corresponded with United States Supreme Court justice Joseph Story, then riding the New England circuit. The conservative Story — who would later preside over several cases arising from the Dorr rebellion — was equally partisan. "If ever there was a case that called upon a judge to write and speak openly and publicly, it was the very case then before you," he advised Pitman.

---

[15] Henry C. Dorr to TWD, January, 1842, DC, Vol. III.

According to Story's Whig view "the Constitution of Rhode Island was to be overturned by a self-created body"; and he knew "no duty more sacred in every citizen than upon such an emergency to come forth and resist, by all the just and moral means in his power, such proceedings." [16] Job Durfee agreed with this extreme judicial activism. In early March his three-judge court (which included William R. Staples and Levi Haile, a leader of the old Constitutional party) issued a public letter asserting the illegality of the People's Constitution and contending that any attempt to carry it into effect would be "treason against this State."

Justice Durfee, erstwhile poet, former congressman, and formidable orator, was not content with a single swipe at the "mobocratic" suffragists. On March 15 he delivered a charge to a Bristol grand jury which they subsequently published reaffirming his belief that support of the People's Constitution was treasonous and expounding a persuasive and logical refutation of popular constituent sovereignty. In attempting to define "the people," Durfee distinguished between the "natural people" — the entire human population regardless of age, sex, color, citizenship, legal or mental status — and the "corporate people" — the legal voters in whom alone sovereignty resides. For him, sovereignty was not some vague primal right in the hands of a majority of natural people, but a carefully defined, limited power to be exercised by the people's representatives under established, legitimate modes. Durfee's distinction was followed by other Law and Order apologists including John Whipple and Daniel Webster when they defended the Charter regime before the United States Supreme Court in the case of *Luther v. Borden* (1849). These conservatives, in the tradition of Hamilton, stressed the primacy of order and authority, while Dorrites argued in Jeffersonian fashion that order was not possible without liberty and

---

[16] [John Pitman], *To the Members of the General Assembly of Rhode Island* (Providence, 1842); Pitman to Joseph Story, January 26, 1842, Pitman-Story Correspondence, William L. Clements Library, University of Michigan; William W. Story, *The Life and Letters of Joseph Story* (Boston, 1851), II, 415–19, 516–17.

that liberty was possible only when the people controlled their government.[17]

Another extremely potent maneuver by Charter adherents was their appeal to the class, sectional and ethno-religious sentiments of Rhode Islanders. The Law and Order party conducted an inconsistent but effective propaganda campaign against the People's Constitution via broadsides, pamphlets, and the pages of the *Providence Journal*. Conservatives warned well-to-do urbanites and farmers that the proposed basic law would bring the city under domination of the idle, ignorant and poorer class; they alarmed the farmer by contending that its reapportionment plan would place the agrarian interest at the mercy of the industrial and shift the basis of taxation from business to land; and they excited entrepreneurs by emphasizing the reformers' anti-corporate philosophy of Equal Rights.[18] Propagandists, especially Henry Bowen Anthony and Professor William G. Goddard, played upon fears of native-born Protestants, warning them that the liberal suffrage clause of the People's Constitution would pave the way for the political ascendancy of those Irish Catholic immigrants who were swarming into the state in ever-increasing numbers.

Political nativism — a potent weapon in the Law and Order

---

[17] Durfee's charge to the Bristol grand jury is reprinted in *Burke's Report*, pp. 706–17. See also the broadside "Citizens of Rhode Island! Read! Mark! Learn!" Broadside File (1842), RIHS. On Durfee generally consult [Thomas Durfee, ed.], *The Complete Works of the Honorable Job Durfee . . .* (Providence, 1849). An extremely impressive analysis and defense of Law and Order thought is William M. Wiecek, "Popular Sovereignty in the Dorr War — Conservative Counterblast," *Rhode Island History*, XXXII, (May, 1973), 35–51. The most learned and persuasive contemporary analysis of the rebellion from the conservative side is Elisha R. Potter, Jr., *Considerations on the Question of a Constitution and Extension of Suffrage in Rhode Island* (Boston, 1842), a tract that drew praise even from libertarian Charles Sumner, Sumner to Potter, April 9, 1844.

[18] *Providence Journal*, October, 1841–March, 1842, especially the articles by "Town Born" (William G. Goddard). On Goddard generally see Francis W. Goddard, ed., *The Political and Miscellaneous Writings of William G. Goddard*, 2 vols. (Providence, 1870). His 1841–42 *Journal* diatribes are reprinted in II, 51–170.

arsenal — was especially evident in the final draft of the Landholders' or Freemen's Constitution, produced in February 1842
by the reconvened session of the Landholders' Convention. This
law and order conclave drafted a compromise document designed to wean moderates from their adherence to the extralegal
People's Constitution. The tactic was highly successful. The Freemen's Constitution contained no lofty appeals to the doctrine of
popular constituent sovereignty nor traces of the locofoco ideology of Equal Rights. It reapportioned but less drastically than
Dorr's document, especially in the upper house, where static and
declining areas were allocated sixty percent of the nineteen senate seats (VI,1–2) to give "great security to the farming interest." [19] The freemen slightly reduced the power of the Assembly,
but they allowed the legislature to retain all its judicial functions
(IV,10) and denied the governor a veto. Their bill of rights
was quite progressive and perhaps even modeled upon the People's Constitution. Surprisingly, the Charterites included a limited restriction on imprisonment for debt.

The most exploitable difference between the two documents
occurred in the area of suffrage. Freemen gave the franchise to
those white, male *native-born* citizens who met age and residency
requirements, but it retained the real estate requirement for
naturalized citizens and actually lengthened the state residency
qualification from one year to three years *after* naturalization.[20]
By resolution of the General Assembly all those who would be

----

[19] This continuing solicitude for the agrarian wing of the Law and
Order coalition — overlooked by most historians — is alluded to by
Samuel Man, a local Whig leader. Man to James F. Simmons, Feb. 21,
1842, Misc. Mss., RIHS, Si 47. It was also criticized in the *New Age,*
March 4, 1842.

[20] The Landholders' or Freemen's Constitution is printed in *Burke's
Report,* pp. 135–48 and in Appendix C of Mowry, pp. 347–66. On the
conservative design of its architects see James F. Simmons to an unidenti-
fied correspondent, February 11, 1842, Simmons Papers. Mowry (pp.
123–26), Dennison (pp. 62–63), Wiecek (p. 91), and nearly all historians
of the rebellion (Gettleman excepted) fail to appreciate the great ideological and the significant substantive differences between the People's
Constitution and the Landholders' document. Such an oversight leads to
the erroneous conclusion that Dorr and his associates were either in-

enfranchised by the Freemen's Constitution were allowed to vote upon its ratification in a three-day referendum scheduled for March 21–23.[21]

These concessions — especially that of suffrage to the native-born — stole the thunder from the Dorrite cause and drove a wedge between extreme and moderate reformers. The *Journal* told natives that the freemen's basic law "extends suffrage for which you originally contended" whereas "foreign elements in the other constitution would neutralize your power and effectiveness." As Henry Anthony admonished: "The great difference between the two constitutions lies in the provision respecting foreigners. Everything else is nothing to this."[22]

In the March campaign over ratification nativistic rhetoric became increasingly inflammatory. One broadside warned men of Rhode Island stock that the People's Constitution would "place your government, your civil and political institutions, your PUBLIC SCHOOLS, and perhaps your RELIGIOUS PRIVILEGES, under the control of the POPE of ROME, through the medium of thousands of NATURALIZED FOREIGN CATHOLICS." This widely disseminated leaflet further advised that support of the Freemen's Constitution was essential unless natives were "prepared to see a Catholic Bishop, at the head of a posse of Catholic Priests, and a band of their servile dependents, take the field to subvert your institutions under the sanction of a State Constitution." [23]

Suffragist Joshua B. Rathbun wrote Dorr from Tiverton that "this right to exclude naturalized citizens is strongly insisted upon here and has perhaps operated against us more than anything else. Men were called upon not to vote for a constitution but to vote against Irishmen." [24] Providence brahmin John

---

credibly stubborn, self-seeking, or blindly radical in urging defeat of the Landholders' Constitution.

[21] Act of the General Assembly, January session 1842, *Burke's Report,* p. 646.

[22] *Providence Journal,* March 7, 1842.

[23] "Native American Citizens! Read and Take Warning!" Broadside File (1842), RIHS, signed by "Roger Williams."

[24] Joshua B. Rathbun to TWD, March 25, 1842, DC, Vol. IV.

Carter Brown privately urged reformer Walter R. Danforth to accept the Freemen's Constitution. "Perhaps you can influence Colonel [Franklin] Cooley to hammer away on the right side, seeing that suffrage is extended to everybody of native growth," Brown told the Suffragist leader. "The Colonel would hardly desire to be governed by the Catholic priesthood." [25] Contemporary broadsides played upon this xenophobia — one expressed the exaggerated opinion that "every Roman Catholic Irishman in Rhode Island is a Dorrite." [26]

The *Journal* utilized the acid pens of Henry Anthony and William Goddard on the eve of the referendum to succinctly state its case:

> The balance of power rests in the hands of the Senators from the agricultural areas of the state. Where will the balance be under Messrs. Dorr, Brown and Company? Where but among 2,500 foreigners and the hundreds more who will be imported. They will league and band together and usurp our native political power. Their priests and leaders will say to a political party as they say in New York City, give us by law every opportunity to perpetuate our spiritual despotism. At the feet of these men will you lay down your freedom. Foreigners still remain foreign and are still embraced by mother church. He still bows down to her rituals, worships the host, and obeys and craves absolution from the priest. He cannot be assimilated. Now is the time to choose between the two systems — the conservative checks or foreigners responsible only to priests.[27]

Conversely, the American Irish press lined up with Dorr. "It is our own Home Rule question in Rhode Island," asserted the *Truth Teller* (New York) in an article upholding the Dorrites' cause. Clearly the Irish-Catholic issue was an essential aspect of the 1842 controversy, both as a scare tactic [28] and a genuine apprehension, despite its suppression by Arthur May Mowry and

---

[25] John Carter Brown to Walter R. Danforth, March 5, 1842, Carter-Danforth Letters, RIHS.

[26] "Comparison," Broadside File (1842), RIHS; "Foreign Voters!" in Sidney S. Rider, comp., Broadsides and Caricatures Relating to Political Affairs in Rhode Island, JHL.

[27] *Providence Journal,* March 19, 1842.

[28] The suffrage papers condemned the Charterites for their exploitation of the Irish question, claiming it was "raised more for political effect." *Providence Express,* March 17, 1842; *New Age,* March 18, 1842.

its neglect by George Dennison, Marvin Gettleman and other historians of the rebellion.[29]

Dorr and his leading associates — moved more by principle than the quest for power — exhorted the "people" to vote down the handiwork of the Landholders' Convention. The electorate responded to this appeal, despite the vote-buying tactics of freeholders, by the ominously narrow margin of 8,689 to 8,013 in a turnout that exceeded the record-breaking December referendum. The negative stance of the ultraconservative faction of the Law and Order party, those opposing any reform whatsoever, saved the day for the Dorrites. The vote of the reformers alone (with naturalized Irish excluded from the referendum) would not have been sufficient to defeat the Freemen's Constitution, but the Suffragists hailed the election as a vindication of the "sovereignty of the people" over the alleged "sovereignty of corporations." [30]

III

The conservatives, though temporarily blocked in their effort to check the Dorrites, were encouraged by the closeness of the March contest and the reduction of the reformers' electoral

---

[29] Mowry wrote a detailed view from the right — a conservative defense of Law and Order; Gettleman presented a well-researched New Left interpretation regarding the rebellion as an episode in the history of American radicalism (see my generally favorable review of his work in *New England Quarterly,* XLVII, March, 1974, 143–45); Dennison penned a provocative theoretical and ideological analysis concerned less with the rebellion as an event in Rhode Island history than with its impact on American constitutional development. Despite the substantial merit of these full-length studies only the briefer accounts of the struggle by Brennan, Williamson, Coleman, Wiecek, and Lemons-McKenna allude to the importance of nativism. This neglect, especially on the part of Mowry, reminds one of the observation made by W.E.B. DuBois in *Black Reconstruction in America, 1860–1880* (New York, 1935), p. 727: "historians of Reconstruction with a few exceptions ignore the Negro as completely as possible, leaving the reader wondering why an element apparently so insignificant filled the whole Southern picture at the time."

[30] *Burke's Report,* pp. 105–06 (vote tabulation); Elisha R. Potter to

strength by more than 5,000 votes since the December constitutional referendum. On March 30, therefore, the Assembly soundly rejected by a margin of fifty-nine to three Samuel Atwell's bill to resubmit the People's Constitution to those electors who had been allowed to vote in the March referendum.[31] As the charter government prepared for the April elections, it took other steps to reverse the Suffragists' momentum. One such tactic was the mobilization of the militia by an executive order which commanded them to be ready to appear armed and equipped at thirty minutes' notice. The Assembly passed on April 2 its so-called "Algerine Law" that imposed severe penalties against those who participated in the upcoming "people's" election and declared anyone who assumed state office under the People's Constitution guilty of treason against the state and subject to life imprisonment.[32] On April 7 Judge John Pitman advised Justice Story that "we are not idle. Full power has been given to the governor to meet the exigency of the crisis and he is doing all he can to put the state in military array." [33]

The Charterites also began to appease Rhode Island's black community. Although the Freemen's Constitution had denied Negro suffrage, some conservatives were now willing to grant that concession in return for black assistance against a forceful

---

John Brown Francis, March 3 and 9, 1842, Francis Collection, RIHS (vote buying); Resolutions of the March 25 meeting of the Providence Suffrage Association, *Providence Express,* March 29, 1842 (the anticorporate statement).

[31] *Burke's Report,* p. 417; Journal of the House, March 30 and 31, 1842, RISA. A bill offered by Eddy Keach of Burrillville providing for repeal of the existing election law and holding the April election under the provisions of the People's Constitution was defeated 59 to 2, *New Age,* April 2, 1842.

[32] *Burke's Report,* pp. 133–35; the official title of the measure was "An Act in Relation to Offenses against the Sovereign Power of the State." Its harshness prompted the Dorrites to label it the "Algerine Law" after the tyrannical Dey of Algiers. It passed by a vote of 60 to 6; in opposition were Representatives Atwell, Keach, Burges, Thurston, Gavitt and Walling, *Might and Right,* pp. 172–91. Dorr's initial reaction to the law was that it was passed "merely to frighten the common sort of folks!" TWD to Aaron White, April 4, 1842, DC, Vol. IV.

[33] Pitman to Story, April 7, 1842, Pitman-Story Correspondence.

effort by the Suffragists.[34] Apparent "unreliability" of the regular state militia, many of whom supported Dorr, prompted Governor Samuel Ward King to apply to President John Tyler so that "such precautionary measures may be taken by the Government of the United States" as may afford the charter government that protection against domestic violence which the Constitution of the United States requires.[35] On April 4, at the instigation of John Pitman, King sent to confer with Tyler a three-man delegation consisting of rural Democrats Elisha Potter, Jr. and John Brown Francis and Whig attorney John Whipple in whose office Dorr had clerked. One week later, after some ambivalence, the states' rights Virginian "assured" King that "should the time arrive, when an insurrection shall exist *against the government of Rhode Island,* and a requisition shall be made upon the Executive of the United States to furnish that protection which is guaranteed to each by the constitution and laws, I shall not be found to shrink from the performance of a duty." Tyler then added a provision which gave a lift to the Law and Order cause: "in such a contingency, the Executive could not look into real or supposed defects of the existing government"; on the contrary it was his duty "to respect the requisitions of that government which has been recognized as the existing government of the State through all time past," until he should be "advised in a regular manner that it has been altered and abolished and another substituted in its place by legal and peaceable proceedings adopted and pursued by the authorities and people of the state." [36]

---

[34] Lemons and McKenna, pp. 10–13; William Goodell, *The Rights and Wrongs of Rhode Island* (Whitesboro, N.Y., 1842), p. 6; and William J. Brown, *The Life of William J. Brown of Providence, R.I.* (Providence, 1883), pp. 172–73. Brown was a leader in the Providence black community.

[35] The King-Tyler correspondence of April–June and supplementary documents are in *Burke's Report,* pp. 656–705; United States House of Representatives, 28 Cong. 1 Sess., House Document No. 225; and James D. Richardson, comp., *A Compilation of the Messages and Papers of the Presidents* (New York, 1897), V, 2136–60.

[36] *Burke's Report,* pp. 656–59; William Sprague to Emanuel Rice, April 7, 1842, Misc. Mss. RIHS, S 74.

With their counteroffensive in full swing, Law and Order forces looked towards the regular annual election on April 20 to sustain themselves in power until the Dorrites' challenge was overcome. The Suffragists, though now on the defensive, were not idle. In February and March they held rallies in various mill villages, and they counteracted the legal challenge to popular constituent sovereignty posed by Durfee and Pitman by drafting the impressive *Nine Lawyers' Opinion* — the most cogent and persuasive statement of suffrage ideology.[37] On April 5 they dispatched Dr. John Brown (who proved to be a naive emissary) to confer with Tyler and leading Democratic congressmen to forestall federal intervention, and on April 18 they fielded a full slate of state officers in defiance of the Algerine Law. Thomas Dorr was their reluctant but courageous candidate for governor (after both Democrat Thomas Carpenter and Whig Wager Weeden had declined) despite a plea from his prestigious parents to save them "from that shame and disgrace which will attend us if you persist, and which will hurry us sorrowing to the grave." [38]

The April elections brought the crisis to a head. When the balloting was done Dorr had polled 6,359 votes on April 18 to become the "people's governor." Two days later incumbent Whig Samuel Ward King defeated Democratic Suffragist Thomas F. Carpenter by a margin of 4,864 to 2,211. Although Dorr's election under the People's Constitution was unopposed and a fierce

---

[37] The nine lawyers were Dorr, Samuel Y. Atwell, Thomas F. Carpenter, Joseph K. Angell, David Daniels, Levi C. Eaton, John P. Knowles, Dutee J. Pearce and Aaron White, Jr. This valuable brief was republished by Sidney S. Rider in *Rhode Island Historical Tracts* (Providence, 1880), No. 11, pp. 68–92. Dorr wrote the opinion and attorney George F. Man assisted with the research.

[38] Wilkins Updike to Elisha R. Potter, April 6, 1842, Potter Collection, is informative on the preparations made by both sides. Also useful is the bound manuscript journal entitled "Incidents in the Life of Hiram Hill," RIHS, hereafter cited Hill's Journal. Its author was a Providence lumber dealer who captained the Third Ward City Guards during the incidents of May–June, 1842. The declinations of Carpenter and Weeden are in DC. The plea from Dorr's parents came via letter on April 8, 1842, DC, Vol. IV. The suffrage meetings are noted in *Burke's Report*, pp. 666–68. On Brown's trip to Washington see *Providence Express*, April 12, 1842.

storm dampened the contest, the turnout was still disappointing. Dorr's total was 2,330 less than the vote against the Freemen's document and 7,585 ballots below that received by the People's Constitution three-and-a-half months earlier.[39] Suffragist support was clearly on the wane, especially in southerly rural areas, and several prominent Rhode Islanders had publicly switched sides. Notable among the defectors were wealthy industrialist and political chameleon William Sprague, who received a United States senatorship in February 1842 for his change of heart, and Constitutionalist Jacob Frieze, historian of Rhode Island suffrage reform. Even state representative Samuel Atwell, the leading suffrage spokesman in the General Assembly, wavered after enactment of the Algerine Law.

Further, those 4,864 votes cast by freeholders for King in the regular election constituted a majority of the whole number of freemen (9,590). Dorrites had claimed this majority in January when they tallied the votes on the People's Constitution, but on April 20 most freeholders allied with the forces of Law and Order.[40]

IV

In the aftermath of the April balloting the Charterites, emboldened by reform's ebbing tide, added new tactics to their counteroffensive. Governor King called a special session of the Assembly that strengthened governmental prerogatives under the riot act, authorized armed volunteer "police companies" in

---

[39] The votes in the People's election are recorded in *Burke's Report,* pp. 452–54. For balloting in the regular contest and all other gubernatorial elections cited hereafter I have used the official count recorded in the *Rhode Island Manual* (biennial). Potter called the storm which held down the People's vote on April 18 "a grand thing for the cause of law and order." Potter to Francis, April 18, 1842, Francis Collection. According to *Might and Right* "a cry was also raised against foreigners and priestcraft," preceding this election, pp. 227–28.

[40] On Sprague's defection after voting for the People's Constitution see *Burke's Report,* p. 354. His correspondent and business partner Emanuel Rice of Natick, a member of the state committee of the Rhode Island Suffrage Association in 1841, also abandoned the cause. Frieze's switch

Providence, and created a Board of Councillors "to advise with the Governor as to the executive measures proper to be taken in the present emergency of the State." This "council of war" consisted of six prominent Whigs and conservative James Fenner, a former Democratic governor. A proposition to call a third constitutional convention was deferred to the next session of the charter assembly after vigorous debate by a vote of 45 to 12. Another move, fraught with ominous consequences for the Suffragists, was the decision by the Tyler administration on May 2 to reinforce the garrison at Fort Adams in Newport by increasing its regular complement of 119 to a total of 302 officers and enlisted men.[41]

A clash appeared imminent as the rival governments prepared to assume power on May 3–4 under their respective basic laws. In Providence on Tuesday, May 3, the Suffragists prefaced their accession to office by staging a colorful parade from the Hoyle Tavern in the west end to the Providence State House on North Main Street. The entourage featured the Providence Brass Band, members of the people's government and a strong military contingent including the sixty-member Dorr Troop of Horse — the governor's personal guard. Only the eventual setting for the People's Legislature diminished the luster and triumph of the occasion. Since the Charterites had locked the State House con-

---

is explained in his *Concise History of the Efforts to Obtain an Extension of Suffrage in Rhode Island From the Year 1811 to 1842* (Providence, 1842), pp. 61–63. On Atwell see the *New Age,* April 19 and 26, 1842. A main point made by Gettleman is that the Algerine Law drove middle class "moderates out of the Suffrage Party" and gave it "a more radical cast" (pp. 92–93, 105–06), a view shared by Newton, pp. 37, 82–85 and expressed by John Whipple in a letter to President Tyler, April 9, 1842, *Burke's Report,* p. 669. Conversely Potter and Francis thought the Algerine Law ill-advised and "impolitic." Potter to Francis, April 18, 1842, Francis Collection.

[41] These statutes are found in the Acts and Resolves of the General Assembly, April, 1842, RISA and summarized by Mowry (pp. 147–49) and the *Providence Express,* April 28, 1842. On the reenforcement of Fort Adams see the statement of Assistant U.S. Adjutant General L. Thomas, *Burke's Report,* p. 699. The seven councillors included Whigs Richard K. Randolph, Edward Carrington, Lemuel H. Arnold, Nathan F. Dixon, Byron Diman and Peleg Wilbur and Democrat James Fenner.

taining the state's seal, its archives, and other symbols of sovereignty, the Suffragists retreated to an unfinished foundry building on Eddy Street near Dorrance (preselected as an alternative site) to conduct their legislative deliberations.[42]

Dorr unsuccessfully opposed such timid acquiescence. Later he ruefully observed "that it was here that the cause was defeated, if not lost." Dorr in chiding his more moderate associates contended that "the period for decided action had now arrived." A valid government, he said, "was entitled to sit in the usual places of legislation, to possess and control the public property, and to exercise all the functions with which it was constitutionally invested. A government without power, appealing to voluntary support, destitute of the ability or disposition to enforce its lawful requisitions, was no government at all and was destined to extinction." Had the State House been seized, lamented Dorr, "right would have been confirmed by possession, the law and the fact would have been conjoined, and the new order of things would have been acquiesced in by all but a minority" of powerless reactionaries.[43]

But the Foundry Legislature, intimidated by the Algerine Law and the threat of federal intervention, preferred ritual to what Dorr termed "the moderate degree of force which was necessary at this critical point of affairs." The gathering (with sixty-six of eighty representatives and nine of twelve senators present) met for two days, chose officers and committees, abrogated the Algerine Law and the Board of Councillors, passed several statutes regulating elections and the selection of militia officers, and chartered the Glocester and Burrillville Greene Artillery Company. Curiously it did not remove the incumbent and hostile state judiciary, an omission which Dorr later termed "a remarkable oversight." Before adjourning it passed, without dissent, an act requiring all persons to deliver to the people's government any public property held by them (e.g. the state armory), relegating the execution of this mandate, with the other laws and

---

[42] *Providence Journal,* May 4 and 5, 1842; *New Age,* May 7, 1842.

[43] "Address to the People of Rhode Island, August 1843," in *Burke's Report,* pp. 738–39.

resolutions, to the future attention of the People's Governor. Then, showing more patriotism than pragmatism, the conclave adjourned until the Fourth of July, leaving Dorr to sustain these quasi-symbolic pronouncements in whatever manner he could. Even the critical study of the rebellion by Arthur May Mowry asserts that such "hasty adjournment threw the whole brunt of the battle upon Governor Dorr." [44]

Apprehensive moderates in the Foundry Legislature also authorized dispatch of a commission to Washington to inform President Tyler that the people of Rhode Island "have formed a written constitution, elected officers, and peaceably organized the government now in full operation." Dorr, a confirmed states' rightist, was unenthusiastic about sending a delegation, but when Burrington Anthony and Dutee Pearce departed for the Potomac, Dorr reluctantly followed after receiving resolutions passed by an informal assemblage of Suffragists urging him to personally present his case in Washington. Dorr made the trip primarily to avert federal intervention and to show moderate Suffragists that "the only hope for success lay in vigorous action within Rhode Island." Dorr left the state "convinced that the Suffragists must implement the will of the people by creating a government of fact as well as right. He returned to the state strengthened in that conclusion." [45]

Dorr's sojourn southward left the reform movement leaderless and in disarray, but it was an interesting and eventful excursion. On May 10 he gained an inconclusive audience with Tyler, who was firm yet "pleasant." Dorr, in a judgment both partisan and unfair, found him lacking in principle and dominated by his conservative secretary of state, Daniel Webster. Tyler's dilemma may have eluded the suspicious Dorr — though the president was a states' rights Virginian his acquiescence in a local majoritarian revolt would be a dangerous precedent which could menace the southern slave system. According to Elisha Potter, Jr.,

---

[44] The proceedings of the Foundry Legislature are printed in *Burke's Report,* pp. 447–69; Mowry's comment is on p. 156.

[45] TWD to Bradford Allen, May 8, 1842, DC, Vol. IV; Dennison, pp. 78–79.

Tyler accepted the premise, suggested to him by the Charterites, that the federal government must uphold "legitimate" state
governments "to prevent Negroes [from] revolutionizing the
South." According to Senator Sprague, the president told Dorr,
Pearce and Burrington Anthony that "their proceedings were
treasonable against the state and if they committed an overt
act and resisted the force of the United States, they would commit treason against the United States" as well.[46]

A movement to bring the alleged validity of the People's Constitution before the Senate, initiated by Dr. John A. Brown during his Washington trip in early April, was also checked by
mid-May. Five prominent Northern Democratic senators — Perry
Smith (Connecticut), Levi Woodbury (New Hampshire), William Allen (Ohio), Thomas Hart Benton (Missouri), and Silas
Wright, Jr. (New York) — wrote letters of encouragement but
counselled caution and moderation in response to an appeal from
the Suffragists. Benton assured Dorr that "the Democracy fully
admit the validity of the constitutional movement of the people
in Rhode Island," but he urged that violence be avoided because "this is not the age, nor the country, in which to settle
political questions by the sword." [47]

Senator Allen, ardent Ohio expansionist, was sufficiently inspired by principle and partisanship to impede possible intervention by Tyler in the Rhode Island embroglio. On April 18, the
day of Dorr's election, Allen introduced a senate resolution which
in substance demanded that the president reveal all the information upon which he was acting in the Rhode Island situation
and all orders and instructions that he had issued to subordinates
such as the secretary of war. The resolution was read, printed,
taken up again two days later and passed over informally. On
April 22, it was tabled by a vote of 24 to 13. Five additional

---

[46] TWD to Walter S. Burges, May 12, 1842 and TWD to Aaron
White, Jr. May 12, 1842, DC, Vol. IV (Dorr on Tyler); Potter, "Memo-
randum," May 6, 1842, and Francis to Potter, March 25, 1842, Potter
Collection (on Southern reaction); John Brown Francis to Potter, May
23, 1842, Potter Collection (information on Tyler's stand received from
Sprague).

[47] The letters are in DC, Vol. IV.

attempts were made by Allen and his associates to gain consideration of the resolution — all failed.[48] William Sprague informed John Brown Francis that many senators were "indignant" over Allen's action and that a Virginia senator remarked
that the Rhode Island rebels "ought to be hung!"[49] Despite
such opposition, the persistent Allen presented new resolutions
against interference by the president and endorsed them in a
long speech on May 17 in which he declared that there were
two governments in operation in Rhode Island and criticized
Tyler for assuming to himself the power to decide between them.
Senator James Fowler Simmons of Rhode Island answered Allen
by upholding the position of the charter government. On the
following day the resolutions were tabled, never to be reintro-
duced. With the issue squarely before it, the Senate, by inaction,
refused to take the view that the president had no authority to
act, or that in acting he was doing so unwisely. In the same
session the upper house also refused to receive a letter from
Dorr in which he claimed to be the governor of Rhode Island.[50]

Successful senatorial opposition to Allen and Dorr was led by
an incongruous coalition of northern Whigs such as Simmons of
Rhode Island and Jabez Huntington of Connecticut; Nathaniel
Tallmadge of New York, a conservative agrarian Democrat who
often aligned himself with the Whigs, and Southern nullifiers,
especially William C. Preston and John C. Calhoun of South
Carolina. By such action the Whigs gave partisan endorsement
to the regime of Samuel Ward King, Tallmadge continued his
war against locofocoism, while Preston and Calhoun sought to
repudiate the majoritarian right of revolution and to provide
support for incumbent state governments. Dorr acknowledged
that most Southerners rejected Suffragist principles because "they
might be construed to take in the Southern blacks and to aid
the abolitionists."[51] A year after the controversy had subsided,

---

[48] *Congressional Globe*, 27 Cong., 2 Sess., pp. 432, 438, 446, 449, 459,
462, 506 and 523; *Senate Documents*, 27 Cong., 2 Sess., IV, 303–04.

[49] John Brown Francis to Potter [April, 1842], Potter Collection.

[50] *Congressional Globe*, 27 Cong., 2 Sess., pp. 509–10, 659; *Senate
Journal*, 27 Cong., 2 Sess., pp. 209, 331.

[51] TWD to Aaron White Jr., May 12, 1842, DC, Vol. IV.

Calhoun justified his vote in an important public letter wherein he expressed sympathy for the suffrage party's quest to enlarge the franchise and denied the propriety of federal intervention so long as the controversy was confined to discussion and agitation. But, after an incisive survey of constitutional precedents, this zealous defender of minority rights declared that it would be the "death-blow of constitutional democracy to admit the right of the numerical majority to alter or abolish constitutions at pleasure" by resort to extra-constitutional means. He also asserted that if the federal government possessed "the right to establish its own abstract standard" of what constitutes a republican form of government, "it would be made absolute master of the States." [52]

V

Back in Rhode Island the Law and Order response to the maneuvers of the people's government was accelerated mobilization and increasingly strong opposition. The charter Assembly convened in a brief two-day session at Newport on May 4, declared that there existed "an insurrection against the laws and constituted authorities" of Rhode Island, and made a requisition upon Tyler "to interpose the authority and power of the United States to suppress such insurrectionary and lawless assemblages, to support the existing government and laws, and protect the State from domestic violence." Governor King immediately dispatched Democratic state senator Elisha Potter and Richard K. Randolph to carry the resolution and a personal letter to Tyler. Randolph was an appropriate emissary being Speaker of the House and a Virginia Whig (like Tyler) who had made the resort town of Newport his permanent home.[53]

---

[52] Calhoun to William Smith (A Public Letter on the Subject of the Rhode Island Controversy), July 3, 1843, *The Works of John C. Calhoun,* ed. Richard K. Crallé (New York, 1854–57), VI, 229–34.

[53] King to Tyler, May 4, 1842, *Burke's Report,* pp. 672–73. On Randolph see Abraham Payne, *Reminiscences of the Rhode Island Bar* (Providence, 1885), p. 51. For an expert analysis of the guarantee clause (Art. IV, Sec. 4) and the Dorr Rebellion see William M. Wiecek, *The*

King's request for federal troops, received by the president on May 6, annoyed Webster and placed Tyler in a precarious situation. If the president should accede to King's plea, he would have to deny the legality of the popular movement in Rhode Island; to refuse assistance would leave him vulnerable to charges of timidly acquiescing in rebellion. He replied to the Law and Order governor in a fair and prudent manner expressing great reluctance to employ the military power of the federal government. Assistance could not be given to prevent but only to suppress an insurrection and could not be rendered until actual violence had been committed by the Suffragists. But "if resistance is made to the execution of the laws of Rhode Island by such force as the civil power shall be unable to overcome, it will be the duty of this government to enforce the constitutional guaranty" against domestic violence, asserted Tyler.[54]

Two days later on May 9 Tyler proposed "measures of conciliation" to the desperate King: "*I am well advised,* if the General Assembly would authorize you to announce a general amnesty and pardon for the past, without making any exception, upon the condition of a return to allegiance, and follow it up by a call for a new convention upon somewhat liberal principles, that all difficulty would at once cease. . . . A resort to force, on the contrary, will engender for years to come feelings of animosity." [55]

When the regular General Assembly reconvened on Wednesday, May 11, "the subject of calling a convention immediately, and upon a liberal basis was seriously agitated amongst us," wrote Potter to the president, but "the only objection made was that they did not wish to concede while the people's party continued their threats." Potter's solution to the legislature's impasse was for Dorr to "allow himself to be arrested peaceably and give bail." On May 12 King promised pardon to those "engaged in treasonable or revolutionary designs against the state . . . on

Guarantee Clause of the U.S. Constitution (Ithaca, N.Y. 1972), pp. 84–110.

[54] Tyler to King, May 7, 1842, *Burke's Report,* pp. 674–75.

[55] Tyler to King, May 9, 1842, *Burke's Report,* pp. 676–77.

the condition only that they withdraw themselves from such enterprise and signify their return to their allegiance to the government." In essence both the moderate Potter and the hard-nosed King were requesting that Dorr and the "people's government" capitulate.[56]

A last-ditch attempt to avert forceful confrontation was made at a secret New York conference held at the Howard House on Saturday, May 14, at which Daniel Webster presided. Burrington Anthony, Dutee Pearce, and John S. Harris represented the Suffragists and John Whipple volunteered to attend as an unofficial spokesman for Law and Order, though he thought King's conduct too inflexible. Dorr was a reluctant participant because he believed, like King, that disbanding the opposition government was the only acceptable solution. Whipple proposed that the United States Circuit Court promptly decide the validity of the People's Constitution with the "facts to be first ascertained by a suitable committee, to be chosen by agreement of the parties.'" In the interim, the Algerine Law would be suspended but the charter government was "to remain in the full exercise of their authority and the persons claiming to exercise authority under the People's Constitution to omit such exercise altogether." For Dorr to accept any proposals for judicial determination of the dispute — such as those advanced by Potter and Whipple — was tantamount to surrender. Dorr and his opponents were well aware of the verdict to be expected from Job Durfee, John Pitman or Justice Joseph Story, who would preside in circuit court if Whipple's compromise were accepted.[57]

As the New York peace parley collapsed, chieftains of New

---

[56] Elisha R. Potter to Tyler, May 15, 1842 and King to Tyler, May 12, 1842, *Burke's Report,* pp. 677–78.

[57] On this conference see *Might and Right* which prints Whipple's proposal, pp. 258–59; [John S. Harris, memorandum of New York Conference of May, 1842], Miller Collection, RIHS; *New Age,* May 28 and June 4, 1842; *Providence Journal,* May 18 and 26, 1842; Newton, pp. 109–10, which cites accounts of the conclave from New York papers; and Mowry, pp. 191–93. A letter from Francis to Potter, April 1842, Potter Collection, optimistically anticipates the question of the legitimacy of Dorr's movement going before "Story's Court."

York's Democratic machine — Tammany Hall — called councils of war. Tammany leaders warmly received the People's Governor during his three-day sojourn in the metropolis. William Cullen Bryant's influential *Evening Post* supported his cause; and the New York Democracy staged a huge mass meeting and colorful parade in Dorr's honor attended by John L. O'Sullivan, editor of the *Democratic Review,* Levi Slamm, editor of the *New Era,* and prominent politicians such as Samuel J. Tilden, Elijah F. Purdy and Ely Moore. The enthusiasm shown for the reform cause by Tammany, the promise of armed assistance from several units of New York militia, the urging of well-intentioned zealots, and the support of such militants as Big Mike Walsh's "Spartan Band" fortified Dorr for the task ahead.[58] He had recommended modest force at the State House on May 3; en route to Washington on May 8 he had written that "it may be expedient to strike a blow as soon as I return"; and upon his arrival in New York on May 12 he had written his trusted confidants Aaron White and Walter S. Burges that he would make "personal application for military aid" in the event of federal intervention and he vowed "to return to Providence as soon as possible, and . . . forthwith call on the military to protect me and others from arrest under the Algerine Law." His New York reception convinced Dorr that his anticipated use of force would enable the People's Government to prevail.[59]

It is most important to note that Dorr spoke of military action mainly in defensive terms. He sought outside aid only in response to outside intervention by federal troops, and he spoke of using his local militia primarily to protect himself and his associates from what he regarded as the unauthorized and invalid aggression of the defunct charter government operating

---

[58] Mowry, pp. 166–74, 193–94, based on accounts in the New York press, is still the best description of Dorr's sojourn with New York City's Tammany leaders. See also Mowry's "Tammany Hall and the Dorr Rebellion," *American Historical Review,* III (Jan. 1898), 292–301.

[59] TWD to Crawford Allen, May 8, 1842, TWD to Walter S. Burges, May 12, 1842, and TWD to Aaron White, Jr., May 12, 1842, DC, Vol. IV.

under the Algerine Law that had been repealed by the Foundry Legislature.

Specifically Dorr reacted to the series of arrests perpetrated by charter officials against members of his government. The first victim was Daniel Brown, People's representative from Newport who was served a warrant for treason under the Algerine act on May 4, and then released under a bail bond of $5,000 restraining him from further illegal acts. On two succeeding days, Dutee Pearce and Burrington Anthony suffered an identical fate giving even greater urgency to their Washington mission. Others apprehended under the Algerine act included Attorney General Jonah Titus, General Treasurer Joseph Joslin and House Speaker Welcome B. Sayles. A warrant was issued for Dorr himself, but Sheriff Roger Potter was unable to serve the People's Governor prior to Dorr's departure for Washington. Such bold and vigorous prosecution of the law by the Charterites during Dorr's absence caused many moderate or timid Suffragists to abandon the cause and resign their offices. Dorr was kept informed of these developments and knew that forceful countermeasures were essential upon his return if his government were to survive. Sincerely convinced beyond doubt that he was the legitimate governor, Dorr decided that a good offense was the best defense against the stubborn charter regime.[60]

After a rousing Tammany send-off with promises of armed support ringing in his ears, Thomas Dorr traveled by boat to Stonington, Connecticut and then proceeded overland by special train to Providence. He arrived at 10:00 a.m. Monday, June 16, entered a waiting coach-and-four, and rode triumphantly in a procession of 1,200 cheering men, one-fifth of whom were armed, to the home of Burrington Anthony on a rise of land called "Federal Hill" in the west side of the city. Here Dorr, "fatigued and covered with dust," addressed the crowd, brandished a sword, warned against the consequences of federal interference with his government, and vowed that he was willing to die with his sword in hand if need be to sustain the People's Constitu-

---

[60] *Providence Journal*, May 5–14, 1842 for the arrests and resignations. See also *Might and Right*, pp. 236–42; and Mowry, pp. 162–64.

tion. Dorr promptly established a headquarters at the Anthony house and began to formulate plans to ensure the supremacy of his government.[61] He issued a proclamation promising his followers massive outside support in the event of federal intervention asserting that "they who have been first to ask assistance from abroad can have no reason to complain of any consequences which may ensue." He vowed that "no further arrests under the law of pains and penalties [the Algerine Law] will be permitted" and directed his militia to prevent enforcement of this "detestable" measure.

Foes of Dorr were greatly alarmed by his determination and bravado — "he looked more like a fiend than a man," said one apprehensive observer. Excitement and tension reached a fever pitch on the following day when more than sixty armed Dorrites raided the Providence armory of the United Train of Artillery

---

[61] This account of events surrounding the so-called arsenal incident from Dorr's arrival in Providence on the morning of May 16 until the collapse of resistance on the morning of May 19 has been principally drawn from diverse and sometimes conflicting sources: *viz.*, the testimony of witnesses at Dorr's treason trial contained in *Burke's Report* and George Turner and Walter Burges, *Report of the Trial of T. W. Dorr for Treason* (Providence, 1844), especially the remarks of Dorr, John S. Harris, John S. Dispean, Col. Leonard Blodget, Col. Charles Carter, Sheriff Roger W. Potter, Horace A. Pierce, George B. Aldrich, Welcome B. Sayles, Jedediah Sprague, and Dutee J. Pearce; the accounts in the *Providence Journal*, the *New Age*, and the *Providence Express; Might and Right*, pp. 242–56; The Dorr War Letters of Henry Joshua Spooner (May 3 to May 21, 1842), Misc. Mss., RIHS, S 764; the letters from W. C. Simmons to James Fowler Simmons, May–June, 1842, Simmons Papers; Dorr's 1843 "Address to the People"; the Dorr Correspondence; "Records of the Commissioners Appointed by the General Assembly of the State of Rhode Island in June, 1842, to Examine the Prisoners Arrested During the Late Rebellion," Mss., JHL; Hill's Journal, RIHS; Almon D. Hodges, Jr., ed., *Almon Danforth Hodges and His Neighbors* (Boston, 1909), pp. 171–205 ("Military Service in Rhode Island"); and Catherine R. Williams, "Recollections of the Life and Conversation of Thomas W. Dorr," D Mss. The two best secondary accounts of military operations have neither been published nor consulted in any published work. One is a 102 page manuscript by John J. Richards (state adjutant general, 1924–26) that is catalogued as the "History of the Collapse of Compulsory Militia Service in Rhode Island, 1836–1842" at RIHS; the other is Sidney S. Rider, "The Development of Constitutional Government in Rhode Island . . .," Vols. XXI–XXIII, also at RIHS.

and seized with no resistance two Revolutionary War cannon that had been confiscated from Burgoyne at Saratoga. The field pieces (minus their ammunition) were transported to Federal Hill where Dorr and his most radical adherents were formulating plans to capture the state arsenal on Cranston Street adjacent to the Dexter Training Grounds. Despite strenuous objections from more moderate and genteel Suffragists — "professionals and tradesmen" — "many of the lower-class members of the suffrage party — farmers, housewrights, shoemakers, blacksmiths, stonemasons and factory hands who had loudly demanded equal political rights" — were now ready to fight for them.[62] Dorr later justified his violent course explaining that "to submit to an arrest, and to the breakup of the government, without an effort in its behalf . . . would have been in the general opinion and in fact a dishonorable abandonment of the means apparently placed at my disposal, to maintain my own, and the rights entrusted to my keeping."

After their confiscation of the cannon, the Dorrites realized they must strike quickly before the Charter government could fully mobilize and receive reenforcements from the southern portions of the state. They waited only for the arrival of volunteers from the northern mill villages. After midnight on May 18, the fateful march to the arsenal began with Dorr's army approaching the fortress from the northeast. The People's Governor, despite urging from advisors, marched with his men as church bells rang out to alert townspeople to the impending confrontation.

Dorr never fully articulated the reason for the decision to take this building. The Foundry Legislature had given him authorization to assume control over all public property, and from a military standpoint this structure was the most formidable and its contents — field pieces, muskets and ammunition — the most useful. Its succesful seizure would perhaps intimidate the charter forces and prompt their capitulation. It also appears that Dorr harbored a naive expectation that the armory's de-

---

[62] This quote is from Gettleman, p. 119.

fenders would surrender without a fight. If he so believed, he was grossly misinformed. King was equally determined to sustain the charter government. On the evening of May 17 he placarded the walls of Providence with notices to "repair to the state arsenal and take arms," dispatched messengers to the southern counties, and sent a steamboat down Narragansett Bay to bring back Newport County's brigade of militia and several chartered commands such as the Newport Artillery and independent artillery companies from Bristol and Warren.

When Dorr and his force of 234 men under the field command of Colonel Jonathan M. Wheeler assembled before the armory at 2:00 a.m. on that dark and foggy night, they found the two-story stone building defended by 200 volunteers under Colonel Leonard Blodget with five six-pound cannon behind its 18-inch walls. Among the defenders were Dorr's father, his younger brother Sullivan Jr., his two uncles Zachariah and Crawford Allen, and his brother-in-law Quartermaster General Samuel Ames — all as determined as the People's Governor to vindicate the family's honor.

When Dorr's guns were in place, Colonel Charles W. Carter advanced under a flag of truce to demand surrender of the building in the name of Colonel Wheeler and Governor Dorr. Blodget defiantly replied: "I know no such persons by these titles. . . . If you want it come and take it." Shortly thereafter Dorr ordered the cannon to be discharged but the antiquated relics misfired. Carter later explained that "the guns were entirely unserviceable. The powder was old and poor; and becoming damp had hardened so that the priming wire would not go through it. . . . After the flash the men began to scatter, so that soon there were hardly enough left to carry off the guns." At daybreak Dorr and fifty associates (minus Colonel Wheeler) hauled the cannon back to headquarters where they were greeted by a hastily drawn handbill announcing the resignation of the entire Providence delegation to the People's Legislature and calling Dorr's action "deplorable." At the urging of his associates Dorr fled to Woonsocket at 8:30 a.m. to regroup his forces while Colonel Henry D'Wolf, a former Rhode Islander from

Uxbridge, Massachusetts, took command of the Providence operation.

Soon after his flight, Governor King and Sheriff Potter arrived at Anthony's house with a warrant for Dorr's arrest, but their bold conduct so antagonized the remaining Suffragists that King had to make an "escape down the back stairs and over the fence in the rear of the house." Sixty armed rebels who remained determined to hold their ground before a superior force which numbered, according to various estimates, between 500 to 1,000 after arrival of the steamboat from Newport and Bristol and the arming of many "loyal" citizens of Providence by Mayor Thomas M. Burgess. Desiring to avert bloodshed, the charter army under Colonel Blodget kept at bay during the day and evening of May 18. When D'Wolf's repeated calls for additional recruits proved fruitless, he abandoned his position at eight o'clock the following morning. As one die-hard defender described it: "Having no horses or the means to procure any to remove the [artillery] pieces, we left the field; and thus ended the bloodless campaign in which none were killed, none wounded and none taken prisoners."

The arsenal fiasco was the death knell of the Dorrite cause, but Dorr in exile refused to accept the inevitable. From New York he wrote that the People's Constitution, "being founded in right and justice, cannot be overthrown by a failure of arms, or by the resignation of those elected to office under it . . . the duty to maintain it has not been effaced by recent events." Less than a week after the arsenal raid Andrew Jackson sided with Dorr: "The people are the sovereign power and agreeable to our system, they have a right to alter and amend their system of Government when a majority wills it, as a majority have a right to rule." Close associate Aaron White conveyed to the stubborn People's Governor on May 25 a more realistic message: "Your idea of using force must be abandoned entirely; there is no hope in that remedy now. I verily believe that if you were to come on with 1,000 men to aid the Suffrage Party just now, you would have to fight suffrage men, just so completely have the minds of many been turned by recent misfortunes. . . . I can hardly find a suffrage man in the city with whom to advise or consult, so completely have we been defeated." [63]

Governor King and his advisors felt that they must exercise constant vigilance to preclude another challenge from Dorrites to the Law and Order government. Moderates on both sides firmly believed that timely concessions in the form of a new constitution could defuse the Rhode Island powder keg. John Brown Francis observed "we must have free suffrage or civil war." [64] John Whipple, Richard Randolph, William Sprague and other leading politicians agreed. [65] During late May and June 1842, vigorous suppression of radicalism and modest concessions to reform became the strategy of King's administration. Arrests of defiant Suffragists under the Algerine Law continued, appeals were made to neighboring governors for Dorr's apprehension and rendition, a reward of $1,000 was offered for his capture, new militia companies were chartered and drilled, many loyal units were given generous funding, suspect companies were purged or disarmed (two had their charters vacated), and several further appeals were made to President Tyler for protection. [66]

Overreaction to the bluster of local radicals and King's acceptance of exaggerated rumors concerning Dorr's plans and movements prompted these repeated requests for federal intervention. Even Senator Sprague reported from Washington on May 27 that "Dorr is organizing an army to . . . pillage Providence."

---

[63] Dorr, quoted from Boston *Daily Advertiser and Patriot,* May 31, 1842, in Gettleman, p. 125; Aaron White to TWD, May 25, 1842, DC, Vol. IV; and Andrew Jackson to Francis P. Blair, May 23, 1842, *The Correspondence of Andrew Jackson,* ed. John Spencer Bassett (Washington, 1926–35), VI, 153.

[64] John Brown Francis to E. R. Potter, June 1842, Potter Collection.

[65] Sprague to E. R. Potter, June 10, 1842, Potter Collection and Sprague to Emanuel Rice, June 6, 1842, Misc. Mss., RIHS, S 74. On the conciliatory spirit of Randolph and Whipple see Francis to Potter, May 23, 1842, Potter Collection.

[66] *Burke's Report,* pp. 678, 681, 792–95, 819–24; *Providence Journal,* May–June 1842; Aaron White to TWD, June 3 and 5, 1842; Mowry, pp. 198–205; Gettleman, pp. 128–29; Dennison, pp. 87–90.

Ten days later he erroneously contended that "there is an effort by Dorr and by a large number of desperate men out of the state to invade it and to take possession of it at all hazards." [67] On May 28 Tyler confessed he was "slow to believe" the imminence of armed invasion in Rhode Island, but he directed Colonel James Bankhead, commandant at Fort Adams, John C. Spencer, secretary of war, and Daniel Webster to investigate the situation.[68] Webster sent an anonymous emissary to Rhode Island who made a personal inspection and reported on June 3 that "Governor King and his council alone of all intelligent persons with whom I consulted, fear an eruption upon them of an armed force to be collected in other states. . . . The supposition that Rhode Island is to be invaded by a foreign force, when that force would neither be led nor followed by any considerable number of the people of the State, does not seem, to say the least, a very reasonable one." This report prevented issuance of a prepared presidential proclamation commanding "all insurgents, and all persons connected with such insurrection to disperse" and led to a reduction in the garrison at Fort Adams from 302 to 190 on June 17.[69] Nevertheless fear and apprehension persisted throughout the month of June, for Dorr had indeed determined to return — not to fight but to reconvene the People's Legislature on July 4.[70]

Dorr chose for his assembly session Chepachet, a village in

---

[67] Sprague to Emanuel Rice, May 27 and June 6, 1842, Misc. Mss., RIHS, S 74.

[68] *Burke's Report,* pp. 682–84.

[69] *Ibid.,* pp. 685–87, 699. A letter written from Worcester on June 3, 1842 by J. Davis to an unnamed correspondent expresses views identical to those of Webster's confidant. Davis contended that Rhode Island authorities were "only industrious in gathering up all the floating rumors which are put adrift and magnifying them into importance." Peck Mss., XIII, #47, RIHS.

[70] Dennison (p. 94) is the first historian to contend that Dorr's return in June was motivated primarily by a desire to peacefully reconvene the People's legislature. Such a purpose can be discerned from the testimony of Dorr and several associates found in *Burke's Report* (*e.g.,* George B. Aldrich, p. 895, General Jedediah Sprague, p. 896, Dutee J. Pearce, pp. 898–99, Laban Wade, p. 900, Col. William H. Potter, p. 902, Col. Charles W. Carter, p. 910). Most historians have gullibly accepted the hysterical

the northwestern town of Glocester, handy to the Connecticut border and accessible to the friendly mill villages of Smithfield and Cumberland where working-class supporters of reform could still be relied upon to defend the People's government. The basis of rebel power had shifted northward by June and the remaining Suffragist leadership was more plebian in character.[71]

Dorr moved with ease through adjacent Connecticut in the days preceding his return, freely visiting Norwich, Killingly and other towns, because Democratic Governor Chauncey Cleveland was sympathetic to the rebel cause. In the eyes of Law and Order men, Cleveland had made Connecticut "the Texas of New England." Pro-Dorr rallies were held at various points in northern Rhode Island from Chepachet to Woonsocket to Diamond Hill in anticipation of the arrival of the People's Governor on June 25. New militia units formed bearing names that often reflected the mentality of their organizers — Dorr's Invincibles, Johnston Savages, Pascoag Ripguts, Glocester Volunteers, Pawtucket Invincibles, Diamond Hill Volunteers and Harmonious Reptiles. Suffragists held military drills and stockpiled supplies. Armed night patrols roamed the northern highways, attempted raids on charter munition depots in Warren and Providence, and threatened another confrontation.[72]

The charter government had prepared well for Dorr's return, politically and militarily. On June 23, in response to several town petitions and town meeting resolves, the General Assembly debated, amended and approved a resolution presented two days earlier by David Daniels calling for a new constitutional convention to convene at Newport on the second Monday of September 1842. Voters would choose delegates in a ratio similar to that which the Assembly conceded in May 1841 for appor-

---

fears of the Charterites as proof of the offensive nature of Dorr's mission. On June 26 Hiram Hill observed in his "Journal" that many townspeople of Providence feared the city would be "sacked and burnt by Dorr's forces."

[71] Gettleman, pp. 130–31.

[72] Richards, pp. 42–51 contains the best description of these Dorrite maneuvers. The analogy to Texas was made by the *Providence Journal,* June 24, 1842.

tionment of the Landholders' Convention — a procedure much
more equitable that the charter's allocation but far short of the
"one man-one vote" standard. Providence and expanding towns
would still be underrepresented. Unlike the Landholders' Convention which was limited to freemen, most adult males now
were allowed to participate — all those who were qualified to
vote for general officers by existing laws plus "all native male
citizens of the United States of the age of twenty-one years
and upwards" who had lived in Rhode Island for three years.
Excluded were naturalized citizens lacking the freehold and Narragansett Indians; included were blacks — a reward for their
military alliance with the forces of Law and Order.[73] Although
some opposed this concession, "there is not so much scolding
about letting the blacks vote as was expected," observed the
perceptive Elisha Potter, "they would rather have the negroes
vote than the d----d Irish." [74]

This convention call was a conciliatory maneuver that ap-
peased most Suffragists, especially those middle-class reformers
whom Dorr derisively called "no-force constitutionalists." Quite
understandably, few would go to the barricades for abstract
issues of equal rights or popular constituent sovereignty, and
fewer still would fight for the political rights of naturalized but
landless Irish Catholics. Even Dorr's close friend and confidant,
Walter S. Burges, co-published a broadside in support of the
proposed convention. "Law and Order, justice and political
Equality are no longer enemies," exclaimed Burges and other
Suffragists. "Who will fight for *any form,* when the substance
can be gained by peace?" [75] was their rhetorical query. Although
it proved naive, this expectation of justice and genuine reform

---

[73] *Burke's Report,* pp. 444–46.

[74] Potter to John Brown Francis, July 22, 1842, Francis Collection.
Potter, a Van Buren Democrat, later explained to the ex-president that the
prevalence of manufacturing in Rhode Island necessitated restrictions
against foreign workingmen who would soon inundate the state and possibly dominate its political fortunes. Potter to Van Buren, Nov. 30, 1842
summarized in Gettleman, pp. 146–47.

[75] *Providence Journal,* June 25, 1842; *Providence Express,* June 27,
1842; broadside letter, June 25, 1842, DC, Vol. IV.

from King and his councillors dashed any chance for reconvening the People's Legislature in the inauspicious setting of
Chepachet.

The charter government's military preparations were equally
effective. As Dorrite activity increased during mid-June, the
Providence Journal spread the unfounded rumor that the "rebels"
intended to attack Providence, raid its banks and stores, and loot
its homes. Paranoiac Governor King fell victim to this propaganda. Alluding to recent Dorrite maneuvers — the theft of
armament, the establishment of "a kind of martial law" in
Chepachet and Woonsocket, the seizure and detention of four
charter scouts "under pretense of being spies," and the imminent
arrival of Dorr — King, in a letter hand-carried to Tyler by
Senator Sprague, contended that such "open violence" made
federal military aid "imperatively required." Despite corrobora-
tion of these assertions by Mayor Burgess and Colonel Bankhead, Tyler deftly sidestepped the appeal on June 25, using a
technical excuse. Citing a 1795 federal statute, he informed King
that the request for aid must "be made by the legislature if in
session" rather than the governor. Such an evasion prompted an
additional plea on June 27 from senators Sprague and Simmons
and Congressman Joseph L. Tillinghast. When Tyler finally dispatched Secretary of War John Spencer to Rhode Island on
June 29 with discretionary power to promulgate the suspended
cease and desist proclamation, summon militia from Massachusetts and Connecticut, and employ federal troops to defend
Providence, the crisis had passed.[76]

Actually King and his military advisors were equal to their
task, for the threat from Dorr was greatly exaggerated. On
June 23, the charter governor issued orders for military mobilization that directed the state's southern militia companies and
selected independent commands to assemble at Providence.[77]
During the next day a steamship arrived bearing 350 men of
the Newport, Bristol and Warren artillery companies, seven field

[76] This correspondence is printed in *Burke's Report*, pp. 681–99.

[77] My account of the Acote's Hill campaign is drawn from most of the
same sources cited in footnote 61 *supra*.

pieces, and a plentiful supply of muskets and ammunition. The ship then steamed down the bay for more. Next a provisional Providence regiment composed of four loyal chartered units and the armed police (the City Guards) prepared for immediate service under the command of Colonel William W. Brown and Lt. Colonel Almon D. Hodges. The unit's chaplain was the nativistic president of Brown University, Reverend Francis Wayland, an arch-foe of the Dorrites who penned several vitriolic pamphlets condemning their movement.[78]

West Pointer William Gibbs McNeill, army engineer and a builder of the Providence and Stonington Railroad, arrived from his home in Stonington to assume command of the special division formed to do battle with Dorr. King and his council in creating the new army disregarded the existing state militia division. Much of it was poorly organized and its largest component — the second brigade of Providence County — contained many Dorr sympathizers. Major General McNeill's force consisted of loyal militia from the southern counties, several efficient chartered commands and some newly created volunteer companies. Elisha Dyer was his adjutant general and Samuel Ames his quartermaster. By Saturday June 25, when the General Assembly proclaimed martial law throughout the state, between 2,500 and 3,000 troops had assembled in Providence. They were quartered at Brown University, in the private homes of Charterites, and in the several city arsenals or encamped on Smith's

---

[78] See Wayland's *The Affairs of Rhode Island* (Providence, 1842) and *A Discourse Delivered in the First Baptist Church Providence, Rhode Island on the Day of Public Thanksgiving, July 21, 1842* (Providence, 1842). On his life consult H. L. and Francis Wayland [Jr.], *A Memoir of the Life and Labors of Francis Wayland*, 2 vols. (New York, 1867). For expressions of Wayland's nativism see his letter to his uncle, Aug. 22, 1842 and Wayland to Basil Manly, Feb. 9, 1843, Wayland Papers, JHL. The philippics of the Brown president prompted a formidable rebuttal by Boston lawyer John A. Bolles, *"The Affairs of Rhode Island" Being a Review of President Wayland's "Discourse"; A Vindication of the Sovereignty of the People* . . . (Boston, 1842). A recent analysis of Wayland's political views is Wilson Smith, *Professors and Public Ethics: Studies of Northern Moral Philosophers before the Civil War* (Ithaca, N.Y., 1956), Chapter 7 ("Francis Wayland and the Dorr War"), pp. 128–46.

Hill. That afternoon McNeill and his staff reviewed 1,600 of these citizen-soldiers before the general retired to his headquarters at Tockwotton Hotel on India Point to devise strategy.

While this rapid and efficient mobilization transpired in Providence, the Suffragists, commanded by Colonel D'Wolf, hastened to defend Chepachet by fortifying Acote's Hill, an eighty-foot rise of land at the southeastern end of the village overlooking the road from Providence. At 2:00 a.m. on June 25 Dorr appeared with Big Mike Walsh of New York and approximately a dozen of Walsh's "Spartan Band," a political gang of militants and rowdies from New York's notorious Five Points ghetto. The People's Governor soon established headquarters at Sprague's Hotel, reviewed the troops, conducted an inventory of supplies (some of which had come from New York, Connecticut and Massachusetts), and issued a call for reconvening his General Assembly on July 4. Estimates vary on the size of the force that greeted Dorr at Chepachet and ranged as high as 1,000 men. Of this number many were merely spectators, villagers, or unarmed sympathizers. Others who came with arms dispersed when news of King's massive mobilization filtered into Chepachet. On Monday June 27 only 225 courageous die-hards remained and no legislators heeded Dorr's call. At this juncture Dorr, urged by such visitors as his father and Dutee Pearce, decided to disband his small, underprovisioned military guard. At 4:00 p.m. he sent a copy of the dispersal order to Walter S. Burges with instructions to print it in the suffrage daily, the *Providence Express*. Early that evening Dorr bade goodbye to his supporters and went into exile for the second and final time. He spent that night in nearby Thompson, Connecticut at the Vernon Stiles Hotel. Ultimately, with the price on his head raised to $5,000, he found refuge in New Hampshire under the protective care of Democratic Governor Henry Hubbard and Congressman Edmund Burke.

By the time of Dorr's departure, General McNeill had organized and equipped his force, now totalling over 3,500. Several advance units marched toward the enemy with plans to confront

Dorr at Chepachet, occupy Woonsocket, and cut off any retreat into Massachusetts or Connecticut. To prevent Dorr's Massachusetts sympathizers from reenforcing his Chepachet garrison, the Kentish Guards of Warwick and East Greenwich deployed at the Pawtucket bridge over the Blackstone River where they joined the Pawtucket and Central Falls Volunteers; some City Guards defended the India Point Bridge over the Seekonk; while the Westerly Infantry patrolled the state's southeastern border along the Pawcatuck River to deter potential Connecticut interlopers.

Colonel Brown had encamped at Greenville, midway between Providence and Chepachet, when a charter patrol apprehended the messenger carrying Dorr's order to disband and a letter to Walter Burges. Colonel Edwin Hazard carried the notice to Burges, who read his friend's parting missive: "Believing that a majority of the people who voted for the constitution are opposed to its further support by military means, I have directed that the military here assembled be dismissed." Hopefully, Dorr added, "no impediments will be thrown in the way of the return of our men to their homes." Hazard then carried the order — meant for publication in the *Express* — to General McNeill who conferred with King, his councillors, Mayor Burgess and Colonel Bankhead. They decided to delay publication until Colonel Brown's force could "capture" Dorr's fort and apprehend as many "combatants" as possible. Such a daring victory, they reasoned, would discourage any future forceful effort against the charter government. They ordered Brown to advance swiftly the same evening, but a severe rainstorm delayed him until 6:00 a.m. on June 28, when he moved out in company with some federal officials and other dignitaries including Whig potentate Thurlow Weed, advisor to New York governor William Seward.

Several Suffragists heading back to Providence, North Providence or Johnston were seized by the Law and Order army en route to Chepachet. Then, according to Colonel Brown's report, charter troops "stormed the insurgent fortification" on Acote's Hill at 7:45 a.m., sustaining no casualties. Jubilant and rowdy charter forces then searched and looted homes and stores in and around the village, ransacked Sprague's Hotel, forayed through the adjacent countryside and took a total of 100 prisoners whom they suspected of disloyalty. They subjected these captives and others seized elsewhere to harsh treatment, harassment, incarceration in crowded, unsanitary and poorly ventilated cells, and denial of civil rights.

On June 28, another charter force under Colonel Josiah H. Martin occupied the village of Woonsocket Falls, a hotbed of rebel activity. Just after midnight on June 30 this aggressive exponent of Law and Order sent twenty raiders under William P. Blodgett to Crooks Tavern in Bellingham, Massachusetts to seize several Dorr supporters. By ignoring state boundaries, the Blodgett raid eventually earned for its perpetrator conviction in a Massachusetts court for assault, burglary and false arrest.

Two fatalities occurred in the abortive and farcical war. Lt. Colonel Almon D. Hodges tersely recollected that "a member of a company from Westerly became insane through excitement," shot and killed his brother, an officer of the unit. The second victim, Alexander Kelby of Pawtucket, Massachusetts, an innocent by-stander, was shot on his own side of the state boundary by a tense and harassed militiaman confronted earlier by an unruly, menacing, rock-throwing crowd while guarding the Pawtucket Bridge. The indiscriminate firing that took Kelby's life wounded two other men.

Fortunately by July 2, all of McNeill's troops had returned to their home stations and resumed civilian pursuits. On July 4 — the date scheduled to reconvene the extinct People's Legislature — Providence militia turned out in a massive parade to celebrate their victory. On the following day General Winfield Scott, the nation's highest ranking military officer, congratulated General McNeill for such "admirable success, without federal aid in the suppression of domestic violence. Rhode Island has covered herself with glory, and may well be termed the great conservatrix of law and order." [79] Though martial law endured until August

---

[79] General Winfield Scott to William Gibbs McNeill, July 5, 1842, Misc. Mss., RIHS, Sco 86.

8 and over 300 indiscriminate arrests and irregular interrogations occurred during its operation, the Dorr war had ended; the freemen had prevailed.[80]

VI

The Algerine convention, as Dorrites called the Law and Order conclave of 1842, met as scheduled in Newport on September 12. Before the end of the month the conservative body — over which James Fenner and Henry Y. Cranston presided — produced a draft constitution and adjourned to November to allow the delegates to discuss the document with their constituents. Senator James Fowler Simmons and the Whig faction that he directed loomed large in the deliberations which produced a basic law modeled on the Landholders' Constitution. In early November the convention reconvened in East Greenwich and quickly sent its handiwork to the General Assembly then sitting in that town.

The Assembly designated November 21–23 as the referendum dates. After a relatively small turnout, tallied ballots revealed a vote that was nearly unanimous (7,024 to 51) because the Suffragists boycotted the entire procedure. Dorr urged this course of inaction in letters from New Hampshire because he believed his constitution to be still in force, making the Algerine constitution superfluous.[81]

---

[80] On martial law see *Burke's Report,* pp. 472, 767–68, 771–816 and the discussion *infra* of *Luther v. Borden.* On Dorr's exile and King's attempt to retrieve him see *Letters of the Hon C. F. Cleveland and Hon. Henry Hubbard, Governors of Connecticut and New Hampshire to Samuel Ward King, Refusing to Deliver Up Thomas Wilson Dorr. . . .* (Fall River, Mass., 1842).

[81] "Journal of the Convention Assembled to Form a Constitution at Newport, September 12, 1842," in folder labeled "Constitutions 1841–42," RISA. The *Providence Journal,* the *New Age,* the *Providence Express* and the regular Democratic paper, the *Republican Herald* conducted a running commentary on the document in September, October and November, 1842. On Dorr's strategy see his "Address," *Burke's Report,* pp. 762–63 and *Might and Right,* pp. 306–07. Thomas Allen Jenckes, secretary to both Law and Order conventions and clerk of the General Assembly (1840–44), later became a U.S. Representative from Rhode Island

Since those in power intended to hold general elections under the new constitution on the first Wednesday in April 1843 and put their basic law into effect on the first Tuesday in May, Dorr and his followers altered their strategy. In mid-December, with Wilmarth N. Aldrich presiding, they held a convention in Providence "for the reorganization of the Democratic party" to battle with the forces of law and order in the upcoming April elections. Dominant at this conclave were Aldrich, then under indictment for violation of the Algerine Law, and such suffrage stalwarts as Dutee Pearce, John R. Waterman, Philip B. Stiness, Dexter Randall, John S. Harris, Jonah Titus, Ariel Ballou and Thomas F. Carpenter. These reformers drafted a platform reaffirming Dorrite principles and castigated those Democratic moderates who had supported the Law and Order party such as Elisha R. Potter, John Brown Francis, and Senator William Sprague. They refused to hold "political fellowship or communion" with such traitors to "democracy and equal rights," while the rejected Potter expressed the conviction that "no decent man can continue with a party led by such Jacobites." When Potter and Francis failed in their attempt to "prevent the Democratic Party [from] falling into the Dorr Party" they found themselves in political limbo. They deplored "the extremes of their party"; and first asserted that they could not "support Fenner and the Algerines." Eventually these moderate rural Democrats were forced to choose, so they cast their lot again with Law and Order. Governor Francis resolved his dilemma this way: "Why should I trouble myself to make this a Whig state and then be rode over by the Simmons clique of the Whigs rough shod? But this is better than the tender mercies of Dorrism, which after all we must try to keep down." [82]

(1863–71) and left a huge collection of his papers to the Library of Congress. Unfortunately they are almost barren for the critical events of 1842.

[82] The proceedings of the December convention and subsidiary ward and town meetings are published in *Burke's Report,* pp. 239–46. On the attempt of the Potter-Francis clique to assume the leadership of the Democratic Party see Potter to Francis, Nov. 27, 28, 29, Dec. 15 and 17, 1842 Francis Collection; Francis to Potter, Dec. 18 and 19, 1842, Ben-

This realignment of parties in the wake of the Dorr Rebellion is highly significant. Moderates and conservatives sought refuge in the *ad hoc* Law and Order party that was Whig dominated. Advocates of Equal Rights, locofoco ideologues, and grateful workingmen — newly armed with the ballot — combined to give the Democratic party a liberal, urban composition. In 1843 the Law and Order coalition nominated the prestigious James Fenner — arch-conservative, former governor, and the only Democrat on King's emergency council — to head a five-man ticket composed of three Whigs and two Democrats. Dorr Democrats countered with the able and well-respected Thomas F. Carpenter, former state adjutant general and Democratic standard bearer in 1840 and 1842.

Dorr, like a coach on the sidelines, had developed a plan whereby his party would contest the April election to be held under the "minority constitution" and, if victorious, call a new convention to frame a liberal basic law modeled upon the People's Constitution and submit it for popular ratification. "The only course remaining to the Suffrage party," he told supporters, "was to enter upon Algerine ground." Victory seemed imperative because "the continuance of the Algerine Power, by a successful election in the spring, would be fatal to our party, or indefinitely postpone its expectations, as the reliance on the Supreme Court of the United States, on Congress, and on aid from abroad generally is delusive and frail." Dorr wanted victory not for partisan gain but for principle. He informed Elisha G. Smith of Warren that "if there be any in the Democratic ranks who, as you suggest, care more for a mere party triumph than for the establishment of the Constitution, their narrow and selfish views are to be deplored." [83]

---

jamin Thurston to Potter, Dec. 26, 1842, and Philip Allen to Potter, Dec. 2 and 7, 1842, Potter Collection. See also the contemporary press accounts in the *Providence Journal*, the *New Age* and the *Republican Herald*. Francis's statement of his political dilemma was made retrospectively on Dec. 17, 1843, Potter Collection, but a year later his position had not changed.

[83] Dorr detailed his plans in several letters to his Rhode Island adherents. The quotes are taken from TWD to Elisha Smith, M. Barney and

With so much at stake both sides desperately waged their April 1843 campaigns. A week before the election Dorr visited the border town of Pawtucket, Massachusetts, to personally encourage and exhort his party. Conversely, administration forces went all-out to avert defeat. Conservative businessmen, in the absence of a secret ballot, resorted to pressure and intimidation, such as the threat to fire Dorrite employees. Vote-buying under the new $1.00 registry tax was common, and the *Providence Journal* resumed its hysterical propagandizing. Such exertions produced the highest turnout ever; and in Providence "the ward rooms were completely jammed at the hour of opening." When the results were tallied Fenner outpolled Carpenter by a vote of 9,107 to 7,392. In a prophetic realignment, the Democrats made a strong showing in northern industrial towns once solidly Whig, and Fenner rolled up impressive pluralities in previously Democratic South County. The Suffragists were crushed. Welcome Sayles lamented to Metcalf Marsh that the "fatal election from which we hoped so much proved so disastrous." Informed of the result, distraught Dorr exclaimed to Aaron White: "If our party will not fight or vote, in God's name what will they do!" [84]

B. M. Bosworth, Feb. 15, 1843, Dorr Collection, RIHS (formerly catalogued in RIHS Mss., XVII, 111). Similar strategy was previously urged in TWD to William Simons, Dec. 29, 1842 and Jan. 7, 1843 and TWD to Franklin Cooley, *et al.,* Feb. 1, 1843 in DC, Vols. V and VI. These and other correspondents such as John S. Harris, Aaron White, F. L. Beckford, Samuel Low and William H. Smith kept Dorr apprised of political developments during the 1843 election campaign. William G. Goddard campaigned vigorously for Law and Order as "Old Narragansett" via articles and open letters in the *Providence Journal* collected in Goddard, II, 171–335 (Nov. 29, 1842–March 30, 1843).

[84] *Burke's Report,* pp. 648–50 contains the official results. They differ from those in Gettleman's voting tables because he used the preliminary tally printed in the *Providence Journal* on April 6, 1843. See George D. Cross to E. R. Potter, March 26, 1843; Potter Collection; *Might and Right,* pp. 307–09; and several letters to Dorr in DC, Vol. VI, for allusions to vote-buying, intimidation and fraud. More damning is the testimony of Providence businessman Hiram Hill, a Law and Order adherent: "Those persons who employ many hands are determined to discharge such as will not agree to support the laws and constitution as now adopted; proscription will be the cry but let it come; no person can be justly blamed for discharging hands that he can do without, when they have

Eventually the disillusioned People's Governor decided to come home and make his final stand. After drafting a justificatory "Address to the People of Rhode Island" fully defending and explaining his entire course of action, he left his New Hampshire sanctuary to face his vindictive conquerors. They immediately arrested and jailed him when he returned to Providence on October 31, under an indictment of high treason against the state made by Newport County's grand jury on August 25, 1842.[85] Despite his challenge to Newport's jurisdiction because his alleged offenses had been committed in Providence County, he was transferred to that politically hostile town on February 29, 1844. His case came before the state's full supreme court with draconian Job Durfee presiding on April 26, before a jury composed entirely of "Whigs and Algerines." [86] When Samuel Atwell

---

and now are doing all they can to bring about measures that will operate to his injury and disadvantage, and be of no possible benefit to themselves," Hill's Journal, entries of December 31, 1842, March 24, April 4 and 5, 1843. John Whipple made a similar claim against the Democrats — *Address of John Whipple To the People of Rhode Island, on the Approaching Election* (Providence, 1843). On the despair of Dorr and Sayles see TWD to Aaron White, April 10 and 27, 1843, DC, Vol. VII; and Sayles to Marsh, Aug. 19, 1843, Marsh Papers. Williamson (p. 258), Gettleman (pp. 149–54), and Dennison (p. 98–101) render good accounts of the 1843 campaign. Also of interest is Donald McKinley Freeman, "South County Reaction to the Dorr Rebellion as Illustrated by Elisha Reynolds Potter" (unpublished master's thesis, University of Rhode Island, 1955).

[85] The "Address" is printed in *Burke's Report,* pp. 731–66. It is Dorr's retrospective and revealing statement of his principles, motives, and course of action.

[86] There are several editions of Dorr's trial. One is printed in *Burke's Report,* pp. 865–1048; another was prepared by Joseph H. Pitman, *Report of the Trial of Thomas W. Dorr for Treason* (Boston, 1844); a third was published by George Turner and Walter S. Burges, Dorr's counsel — *Report of the Trial of Thomas W. Dorr for Treason* (Providence, 1844) and Turner, *Case of Thomas W. Dorr Explained* (Providence, 1845). The subsequent career of Dorr's counsel and confidant, Walter S. Burges, is most interesting to the student of Rhode Island constitutional development. Burges became federal district attorney for Rhode Island under President Polk (1845–49), state attorney general (1851–54, 1860–63), and the selection of a Republican Assembly for associate justice of the Rhode Island Supreme Court (1868–81). It was to Burges that Dorr left his voluminous papers and correspondence. Burges entrusted these manu-

fell ill Dorr conducted his own defense assisted by George Turner of Newport and Walter S. Burges. Conservative Democratic Attorney General Joseph A. Blake led the state's prosecution. The trial went poorly for Dorr as the partisan Justice Durfee disallowed his principal lines of defense. Dorr's closing argument, Blake's refutation and Durfee's strict charge to the jury concluded by 11:00 p.m. Monday, May 6. Three hours later the jury delivered its verdict of guilty — "the court made everything plain for us," recalled one of the twelve. When Dorr's motion for a new trial, offering eighteen exceptions, was systematically dismissed, the time arrived for sentencing. Dispassionately Chief Justice Durfee ordered the People's Governor "imprisoned in the State prison at Providence, for the term of his natural life, and there kept at hard labor in separate confinement." On June 27 convict Dorr entered state prison in conformity with the order of the court. There he joined a young Irishman by the name of John Gordon who had been convicted on circumstantial evidence of the murder of industrialist Amasa Sprague. Gordon, a victim of the anti-Irish hysteria that permeated the state, was executed in February 1845, in Rhode Island's preview of Sacco-Vanzetti, after his Dorrite lawyers, Atwell and Carpenter, failed in their efforts to obtain clemency.[87]

The verdict and especially the sentence against Thomas Dorr

---

scripts to historian Sidney S. Rider who used them and other documents to compile a constitutional history of Rhode Island (1636–1843) from the Dorrite perspective. This work in twenty-seven scrapbooks was destined for publication in three volumes, but inexplicably, the printed work never appeared. The cantankerous Rider (who denied Arthur May Mowry access to these unique sources) donated his massive collection, including Dorr's papers, to the John Hay Library; the scrapbook history went to the Rhode Island Historical Society. Mine is the first study to use or acknowledge Rider's detailed, highly informative, and carefully written narrative. On Burges consult John H. Stiness, *Memorial Address: Walter Snow Burges* (Providence, 1892); for Rider's projected history see his prepublication "prospectus," RIHS.

[87] On the Gordon murder trial see Edward C. Larned and William Knowles, eds., *The Trial of John Gordon and William Gordon Charged with the Murder of Amasa Sprague*, 2nd ed. (Providence, 1844). On the relation between the Dorrites and the Gordons see Conley and Smith, pp. 52–55 and George Potter, *To the Golden Door: The Story of the Irish*

outraged his supporters and troubled his more moderate opponents, some of whom were motivated by humane feelings and others by fear of political repercussions. As early as May 22, 1842, John Brown Francis had asked rhetorically: "Why make a martyr of this parricide?" That question's wisdom would soon become painfully evident to the forces of law and order.[88]

Reaction to Dorr's imprisonment was quite predictable for during the rebellion itself the press had distorted the nature of the conflict for partisan gain. Whig papers throughout the country had praised Governor King's administration for its courageous stand against radicalism and anarchy, while the northern Democratic organs simplistically depicted the struggle as one between progressive, enlightened Democrats led by Dorr and reactionary Whigs. The substantial Democratic contribution to the cause of law and order — extremists such as the Fenner-Gibbs clique and moderates like Sprague, Francis and Potter — were ignored. As Francis remarked in 1842, "the course of all the papers has been infamous — coining political capital out of our blood." [89] Most notable and enduring of these national fulminations was the epic debate on political theory waged in the pages of the *Democratic Review* during 1842–43 between former suffrage agitator Orestes Brownson — who defended the minoritarian principles of law and order — and the *Review's* locofoco editor, John L. O'Sullivan — longtime friend of Dorr who supported the majoritarian doctrine of popular constituent sovereignty.[90]

In Ireland and America (Boston, 1960), pp. 441–46. General Carpenter eventually converted to Catholicism.

[88] Francis to Elisha R. Potter, May 22, 1842, Potter Collection.

[89] Francis to Potter, May 22, 1842, Potter Collection. I surveyed the national reaction to the Dorr Rebellion, both by the press and by leading contemporaries, in a doctoral research paper written at the University of Notre Dame and now in my possession. My generalization is based on this seventy-two page analysis.

[90] *The United States Magazine and Democratic Review*, Vols. X–XIV (1842–44) and *Brownson's Quarterly Review*, I (Oct., 1844), 532–44 and II (Oct., 1845), 514–30. Brownson's analysis of the Rebellion (the "origin and ground" of government) was rewritten, and, with some additions, published after the Civil War under the title of *The American*

In a presidential election year, Dorr's plight again became grist for the political mill under the banner of "Polk, Dallas and Dorr." Even before the trial the propaganda value of the episode became apparent to Democrats in Rhode Island and elsewhere. On February 1, 1844, the twenty-six member Democratic minority — seven senators and eighteen representatives from seven towns in Providence County and the senator from Jamestown — sent a memorial to the United States House of Representatives requesting Congress to inquire into the "interference" by Tyler in Rhode Island affairs from April through June 1842. Local Dorrites also challenged the right of Representatives Henry Cranston and Elisha Potter to their seats in Congress and requested that the House apply the federal guarantee clause relating to a "republican form of government" (Article IV, Section 4) in favor of the legitimacy of the People's Constitution. Dorr's former protector, Congressman Edmund Burke, presented the Rhode Island memorial to the Democratic-controlled House on February 19; after considerable debate it was printed and referred to a five-man committee chaired by Burke himself. After seventeen sessions a majority report was prepared and adopted by the three Democrats on the panel — Burke, George Rathbun (N.Y.) and John A. McClernand (Ill.). Slave-state Whigs Jacob Preston and John Causin, both of Maryland, subsequently compiled a minority report vindicating Tyler and the Law and Order party — a course of action recommended by William Goddard even before the Burke committee began its investigation because Goddard knew that the sponsors of the memorial hoped "to make the Rhode Island Question one of the main issues in the approaching presidential election."

Burke's Report, as the majority brief was known, was far from neutral — the first imprinted page, the frontispiece, displayed an

---

Republic; see H. F. Brownson, *Orestes A. Brownson's Early Life* (Detroit, 1898), p. 148. Brownson was originally a supporter of the Suffragists, having addressed their association in 1841 and written a letter of encouragement to "Governor" Dorr in May 1842, H. F. Brownson, pp. 342–43 and Brownson to TWD, May 14, 1842, DC, Vol. IV. On the reason for Brownson's change in sentiment see *Brownson's Quarterly Review,* I (Oct., 1844), 532–44, a review of *Might and Right.*

engraved daguerrotype of "T. W. Dorr, Inaugurated Governor
of Rhode Island, May 3, 1842." From that point onward, through
eighty-six pages of formal conclusions and nearly a thousand
more of documents, depositions, court records and voting lists,
the report upheld the philosophy of Dorrism, censured Whig
president John Tyler for "interfering," and criticized Rhode
Island "Algerines" for their forceful resistance to popular constituent sovereignty. Dorr and his associates furnished Burke with
his documentary evidence and Benjamin F. Hallett, former
Rhode Island suffragist editor, obtained depositions from witnesses to the events of 1841–42. Devotees of law and order,
alleging unfounded congressional intermeddling, were uncooperative. Governor James Fenner caustically observed that "a
more villainous business never was entertained by the House."

Unquestionably Burke made a sincere attempt to vindicate
the philosophy of Equal Rights which he himself espoused; just
as certain, both Burke and Dorr intended and timed the report
— 5,000 copies were printed in June 1844 — to discredit Whiggery and bolster the Democratic cause in the presidential election
of 1844. *Burke's Report,* still the most valuable published source
on the Dorr Rebellion, was also a political campaign document.
Once the election had passed it became primarily of interest to
historians, and apart from printing a second edition in early
1845 and engaging in brief desultory debate, the House took
no action on Burke's findings.[91]

While the House conducted its investigation, affairs in Rhode
Island continued tranquil except for a petition circulated and

---

[91] All the pertinent documents referred to in the text, including the
February 1844 memorial, are found in *Burke's Report.* The shorter
minority report by Causin was published as 28 Cong., 1 Sess., House
Report No. 581. For a critique of congressional interference, see the statement by Congressman Elisha Potter, *Speech on the Memorial of the Democratic Members of the Rhode Island General Assembly* (Washington,
1844). On Goddard's suggestion, see Goddard to Potter, Feb. 26, 1844;
Fenner's criticism was voiced in a letter to Potter, May 17, 1844, both
in the Potter Collection. There are several letters between Dorr and
Burke in DC and in the Edmund Burke Papers, Library of Congress.
Burke's Report attempted to identify Henry Clay, Whig presidential candidate in 1844, with the forces of Law and Order, pp. 768–71. Both Dorr

sent to Congress in April 1844 by Irish leader Henry J. Duff and
other naturalized Rhode Islanders alleging that their state's new
suffrage law deprived them of their proper privileges as citizens
of the United States. Samuel Ames, describing Duff as a "rabid
Dorrite," thought the petition might arouse the support of
Southerners because in Rhode Island "a white foreigner is required by our constitution to have a higher qualification to vote
than a native Negro." Ames's apprehensions proved unfounded.
Duff got no relief from Congress, and when he turned to the
General Assembly in May 1846 his petition was referred to committee, studied, then flatly denied in a report that defended the
voting discrimination, lectured Duff's Irish signatories that "they
must not expect to be placed on a perfect equality with native
citizens," and asserted that the request would "lead to acrimonious debate and serve to increase the ill feeling and prejudice
which the petitioners complain now exist between them and
native citizens." [92]

Despite Dorr's observation in February 1843 that appeals to

---

and Burke strongly and sincerely believed that Tyler's role was decisive
in the defeat of the People's Government. Conversely King, Francis,
Sprague and other Law and Order stalwarts were sharply critical of the
president's nonintervention ism (e.g., Francis to Potter, July 8, 1842,
Potter Collection). Historians have oscillated from a judgment of
"cautious" and "conservative" (Mowry, pp. 200–01, 212, 251), to
"feeble" and politically motivated (Gettleman, pp. 97, 113), to a violation of local self-government (Dennison, pp. 121–22). Tyler's biographers,
calling the Dorr Rebellion "the chief domestic disturbance of his administration," view his actions most favorably: Oliver Perry Chitwood,
John Tyler, Champion of the Old South (New York, 1939), pp. 326–27;
Robert J. Morgan, *A Whig Embattled: The Presidency under John Tyler*
(Lincoln, Neb., 1954), pp. 100–01. Bennett M. Rich, *The Presidents and
Civil Disorder* (Washington, 1941), pp. 54–56 and Wiecek, *Guarantee
Clause,* p. 107 also render affirmative judgments. I agree with Wiecek
that "Tyler had acted with balance, firmness, and tact in meeting the
challenge of the Dorr Rebellion. He had the satisfaction of seeing his
policies of caution and conciliation vindicated at no cost to his consistency
or to national stability."

[92] *Congressional Globe,* 28 Cong., 1 Sess., p. 464; Samuel Ames to
Elisha R. Potter, April 8, 1844, Potter Collection; Petitions Not Granted
(1847), RISA; and Sylvester G. Sherman, *Report of the Committee on
the Petition of Henry J. Duff and Others* (Providence, 1847).

Congress or the Supreme Court are "delusive and frail," he eventually grasped at both these remaining straws to vindicate his cause.[93] While Burke investigated and liberationists agitated, Dorr, Burges, Atwell, George Turner, and Benjamin Hallett moved to place the People's Constitution before the United States Supreme Court for a test of its validity and for the ultimate vindication of the people's cause.[94] The agent for this appeal to the nation's highest tribunal was Martin Luther, one of approximately three dozen Suffragists formally indicted and jailed for violation of the Algerine Law. Instead of accepting his fate passively, Luther and his mother Rachel waged a legal counterattack in the form of suits for trespass. His $5,000 damage claim

---

[93] TWD to Elisha G. Smith, Feb. 15, 1843, Dorr Collection, RIHS. Leaving no stone unturned, Dorr even prepared a set of resolutions supportive of Suffragist principles for introduction at the Democratic National Convention of 1844. See TWD to Aaron White, Dec. 3, 1843, DC, Vol. VII, TWD to Walter S. Burges, May 23, 1844, Hezekiah Willard to TWD, May 11, 1844, DC, Vol. VIII; and Welcome B. Sayles to Metcalf Marsh, Nov. 6, 1843, Marsh Papers. Southern Democrats prevented their adoption.

[94] On the Luther litigation see 7 Howard 1 (1849); 12 L. Ed. 581; and *Thomas W. Dorr v. Rhode Island,* Supreme Court Records, National Archives (this unargued and unreported case was dropped by Dorr after the Luther verdict). I have relied on several excellent analyses of Luther, the best of which are Dennison, pp. 140–92; Gettleman, pp. 174–99; Wiecek, pp. 111–29; and C. Peter Magrath, "Optimistic Democrat: Thomas W. Dorr and the Case of *Luther v. Borden*," *Rhode Island History,* XXIX (Aug.–Nov., 1970), 94–112. Also useful were Mowry, pp. 231–36; Mahlon H. Hellerich, "The Luther Cases in the Lower Courts," *Rhode Island History,* XI (Apr., 1952), 33–45; Michael A. Conron, "Law, Politics, and Chief Justice Taney: A Reconsideration of the *Luther v. Borden* Decision," *American Journal of Legal History,* XI (Oct., 1967), 377–88; Charles Warren, *The Supreme Court in United States History* (Boston, 1926), II, 186–95; Charles O. Lerche, "The Dorr Rebellion and the Federal Constitution," *Rhode Island History,* IX (Jan., 1950), 1–10; Maurice G. Baxter, *Daniel Webster and the Supreme Court* (Amherst, Mass., 1966), pp. 58–64; and Charles G. Post, *The Supreme Court and Political Questions* (Baltimore, 1936), pp. 52–65. Important letters in DC alluded to or quoted in my narrative include Levi Woodbury to TWD, April 15, 1842, Vol. IV; Luther to TWD, March 28, 1844, TWD to Burges, Nov. 12, 1844, Aaron White to TWD, Feb. 9, 1844 and March 14, 1844, Vol. VIII; the correspondence between Nathan Clifford, Benjamin Hallett, Aaron White and TWD, Vols. XI

arose from the invasion of his Warren home by a group of nine armed charter militiamen acting under their government's declaration of martial law. On June 29, 1842 this charter force, under command of Luther M. Borden, had broken into Martin Luther's private dwelling, roused and rousted his elderly mother and conducted a fruitless search for Luther — a Warren town moderator serving under the People's Constitution — who had fled to the adjacent town of Swansea, Massachusetts where he established domicile and eventually filed suit against Borden and his comrades-in-arms in United States Circuit Court using diversity of citizenship to secure federal jurisdiction in the case.

In form this claim was a routine trespass action, but in reality it raised profound issues relating to the guarantee clause of the federal constitution, the doctrine of political questions, and the exercise of martial law. Luther's case was potentially a vehicle whereby the Supreme Court would be called upon to decide between the legality of the People's government or the charter government. According to the Dorrites, the People's Constitution had replaced the charter on May 3, 1842. If this assertion were legally valid, then Luther acted properly as an official in the new regime and Borden committed actionable trespass taking orders from a defunct government that had no power to proclaim martial law — Borden not Luther would become the insurrectionist.

When Luther finally returned to Rhode Island he was tried, fined and imprisoned for six months for violating the Algerine Law. From jail he wrote to Dorr who was also incarcerated awaiting trial. By late 1844 the People's Governor had become convinced that "the great question of sovereignty" could not be developed clearly in his treason case (*State v. Dorr*), but it could be "fully and perfectly presented in the case of Luther."

---

and XII *passim;* and TWD to George Turner letters at the Newport Historical Society. See also the published arguments: Daniel Webster and John Whipple, *The Rhode Island Question* (Washington, 1848) and Benjamin F. Hallett, *The Right of the People to Establish Forms of Government* . . . (Boston, 1848). Many of the papers filed in the Luther case are published in *Burke's Report,* pp. 357–473, and Story's Circuit Court charge to the jury is printed in *Causin's Report,* pp. 163–67.

To his legal colleague Walter Burges, Dorr pleaded "for God's sake do not let that case fall through." As he wrote the issue was docketed with the Supreme Court, having been expeditiously disposed of in the lower federal court during its November 1843 term by those twin legal nemeses of Dorrism — John Pitman and Joseph Story. Their strategy, agreed to by Hallett, was to use a pro forma decision to construct grounds for an appeal to the high court because of the momentous issues at stake. Rachel Luther's action for personal trespass, raising questions posed by Aaron White and others concerning the validity of the charter government's declaration and use of martial law, also went to the high court as a companion suit. In addition, Dorr's own appeal for a writ of error on his treason conviction (*Thomas W. Dorr v. Rhode Island*) was filed on February 7, 1845 as a parallel case.

Dorr's letters and memoranda indicate that he stage-managed the Luther litigation to its bitter conclusion in 1849. He drew an assist from two nationally known attorneys — members of the Democratic administration of James Knox Polk — crafty Robert J. Walker, secretary of the treasury, and learned Nathan Clifford of Maine, attorney general and future Supreme Court justice (1858–1881). With such top-level assistance before a high court composed mainly of Jacksonian jurists, Dorr entertained strong expectations for a retroactive vindication of his cause, but Aaron White and Benjamin Hallett were pessimistic, especially after Daniel Webster agreed to join John Whipple in defending Law and Order.

After several exasperating delays, oral arguments were presented in the Luther litigation for six days in early 1848. Hallett and Clifford eloquently sought judicial approval for their doctrine of popular constituent sovereignty upon which there were only two federal constitutional limitations according to Dorr: the constitution drafted by the people must be republican and the people must proceed without domestic violence. The People's Constitution was prima facie evidence that the first requirement had been met, and events up to May 3, 1842 were certainly non-violent. Thereafter, asserted the plaintiffs, the charter adherents became the insurrectionaries by refusing to acquiesce peacefully in the will of the majority. Appellants' basic claim was that the People's Constitution superseded the charter, since it had been adopted by a majority of the state's adult male voters. They refrained, however, from demanding that the Court issue a decision that would retroactively install the People's government, realizing that such a request would doom their appeal and produce political chaos. Therefore they acknowledged that the people of Rhode Island had "permitted" the establishment of a valid government in May 1843 under a new written state constitution that superseded the Dorrite document.

Webster and Whipple countered with an impressive defense of King and the charter government. Eloquent Webster, in accord with the judicial and extra-judicial opinions of Pitman and Durfee, admitted that the people were indeed sovereign, but he persuasively argued that this sovereignty had to assert itself through the forms of law and the mechanics of representation. The foremost prerequisite for change was consent of the existing government. He further argued that federal authorities had recognized the legitimacy of the charter regime — Tyler had promised it support in the event of insurrection and Congress had continued to seat its senators and representatives with no serious challenge from the Dorrites. Further, the Supreme Court of Rhode Island, in the trials of Dorr and his leading associates, had confirmed the illegitimacy of the People's Constitution. The United States Supreme Court was not the proper authority to conduct a detailed retroactive investigation of the rival claims to sovereignty, Webster concluded. That determination belonged to the political branches of government — Congress and the President — and by their actions they had decided in favor of Law and Order.

In a five to one opinion handed down in January 1849, when election fever had subsided, Chief Justice Roger Taney accepted the main points of Webster's argument. The Luthers had presented a political question that was not justiciable, said Taney, in a conclusion influenced by expedience and practicality. Responsibility to decide questions of disputed sovereignty was not vested with the Court but rather with the political branches — Congress and the President, the state legislature and the governor. In response to the Dorrite request that Taney apply the guarantee clause to the Rhode Island situation the Maryland jurist insisted that:

> Congress must necessarily decide what government is established in the State before it can determine whether it is republican or not. And when the senators and representatives of a state are admitted into the councils of the Union, the authority of the government under which they are appointed, as well as its republican character, is recognized by the proper constitutional authority. And its decision is binding on every other department of the government, and could not be questioned in a judicial tribunal.

Congressional acceptance of the charter delegation and Dorr's failure to send rival congressmen, could be construed as implicit recognition of the Law and Order government. Further, Tyler's mere promise of federal support to King under the power delegated to the president by Congress to protect states from domestic violence or invasion was "as effectual as if the militia had been assembled under his orders" to suppress the Dorrites, ruled the chief justice. The High Court would abide, said Taney, by the implicit and explicit actions of the political branches and by the determination of Judge Durfee's court.

Levi Woodbury of New Hampshire, a Dorr sympathizer in 1842, filed the lone dissent, but confined his objection to a learned discussion of martial law. His detailed and well-researched opinion that the charter forces used this power arbitrarily, extravagantly and unconstitutionally, failed to dissuade the majority from its belief that "the established government resorted to the rights and usages of war to maintain itself and to overcome unlawful opposition." With such a rude dismissal, the Dorr rebellion ceased to vex the federal government.[95]

---

[95] Ironically, Taney speaking for the majority, Woodbury in dissent, and Whipple in his argument repudiating the right of peaceable revolution all implied that success was the essential criterion which justified revolution against existing authority (*e.g.*, the American Revolution). Dorr in appraising the Luther litigation wrote: "So far . . . from deciding the Rhode Island Question against the claims of the people . . ., the Court [held] . . . that they did not go far enough; they did not

VII

In February 1844 William Goddard noted that Governor Fenner "is doing well. Our state election excites no interest." Dorr Democrats, discouraged by defeat in 1843 and imprisonment of their leader, declined to battle the Law and Order party — Fenner was reelected in April by default.[96] However, the harsh sentence imposed upon Dorr in June 1844 was a political blunder which reactivated liberal Democrats and split the forces of Law and Order. Samuel Ames and others had urged general amnesty rather than vengeance, but Fenner, Cranston, Goddard, ex-governor William C. Gibbs, Henry Anthony and other prominent Algerines preferred the latter course. "The difficulty lies in this," said Ames, "that if any one of our party attempts to move in the matter [of amnesty], he is cried down by certain violent men as a deserter from the Law and Order ranks." [97] Such vindictiveness and maltreatment of the imprisoned reformer hurt the Whig image nationally in 1844, enraged local Dorrites, elicited sympathy from conservative humanitarians, and invited political opportunism. By early 1845 "liberation" was the major issue in Rhode Island politics and a rift in Law and Order ranks developed.

In a bold maneuver Whig moderates and opportunists led by

---

take the necessary measures to make their government a reality, a fact such as the Court can regard." As George Dennison has observed: "After all had been done and said peaceable revolution meant violent revolution unless the government acquiesced," pp. 162–63, 175, 185. Dorr in a letter to Hallett correctly observed that the justices "regard the government in fact as the government in right," Jan. 15, 1849, DC, Vol. XII.

[96] Goddard to Potter, Feb. 26, 1844, Potter Collection. On the "purchase" of the registry voters prior to the 1844 election, the observation by John Brown Francis speaks volumes on an abuse that was to endure in Rhode Island until 1888: "Our meeting [of the Law and Order Party] was well attended this P. M. and there were 250 names reported as necessary to be paid for. Sprague's man told me that not one of their workmen would advance a cent. Their hearts were nearly all against us, tho if their tax was paid we might have their votes. In my opinion, both parties will soon get tired of this dollar tax." Francis to Potter, Dec. 26, 1843, Potter Collection.

[97] Ames to Potter, May 15, 1844, Potter Collection. On the legislative

Senator Simmons and former governor Lemuel Arnold united with Dorr Democrats to field a "liberation" slate headed by Charles Jackson that outmaneuvered and outvoted hard-nosed incumbents like Fenner and moderate rural Democrats like Congressman Potter. Fenner lost 8,010 to 7,800. Potter summarized the election tersely: "The Simmons Whigs, Arnold and Charles Jackson have joined the Dorrites and come out for liberation and defeated us. Charles Jackson is Governor over Fenner, and Arnold got 150 majority over me. The Dorrites all went straight for Jackson and Arnold and Whigs enough [supported liberation] to elect them. It is a piece of treachery unparalleled, I believe, in the history of our politics."[98]

Actually more electors favored Dorr's release than those who voted for Jackson in 1845. Many Law and Order men knew that Dorr "was subject to violent attacks of acute rheumatism and they feared, if he should die in prison," enemies of the party would derive great emotional support from the people. As early as October 1844 Law and Order legislators had caucused at the Bristol session of the Assembly and "after a stormy debate" Speaker Samuel Ames appointed a committee of three, chaired by Almon D. Hodges, to consider the subject of amnesty. After extensive hearings that included a moving plea by distinguished Sullivan Dorr, the committee unanimously reported a resolution for the discharge from prison of the People's Governor upon his taking an ordinary oath of allegiance to the Algerine constitution. All the Dorrites in the legislature voted against this procedure, and Dorr declined to take the oath. Simmons' Whigs and

---

resolutions of 1843 pardoning lesser offenders see *Causin's Report,* pp. 143–44.

[98] Elisha R. Potter to Thomas Potter, April 4 and May 18, 1845, Potter Collection. There is interesting material on the 1845 campaign in the Dorr Correspondence, the Simmons Papers, the Francis Collection, Dexter Randall, *Democracy Vindicated and Dorrism Unveiled* (Providence, 1846); and Goddard, II, 362–511, as well as in the Potter Collection. Gettelman makes the best attempt thus far to analyze the 1845 contest (pp. 169–73), but he attaches too much significance to the long-range consequences of these temporary realignments. The seedbed of modern party development in Rhode Island is not 1845 but rather 1853–56.

Dorr's supporters then joined hands to advocate unconditional freedom.[99] A Dorr Liberation Society formed, sold liberation stock, and New York lawyer Francis C. Treadwell made an unsuccessful and unauthorized appeal of Dorr's conviction to the United States Supreme Court.[100] After the liberationists staged their upset victory Dorr was freed on June 27, 1845. Counting the time he spent awaiting trial, he had served nearly twenty months in jail — an ordeal that shattered his fragile health and contributed to his political and physical demise.

Law and order regulars branded Dorr's temporary Whig allies "four traitors" — Jackson, Arnold, Simmons, and Samuel F. Man — for the manner in which they achieved his liberation. In 1846 Fenner's lieutenant governor Byron Diman got revenge, outpolling Jackson by a plurality of eighty-eight and forcing the General Assembly in Grand Committee to resolve the contest. Diman and the regular Law and Order men prevailed but, the crisis over, his coalition gradually dissolved. For the remainder of the decade the Whig party under the direction of Henry Bowen Anthony maintained political dominance over a badly divided Democratic organization so demoralized that it did not oppose Anthony in the 1850 gubernatorial election.[101]

Democrats grudgingly united in 1851 and rose phoenix-like

---

[99] Legislative committee chairman Almon Hodges provides the most informed account of the mechanics of liberation, Hodges, pp. 207–09.

[100] *Ex Parte Dorr*, 3 Howard 103 (1845), wherein the Supreme Court denied Treadwell's request for a writ of *habeas corpus* on jurisdictional grounds. See also [Francis C. Treadwell], *The Conspiracy to Defeat the Liberation of Gov. Dorr* . . . (New York, 1845). The organ of the New York liberationists was the *Working Man's Advocate* (New York), affiliated with the National [Land] Reform Association of George Henry Evans. This group sent Treadwell to rescue Dorr from the "land aristocrats" of Rhode Island. In its issue of July 6, 1844, the paper dedicated itself to the cause of Dorr's liberation, and thereafter it published a running account of its efforts. On May 25, 1844 the *Working Man's Advocate* had reprinted an article from a leading English Chartist journal, the *Northern Star* (Leeds), expressing support for the cause of "universal suffrage" in Rhode Island.

[101] "The Four Traitors," Broadside File (1846), RIHS, reproduced in Mowry, p. 258. The *Rhode Island Manual* lists the contestants, official statistics, and party affiliations in these elections. On October 29, 1846

to victory for three successive years behind Philip Allen, well respected industrialist and humanitarian, friend of Potter and Francis, and uncle of Thomas Dorr. Before the end of Allen's first term it became quite obvious that he and his leading associates — among them his nephew — supported the liberal doctrine of Equal Rights. Strongly advocating extension of suffrage to naturalized immigrants on the same basis enjoyed by native citizens, these locofocos made several abortive attempts to achieve this reform during their brief period of ascendancy. Allen's victories over a declining Whig party in 1852 and again in 1853 revived the old anti-Dorr sentiments as demonstrated by a *Providence Journal* comment on the danger of removing the suffrage restriction: "Rhode Island will no longer be Rhode Island when that is done. It will become a province of Ireland: St. Patrick will take the place of Roger Williams, and the shamrock will supersede the anchor and Hope." [102]

When the Democratic-controlled legislature offered a referendum in 1853 on calling a new constitutional convention to liberalize suffrage and implement other Dorrite proposals, the issue became clear-cut. The Whig party, then dividing over the slavery question, mobilized to resist the convention, rural Democrats defected, and the call was soundly defeated. Later in the year the Whigs decisively rejected a second referendum on a limited convention, so Democrats then tried to achieve reform by proposing nine constitutional amendments.[103] This attempt "to

---

Dorr lost the vote in Grand Committee for United States Senator to Whig industrialist John H. Clarke 59 to 34. Of the five remaining ("scattered") votes, Charles Jackson and Job Durfee each received one.

[102] The pages of the *Journal* from 1851 through 1854 (especially at election time) are replete with nativistic statements in opposition to any reform which would enfranchise the naturalized Irishman. Its alarmism prepared the way for the Know-Nothing ascendancy, *e.g.,* Jan. 25, 28, 30, 31, April 1 and 5, 1851, March 4, 1852, March 26, 30 and April 3, 1853.

[103] Despite Allen's victories in 1851, 1852 and 1853, the Democrats did not safely control the Assembly until the 1853–54 legislative year. In 1851–52 they elected 35 representatives, and 17 senators, the Whigs 37 and 14 respectively; in 1852–53 the line-up for the Democrats was 31 and 15, while the Whigs dominated both houses with 40 representatives

foister upon the people of Rhode Island" the People's Constitution caused nativist Whigs to realign themselves with those
agrarian Democrats from South County and the western hill
towns who feared the liberalism of their party's urban wing.
Similar to the Law and Order faction that had vanquished Dorr,
this coalition was supplemented by many native-born newcom-
ers to politics from the working classes who were restless and
disgusted with the existing leadership of the two major parties.
The novelty of the emergent American party, its chauvinistic
nativism, the chance it offered the common man for participation in the decision-making process, and its repudiation of
the political establishment made it an attractive alternative
for these disgruntled voters, many of whom had gratefully
sided with the Democrats in the immediate wake of the Dorr
Rebellion.

By 1855 the Whig party disintegrated and the Democrats
(minus many farmers and native workingmen) were eclipsed by
a combination of antislavery and nativist factions that built separate organizations but nominated almost identical state tickets.
These factions — the antislave Republicans and the nativistic
American party — were politically dominant during the mid-
1850s. Gradually they fused under the Republican label with
suffrage restriction a common bond.

A curious sidelight of this emergent Republican ascendancy
was provided by three successive and decisive defeats suffered

---

and 17 senators. In the April 1853 elections, however, the Democrats
achieved an eighteen vote majority in the House and a two vote edge in
the Senate. Because of their broad suffrage proposals and bold convention
calls, many natives abandoned the party. It succumbed to the Whigs in
April 1854, and did not control both the governorship and the Assembly
again until Jan. 1, 1935. See Laurence Bruce Raber, "The Formation and
Early Development of the Republican Party in Rhode Island, 1850–
1865" (unpublished master's thesis, University of Rhode Island, 1965),
pp. 16–63; and Charles Carroll, *Rhode Island: Three Centuries of
Democracy* (New York, 1932), I, 576–81. The Whig General Assembly
of 1854 refused assent to the four most liberal Democratic amendments
and sent the other five to an electorate that ratified three and rejected
two. The successful proposals became the first three amendments to the
Rhode Island constitution.

by Democratic gubernatorial candidate Americus V. Potter, once Dorr's major general of militia. The first two setbacks (1855 and 1856) came at the hands of Know Nothing-Republican Governor William W. Hoppin, and the *coup de grace* in 1857 was delivered by Republican Elisha Dyer, Law and Order adjutant general during the Dorr Rebellion.[104]

During the Allen ascendancy an attempt was made to vindicate Thomas Dorr. As soon as the 1851 Democratic Assembly organized, it passed a resolution restoring to Dorr his political rights.[105] Then in 1854, before succumbing to the tidal wave of nativism, the Democratic legislature passed an act reversing and annulling the judgment of the Rhode Island Supreme Court in Dorr's treason trial. In a move both tragic and ironic, the Supreme Court, still under Algerine control, responded by asserting its independence — for which Dorr had fought — by denying the power of the General Assembly to reverse its judgment.[106] In April 1854 the Democrats were ousted and relegated to a minority status that they maintained during the next four generations. The beginning of hard times for Rhode Island Democrats coincided with the end of hard times for Dorr. On December 27, 1854 he died in Providence at the age of forty-nine in the midst of the local Know-Nothing campaign to prevent naturalized Irish Catholics from attaining equal rights.

---

[104] On these developments see Raber, pp. 16–101; Carroll, pp. 576–94; Brennan, pp. 131–37; Coleman, pp. 242–48; Conley and Smith, pp. 76–83; Charles Stickney, "Know-Nothingism in Rhode Island," Rhode Island Historical Society, *Publications,* I (1894), 243–57; John Michael Ray, "Anti-Catholicism and Know-Nothingism in Rhode Island," *American Ecclesiastical Review,* CXLVIII (Jan., 1963), 27–36; Larry Anthony Rand, "The Know-Nothing Party in Rhode Island," *Rhode Island History,* XXIII (Oct., 1964), 102–16; and Mario R. DiNunzio and Jan T. Galkowski, "The Disruption of Rhode Island Politics: A Computer Study of Party Loyalty in the 1850s" (research paper, Providence College, 1975) to be published in *Rhode Island History,* XXXVI (Aug. 1977).

[105] *Rhode Island Acts and Resolves,* May session, 1851, pp. 3–4.

[106] *Rhode Island Acts and Resolves,* January session, 1854, pp. 249–51 and June session, pp. 3–14; 3 *Rhode Island Reports* 299; *Providence Journal,* Feb. 25 to March 4, 1854.

VIII

The constitution that emanated from the autumn deliberations in 1842 — as amended — is still the state's basic law. The document was similar in most respects to the Landholders' Constitution rejected the previous March, but some notable changes occurred. The Declaration of Rights and Principles now began with an explicit repudiation of the doctrine of popular constituent sovereignty: "We declare that the basis of our political systems is the right of the people to make and alter their constitutions of government; but that the constitution which at any time exists, till changed by an explicit act of the whole people, is sacredly obligatory upon all." The experience of the preceding months had interpreted this statement (read in conjunction with Article XIII on Amendments) to mean that change must come via divested sovereignty through legally prescribed forms. This constitution, however, contained no provision for the calling of future conventions.

Another basic change in the bill of rights was a justificatory addendum to the proviso that the military shall be held in strict subordination to the civil authority — "the law martial shall be used and exercised in such cases only as occasion shall necessarily require."

The suffrage article contained important revisions. Blacks, after some opposition, secured a separate referendum on their right to vote as a reward for their help in suppressing the rebellion. Some Law and Order men upheld their bargain and acquiesced in this arrangement, feeling that Rhode Island's blacks were "conservative and go with the wealthy part of the community" by whom most were employed.[107] A concession was also given to women by insertion of a clause that allowed non-electors to be members of a school committee. A most important and un-

---

[107] Elisha R. Potter to John Brown Francis, November 14, 1842, Francis Collection; and Goodell, p. 6. In 1844 Samuel Ames also discussed the political conservatism of Rhode Island blacks, Ames to Potter, April 8, 1844, Potter Collection. The special referendum favored black suffrage 4,031 to 1,798, *Causin's Report,* p. 143.

fortunate omission was the failure of the delegates to provide for secrecy of the ballot.

The distinction in the Landholders' Constitution between native-born citizens with real estate and those without was retained. Freeholders needed only one year's residence to vote on all political and financial questions at every level of government. Those natives who lacked real estate were subject to a two-year residency qualification, but if these landless citizens paid taxes on $134.00 worth of personal property they could also vote in all elections. In addition to these fully enfranchised voters (i.e. those who paid taxes on at least $134.00 worth of real or personal property) the new constitution established a second-class category of native-born electors known as registry voters. These individuals could be enfranchised either by paying at least $1.00 in taxes or by performing at least one day of volunteer service in the militia per year,[108] but registry voters could not participate in council elections in the city of Providence nor could they vote on financial questions in any municipality. The final and most demanding electoral category was reserved for naturalized citizens. They were still subjected to the old real estate qualification — a restriction which made Rhode Island's new basic law the most nativistic in the nation from the moment of its inception.[109]

---

[108] The ineptitude or the disloyalty of the regular state militia during the Dorr Rebellion led to the abolition of compulsory militia duty in peacetime and a reliance on those independent, volunteer chartered commands that had strongly supported the charter government. Richards, pp. 102–03. According to Governor Francis "the disorganization of the militia was the cause of our troubles!" Francis to Potter, Sept. 1, 1842, Potter Collection. In 1843 Dorr observed that the new militia law "exempts the great majority — the enrolled militia — the suffrage men — from military duty, and thus gets rid of their military qualification as voters — and also taxes them (and not the community at large) for the support of the active militia, the charter men. . . ." *Burke's Report*, p. 765.

[109] On the effect of this exclusion see Conley and Smith, pp. 51–52, 76–83, 96–103; Charles E. Gorman, *An Historical Statement of the Elective Franchise in Rhode Island* (Providence, 1879); and Chilton Williamson, "Rhode Island Suffrage Since the Dorr War," *New England Quarterly*, XXVIII (March, 1955), 34–50. Henry Bowen Anthony, Re-

The major change in the judiciary mandated the Supreme Court to render advisory opinions at the request of the governor or the General Assembly. The cumbersome and inflexible article on amendments (requiring passage by two successive legislatures, a general election intervening, and approval by three-fifths of the electors voting thereon) remained intact as a bulwark against reform. Apportionment clauses of the new basic law underwent significant change. In the House the nine expanding towns immediately obtained fifty-two percent of the state's representatives (36 of 69), an allocation even more generous than the forty-six percent allowed by the People's Constitution.[110] Nevertheless the upper limit of twelve seats for any municipality regardless of size immediately deprived Providence of two seats and checked any growth in its political power. The expanding towns paid dearly for their gain in the lower house, because the most striking alteration in the new constitution was the veto power given to the rural towns in the Senate. In place of the at-large method that prevailed under the charter and the regional districts proposed in the People's and Landholders' Constitutions, a town system was established whereby the lieutenant governor and each municipality, regardless of size, had one senate vote. Conservative rural members of the Law and Order coalition were thereby rewarded with a veto as absolute in practice as Calhoun's "concurrent majority" was in theory. South County had prevailed; the "agrarian interest" was secure. Wilkins Up-

---

publican party leader and United States Senator, led the opposition to the liberalization of the suffrage until his death in 1884. He was even instrumental in restricting the Fifteenth Amendment of the United States Constitution to blacks alone so that Rhode Island's Irish-born citizens would not be enfranchised by this voting rights amendment. See William Gillette, *The Right to Vote: Politics and the Passage of the Fifteenth Amendment* (Baltimore, 1965), pp. 58–59, 150–53; and Henry Bowen Anthony, "Limited Suffrage in Rhode Island," *North American Review,* CXXXVII (Nov., 1883), 413–21; *Defense of Rhode Island, her Institutions, and her Right to her Representatives in Congress* (Washington, 1881); and *Congressional Record,* 46 Cong., 3 Sess., pp. 1490–99.

[110] An upper limit of seventy-two representatives was reached after the census of 1850. The new constitution also replaced the charter system of semi-annual elections for the lower house with one-year terms for state representatives.

dike, a principal architect of the new Senate, was later praised for enabling the country folk "to hold a salutary check on many of the plans" of their "more wealthy and aspiring neighbors."[111]

Most of the constitutional crises which convulsed Rhode Island during the century and a quarter following adoption of the 1843 constitution would have been avoided had the People's Constitution prevailed. Dorr lost the battle but much that the Dorrites proposed has been added to the organic law of the state. What has died is Dorr's doctrine of popular constituent sovereignty, that even in 1842 was an archaic and potentially dangerous relic of our Revolutionary era. Dead also is the anti-bank and anti-corporate economic dimension of Equal Rights, the passing passion of an atomistic pre-industrial age.

But much still lives. In 1856, Dorr's brother-in-law and rival, Chief Justice Samuel Ames, in *Taylor v. Place* interpreted the nebulous language of the 1843 document as an unequivocal statement of judicial independence — a doctrine explicitly asserted by the People's Constitution.[112]

The nativistic freehold qualification was removed in 1888 by the Bourn Amendment (VII) under sustained pressure from an "Equal Rights Movement" that invoked the memory of Dorr. This change was strategically conceded, however, by the dominant Republican party primarily to gain the votes of newer immigrants from French and British Canada, England and Italy against the rising threat of *native* Irish Democratic power. Only a half-loaf in another respect, this "reform" maintained the real or personal property requirement for voting in council elections and broadened its application from Providence to include all cities. Not abandoned until 1928 (Amendment XX), the property tax operated in a strong council-weak mayor system to deprive nearly sixty percent of city dwellers — most of them

---

[111] A Citizen of Narragansett, "To the Electors of the Western Congressional District," Broadside File (1847), RIHS, a tract detailing Updike's political achievements while boosting him for Congress as a Whig in 1847.

[112] *Taylor v. Place*, 4 *Rhode Island Reports* 324. Consult C. Peter Magrath, "Samuel Ames: The Great Chief Justice of Rhode Island," *Rhode Island History*, XXIV (July, 1965), 65–76.

lower-class immigrants — of control over their local government. In the decades before 1928 the ceremonial mayor was usually Democratic, while the powerful council was Republican.[113]

In 1889 after several investigations had revealed undue political pressure exerted over workers by employers, especially in the mill villages, a permanent and effective Australian or secret ballot law was enacted; and in 1909 the governor was finally given the veto that the Dorrites had proposed nearly seventy years earlier (Amendment XV).

The rotten-borough senate that represented towns rather than people provided the major source of political contention. From 1901 to 1935 under the infamous Brayton Law it possessed not only a legislative veto but control over state appointments and the state budget.[114] Senate malapportionment caused bitter complaint — especially during the 1920s when West Greenwich (population 407) could checkmate Providence (population 267,-918). Amendment XIX offered mild relief from this extreme inequity in 1928, but it took the United States high court in *Baker v. Carr* (1962) and *Reynolds v. Sims* (1964) to mandate a 1965 state legislative reapportionment based on the "one man, one vote" principle.[115] Both decisions also modified the political

---

[113] On the effect of the city council restriction see the testimony of contemporary political scientists: Hubbard, pp. 211–15; James Quayle Dealey, *Political Situations in Rhode Island* [Providence, 1928], pp. 9–11, 36–38, 51–53, 69; and William Kirk (ed.), *A Modern City: Providence, Rhode Island, and Its Activities* (Chicago, 1909), pp. 145–63. I have hypothesized concerning Brayton's motivation for supporting the Bourn Amendment; the "Boss" left no letters or memoirs.

[114] *Public Laws,* Chap. 731 (1889) as amended and strengthened by *Public Laws,* Chap. 894 (1890) and Chap. 920 (1891). The Democrats had passed a rudimentary "blind" or secret ballot law in 1851 (*Acts and Resolves,* June session, 1851, pp. 25–28), but the Whigs immediately amended and weakened it when they came to power in May, 1854 (*Acts and Resolves,* May session, 1854, p. 1). That the absence of the secret ballot led to intimidation of working-class electors is verified by the reports of an investigating committee of the United States Senate chaired by William A. Wallace of Pennsylvania (46 Cong., 2nd Sess., Senate Reports Nos. 427 and 572, April–May, 1880), excerpts from which are reprinted in Conley and Smith, p. 101.

[115] The federal and state censuses reveal the extreme imbalance in the Rhode Island Senate where in 1925 rural towns with eight percent of

question doctrine propounded in *Luther v. Borden* and vindicated Dorr's belief that the Supreme Court should act "to evolve substantive standards of republican government and to enforce these on state governments." [116]

Failure of the basic law of 1843 to provide a mechanism for calling future constitutional conventions posed a major problem for nearly a century. In 1883 a conservative, Republican-dominated state Supreme Court — in an attempt to block the Equal Rights Movement — rendered an advisory opinion to the House of Representatives declaring that a constitutional convention could not be convened by the people or the Assembly. That incredible and reactionary decision endured until after the Democrats seized power in the "Bloodless Revolution" of 1935, and threw out the Republican Court. New Deal governor Theodore Francis Green, descendant of George Burrill and Walter S. Burges, declared that "the spiritual presence of Thomas Wilson Dorr" and his "indomitable advocacy of the rights of the people" inspired those actions.[117]

---

the total population had twenty-two of the thirty-nine Senate votes. On the Senate and the Brayton Law, P.L., Chap. 809, Secs. 62–63 (1901), see Hubbard, pp. 227–31; Dealey, pp. 11–15; and Amasa M. Eaton, *Brief Showing the Unconstitutionality of Sections 62 and 63 of Chapter 809 of the Public Laws* (n.p., n.d.). The inequity and corruption of this system even drew the attention of national reformers, *e.g.*, Lincoln Steffens, "Rhode Island: A State for Sale," *McClure's Magazine*, XXIV (Feb., 1905), 337–53. See also John D. Buenker, "Urban Liberalism in Rhode Island, 1909–1919," *Rhode Island History*, XXX (May, 1971), 35–51; Buenker, "The Politics of Resistance: The Rural-Based Yankee Republican Machines of Connecticut and Rhode Island," *New England Quarterly*, XLVII (June, 1974), 212–37; Duane Lockard, *New England State Politics* (Princeton, 1959), pp. 172–227; Jerome L. Sternstein, "Nelson W. Aldrich: The Making of the 'General Manager of the United States,' 1841–1886" (unpublished doctoral dissertation, Brown University, 1968); Mary Cobb Nelson, "The Influence of Immigration on Rhode Island Politics, 1865–1910" (unpublished doctoral dissertation, Harvard University, 1954); and Robert C. Power, "Rhode Island Republican Politics in the Gilded Age" (unpublished honors thesis, Brown University, 1972).

[116] Wiecek, *Guarantee Clause,* pp. 126–29.

[117] *In Re The Constitutional Convention,* 14 Rhode Island Reports 649 (1883); *In Re Opinion to the Governor,* 55 R.I. 56 (1935). For criticisms of the 1883 opinion see [Charles S. Bradley], *The Methods of Changing the Constitutions of the States Especially That of Rhode Island*

With the court ban on conventions removed, reformers relied on the device of *limited* constitutional conclaves to circumvent the difficult amendment procedure that had become even more cumbersome when the legislature went from one to two year sessions in 1912 (Amendment XVI). One such limited convention in 1973 not only established specific procedures for the regular call of constitutional conventions, but also applied the simple majoritarian principle of the People's Constitution to the process of amendment in place of the three-fifths rule. In addition, this gathering removed the last vestige of the property holding requirement by opening financial town meetings to all electors.[118]

Dorr's 1843 lament — "All is lost save honor" — may well have been the story of his rebellion and his life, but it is not his legacy nor the ultimate verdict of history. At the conclusion of his trial for treason, Dorr made an impassioned plea: "From the sentence of the court I appeal to the People of our State and of our Country. They shall decide between us. I commit myself without distrust to their final award." [119] To his credit — and to ours — the confidence of this optimistic, if somewhat naive democrat continues to experience an inexorable though painfully gradual vindication. In the many decades since his defeat and death, the judgment against him

---

(Boston, 1885); Samuel R. Honey, *Constitutional Reform* (Providence, 1894); Dealey, pp. 7–9, 43–45; Amasa M. Eaton, *Constitution-Making in Rhode Island* (Providence, 1899), pp. 1–34; *Advisory Opinion of the Supreme Court of Rhode Island Upon Questions Relating to a Constitutional Convention, April 1, 1935, Affirmative and Negative Briefs Submitted* (Providence, 1935); and Fred J. Volpe, "Rhode Island Advisory Opinions: Ghosts that Slay?" *Rhode Island Bar Journal,* XXV (Feb., 1977), 2–3, 8, 13, 15–17, 19. On the "Bloodless Revolution" and Green's remark see Erwin L. Levine, *Theodore Francis Green: The Rhode Island Years* (Providence, 1963), pp. 173–87.

[118] Patrick T. Conley, ed., *The Proceedings of the Rhode Island Constitutional Convention of 1973* (Providence, 1973). Convention secretary, Patrick T. Conley of Cranston, sponsor of the convention-amendment proposal, invoked the principles of Dorr while urging its passage, pp. 122–23; see also Conley's historically oriented speech supporting removal of the final property requirement for voting, p. 82.

[119] *Burke's Report,* pp. 1045–46.

from a biased court has been properly overruled by time and experience. From 1776 to 1841 Rhode Island was a democracy in decline. More than any other, Thomas Wilson Dorr began the reversal of that unfortunate trend.

Bibliography

This bibliography is intended to be inclusive for the period under direct analysis — 1776 to 1841. The listing is selective for the Colonial Era and the Dorr Rebellion. For works which deal with the aftermath and legacy of the rebellion, especially the post-1849 era, consult the footnotes in chapter thirteen. The bibliography has been divided into classifications based upon the type of sources used. Annotations, analyses, or historiographical commentary relating to these sources are often contained in the footnotes that parallel the text.

PRIMARY MATERIAL

I. UNPUBLISHED (Listed by depository)

A. *John Carter Brown Library (Brown University)*
   Welcome Arnold Papers
   Brown Papers
B. *John Hay Library (Brown University)*
   Dorr Collection
   Thomas A. Jenckes Manuscripts
   James Manning Papers
   Records of the Commissioners Appointed by the General Assembly
      of the State of Rhode Island in June, 1842, to Examine the
      Prisoners Arrested During the Late Rebellion.
   The Sidney S. Rider Collection. This mammoth collection contains
      thousands of published and unpublished documents relating to
      Rhode Island history. Among those especially useful in the prep-
      aration of this work were:
   Broadsides and Caricatures Relating to Political Affairs in
      Rhode Island
   Dorr Correspondence. 14 vols.
   Dorr Manuscripts. 46 vols.

Dorr Papers. *ca.* 100 folders.

Documents relating to the alleged political trade between Nehemiah R. Knight and Tristam Burges . . . 1836.

Original documents relating to a movement in Providence and adjoining towns in opposition to the operation of the new estimate law, setting forth the imperfection of our judicial system and calling attention to the want of a constitution of state government in Rhode Island.

Private Letters from Prominent Rhode Island Men to Samuel F. Man Relating to the Political Affairs of Rhode Island. 3 vols.

Private Papers and Letters of Jonah Titus from Many Prominent in Rhode Island Politics, 1830–1860.

Francis Wayland Manuscripts

C. *Library of Congress — Manuscripts Division*
    Edmund Burke Papers
    Thomas A. Jenckes Papers
    James F. Simmons Papers
    Levi Woodbury Papers

D. *University of Michigan — William L. Clements Library*
    The John Pitman–Joseph Story Correspondence

E. *Newport County Court House*
    Rhode Island Supreme Court Records (Newport Session)

F. *Newport Historical Society*
    William Ellery, Loan Office and Custom House Letter Book, 1786–1794
    Miscellaneous Manuscripts, especially the letters of TWD to George Turner

G. *North Smithfield Heritage Association*
    Metcalf Marsh Papers

H. *Rhode Island Historical Society*
    James Brown Papers
    Moses Brown Papers
    Carter-Danforth Papers
    Champlin Papers
    Channing-Ellery Papers
    Clark-Nightingale Papers
    Byron Diman Papers
    Dorr Manuscripts
    Durfee Papers
    Samuel Eddy Papers
    Theodore Foster Papers
    John Brown Francis Collection
    Albert C. and Richard Ward Greene Collection
    Hiram Hill Journal ("Incidents in the Life of Hiram Hill")
    Enos Hitchcock Papers
    List of the Freemen of the City of Providence Who Voted at the Presidential Election, 1840 [with an indication of their party preference]
    William Davis Miller Collection (from which the Potter and Francis Papers were subsequently culled)
    Miscellaneous Manuscripts, especially the Dorr War letters of Henry Joshua Spooner and the letters of William Sprague to Emanuel Rice
    Jeremiah Olney Papers

Peck Manuscripts
Potter Collection
Providence Town Papers
Rhode Island Historical Society Manuscripts
Rhode Island Manuscripts
Shepley Collection
Updike Papers
Warwick Manuscripts (the political papers of John R. Waterman)

I. *Rhode Island State Archives*

Acts and Resolves of the Rhode Island General Assembly

Constitutions, 1841–42, especially Journal of the Convention Assembled to Form a Constitution at Newport, September 12, 1842.

Ellery-Huntington Correspondence

General Treasurer's Papers: Lodged Money.

Grand Committee Office, Account Books A & B, 1786–1803

The Journal of the Convention . . . 1824.

Journal of the House of Representatives

Journal of the Senate

Laws and Acts, made from the First Settlement of Her Majesties Colony of Rhode Island and Providence Plantation [1705].

Letters from the Governor

Letters to the Governor

Miscellaneous Letters

Miscellaneous Papers of the General Assembly

Miscellaneous Papers Relating to the Estimates of 1796, 1823 and 1849.

Papers Relating to the Adoption of the Constitution of the United States

Petitions to the General Assembly

Records of the Rhode Island General Assembly (published in part by J. R. Bartlett for the period up to 1792)

Reports of Committees to the General Assembly

Rhode Island Equity Court: File Papers, Sept. 1741–Dec., 1743. 7 vols.

J. *Rhode Island State Records Center*

Rhode Island Supreme Court Records (Providence session)

K. *Town Meeting Records*

The town meeting records of Rhode Island's communities have been consulted at random for those periods during which the towns played a major role in the state's constitutional development, *e.g.* 1786–1790, 1796, 1824, 1829, 1833–34, etc. The records are to be found in the clerk's office of the respective municipalities unless otherwise indicated. The towns extant in the period up to 1842 whose records have been consulted are as follows:

Bristol
Burrillville
Charlestown
Coventry
Cranston
Cumberland
East Greenwich
Exeter (Rhode Island Historical Society)
Foster
Glocester

Hopkinton
Jamestown
Johnston (Providence City Hall)
Little Compton
Middletown
Newport (Newport Historical Society)
North Kingstown
North Providence (Pawtucket City Hall)
Portsmouth
Providence (City Council Records, 1832–1841)
Richmond
Scituate
Smithfield (Central Falls City Hall)
Tiverton
Warren
Warwick
West Greenwich (Rhode Island State Archives)
Westerly

II. PUBLISHED (Public Documents, Pamphlets, Letters, Memoirs, Gazetteers, Broadsides, etc.).

Abstract of the Returns of the Fifth Census [1830]. 22 Cong. 1 Sess., House Document No. 263. Washington, D.C.: Duff Green, 1832.

Acts and Laws of His Majestie's Colonie of Rhode Island and Providence Plantations in America. Boston: John Allen and Nicholas Brown, 1719.

Acts and Laws, Of His Majesty's Colony of Rhode Island, and Providence Plantations, in America. Newport: James Franklin, 1730.

Acts and Laws, of His Majesty's Colony of Rhode Island, and Providence Plantations, in New England, In America. Newport: The Widow Franklin, 1745.

Acts and Laws of His Majesty's Colony of Rhode Island, and Providence Plantations, in New England, In America. From Anno 1745, to Anno, 1752. Newport: J. Franklin, 1752.

Acts and Laws of the English Colony of Rhode Island and Providence Plantations, in New England, in America. Newport. Samuel Hall, 1767.

Acts and Laws of the English Colony of Rhode Island and Providence Plantations, in New England, in America: Made and passed since the Revision in June, 1767. Compared and Corrected by the Secretary. Newport: Solomon Southwick, 1772.

Adams, John. *Defence of the Constitutions of Government of the United States.* . . . 3rd ed. 3 vols. Philadelphia: Budd and Bartram, 1797.

Adams, John Quincy. *The Memoirs of John Quincy Adams.* Edited by Charles Francis Adams. 12 vols. Philadelphia: J. B. Lippincott, 1874–77. Vols. XI–XII.

Address to the Freemen of the Agricultural and Manufacturing Interests of Rhode Island. Providence: The Republican Herald, 1829. (at RIHS).

An Address to the Freemen of Rhode Island by a Landholder. Providence: Republican Herald, 1831. (at RIHS).

Address to the Freemen of Rhode Island on the Annual Election of State Officers . . . 1828. n.p., n.d., (at RIHS).

Anon. *To the Farmers of Rhode Island.* n.p., 1835.

Anthony, Henry Bowen. "Limited Suffrage in Rhode Island," *North American Review*, CXXXVII (1883), 413–421.

Aristides [Thomas Wilson Dorr]. *Political Frauds Exposed. . . .* Providence: n.p., [1838].

Balch, William S. *Popular Liberty and Equal Rights: An Oration, delivered before the Mass Convention of the R.I. Suffrage Association . . . July Fifth, 1841.* Providence: B. F. Moore, 1841.

Bartlett, John R. (comp.). *Census of the Inhabitants of the Colony of Rhode Island and Providence Plantations . . . 1774.* Providence: Knowles, Anthony & Co., 1858.

————— (ed.). *Records of the Colony of Rhode Island and Providence Plantations in New England.* 10 vols. Providence: A. Crawford Greene, 1856–1865.

Birney, James Gillespie. *Letters of James Gillespie Birney, 1831–1857.* Edited by Dwight L. Dumond. 2 vols. New York: D. Appleton-Century Co., 1938. Vol. I.

[Bolles, John A.]. *The Affairs of Rhode Island.* Boston: Benjamin B. Mussey, 1842.

Borden, Morton (ed.). *The Antifederalist Papers.* East Lansing, Mich.: Michigan State Univ. Press, 1965.

Bowen, Henry L. *Memoir of Tristam Burges.* Providence: Marshall, Brown & Co., 1835.

[Brigham, Clarence S. (ed.)]. *The Early Records of the Town of Portsmouth.* Providence: E. L. Freeman & Sons, 1901.

Broadside File. Rhode Island Historical Society.

Brown, William J. *The Life of William J. Brown of Providence, R.I., with Personal Recollections of Incidents in Rhode Island.* Providence: Angell and Co., 1883.

Brownson, Orestes A. *The Works of Orestes A. Brownson.* Edited by Henry F. Brownson. 20 vols. Detroit: Thorndike Nourse, 1882–87. Vol. XV.

[Burges, Tristam]. *Address to the Landholders and Farmers of Newport County . . . August 7, 1829.* Providence: The Daily Advertiser, 1829.

[Burges, Tristam]. *What a Ploughman Said about the "Hints to Farmers" Made Last April by "Men of Trade."* Kingston: n.p., 1829.

Burnaby, Rev. Andrew. *Travels Through the Middle Settlements in North America in the Years 1759 and 1760.* 2nd. ed. London: Printed for T. Payne, 1775.

Burnett, Edmund C. (ed). *Letters of Members of the Continental Congress.* 8 vols. Washington, D.C.: The Carnegie Institution, 1921–1936.

[Burrill, George R.]. *A Few Observations on the Government of the State of Rhode Island.* Providence: John Carter, 1807.

Calhoun, John C. *The Works of John C. Calhoun.* Edited by Richard K. Crallé. 6 vols. New York: D. Appleton, 1854–57. Vol. VI.

Causin, John. [*Minority Report of the Select Committee to Whom Were Referred the Memorial of the Democratic Members of the Rhode Island Legislature*]. 28 Cong. 1 Sess., House Report No. 581 [1844].

Chafee, Zechariah, Jr. (ed.). *Documents on Fundamental Human Rights.* 3 vols. Cambridge: Harvard Univ. Press, 1951–52.

—————. "Records of the Rhode Island Court of Equity, 1741–1743," *Publications of the Colonial Society of Massachusetts,* XXXV (1951), 91–118.

Chapin, Howard M. (ed.). *Documentary History of Rhode Island*. 2 vols. Providence: Preston and Rounds, 1916–1919.

———— (ed.). *The Early Records of the Town of Warwick*. Providence: 1926.

———— (ed.). *Rhode Island Court Records* [1647–1670]. 2 vols. Providence: Rhode Island Historical Society, 1920–22.

Charter and Ordinances of the City of Providence, with the Acts of the General Assembly Relating to the City. Providence: Knowles & Vose, 1845.

Charters and Legislative Documents Illustrative of Rhode Island History. Providence: Knowles & Vose, 1844.

Clarke, John. *Ill Newes from New-England*. London: Henry Hills, 1652. Reprinted in Massachusetts Historical Society, *Collections*, 4th Ser., II (1854).

Congdon, Charles T. *Reminiscences of a Journalist*. Boston: James R. Osgood, 1880.

Cooke, Jacob (ed.). *The Federalist*. Middletown, Conn.: Wesleyan Univ. Press, 1961.

Corning, Howard (ed.). "Letters of Sullivan Dorr," *Massachusetts Historical Society Proceedings*, LXVII (1941–44), 178–364.

Corwin, Edward S., Norman J. Small and Lester S. Jayson (eds.). *The Constitution of the United States of America: Analysis and Interpretation*. 88 Cong., 1 Sess., Senate Doc. No. 39. Washington, D.C.: Government Printing Office, 1964.

Cotner, Robert C. (ed.). *Theodore Foster's Minutes of the Convention Held at South Kingstown, Rhode Island, in March, 1790, Which Failed to Adopt the Constitution of the United States*. Providence: Rhode Island Historical Society, 1929.

Danforth, Walter R. "Pictures of Providence in the Past, 1790–1820: The Reminiscences of Walter R. Danforth," edited by Clarkson A. Collins, 3rd, *Rhode Island History*, X (Jan.–Oct., 1951), 1–13, 45–60, 85–96, 119–129; XI (Jan.–April, 1952), 17–29, 50–63.

Darby, William and Theodore Dwight, Jr. (comps.). *A New Gazetteer of the United States . . . With the Population of 1830*. Hartford, Conn.: Edward Hopkins, 1833.

DeBow, J.D.B. (comp.). *Statistical View of the United States . . . Being a Compendium of the Seventh Census*. Washington, D.C.: Beverley Tucker, 1854.

Dexter, Franklin Bowditch (ed.). *Extracts from the Itineraries and Other Miscellanies of Ezra Stiles, 1755–1794, with a Selection From His Correspondence*. New Haven: Yale Univ. Press, 1916.

———— (ed.). *The Literary Diary of Ezra Stiles*. 3 vols. New York: Charles Scribner's Sons, 1901.

Dexter, George (ed.). "Letters of Henry Wheaton," *Massachusetts Historical Society Proceedings*, XIX (1881–1882), 360–376.

Documentary History of the Constitution of the United States of America, 1788–1870. 5 vols. Washington, D.C.: Dept. of State, 1894–1905.

[Dorr, Thomas W., et al.]. *An Address to the People of Rhode Island from the Convention . . . to Promote the Establishment of a State Constitution*. Providence: Cranston and Hammond, 1834.

[Dorr, Thomas W., et al.]. *The Nine Lawyers' Opinion [on the Right of the People of Rhode Island to Form a Constitution]*. In Vol. XI, 1st Series of the Rhode Island Historical Tracts. Edited by Sidney S. Rider. Providence: S.S. Rider, 1880.

[Dorr, Thomas Wilson (comp.)]. [Political scrap book, being cuttings from newspapers between the years 1836–1840 relating to political and economic affairs]. John Hay Library, Brown University.

Draft of Constitution of the State of Rhode Island and Providence Plantations . . . November, 1841. Providence: The New Age, 1841.

[Durfee, Thomas (ed.)]. *The Complete Works of the Honorable Job Durfee. . . .* Providence: Gladding and Proud, 1849.

Dyer, Elisha (comp.). *Valuation of the Cities and Towns in the State of Rhode Island. . . .* Providence: Providence Press Co., 1871.

Elliot, Jonathan (comp.). *The Debates in the Several State Conventions on the Adoption of the Federal Constitution as Recommended by the General Convention at Philadelphia in 1787.* 2nd ed. 5 vols. Philadelphia: J. B. Lippincott, 1861.

First Social Reform Society of New York. *An Address to the Citizens of Rhode Island Who Are Denied the Right of Suffrage.* n.p., 1840. (in Rider Collection, JHL).

Fitzpatrick, John C. (ed.). *The Diaries of George Washington, 1748–1799.* 4 vols. Boston and New York: Houghton Mifflin, 1925. Vol. IV.

Ford, Paul Leicester (ed.). *Essays on the Constitution of the United States, 1787–1788.* Brooklyn, N.Y.: Historical Printing Club, 1892.

————— (ed.). *Pamphlets on the Constitution of the United States.* Brooklyn, N.Y.: Historical Printing Club, 1888.

Ford, Worthington C., *et al.* (eds.). *Journals of the Continental Congress.* 34 vols. Washington, D.C.: Government Printing Office, 1904–37.

Frieze, Jacob. *A Concise History of the Efforts to Obtain an Extension of the Suffrage in Rhode Island from the year 1811 to 1842.* Providence: Benjamin F. Moore, 1842.

Goddard, William G. *The Political and Miscellaneous Writings of William G. Goddard.* Edited by Francis W. Goddard. 2 vols. Providence: Sidney S. Rider & Brother, 1870.

Goodell, William. *The Rights and Wrongs of Rhode Island.* Whitesboro, N.Y.: Press of the Oneida Institute, 1842.

Gorton, Samuel. *Simplicity's Defence Against Seven-Headed Policy.* Edited by William R. Staples. Vol. II of the Rhode Island Historical Society, *Collections.* Providence: Marshall, Brown & Co., 1835.

Great Britain, Privy Council. *Acts of the Privy Council of England, Colonial Series . . . 1613–1783.* Edited by William L. Grant and James Munro. 6 vols. Hereford: Anthony Brothers, 1908–1912.

Great Britain. Public Record Office. *Calendar of State Papers: Colonial Series. . . .* Edited by W. N. Sainsbury, et al. 43 vols. to date. London: His Majesty's Stationary Office, 1860—

Great Britain. *Statutes at Large, from Magna Charta to . . . 1866.* Edited by Danby Pickering, *et al.* 106 vols. Cambridge and London: J. Bentham, G. E. Eyre and W. Spottiswood, 1762–1866.

Hallett, Benjamin F. *The Right of the People to Establish Forms of Government: Mr. Hallett's Argument in the Rhode Island Causes, Before the Supreme Court of the United States.* Boston: Beals & Greene, 1848.

Haskel, Daniel and J. Calvin Smith (comps.). *A Complete Descriptive and Statistical Gazetteer of the United States of America . . . With an Abstract of the Census and Statistics for 1840.* New York: Sherman & Smith, 1845.

Hayward, John (comp.). *The New England Gazetteer and Census of 1840*. Boston: John Hayward, 1841.

Hazard, Benjamin. *Report of the Committee on the Subject of An Extension of Suffrage*. Providence: n.p., 1829.

Hodges, Almon Danforth, Jr. (ed.). *Almon Danforth Hodges and His Neighbors*. Boston: T.R. Marvin and Son, 1909.

Hutchinson, Peter Orlando (comp.). *The Diary and Letters of His Excellency Thomas Hutchinson, Esq.* 2 vols. Boston: Houghton Mifflin, 1884.

Jackson, Andrew. *The Correspondence of Andrew Jackson*. Edited by John Spencer Bassett. 7 vols. Washington: Carnegie Institution, 1926–35. Vol. VI.

Jackson, Charles T. *Report on the Geological and Agricultural Survey of the State of Rhode Island*. Providence: B. Cranston, 1840.

Jefferson, Thomas. *Writings*. Edited by Paul Leicester Ford. 10 vols. New York: G.P. Putnam's Sons, 1892–1899.

————. *Writings*. Edited by Andrew A. Lipscomb and Albert Ellery Bergh. 20 vols. Washington, D.C.: The Thomas Jefferson Memorial Association, 1905.

Jensen, Merrill (ed.). *American Colonial Documents to 1776*. Vol. IX of English Historical Documents. Edited by David C. Douglas. New York: Oxford Univ. Press, 1955.

Kimball, Gertrude Selwyn (ed.). *The Correspondence of the Colonial Governors of Rhode Island, 1723–1775*. 2 vols. Boston and New York: Houghton Mifflin, 1902–03.

———— (ed.). *Pictures of Rhode Island in the Past, 1642–1833 by Travellers and Observers*. Providence: Preston and Rounds, 1900.

King, Dan. *The Life and Times of Thomas Wilson Dorr*. Boston: Published by the author, 1859.

Knollenberg, Bernhard (ed.). *Correspondence of Governor Samuel Ward, May, 1775–March 1776*. Providence: Rhode Island Historical Society, 1952.

Larned, Edward C. and William Knowles (ed.). *A Full Report of the Trial of John Gordon and William Gordon Charged with the Murder of Amasa Sprague*. 2nd ed. Providence: Daily Transcript, 1844.

Lawson, John D. (ed.). *American State Trials*. 17 vols. St. Louis: F. H. Thomas Law Book Co., 1914–1936. Vol. IV.

Letters of the Hon. C.F. Cleveland and Hon. Henry Hubbard, Governors of Connecticut and New Hampshire to Samuel Ward King, Refusing to Deliver Up Thomas Wilson Dorr. . . . Fall River, Mass.: Thomas Almy, 1842.

Luther, Seth. *An Address on the Right of Free Suffrage*. Providence: S. R. Weeden, 1833.

Maclay, William. *The Journal of William Maclay: United States Senator from Pennsylvania, 1789–1791*. Edited by Edgar S. Maclay with an Introduction by Charles A. Beard. New York: Frederick Ungar, 1965.

Manual With Rules and Orders for the Use of the General Assembly. 1937–38, 1965–66.

[McDougall, Frances H.]. *Might and Right*. Providence: A.H. Stillwell, 1844.

[McLane, Louis, (comp.)]. *Documents Relating to the Manufactures in the United States.* . . . 22 Cong. 1 Sess, House Executive Document no. 308. 2 vols. Washington, D.C.: D. Green, 1833.

Moore, Benjamin F. *The Providence Almanac, embracing a business directory of Providence, Newport, Warren, Bristol, Pawtucket and Woonsocket, R.I.* . . . *1844.* Providence: B.F. Moore, 1844.

Morison, Samuel Eliot (ed.). *Sources and Documents Illustrating the American Revolution and the Federal Constitution, 1764–1788.* Oxford: The Clarendon Press, 1929.

Payne, Abraham. *Reminiscences of the Rhode Island Bar.* Providence: Tibbitts & Preston, 1885.

Pease, John C. and John M. Niles. *A Gazetteer of the States of Connecticut and Rhode Island.* Hartford: William S. Marsh, 1819.

"The Petition to Revoke the City Charter of Newport, R.I., 1786," *Newport Historical Magazine,* I (1880), 224–229.

[Pitman, John]. *To the Members of the General Assembly of Rhode Island.* Providence: Knowles & Vose, 1842.

Pitman, Joseph H. *Report of the Trial of Thomas Wilson Dorr for Treason.* . . . Boston: Tappan & Dennet, 1884.

Polishook, Irwin H. (ed.). "Peter Edes's Report of the Proceedings of the Rhode Island General Assembly, 1787–1790," *Rhode Island History,* XXV (Apr., July, Oct., 1966), 33–42, 87–97, 117–129; XXVI (Jan., 1967), 15–31.

Potter, Elisha R. [Jr.]. *Considerations on the Questions of the Adoption of a Constitution and Extension of Suffrage in Rhode Island.* Boston: Thomas H. Webb, 1842.

———. *Speech on the Memorial of the Democratic Members of the Rhode Island General Assembly.* Washington: The Globe, 1844.

Preamble and Constitution of the Rhode Island Suffrage Association Adopted Friday Evening, March 27, 1840. Providence: B.T. Albro, 1840.

Proceedings of the Antimasonic State Convention Held January 16, 1835. . . . Providence: W. Simons Jr., 1835.

Proposed Constitution of the State of Rhode Island and Providence Plantations as finally adopted by the People's Convention Assembled at Providence on the 18th Day of November, 1841. Providence: n.p., 1841. (at JHL).

Providence City Charters (a bound volume of pamphlets at the RIHS relating to the formative period of the *city* government).

The Providence Directory. . . . Providence: Brown and Danforth, 1824; Carlile and Brown, 1826; H.H. Brown, 1828, 1830, 1832, 1836, 1838, 1841.

Providence Tax Books, 1832–1841.

The Public Laws of the State of Rhode Island and Providence Plantations, . . . *1798.* Providence: Carter and Wilkinson, 1798.

Public Laws of the State of Rhode Island and Providence Plantations Passed Since the Session of the Hon. General Assembly in January, 1798. Providence: Jones & Wheeler, 1810.

Public Laws of the State of Rhode Island and Providence Plantations. Providence: Miller & Hutchens, 1822.

Public Laws of the State of Rhode Island and Providence Plantations, Passed at and since the Session of the General Assembly, in January, 1822. Providence: n.p., 1839.

Public Laws of the State of Rhode Island and Providence Plantations. Providence: Knowles and Vose, 1844.

Randall, Dexter. *Democracy Vindicated and Dorrism Unveiled*. Providence: H. H. Brown, 1846.

Rhode Island State Map Collection. Rhode Island Historical Society.

Rhode Island Supreme Court. *Rhode Island Reports*.

Richardson, James D. (comp.). *A Compilation of the Messages and Papers of the Presidents*. 20 vols. New York: National Institute of Literature, 1897–1917. Vol. V.

Rogers, Horatio, George M. Carpenter, and Edward Field (eds.). *The Early Records of the Town of Providence*. 21 vols. Providence: Snow and Farnham, 1892–1951.

Sawyer, F. *Facts Involved in the Rhode Island Controversy*. Providence: n.p., 1842.

Schedules [Acts and Resolves] *of the* [Rhode Island] *General Assembly*. (Published at the conclusion of each Assembly session).

Seward, William H. *The Works of William H. Seward*. Edited by George E. Baker. 3 vols. New York: Redfield, 1853. Vol. II.

Sherman, Sylvester J. *Report of the Committee on the Petition of Henry J. Duff and Others*. Providence: M. B. Young, 1847.

Snow, Edwin M. (comp.). *Census of the City of Providence Taken in July, 1855 . . . and An Appendix Giving an Account of Previous Enumerations of the Population of Providence*. 2nd ed. Providence: Knowles, Anthony & Co., 1856.

———— (comp.). *Report Upon the Census of Rhode Island, 1865*. Providence: Providence Press Co., 1867.

Staples, William R. (ed.). *Proceedings of the First General Assembly of the Incorporation of Providence Plantations, and the Code of Laws Adopted by That Assembly in 1647, with Notes Historical and Explanatory*. Providence: n.p., 1847.

———— (comp.). *Rhode Island in the Continental Congress, With the Journal of the Convention that Adopted the Constitution, 1765–1790*. Providence: Providence Press Co., 1870.

Stokes, Anthony. *A View of the Constitution of the British Colonies in North America and the West Indies. . . .* London: B. White, 1783.

Stone, Edwin M. (ed.). *The Life and Recollections of John Howland*. Providence: George H. Whitney, 1857.

Story, Joseph. *Charge of Mr. Justice Story on the Law of Treason Delivered to the Grand Jury of the Circuit Court of the United States Holden at Newport for the Rhode Island District, June 15, 1842*. Providence: H. H. Brown, 1842.

Tansill, Charles C. (ed.). *Documents Illustrative of the Formation of the Union of the American States*. 69 Cong., 1 Sess., House Doc. No. 398. Washington, D.C.: Government Printing Office, 1927.

Thorpe, Francis Newton (ed.). *The Federal and State Constitutions, Colonial Charters and Other Organic Laws. . . .* 7 vols. Washington, D.C.: Government Printing Office, 1909.

Toppan, Robert N. and Alfred T. S. Goodrick (eds.). *Edward Randolph: Including His Letters and Official Papers . . . 1676–1703*. 7 vols. Boston: The Prince Society, 1898–1909.

Towle, Dorothy S. (ed.). *Records of the Vice-Admiralty Court of Rhode Island, 1716–1752*. Washington, D.C.: American Historical Association, 1936.

[Treadwell, Francis C.]. *The Conspiracy to Defeat the Liberation of Gov. Dorr. . . .* New York: John Windt, 1845.

Tucker, George. *Progress of the United States in Population and Wealth in Fifty Years, as Exhibited by the Decennial Census.* New York: Press of Hunt's Merchants' Magazine, 1843.

Turner, George. *Case of Thomas W. Dorr Explained.* Providence: n.p., 1845.

————— and Walter S. Burges. *Report of the Trial of Thomas W. Dorr for Treason.* . . . Providence: B. F. Moore, 1844.

Tyler, Leon G. *The Letters and Times of the Tylers.* 3 vols. Richmond: Whittet and Shepperson, 1884–85. Vol. II.

U.S. Census Office. *Compendium of the Enumeration of the Inhabitants and Statistics of the United States* . . . *from the Returns of the Sixth Census.* Washington, D.C.: Blair and Rives, 1841.

—————. *Fifth Census: or, Enumeration of the Inhabitants of the United States* . . . *1830.* Washington, D.C.: D. Green, 1832.

U.S. Congress. *Annals of the Congress of the United States, 1789–1824.* 42 vols. Edited by J. Gales and W. W. Seaton. Washington, D.C.: Gales & Seaton, 1834–1856. 1st Congress, Vols. I–II; and *Congressional Globe,* 27th and 28th Congress.

U.S. President. *United States Troops in Rhode Island.* Washington: Blair and Rives, 1844 (28th Congress, 1 Sess., House Executive Document No. 225).

U.S. Supreme Court. *The Providence Bank v. Alpheus Billings and Thomas G. Pittman* (1830), 7 L. Ed. 514; *Luther v. Borden* (1849), 7 Howard 1; 12 L. Ed. 581; and *Ex Parte Dorr* (1845), 3 Howard 103.

[Updike, Wilkins, *et al.*]. *Hints to the Farmers of Rhode Island by a Freeman.* Providence: Republican Herald, 1829. (at RIHS).

Varnum, James M. *The Case, Trevett against Weeden.* . . . . Providence: John Carter, 1787.

Wayland, Francis. *The Affairs of Rhode Island.* Provdence: B. Cranston, 1842.

—————. *A Discourse Delivered in the First Baptist Church, Providence, Rhode Island on the Day of Public Thanksgiving, July 21, 1842.* Providence: Knowles & Vose, 1842.

—————. *The Duty of Obedience to the Civil Magistrate.* Boston: Charles C. Little and James Brown, 1847.

—————. *The Duties of An American Citizen.* Boston: James Loring, 1825.

—————. *Occasional Discourses.* Boston: James Loring, 1833.

—————. *University Sermons.* Boston: Gould and Lincoln, 1854.

Webster, Daniel. *The Writings and Speeches of Daniel Webster.* National Edition. 18 vols. Boston: Little, Brown, 1903. Vol. XI.

————— and John Whipple. *The Rhode Island Question.* . . . . Washington, D.C.: J. & G. S. Gideon, 1848.

Weed, Thurlow. *Autobiography.* Edited by Harriet A. Weed. Boston: Houghton Mifflin, 1883.

What a Ploughman Said. . . . Kingston, R.I.: n.p., 1829. (at RIHS).

Whipple, John. *Address* . . . *To the People of Rhode Island, on the Approaching Election.* Providence: Knowles & Vose, 1843.

Williams, Roger. *The Complete Writings of Roger Williams.* Introduction by Perry Miller. 7 vols. New York: Russell and Russell, 1963.

III. NEWSPAPERS AND MAGAZINES (All of the following are located either in the original or on microfilm at the Rhode

Island Historical Society or at Brown University Library except as otherwise indicated.)

Beacon (Providence). 1824–1826.

Brownson's Quarterly Review (Boston). 1844–45.

Columbian Phenix (Providence). 1808–12 (a continuation of the *Providence Phenix*).

Manufacturers' and Farmers' Journal (Providence). 1820–1841.

Morning Courier and General Advertiser (Providence). 1836–1840. Misc. issues at the American Antiquarian Society, Worcester, Massachusetts.

Microcosm (Providence). 1828–1829.

New Age and Constitutional Advocate (Providence). 1840–1843 (merged with the *Providence Express* in 1842–43).

New England Artisan. 1832–33. American Antiquarian Society.

New Era (New York City). 1839. New York Public Library.

Newport Mercury. 1785–1841.

Niles' Register (Baltimore). Vols. LXII–LXVIII (1842–45).

Northern Star and Constitutionalist (Warren). 1834–1837.

Providence Daily Journal. 1829–57.

Providence Gazette. 1785–1825.

Providence Patriot. 1817–1824, 1829 (successor to *Columbian Phenix*).

Providence Phoenix. 1802–1808 (predecessor of *Columbian Phenix*).

Republican Herald (Providence). 1828–1843.

Rhode Island American (Providence). 1808–12, 1817–24, 1829 (began in 1808 as the *American*).

Rhode Island Constitutionalist. (Providence). 1834.

Rhode Island Republican (Newport). 1809–1812, 1817–1824, 1829, 1833–1842.

The Suffrage Examiner (Providence). 1841.

United States Chronicle (Providence). 1784–1800.

United States Magazine and Democratic Review (Washington, D.C. and New York City). 1837–1845.

Woonsocket Patriot. 1833–1842.

Working Man's Advocate (New York City). 1844–45.

SECONDARY MATERIALS

I. BOOKS

Abrahamson, Shirley S. (comp.). *Constitutions of the United States: National and State.* 2 vols. Dobbs Ferry, N.Y.: Oceana Publications, 1962.

Academy of Political Science. *The Revision of the State Constitution.* Proceedings of the Academy of Political Science, Volume V, nos. 1 and 2 (October, 1914, January, 1915).

Adams, William Forbes. *Ireland and Irish Emigration to the New World from 1815 to the Famine.* New Haven: Yale Univ. Press. 1932.

Akagi, Roy H. *The Town Proprietors of the New England Colonies.* Philadelphia: Univ. of Pennsylvania Press, 1924.

Alden, John Eliot (comp.). *Rhode Island Imprints, 1727–1800.* New York: R. R. Bowker, 1949.

Andrews, Charles McLean. *The Colonial Period of American History.* 4 vols. New Haven: Yale Univ. Press, 1934–38. Vol. II.

Arnold, Samuel G. *History of the State of Rhode Island and Providence Plantations*. 2 vols. New York: D. Appleton, 1859–1860.

Association of American Law Schools. *Select Essays in Anglo-American Legal History*. 3 vols. Boston: Little, Brown, 1907.

——. *Selected Essays on Constitutional Law*. 4 vols. Chicago: The Foundation Press, 1938.

Austin, John O. *Genealogical Dictionary of Rhode Island*. Albany, N.Y.: Joel Munsell's Sons, 1887.

Bailyn, Bernard. *The Ideological Origins of the American Revolution*. Cambridge: Harvard Univ. Press, 1967.

Bancroft, George. *History of the United States from the Discovery of the American Continent*. 10 vols. Boston: Little, Brown, 1834–1875. Vol. II.

Barnes, Viola F. *The Dominion of New England*. New Haven. Yale Univ. Press, 1923.

Bartlett, Irving H. *From Slave to Citizen: The Story of the Negro in Rhode Island*. Providence: Urban League of Greater Providence, 1954.

Bartlett, John R. (comp.). *Bibliography of Rhode Island*. Providence: Alfred Anthony, 1864.

Bates, Frank Greene. *Rhode Island and the Formation of the Union*. Vol. X, no. 2 in the Columbia Studies in History, Economics and Public Law. New York: Macmillan, 1898.

Battis, Emery. *Saints and Sectaries: The Antinomian Controversy in the Massachusetts Bay Colony*. Chapel Hill, N.C.: Univ. of North Carolina Press, 1962.

Baxter, Maurice G. *Daniel Webster and the Supreme Court*. Amherst, Mass.: Univ. of Massachusetts Press, 1966.

Bayles, Richard M. (ed.). *History of Newport County, Rhode Island*. New York: L. E. Preston, 1888.

—— (ed.). *History of Providence County*. 2 vols. New York: W. W. Preston, 1891.

Beard, Charles A. *An Economic Interpretation of the Constitution of the United States*. New York: Macmillan, 1935.

Benson, Lee. *Turner and Beard: American Historical Writing Reconsidered*. New York: The Free Press, 1960.

——. *The Concept of Jacksonian Democracy*. Princeton, N.J.: Princeton Univ. Press, 1961.

Berthoff, Rowland. *An Unsettled People: Social Order and Disorder in American History*. New York: Harper & Row, 1971.

Bicknell, Thomas Williams. *The History of the State of Rhode Island and Providence Plantations*. 6 vols. New York: The American Historical Society, 1920.

——. *Story of Dr. John Clarke*. Providence: Published by the Author, 1915.

Bidwell, Percy W. and John I. Falconer. *History of Agriculture in the Northern United States, 1620–1860*. Washington, D.C.: The Carnegie Institution, 1925.

Billington, Ray Allen. *The Protestant Crusade, 1800–1860: A Study of the Origins of American Nativism*. New York: Macmillan, 1938.

—— (ed.). *The Reinterpretation of Early American History: Essays in Honor of John Edwin Pomfret*. San Marino, Cal.: Henry E. Huntington Library, 1966.

Biographical Cyclopedia of Representative Men of Rhode Island. Providence: National Biographical Publishing Co., 1881.

Bishop, Cortlandt F. *History of Elections in the American Colonies.* Vol. III, no. 1 of the Columbia University Studies in History, Economics and Public Law. New York: Macmillan, 1893.

Bishop, Hillman Metcalf. *Why Rhode Island Opposed the Federal Constitution.* Providence: Roger Williams Press, 1950. A pamphlet reprint of four articles which appeared serially in *Rhode Island History,* VIII (1949).

Black, Robert C. III. *The Younger John Winthrop.* New York: Columbia Univ. Press, 1966.

Blau, Joseph L. (ed.). *Social Theories of Jacksonian Democracy.* Indianapolis: Bobbs Merrill, 1954.

Bloom, Sol (comp.). *History of the Formation of the Union Under the Constitution.* Washington, D.C.: Government Printing Office, 1943.

Bowen, Richard LeBaron. *The Providence Oath of Allegiance and Its Signers, 1651–52.* Concord, New Hampshire: Rumford Press, 1943.

[Bradley, Charles Smith]. *The Methods of Changing the Constitutions of the States, Especially That of Rhode Island.* Boston: Alfred Mudge & Son, 1885.

Bradley, Francis J. *A Brief History of the Diocese of Fall River, Mass.* Fall River: Privately printed, 1931.

Brant, Irving. *James Madison: A Biography.* 6 vols. Indianapolis: Bobbs Merrill, 1941–61.

Brennan, Brother Joseph, F.S.C. *Social Conditions in Industrial Rhode Island: 1820–1860.* Washington, D.C.: The Catholic Univ. of America, 1940.

Brennan, Ellen E. *Plural Office-Holding in Massachusetts, 1760–1780.* Chapel Hill: Univ. of North Carolina Press, 1945.

Bridenbaugh, Carl. *Fat Mutton and Liberty of Conscience: Society in Rhode Island, 1636–1690.* Providence: Brown Univ. Press, 1974.

————. *Silas Downer: Forgotten Patriot.* Providence: Rhode Island Bicentennial Foundation, 1974.

Brigham, Clarence S. (comp.). *History and Bibliography of American Newspapers, 1690–1820.* 2 vols. Worcester, Mass.: American Antiquarian Society, 1947.

————. *History of the State of Rhode Island and Providence Plantations.* Boston and Syracuse: Mason Publishing Co., 1902.

Brockunier, Samuel H. *The Irrepressible Democrat: Roger Williams.* New York: Ronald Press, 1940.

Bronson, Walter C. *The History of Brown University, 1764–1914.* Providence: Published by the University, 1914.

Brown, H. Glenn and Maude O. Brown. *A Directory of Printing, Publishing, Bookselling & Allied Trades in Rhode Island to 1865.* New York: New York Public Library, 1958.

Brown, Robert E. *Charles Beard and the Constitution: A Critical Analysis of "An Economic Interpretation of the Constitution."* Princeton, N.J.: Princeton Univ. Press, 1956.

————. *Middle-Class Democracy and the Revolution in Massachusetts, 1691–1780.* Ithaca, N.Y.: Cornell Univ. Press, 1955.

Brown, William Garrott. *The Life of Oliver Ellsworth.* New York: Macmillan, 1905.

Brownson, Henry F. *Orestes A. Brownson's Early Life, 1803–1844.* Detroit: H. F. Brownson, 1898.

Bulkley, Abby Isabel. *The Chad Browne Memorial.* Brooklyn: Privately printed, 1888.

Burnett, Edmund Cody. *The Continental Congress.* New York: Macmillan, 1941.

Butler, Charles. *Historical Memoirs of the English, Irish, and Scottish Catholics, Since the Reformation.* 5 vols. 3rd ed. London: J. Murray, 1822.

Cady, John Hutchins. *The Civic and Architectural Development of Providence, 1636–1950.* Providence: The Book Shop, 1957.

———. *Rhode Island Boundaries, 1636–1936.* Providence: Rhode Island Tercentenary Commission, 1936.

Cairns, Margaret Therese. *A Checklist of Rhode Island Imprints, 1831–1834.* Washington, D.C.: The Catholic Univ. of America, 1959.

Callender, John. *An Historical Discourse on the Civil and Religious Affairs of the Colony of Rhode Island.* Edited by Romeo Elton. Vol. IV of the *Collections* of the Rhode Island Historical Society. Providence: Knowles, Vose, 1838.

Carpenter, Esther Bernon. *South County Studies.* Boston: Printed for the Subscribers, 1924.

Carroll, Charles. *Public Education in Rhode Island.* Providence: E. L. Freeman, 1918.

———. *Rhode Island: Three Centuries of Democracy.* 4 vols. New York: Lewis Historical Publishing Co., 1932.

[Carroll, William, *et al.*]. *Printers and Printing in Providence, 1762–1907.* Providence: Providence Printing Co., 1907.

Cave, Alfred A. *Jacksonian Democracy and the Historians.* No. 22 of the University of Florida Monographs. Gainesville, Fla.: Univ. of Florida Press, 1964.

Channing, Edward. *A History of the United States.* 6 vols. New York: Macmillan, 1905–1925. Vol. I.

Channing, Edward T. *Life of William Ellery* in 1st Series, Vol. VI of the Library of American Biography. Edited by Jared Sparks. Boston: Hilliard, Gray & Co., 1836.

Chitwood, Oliver Perry. *John Tyler; Champion of the Old South.* New York: Appleton-Century, 1939.

Chupack, Henry. *Roger Williams.* New York: Twayne Publishers, 1969.

Chute, Marchette. *The First Liberty: A History of the Right to Vote in America.* New York: E. P. Dutton, 1969.

Chyet, Stanley F. *Lopez of Newport: Colonial American Merchant Prince.* Detroit: Wayne State Univ. Press, 1970.

Clark, Victor S. *History of Manufactures in the United States.* 3 vols. Washington, D.C.: The Carnegie Institution, 1929.

Clauson, J. Earl. *Cranston: A Historical Sketch.* Providence: T. S. Hammond, 1904.

Cole, J. R. (comp.). *History of Washington and Kent Counties, Rhode Island.* New York: W. W. Preston, 1889.

Coleman, Peter J. *The Transformation of Rhode Island, 1790–1860.* Providence: Brown Univ. Press, 1963.

Commager, Henry Steele. *The Era of Reform, 1830–1860.* Princeton, N.J.: D. Van Nostrand, 1960.

Commons, John R. et al. *History of Labour in the United States.* 4 vols. New York: Macmillan, 1918–1935.

Conley, Patrick T. and Matthew J. Smith. *Catholicism in Rhode Island: The Formative Era.* Providence: Diocese of Providence, 1976.

Cook, Edward M., Jr. *Fathers of the Towns: Leadership and Community Structure in Eighteenth-Century New England.* Baltimore: Johns Hopkins Univ. Press, 1976.

Cooley, Thomas McIntyre. *General Principles of Constitutional Law in the United States.* 3rd ed. revised by Andrew C. McLaughlin. Boston: Little, Brown, 1898.

————. *Treatise on the Constitutional Limitations which Rest Upon the Legislative Power of the States of the American Union.* 6th ed. with additions by A. C. Angell. Boston: Little, Brown, 1890.

Corwin, Edward S. *The Doctrine of Judicial Review: Its Legal and Historical Basis and Other Essays.* Gloucester, Mass.: Peter Smith, 1963.

Crane, Theodore. *Francis Wayland: Political Economist as Educator.* Providence: Brown Univ. Press, 1962.

Cullen, Thomas F. *The Catholic Church in Rhode Island.* North Providence, R.I.: Franciscan Missionaries of Mary, 1936.

Cunliffe, Marcus. *The Nation Takes Shape, 1789–1837.* Chicago: Univ. of Chicago Press, 1959.

Curti, Merle. *The Growth of American Thought.* 3rd ed. New York: Harper and Row, 1964.

Dangerfield, George. *The Awakening of American Nationalism, 1815–1828.* New York: Harper and Row, 1965.

Dargo, George. *Roots of the Republic: A New Perspective on Early American Constitutionalism.* New York: Praeger, 1974.

Darling, Arthur B. *Political Changes in Massachusetts, 1824–1848.* New Haven: Yale Univ. Press, 1925.

Dealey, James Q. *Growth of American State Constitutions.* Boston and New York: Ginn & Co., 1915.

DeGrazia, Alfred. *Public and Republic: Political Representation in America.* New York: Alfred A. Knopf, 1951.

Dennison, George M. *The Dorr War: Republicanism on Trial, 1831–1861.* Lexington: The Univ. Press of Kentucky, 1976.

Dickerson, Oliver M. *American Colonial Government, 1696–1765.* Cleveland: The Arthur H. Clark Co., 1912.

Dixon, Robert G., Jr. *Democratic Representation: Reapportionment in Law and Politics.* New York: Oxford Univ. Press, 1968.

Dodd, Walter F. *The Revision and Amendment of State Constitutions.* Extra vol., new ser. no. 1 of The Johns Hopkins University Studies in Historical and Political Science. Baltimore: The Johns Hopkins Univ. Press, 1910.

Dorfman, Joseph. *The Economic Mind in American Civilization.* 5 vols. New York: Viking Press, 1946–1959. Vol. II.

Dorr, Henry C. *The Planting and Growth of Providence.* No. 15 of the Rhode Island Historical Tracts, 1st Series. Edited by Sidney S. Rider. Providence: S. S. Rider, 1882.

Dunn, Richard S. *Puritans and Yankees: The Winthrop Dynasty of New England, 1630–1717.* Princeton, N.J.: Princeton Univ. Press, 1962.

Durfee, Thomas. *Gleanings from the Judicial History of Rhode Island.* No. 18 of the Rhode Island Historical Tracts, 1st Series. Edited by Sidney S. Rider. Providence: S. S. Rider, 1883.

Easton, Emily. *Roger Williams: Prophet and Pioneer.* Boston and New York: Houghton Mifflin, 1930.

Eaton, Amasa. *Constitution-Making in Rhode Island.* Providence: E. L. Freeman, 1899.

Ernst, James E. *The Political Thought of Roger Williams.* Seattle: Univ. of Washington Press, 1929.

Farrand, Max. *The Framing of the Constitution of the United States.* New Haven: Yale Univ. Press, 1913.

Ferguson, E. James. *The Power of the Purse: A History of American Public Finance, 1776–1790.* Chapel Hill, N.C.: Univ. of North Carolina Press, 1961.

Fessenden, G.M. *History of Warren.* Providence: H. H. Brown, 1845.

Field, Edward (ed.). *State of Rhode Island and Providence Plantations at the End of the Century: A History.* 3 vols. Boston: Mason Pub. Co., 1902.

Finlayson, Geoffrey B.A.M. *Decade of Reform: England in the Eighteen Thirties.* New York: W. W. Norton, 1970.

Fischer, David Hackett. *The Revolution of American Conservatism: The Federalist Party in the Era of Jeffersonian Democracy.* New York: Harper and Row, 1965.

Fitton, Rev. James. *Sketches of the Establishment of the Church in New England.* Boston: Patrick Donahoe, 1872.

Flaherty, David H. (ed.). *Essays in the History of Early American Law.* Chapel Hill, N.C.: Univ. of North Carolina Press, 1969.

Foner, Philip S. *Frederick Douglass.* New York: Citadel Press, 1964.

————. *The Life and Writings of Frederick Douglass.* 4 vols. New York: International Publishers, 1950–55. Vol. I.

Foster, William E. *Stephen Hopkins; A Rhode Island Statesman.* No. 19 of the Rhode Island Historcial Tracts, 1st Series. Edited by Sidney S. Rider. Providence: S. S. Rider, 1884.

Fox, Dixon Ryan. *The Decline of the Aristocracy in the Politics of New York, 1801–1840.* New York: Columbia Univ. Press, 1919.

Fuess, Claude M. *Daniel Webster.* 2 vols. Boston: Little, Brown, 1930. Vol. II.

Fuller, Oliver P. *History of the Town of Warwick, R.I., from its Settlement, 1642 to the present time.* Providence: Angell, Burlingame & Co., 1875.

Gabriel, Ralph Henry. *The Course of American Democratic Thought.* 2nd ed. New York: Ronald Press, 1956.

Garrett, John. *Roger Williams: Witness Beyond Christendom, 1603–1683.* New York: Macmillan, 1970.

Gettleman, Marvin E. *The Dorr Rebellion: A Study in American Radicalism, 1833–1849.* New York: Random House, 1973.

Goodrich, Massena. *Historical Sketch of the Town of Pawtucket.* Pawtucket, R.I.: Nickerson, Sibley & Co., 1876.

Gorman, Charles E. *An Historical Statement of the Elective Franchise in Rhode Island.* Providence: n.p. 1879.

Green, Fletcher M. *Constitutional Development in the South Atlantic States, 1776–1860.* Chapel Hill, N.C.: Univ. of North Carolina Press, 1930.

Green, John H. "The Story of Early Catholicism in Newport and the History of Saint Joseph's Parish," in *The St. Joseph's Church Reference Book, Golden Jubilee, 1885–1935.* Newport: Privately printed, 1935.

Greene, Evarts B. *The Provincial Governor in the English Colonies of North America.* New York: Longmans, Green, 1898.

————. *Religion and the State.* New York: New York Univ. Press, 1941.

Greene, Lorenzo Johnston. *The Negro in Colonial New England.* New York: Columbia Univ. Press, 1942.

Greene, Welcome Arnold. *The Providence Plantations for Two Hundred and Fifty Years.* Providence: J. A. & R. A. Reid, 1886.

Grieve, Robert. *An Illustrated History of Pawtucket, Central Falls, and Vicinity.* Pawtucket: Pawtucket Gazette and Chronicle, 1897.

Griffin, C. S. *The Ferment of Reform, 1830–1860.* New York: Thomas Y. Crowell, 1967.

Guild, Reuben A. *Early History of Brown University Including the Life, Times and Correspondence of President Manning, 1756–1791.* Providence: Snow & Farnham, 1897.

Gutstein, Morris A. *The Story of the Jews of Newport.* New York: Block Publishing Co., 1936.

Haines, Charles Grove. *The American Doctrine of Judicial Supremacy.* Vol. I in the Publications of the University of California at Los Angeles in Social Sciences. Los Angeles: Univ. of California Press, 1932.

Haley, John Williams. *The Lower Blackstone River Valley. . . .* Pawtucket, R.I.: E. L. Freeman, 1936.

Hall, Michael G. *Edward Randolph and the American Colonies, 1676–1703.* Chapel Hill, N.C.: Univ. of North Carolina Press, 1960.

Hammond, Bray. *Banks and Politics in America from the Revolution to the Civil War.* Princeton, N.J.: Princeton Univ. Press, 1957.

Handlin, Oscar. *Boston's Immigrants: A Study in Acculturation.* rev. ed. Cambridge, Mass.: Belknap Press, 1959.

Hansen, Marcus Lee. *The Atlantic Migration, 1607–1860.* Cambridge: Harvard Univ. Press, 1940.

Hartz, Louis. *The Liberal Tradition in America.* New York: Harcourt, Brace, and World, 1955.

Haskins, George Lee. *Law and Authority in Early Massachusetts.* New York: Macmillan, 1960.

Hasse, Adelaide. *Index of Economic Material in Documents of the States of the United States: Rhode Island, 1789–1904.* Washington, D.C.: The Carnegie Institution, 1908.

Havard, William C. and Loren P. Beth. *The Politics of Mis-Representation.* Baton Rouge, La.: Louisiana State Univ. Press, 1962.

Hedges, James B. *The Browns of Providence Plantations: Colonial Years.* Cambridge: Harvard Univ. Press, 1952.

———. *The Browns of Providence Plantations: The Nineteenth Century.* Providence: Brown Univ. Press, 1968.

Hockett, Homer Cary. *The Constitutional History of the United States, 1776–1826.* New York: Macmillan, 1939.

Holbrook, Stewart H. *The Yankee Exodus.* New York: Macmillan, 1950.

Holdsworth, William. *History of English Law.* 16 vols. London: Methuen & Co., Ltd., 1903–66. Especially XI.

Horton, John Theodore. *James Kent: A Study in Conservatism, 1763–1847.* New York: Appleton-Century, 1939.

Howard, George E. *An Introduction to the Local Constitutional History of the United States.* Extra vol. IV in The Johns Hopkins University Studies in Historical and Political Science. Baltimore: The Johns Hopkins Univ. Press, 1889.

Hugins, Walter. *Jacksonian Democracy and the Working Class: A Study of the New York Workingmen's Movement.* Stanford, Calif.: Stanford Univ. Press, 1960.

————— (ed.). *The Reform Impulse, 1825–1850.* New York: Harper and Row, 1972.

Hurst, James Willard. *The Growth of American Law: The Law Makers.* Boston: Little, Brown, 1950.

Jackson, Henry. *An Account of the Churches in Rhode Island.* Providence: George H. Whitney, 1854.

Jacobson, David L. (ed.). *The English Libertarian Heritage.* Indianapolis: Bobbs Merrill, 1965.

James, Sydney V. *Colonial Rhode Island: A History.* New York: Charles Scribner's Sons, 1975.

Jameson, J. Franklin (ed.). *Essays in the Constitutional History of the United States in the Formative Period, 1775–1789.* Boston: Houghton Mifflin, 1889.

Jameson, John A. *Treatise on the Constitutional Convention.* 4th ed. Chicago: Callaghan, 1887.

Jensen, Merrill. *The Articles of Confederation.* Madison: Univ. of Wisconsin Press, 1963.

—————. *The Founding of a Nation: A History of the American Revolution, 1763–1776.* New York: Oxford Univ. Press, 1968.

—————. *The Making of the American Constitution.* Princeton, N.J.: D. Van Nostrand, 1964.

—————. *The New Nation: A History of the United States During the Confederation, 1781–1789.* New York: Alfred A. Knopf, 1950.

Jones, Rufus. *The Quakers in the American Colonies.* London: Macmillan, 1911.

Jones, Samuel. *A Treatise on the Right of Suffrage.* Boston: Otis Broaders & Co., 1842.

Jordan, W. K. *Development of Religious Toleration in England.* 4 vols. Cambridge: Harvard Univ. Press, 1932–1940. Vol. III.

Kammen, Michael. *Deputyes and Libertyes: The Origins of Representative Government in Colonial America.* New York: Knopf, 1969.

Keach, Horace A. *Burrillville, as it was, and is.* Providence: Knowles, Anthony & Co., 1856.

Kelly, Alfred H. and Winfred A. Harbison. *The American Constitution.* 5th ed. New York: W. W. Norton, 1976.

Kenyon, Cecelia M. (ed.). *The Antifederalists.* Indianapolis: Bobbs Merrill, 1966.

Kimball, Everett. *The Public Life of Joseph Dudley.* New York: Longmans, Green & Co., 1911.

Kimball, Gertrude S. *Providence in Colonial Times.* Boston: Houghton, Mifflin, 1912.

Kiven, Arline Ruth. *Then Why the Negroes: The Nature and Course of the Anti-Slavery Movement in Rhode Island, 1637–1861.* Providence: Urban League of Rhode Island, 1973.

Koch, Adrienne. *Jefferson and Madison: The Great Collaboration.* New York: Alfred A. Knopf, 1950.

—————. *The Philosophy of Thomas Jefferson.* New York: Columbia Univ. Press, 1943.

Labaree, Leonard Woods. *Conservatism in Early American History.* New York: New York Univ. Press, 1948.

Leder, Lawrence H. *Liberty and Authority: Early American Political Ideology, 1689–1763.* Chicago: Quadrangle, 1968.

Levy, Leonard W. (ed.). *Essays on the Making of the Constitution.* New York: Oxford Univ. Press, 1969.

Libby, Orin G. *The Geographical Distribution of the Vote of the Thirteen States on the Federal Constitution, 1787–1788*. Madison, Wis.: Univ. of Wisconsin, 1894.

Litwack, Leon F. *North of Slavery: The Negro in the Free States, 1790–1860*. Chicago: Univ. of Chicago Press, 1961.

Lord, Robert H., John E. Sexton, and Edward T. Harrington. *History of the Archdiocese of Boston*. 3 vols. New York: Sheed and Ward, 1944.

Lovejoy, David S. *Rhode Island Politics and the American Revolution, 1760–1776*. Providence: Brown Univ. Press, 1958.

Lynd, Staughton. *Class Conflict, Slavery, and the United States Constitution*. Indianapolis: Bobbs Merrill, 1967.

Madeleine, Sister M. Grace. *Monetary and Banking Theories of Jacksonian Democracy*. New York: Kennikat Press, 1970 reprint of 1943 edition.

Maguire, John Francis. *The Irish in America*. New York: D. & J. Sadlier, 1868.

Main, Jackson Turner. *The Antifederalists: Critics of the Constitution, 1781–1788*. Chapel Hill, N.C.: Univ. of North Carolina Press, 1961.

—————. *The Social Structure of Revolutionary America*. Princeton, N.J.: Princeton Univ. Press, 1965.

—————. *The Sovereign States, 1775–1783*. New York: New Viewpoints, 1973.

—————. *The Upper House in Revolutionary America, 1763–1788*. Madison, Wis.: Univ. of Wisconsin Press, 1967.

Malone, Dumas. *Jefferson and His Time*. 5 vols. to date. Boston: Little, Brown, 1948—

Mason, Alpheus Thomas. *The States Rights Debate: Antifederalists and the Constitution*. Englewood Cliffs, N.J.: Prentice Hall, 1964.

Mason, George Champlin. *Reminiscences of Newport*. Newport: Charles E. Hammett, Jr., 1884.

Mathews, Lois Kimball. *The Expansion of New England*. Boston and New York: Houghton Mifflin, 1909.

Mayer, Kurt B. *Economic Development and Population Growth in Rhode Island*. Providence: Brown Univ. Press, 1953.

McCormick, Richard P. *The Second American Party System*. Chapel Hill, N.C.: Univ. of North Carolina Press, 1966.

McDonald, Forrest. *E Pluribus Unum: The Formation of the American Republic, 1776–1790*. Boston: Houghton Mifflin, 1965.

—————. *We The People*. Chicago: Univ. of Chicago Press, 1958.

MacDonald, Grace E. *Check-list of Legislative Documents in the Rhode Island State Archives*. Providence: Oxford Press, 1928.

McGee, Thomas D'Arcy. *A History of the Irish Settlers in North America from the Earliest Period to the Census of 1850*. Boston: American Celt Office, 1851.

McGrane, Reginald Charles. *The Panic of 1837*. Chicago: Univ. of Chicago Press, 1924.

McKenna, John H. *The Centenary Story of Old St. Mary's Pawtucket, R.I., 1829–1929*. Providence: Vistor Press, 1929.

McLaughlin, Andrew C. *The Confederation and the Constitution, 1783–1789*. Vol. X in the American Nation Series. Edited by Albert Bushnell Hart. New York: Harper and Bros., 1907.

————. *A Constitutional History of the United States.* New York: Appleton-Century-Crofts, 1935.

————. *Foundations of American Constitutionalism.* New York: New York Univ. Press, 1932.

McKay, Robert B. *Reapportionment: The Law and Politics of Equal Representation.* New York: Twentieth Century Fund, 1965.

McKinley, Albert E. *The Suffrage Franchise in the Thirteen English Colonies in America.* Philadelphia: Univ. of Pennsylvania Press, 1905.

Mendcloff, Nathan N. *A Checklist of Rhode Island Imprints, 1821–30, with a Historical Introduction.* Washington, D.C.: The Catholic Univ. of America, 1954.

Meyers, Marvin. *The Jacksonian Persuasion.* New York: Alfred A. Knopf, 1960.

Miller, Perry. *Roger Williams; His Contribution to the American Tradition.* Indianapolis: Bobbs Merrill, 1953.

———— (ed.). *The Legal Mind in America from Independence to the Civil War.* New York: Doubleday, 1962.

Mims, Edwin, Jr. *The Majority of the People.* New York: Modern Age, 1941.

Moeson, Florence. *A Checklist of Rhode Island Imprints from 1839–41.* Washington, D.C.: The Catholic Univ. of America, 1959.

Mohr, Ralph S. *Governors for Three Hundred Years, 1638–1954, Rhode Island and Providence Plantations.* Providence: State of Rhode Island Graves Registration Committee, 1954.

Morgan, Edmund S. *The Gentle Puritan: A Life of Ezra Stiles, 1727–1795.* New Haven: Yale Univ. Press, 1962.

————. *The Puritan Dilemma: The Story of John Winthrop.* Boston: Little, Brown, 1958.

————. *Roger Williams: The Church and The State.* New York: Harcourt, Brace & World, 1967.

———— and Helen M. Morgan. *The Stamp Act Crisis: Prologue to Revolution.* 2nd ed. New York: Collier Books, 1963.

Morgan, Robert J. *A Whig Embattled: The Presidency under John Tyler.* Lincoln, Neb.: Univ. of Nebraska Press, 1954.

Mott, Frank Luther. *American Journalism: A History: 1690–1960.* 3rd ed. New York: Macmillan, 1962.

Mowry, Arthur May. *The Dorr War.* Providence: Preston and Rounds, 1901.

Munro, Wilfred Harold. *The History of Bristol, Rhode Island. . . .* Providence: J. A. and R. A. Reid, 1880.

————. *Tales of an Old Sea Port* [Bristol]. Princeton: Princeton Univ. Press, 1917.

Murphy, William P. *The Triumph of Nationalism: State Sovereignty, the Founding Fathers, and the Making of the Constitution.* Chicago: Quadrangle Books, 1967.

Nettels, Curtis P. *The Emergence of A National Economy, 1775–1815.* Vol. II of the Economic History of the United States. Edited by Henry David, *et al.* New York: Holt, Rinehart and Winston, 1962.

Nevins, Allan. *The American States During and After the Revolution, 1775–1789.* New York: Macmillan, 1924.

Newbold, Robert C. *The Albany Congress and Plan of Union of 1754.* New York: Vantage Press, 1955.

Nye, Russel Blaine. *Society and Culture in America, 1830–1860.* New York: Harper & Row, 1974.

Osgood, Herbert L. *The American Colonies in the Seventeenth Century.* 3 vols. New York: Columbia Univ. Press, 1904–1907.

————. *The American Colonies in the Eighteenth Century.* 4 vols. New York: Columbia Univ. Press, 1924.

Parrington, Vernon L. *Main Currents in American Thought.* 3 vols. New York: Harcourt, Brace and World, 1927–1930, Vol. I.

Parsons, C. W. *Notice on the History of Population in the State of Rhode Island.* [Providence: 1859].

Pessen, Edward. *Jacksonian America: Society, Personality, and Politics.* Homewood, Ill.: The Dorsey Press, 1969.

———— (ed.). *New Perspectives on Jacksonian Parties and Politics.* Boston: Allyn and Bacon, 1969.

Peterson, Merrill D. (ed.). *Democracy, Liberty, and Property: The State Constitutional Conventions of the 1820s.* Indianapolis: Bobbs Merrill, 1966.

Polishook, Irwin H. *Rhode Island and the Union, 1774–1795.* Evanston, Ill.: Northwestern Univ. Press, 1969.

———— (ed.). *Roger Williams, John Cotton and Religious Freedom.* American Historical Sources Series. Edited by Lorman Ratner. Englewood Cliffs, N.J.: Prentice-Hall, 1967.

Pomfret, John E. with Floyd M. Shumway. *Founding the American Colonies, 1563–1660.* New York: Harper and Row, 1970.

Post, Charles G. *The Supreme Court and Political Questions.* Baltimore: The Johns Hopkins Univ. Press, 1936.

Potter, Charles Edward. *History and Genealogies of the Potter Families in America to the Present, with Historical and Biographical Sketches.* Boston: Privately printed, 1880.

Potter, Elisha R. Jr. *The Early History of Narragansett.* Providence: Marshall, Brown and Co., 1835.

———— and Sidney S. Rider. *Some Account of the Bills of Credit or Paper Money in Rhode Island, 1710 to 1786.* No. 8 of the Rhode Island Historical Tracts, 1st Series. Edited by Sidney S. Rider. Providence: S. S. Rider, 1880.

Potter, George. *To the Golden Door: The Story of the Irish in Ireland and America.* Boston: Little, Brown, 1960.

Purcell, Richard J. *Connecticut in Transition, 1775–1818.* Middletown, Conn.: Wesleyan Univ. Press, 1963.

Read, Conyers (ed.). *The Constitution Reconsidered.* New York: Columbia Univ. Press, 1938.

Remini, Robert V. *The Election of Andrew Jackson.* Philadelphia: J. B. Lippincott, 1963.

Representative Men and Old Families of Rhode Island. 3 vols. Chicago: J. H. Beers, 1908.

Rich, Bennett M. *The Presidents and Civil Disorder.* Washington: Brookings Institution, 1944.

Richards, John J. *Rhode Island's Early Defenders and Their Successors* [the Militia]. East Greenwich, R.I.: Rhode Island Pendulum, 1930.

Richardson, Erastus. *History of Woonsocket.* Woonsocket, R.I.: S. S. Foss, 1876.

Richman, Irving B. *Rhode Island: A Study in Separatism.* Boston and New York: Houghton Mifflin, 1905.

Richmond, John W. *Rhode Island Repudiation or the History of the*

Revolutionary Debt of Rhode Island. 2nd ed. Providence: Sayles, Miller & Simons, 1855.

Rider, Sidney S. *An Inquiry Concerning the Origin of the Clause in the Laws of Rhode Island (1719–1783) Disfranchising Roman Catholics.* No. 1 of the Rhode Island Historical Tracts, 2nd Series. Edited by Sidney S. Rider. Providence: S. S. Rider 1889.

————. *Memoirs of Joseph K. Angell, Frances H. (Whipple) Mc-Dougall and Catherine R. Williams.* No. 11 of the Rhode Island Historical Tracts, 1st Series. Edited by Sidney S. Rider. Providence: S. S. Rider, 1880.

Riegel, Robert E. *Young America: 1830–1840.* Norman, Okla.: Univ. of Oklahoma Press, 1949.

Robinson, Caroline E. *The Hazard Family of Rhode Island, 1635–1894.* Boston: Privately printed, 1895.

Robinson, William A. *Jeffersonian Democracy in New England.* New Haven: Yale Univ. Press, 1916.

Rossiter, Clinton. *1787: The Grand Convention.* New York: Macmillan, 1965.

Rudé, George. *The Crowd in History . . . 1730–1848.* New York: John Wiley & Sons, 1964.

Russell, Elmer B. *The Review of American Colonial Legislation by the King in Council.* No. 64 of the Columbia University Studies in History, Economics and Public Law. New York: Columbia Univ. Press, 1915.

Russell, Howard S. *A Long, Deep Furrow: Three Centuries of Farming in New England.* Hanover, N.H.: Univ. Press of New England, 1976.

Rutland, Robert A. *The Birth of the Bill of Rights, 1776–1791.* Chapel Hill, N.C.: Univ. of North Carolina Press, 1955.

————. *Ordeal of the Constitution: The Antifederalists and the Ratification Struggle of 1787–1788.* Norman, Okla.: Univ. of Oklahoma Press, 1966.

Sayles and Allied Families: Genealogical and Biographical, Prepared and Privately Printed for Mary Dorr (Ames) Sayles. New York: The American Historical Society, 1925.

Schlesinger, Arthur M., Sr. *The American as Reformer.* Cambridge: Harvard Univ. Press, 1950.

Schlesinger, Arthur M., Jr. *The Age of Jackson.* Boston: Little, Brown, 1945.

Semi-Centennial of the Providence Journal, 1820–1870. Providence: Knowles, Anthony & Danielson, 1870.

Shannon, William V. *The American Irish: A Political and Social Portrait.* rev. ed. New York: Macmillan, 1966.

Sheffield, W. P. *Random Notes on the Government of Rhode Island.* Newport, R.I.: Daily News Job Print, 1897.

Silbey, Joel H. *The Transformation of American Politics, 1840–1860.* American Historical Sources Series. Edited by Lorman Ratner. Englewood Cliffs, N.J.: Prentice-Hall, 1967.

Smelser, Marshall. *The Democratic Republic, 1801–1815.* New York: Harper & Row, 1968.

Smith, J. Allen. *The Spirit of American Government: A Study of the Constitution: Its Origin, Influence and Relation to Democracy.* New York: Macmillan, 1907.

Smith, Joseph Henry. *Appeals to the Privy Council from the American Plantations.* New York: Columbia Univ. Press, 1950.

Smith, Joseph Jencks. *Civil and Military List of Rhode Island, 1647–1850.* 2 vols. Providence: Preston & Rounds, 1900–01.

————. *New Index to the Civil and Military Lists of Rhode Island.* Providence: Joseph J. Smith, 1907.

Smith, Wilson. *Professors and Public Ethics: Studies of Northern Moral Philosophers Before the Civil War.* Ithaca, N.Y.: Cornell Univ. Press, 1956.

Smyth, J. W. *History of the Catholic Church in Woonsocket and Vicinity.* . . . Woonsocket, R.I.: Charles E. Cook, 1903.

Staples, William R. *Annals of the Town of Providence.* . . . Providence: Knowles and Vose, 1843.

Steere, Thomas. *History of the Town of Smithfield . . . 1730–1871.* Providence: E. L. Freeman, 1881.

Stiness, John H. *Memorial Address: Walter Snow Burges.* Providence: Snow & Farnham, 1892.

Stokes, Anson Phelps. *Church and State in the United States.* 3 vols. New York: Harper & Row, 1950.

Stokes, Howard K. *The Finances and Administration of Providence.* Extra Vol. XXV of the Johns Hopkins University Studies in Historical and Political Science. Baltimore: The Johns Hopkins Univ. Press, 1903.

Story, William Wirt. *The Life and Letters of Joseph Story.* 2 vols. Boston: Little, Brown, 1851. Vol. II.

Swisher, Carl Brent. *American Constitutional Development.* 2nd ed. Cambridge, Mass.: Houghton Mifflin, 1954.

Thayer, James B. *The Origin and Scope of the American Doctrine of Constitutional Law.* Boston: Little, Brown, 1893.

Thompson, Mack. *Moses Brown: Reluctant Reformer.* Chapel Hill, N.C.: Univ. of North Carolina Press, 1962.

Thorpe, Francis Newton. *The Constitutional History of the United States . . . 1765–1895.* 3 vols. Chicago: Callaghan & Co., 1901. Vols. I–II.

Tönnies, Ferdinand. *Community and Society (Gemeinschaft und Gesellschaft).* Translated and edited by Charles P. Loomis. East Lansing, Mich.: The Michigan State Univ. Press, 1957.

Turner, Henry E. *William Coddington in Rhode Island Colonial Affairs.* No. 4 of the Rhode Island Historical Tracts, 1st Series. Edited by Sidney S. Rider. Providence: S. S. Rider, 1878.

Tyler, Alice Felt. *Freedom's Ferment.* Minneapolis: Univ. of Minnesota Press, 1944.

U.S. Congress. *Biographical Directory of the American Congress, 1774–1971.* Washington: Government Printing Office, 1971.

Updike, Wilkins. *History of the Episcopal Church in Narragansett, Rhode Island.* New York: Henry M. Onderdonk, 1847.

————. *A History of the Episcopal Church in Narragansett, Rhode Island.* . . . 2nd ed., rev. and enlarged by Daniel Goodwin. Boston: D. B. Updike, 1907.

————. *Memoirs of the Rhode Island Bar.* Boston: T. H. Webb & Co., 1842.

Uroff, Margaret Dickie. *Becoming a City: From Fishing Village to Manufacturing Center* [Providence, Rhode Island]. New York: Harcourt, Brace, and World, 1968.

Van Deusen, Glyndon G. *The Jacksonian Era, 1828–1848.* New York: Harper and Row, 1959.

Varnum, James M. *A Sketch of the Life and Public Services of James Mitchell Varnum*. Boston: David Clapp & Son, 1906.

Ward, Harry M. *The United Colonies of New England, 1643–90*. New York: Vantage Press, 1961.

Ware, Caroline F. *The Early New England Cotton Manufacture*. New York: Houghton Mifflin, 1931.

Ware, Norman. *The Industrial Worker, 1840–1860*. Boston and New York: Houghton Mifflin, 1924.

Warren, Charles. *The Supreme Court in United States History*. Rev. ed. 2 vols. Boston: Little, Brown, 1926.

Washburne, George A. *Imperial Control of the Administration of Justice in the Thirteen Colonies, 1684–1776*. No. 105 in the Columbia University Studies in History, Economics and Public Law: New York: Longmans, Green, 1923.

Wayland, Francis and H. L. Wayland. *A Memoir of the Life and Labors of Francis Wayland D.D., LL.D.* 2 vols. New York: Sheldon and Co., 1867.

Weeden, William B. *Early Rhode Island: A Social History of the People*. New York: The Grafton Press, 1910.

Welter, Rush. *The Mind of America, 1820–1860*. New York: Columbia Univ. Press, 1975.

Weston, Florence. *The Presidential Election of 1828*. Washington, D.C.: The Catholic Univ. of America, 1938.

White, George S. *Memoir of Samuel Slater*. 2nd ed. Philadelphia: n.p., 1836.

Whitman, Alden. *Labor Parties, 1827–34*. New York: International Publishers, 1943.

Wiecek, William M. *The Guarantee Clause of the U.S. Constitution*. Ithaca, New York: Cornell Univ. Press, 1972.

Williams, Basil. *The Whig Supremacy*. 2nd ed. Oxford, England: Oxford Univ. Press, 1962.

Williams, Robin M. Jr. *American Society: A Sociological Interpretation*. 2nd rev. ed. New York: Alfred A. Knopf, 1960.

Williamson, Chilton. *American Suffrage from Property to Democracy, 1760–1860*. Princeton, N.J.: Princeton Univ. Press, 1960.

Wiltse, Charles M. *The Jeffersonian Tradition in American Democracy*. New York: Hill and Wang, 1960.

Winslow, John. *The Trial of the Rhode Island Judges: An Episode Touching Currency and Constitutional Law*. Brooklyn: Geo. Tremlett, 1887.

Winslow, Ola Elizabeth. *Master Roger Williams*. New York: Macmillan, 1957.

Wood, Gordon S. *The Creation of the American Republic, 1776–1787*. Chapel Hill, N.C.: Univ. of North Carolina Press, 1969.

Wright, Benjamin Fletcher. *Consensus and Continuity, 1776–1787*. Boston: Boston Univ. Press, 1958.

————. *The Growth of American Constitutional Law*. Boston: Houghton Mifflin, 1942.

II. ARTICLES

Adams, James Truslow. "Disfranchisement of Negroes in New England," *American Historical Review*, XXX (Apr., 1925), 543–547.

Adelman, David C. "Strangers: Civil Rights of Jews in the Colony of

Rhode Island," *Rhode Island History*, XIII (July, 1954), 65–77.

Allen, Samuel H. "The Electors of Rhode Island," *The Narragansett Historical Register*, III (1884–85), 144–148; VI (1888), 301–313.

————. "The Federal Ascendancy of 1812," *The Narragansett Historical Register*, VII (Oct., 1889), 381–394.

Andrews, Neil. "The Development of the Nominating Convention in Rhode Island," No. 1 of the Papers from the Historical Seminary of Brown University. Edited by J. Franklin Jameson. Providence: n.p., 1894.

Appleton, Marguerite. "Rhode Island's First Court of Admiralty," *New England Quarterly*, V (Jan., 1932), 148–154.

Arnold, Noah J. "The History of Suffrage in Rhode Island," *The Narragansett Historical Register*, VIII (1890), 305–331.

————. "The Valley of the Pawtuxet: Its History and Development," *The Narragansett Historical Register*, VI (1888), 222–259.

Bartlett, Irving H. "The Inconsistency of Thomas Dorr," *New England Social Studies Bulletin*, XI (May, 1954), 3–7.

Bates, Frank Greene. "Rhode Island and the Impost of 1781," in the *Annual Report of the American Historical Association for 1894*, pp. 351–359.

Bercovitch, Sacvan. "Typology in Puritan New England: The Williams-Cotton Controversy Reassessed," *American Quarterly*, XIX (Summer, 1967), 166–191.

Bidwell, Percy W. "The Agricultural Revolution in New England," *American Historical Review*, XXVI (July, 1921), 683–702.

————. "Population Growth in Southern New England, 1810–1860," *American Statistical Association Quarterly Publications*, n.s., XV (1916–17) 813–839.

————. "Rural Economy in New England at the Beginning of the Nineteenth Century," *Transactions of the Connecticut Academy of Arts and Sciences*, XX (Apr., 1916), 241–399.

Bozeman, Theodore Dwight. "Religious Liberty and the Problem of Order in Early Rhode Island," *New England Quarterly*, XLV (March, 1972), 44–64.

Brigham, Clarence S. "Report on the Archives of Rhode Island," in the *Annual Report of the American Historical Association for 1903*, I, 543–644.

Brunkow, Robert d. "Love and Order in Roger Williams' Writings," *Rhode Island History*, XXXV (Nov., 1976), 115–126.

Calamandrei, Mauro. "Neglected, Aspects of Roger Williams' Thought," *Church History*, XXI (Sept., 1952), 239–259.

Chafee, Zechariah Jr. "Record of the Rhode Island Court of Equity, 1741–1743," *Proceedings of the Colonial Society of Massachusetts*, XXXV (1951), 91–118.

Channing, Edward. "The Narragansett Planters; A Study of Causes," in *The Johns Hopkins University Studies in Political and Social Science*, IV (1886), 105–127.

Chapin, Howard M. "Eighteenth Century Rhode Island Printed Proxies," *The American Collector*, I (1925), 54–59.

Cheyney, Edward P. "The Manor of East Greenwich in the County of Kent," *American Historical Review*, XI (Oct., 1905), 29–35.

Chudacoff, Howard P. and Theodore C. Hirt. "Social Turmoil and Governmental Reform in Providence, 1820–1832," *Rhode Island History,* XXXI (Feb., 1972), 21–31.

Ciaburri, Robert L. "The Dorr Rebellion in Rhode Island: The Moderate Phase," *Rhode Island History,* XXVI (July, 1967), 73–87.

Cohen, Joel A. "Democracy in Revolutionary Rhode Island: A Statistical Analysis," *Rhode Island History,* XXIX (Feb.–May, 1970), 3–16.

————. "Lexington and Concord: Rhode Island Reacts," *Rhode Island History,* XXVI (Oct., 1967), 97–102.

Colegrove, Kenneth. "New England Town Mandates; Instructions to the Deputies in Colonial Legislatures," *Publications of the Colonial Society of Massachusetts,* XXI (Dec., 1919), 411–449.

Coleman, Peter J. "Rhode Island Cotton Manufacturing," *Rhode Island History,* XXIII (July, 1964), 65–80.

Commager, Henry Steele. "The Constitution: Was It An Economic Document?" *American Heritage,* X (Dec., 1958), 58–61, 100–103.

Conley, Patrick T. "Revolution's Impact on Rhode Island," *Rhode Island History,* XXXIV (Nov., 1975), 121–128.

————. "Rhode Island in Disunion, 1787–1790," *Rhode Island History,* XXXI (Nov., 1972), 99–115.

————. "Rhode Island's Paper Money Issue and *Trevett v. Weeden* (1786)," *Rhode Island History,* XXX (Summer, 1971), 95–108.

Conron, Michael A. "Law, Politics, and Chief Justice Taney: A Reconsideration of the *Luther v. Borden* Decision," *American Journal of Legal History,* XI (Oct., 1967), 377–88.

Coogan, Robert A. "The Foundations of the Rhode Island Judicial System," *Rhode Island Bar Annual,* I (Oct., 1964), 1–19.

Cook, Edward M. Jr. "Local Leadership and the Typology of New England Towns, 1700–1785," *Political Science Quarterly,* LXXXVI (Dec., 1971), 586–608.

Corning, Howard. "Sullivan Dorr, China Trader," *Rhode Island History,* III (July, 1944), 75–90.

Corwin, Edward S. "The Progress of Constitutional Theory Between the Declaration of Independence and the Meeting of the Philadelphia Convention," *American Historical Review,* XXX (Apr., 1925), 511–536.

Crane, Theodore S. "Francis Wayland: Political Economist as Educator," *Rhode Island History,* XXI (July–Oct., 1962), 65–90, 105–124.

Curran, William A. "*Trevett v. Weeden:* Its Place in Our History," *Rhode Island Bar Annual,* III (1966), 22–28.

Darling, Arthur B. "The Workingmen's Party in Massachusetts, 1833–1834," *American Historical Review,* XXIX (Oct., 1923), 81–86.

Davies, James C. "Toward a Theory of Revolution," *American Sociological Review,* XXVII (Feb., 1962), 5–19.

Degler, Carl. "The Locofocos: Urban 'Agrarians,' " *Journal of Economic History,* XVI (Sept., 1956), 322–333.

Demos, John. "Families in Colonial Bristol, Rhode Island: An Exercise in Historical Demography," *William and Mary Quarterly,* 3rd Ser., XXV (Jan., 1968), 40–57.

Dodd, William F. "The First State Constitutional Conventions, 1776–1783," *American Political Science Review,* II (Nov., 1908), 545–561.

Donnan, Elizabeth. "Agitation Against the Slave Trade in Rhode Island,

1784–1790," in *Persecution and Liberty: Essays in Honor of George Lincoln Burr*. New York: The Century Co., 1931.

Dunn, Richard S. "John Winthrop, Jr. and the Narragansett Country," *William and Mary Quarterly*, 3rd Ser., XIII (Jan., 1956), 68–86.

Eaton, Amasa M. "The Development of the Judicial System in Rhode Island," *Yale Law Journal*, XIV (Jan., 1905), 148–170.

————. "The Right of Local Self-Government," *Harvard Law Review*, XIII (1899), 441–454, 570–588, 638–658; XIV (1900), 20–38, 116–138.

————. "Thomas Wilson Dorr and the Dorr War," in William Draper Lewis (ed.). *Great American Lawyers*. Philadelphia: John C. Winston, 1908.

Farnham, Charles W. "Rhode Island Colonial Records," *Rhode Island History*, XXIX (Feb. and May, 1970), 36–44.

Farrell, John T. "The Early History of Rhode Island's Court System," *Rhode Island History*, IX (July–Oct., 1950), 65–71, 103–117; X (Jan., 1951), 14–25.

Fingerhut, Eugene R. "Were the Massachusetts Puritans Hebraic?" *New England Quarterly*, XL (Dec., 1967), 521–531.

Foster, William E. "Sketch of the Life and Services of Theodore Foster," *Collections of the Rhode Island Historical Society*, VII (1885), 111–134.

————. "Town Government in Rhode Island," in *The Johns Hopkins University Studies in Political and Social Science*, IV (1886), 69–104.

Franklin, Susan B. "William Ellery: Signer of the Declaration of Independence," *Rhode Island History*, XII (Oct., 1953), 110–119; XIII (Jan.–Apr., 1954), 11–17, 44–52.

Gersuny, Carl. "Seth Luther — The Road from Chepachet," *Rhode Island History*, XXXIII (May, 1974), 47–55.

Gettleman, Marvin E. and Noel P. Conlon. "Responses to the Rhode Island Workingmen's Reform Agitation of 1833," *Rhode Island History*, XXVIII (Aug., 1969), 75–94.

Goebel, Julius, Jr. "King's Law and Local Custom in Seventeenth Century New England," *Columbia Law Review*, XXXI (Mar., 1931), 416–448.

Grant, Philip A., Jr. "Party Chaos Embroils Rhode Island," *Rhode Island History*, XXVI (Oct., 1967), 113–125; XXVII (Jan., 1968), 24–33.

Grimsted, David. "Rioting in Its Jacksonian Setting," *American Historical Review*, LXXVII (Apr., 1972), 361–397.

Hadcock, Editha. "Labor Problems in the Rhode Island Cotton Mills, 1790–1940," *Rhode Island History*, XIV (July–Oct., 1955), 82–85, 88–93, 110–119.

Haffenden, Philip. "The Crown and Colonial Charters, 1675–1688," *William and Mary Quarterly*, 3rd Ser., XV (July–Oct., 1958), 297–311, 452–466.

Hartz, Louis. "Seth Luther: Working Class Rebel," *New England Quarterly*, XIII (Sept., 1940), 401–418.

Hazeltine, Harold D. "Appeals from Colonial Courts to the King in Council, With Especial Reference to Rhode Island," in the *Annual Report of the American Historical Association for the Year 1894*, pp. 299–350.

Hellerich, Mahlon. "The Luther Cases in the Lower Courts," *Rhode Island History*, XI (Apr., 1952), 33–45.

Hunt, Gaillard. "Office Seeking in Washington's Administration," *American Historical Review*, I (Jan., 1896), 270–283.

[Jameson, J. Franklin, (comp.)]. "The Adjustment of Rhode Island Into the Union in 1790," *Publications of the Rhode Island Historical Society*, n.s., VIII (July, 1900), 104–135.

Jensen, Merrill. "Democracy and the American Revolution," *The Huntington Library Quarterly*, XX (Aug., 1957), 321–341.

Jernigan, Marcus W. "The Tammany Societies of Rhode Island," No. 7 of the Papers from the Historical Seminary of Brown University. Edited by J. Franklin Jameson. Providence: Preston & Rounds, 1897.

Kaminski, John P. "Political Sacrifice and Demise — John Collins and Jonathan J. Hazard, 1786–1790," *Rhode Island History*, XXXV (Aug., 1976), 91–98.

Kaplan, Marilyn. "The Jewish Merchants of Newport, 1740–1790," *Rhode Island Jewish Historical Notes*, VII (Nov., 1975), 12–32.

Kellogg, Louise Phelps. "The American Colonial Charter. A Study of English Administration in Relation Thereto, Chiefly After 1688," in the *Annual Report of the American Historical Association for the Year 1903*, I, 185–341.

Kenyon, Cecelia M. "An Economic Interpretation of the Constitution After Fifty Years," *The Centennial Review*, VII (Summer, 1963), 327–352.

————. "Men of Little Faith: The Anti-Federalists on the Nature of Representative Government," *William and Mary Quarterly*, 3rd Ser., XII (Jan., 1955), 3–46.

————. "Republicanism and Radicalism in the American Revolution: An Old-Fashioned Interpretation," *William and Mary Quarterly*, 3rd Series, XIX (Apr., 1962), 153–182.

[King, Eugene P. and Henry King]. "Doctor Dan King and His Sons," *Transactions of the Rhode Island Medical Society*, IV (1891), 344–351.

Kohler, Max J. "The Jews in Newport," *Publications of the American Jewish Historical Society*, no. 6 (1897), 61–80.

LaFantasie, Glenn W. "Act for All Reasons — Revolutionary Politics and May 4, 1776," *Rhode Island History*, XXXV (May, 1976), 39–47.

Lemons, J. Stanley and Michael A. McKenna. "Re-enfranchisement of Rhode Island Negroes," *Rhode Island History*, XXX (Feb., 1971), 2–13.

Lerche, Charles O. "The Dorr Rebellion and the Federal Constitution," *Rhode Island History*, IX (Jan., 1950), 1–10.

Leslie, William R. "The Gaspee Affair: A Study of its Constitutional Significance," *Mississippi Valley Historical Review*, XXXIX (Sept., 1952), 233–256.

Lockridge, Kenneth A. "Land, Population and the Evolution of New England Society 1630–1790," *Past and Present*, XXXIX (1968), 62–80.

Lovejoy, David S. "Equal Rights Imply Equality: The Case Against Admiralty Jurisdiction in America, 1764–1776," *William and Mary Quarterly*, 3rd Ser., XVI (Oct., 1959), 459–484.

————. "Samuel Hopkins: Religion, Slavery, and the Revolution," *New England Quarterly*, XL (June, 1967), 227–243.

Magrath, C. Peter. "Samuel Ames: The Great Chief Justice of Rhode Island," *Rhode Island History*, XXIV (July, 1965), 65–76.

————. "Optimistic Democrat: Thomas W. Dorr and the Case of *Luther* vs. *Borden*," *Rhode Island History*, XXIX (Aug. and Nov., 1970), 94–112.

Main, Jackson T. "Charles Beard and the Constitution: A Critical Review of Forrest McDonald's *We the People*," *William and Mary Quarterly*, 3rd Ser., XVII (Jan., 1960), 86–110.

————. "Government by the People; the American Revolution and the Democratization of the Legislatures," *William and Mary Quarterly*, 3rd Ser., XXIII (July, 1966), 391–407.

Marks, Frederick W. 3rd. "Foreign Affairs: A Winning Issue in the Campaign for Ratification of the United States Constitution," *Political Science Quarterly*, LXXXVI (Sept., 1971), 444–469.

Marsis, James L. "Agrarian Politics in Rhode Island, 1800–1860," *Rhode Island History*, XXXIV (Feb., 1975), 13–21.

Mason, George Champlin. "Nicholas Easton vs. the City of Newport," *Rhode Island Historical Society Collections*, VII (1885), 327–349.

Maxey, Edwin. "Suffrage Extension in Rhode Island Down to 1842," *American Law Review*, (July–Aug., 1908), 541–577.

McCanna, Francis I. "A Study of the History and Jurisdiction of Rhode Island Courts," *Journal of the American Irish Historical Society*, XXII (1923), 170–195.

McCarthy, Charles. "The Anti-Masonic Party: A Study of Political Antimasonry in the United States, 1827–1840," in the *Annual Report of the American Historical Association for the Year 1902*, I, 365–574.

McCormick, Richard P. "New Perspectives on Jacksonian Politics," *American Historical Review*, LXV (Jan., 1960), 288–301.

————. "Suffrage Classes and Party Alignments: A Study in Voter Behavior," *Mississippi Valley Historical Review*, XLVI (Dec., 1959), 399–410.

McDonald, Forrest. "The Anti-Federalists, 1781–1789," *Wisconsin Magazine of History*, XLVI (Spring, 1963), 206–214.

McGiffert, Michael. "Puritan Studies in the 1960s," *William and Mary Quarterly*, 3rd Ser., XXVII (Jan., 1970), 36–67.

Meade, John Richard. "The Truth Concerning the Disfranchisement of Catholics in Rhode Island," *The American Catholic Quarterly Review*, XIX (Jan., 1894), 169–177.

Miller, Frank Hayden. "Legal Qualifications for Office in America, 1619–1899," in the *Annual Report of the American Historical Association for the Year 1899*, I, 87–153.

Miller, William Davis. "The Narragansett Planters," *Proceedings of the American Antiquarian Society*, n.s., XLIII (1934), 49–115.

Moore, Leroy, Jr. "Religious Liberty: Roger Williams and the Revolutionary Era," *Church History*, XXXIV (Mar., 1965), 57–76.

————. "Roger Williams and the Historians," *Church History*, XXXII (Dec., 1963), 432–451.

Morehouse, Frances. "The Irish Migration of the Forties," *American Historical Review*, XXXIII (April, 1928), 579–592.

Morgan, Edmund S. "Miller's Williams," *New England Quarterly*, XXXVIII (Dec., 1965), 513–523.

————. "Perry Miller and the Historians," *Proceedings of the American Antiquarian Society*, LXXIV (Apr., 1964), 11–18.

Morris, Richard B. "The Confederation Period and the American Historian," *William and Mary Quarterly*, 3rd Ser., XIII (April, 1956), 139–156.

Mowry, Arthur May. "The Constitutional Controversy in Rhode Island in 1841," in the *Annual Report of the American Historical Association for the Year 1894*, pp. 361–370.

————. "Tammany Hall and the Dorr Rebellion," *American Historical Review*, III (Jan., 1898), 292–301.

Osgood, Herbert L. "The Classification of Colonial Governments," in the *Annual Report of the American Historical Association for the Year 1895*, pp. 617–629.

O'Toole, Dennis A. "Democratic Balance — Ideals of Community in Early Portsmouth," *Rhode Island History*, XXXII (Feb., 1973), 3–17.

Peace, Nancy E. "Roger Williams — A Historiographical Essay," *Rhode Island History*, XXXV (Nov., 1976), 103–113.

Peckham, Stephen Farnum. "Providence Before 1850," *Journal of American History*, VI (Oct.–Dec., 1912), 661–685.

Perry, Amos. "The Town Records of Rhode Island: A Report," *Publications of the Rhode Island Historical Society*, n.s., I (July, 1893), 101–182.

Pessen, Edward. "The Egalitarian Myth and the American Social Reality: Wealth, Mobility, and Equality in the 'Era of the Common Man,' " *American Historical Review*, LXXVI (Oct., 1971), 989–1034.

————. "The Workingmen's Movement of the Jacksonian Era," *Mississippi Valley Historical Review*, XLIII (Dec., 1956), 428–443.

————. "The Working Men's Party Revisited," *Labor History*, IV (Fall, 1963), 203–226.

Pole, J. R. "Historians and the Problem of Early American Democracy," *American Historical Review*, LXVII (Apr., 1962), 626–646.

Polishook, Irwin H. "The Collins-Richardson Fracas of 1787: A Problem in State and Federal Relations During the Confederation Era," *Rhode Island History*, XXII (Oct., 1963), 117–121.

————. "*Trevett vs. Weeden* and the Case of the Judges," *Newport History*, XXXIII (April, 1965), 45–69.

Rae, John Bell. "The Issues of the Dorr War," *Rhode Island History*, I (Apr., 1942), 33–44.

————. "Rhode Island Pioneers in the Regulation of Banking," *Rhode Island History*, II (Oct., 1943), 105–109.

Rammelkamp, Julian. "The Providence Negro Community, 1820–1842," *Rhode Island History*, VII (Jan., 1948), 20–33.

Reilly, James F. "The Providence Abolition Society," *Rhode Island History*, XXI (Apr., 1962), 33–48.

Rezneck, Samuel. "The Social History of an American Depression, 1837–1843," *American Historical Review*, XL (July, 1935), 662–687.

Rider, Sidney Smith. *Book Notes*. 33 vols. 1883–1916. (The most important articles from this periodical are cited separately).

————. "The History of the Hazard Family in Rhode Island," *Book Notes*, XIII (1896), 181–185.

————. "The History of the Rhode Island Bank Process," *Book Notes*, XXII (1905), 74–77, 89–93.

————. "How the U.S. Senate Forced Rhode Island to Ratify the U.S. Constitution," *Book Notes,* XI (1894), 73–75, 85–86.

————. "The Meaning of the Phrase 'The Manor of East Greenwich in Our County of Kent,' in the Charter of Rhode Island in 1663," *Book Notes,* XXIII (1906), 17–27.

————. "The Origin, Meaning and Duration of Existence in Rhode Island of the Political Word 'Prox,' " *Book Notes,* XXV (1908), 201–204; XXVI (1909), 1–5, 12–15.

————. "The Point Actually Decided by the Rhode Island Supreme Court in the Case *Trevett vs. Weeden,* 1786," *Book Notes,* XXII (1905), 62–63.

Robson, Lloyd A. "Newport Begins." Published serially in *Newport History,* 1964–1967.

Roelker, William G. "Francis Wayland: A Neglected Pioneer of Higher Education," *Proceedings of the American Antiquarian Society,* LIII (April, 1943), 27–78.

Roll, Charles W., Jr. "We, Some of the People: Apportionment in the Thirteen State Conventions Ratifying the Constitution," *Journal of American History,* LVI (June, 1969), 21–40.

Rosenmeier, Jesper. "The Teacher and the Witness: John Cotton and Roger Williams," *William and Mary Quarterly,* 3rd Ser., XXV (July, 1968), 408–431.

Rossiter, Clinton. "Roger Williams on the Anvil of Experience," *American Quarterly,* III (Spring, 1951), 14–21.

Schoolcraft, J. "Inflation in Lilliput; Paper Currency in Colonial Rhode Island," *Virginia Quarterly Review,* XII (Apr., 1936), 220–231.

Simpson, Alan. "How Democratic Was Roger Williams?" *William and Mary Quarterly,* 3rd Ser., XIII (Jan., 1956), 53–67.

Spencer, William B. "A History of the North Branch of the Pawtuxet Valley," *The Narragansett Historical Register,* VI (1888), 122–135.

Stedman, Murray S. Jr. and Susan W. Stedman. "The Rise of the Democratic Party of Rhode Island," *New England Quarterly,* XXIV (Sept., 1951), 329–341.

Stillwell, Margaret Bingham. "A Man Who Dared to Stand Alone — A Sidelight on the Dorr Rebellion, 1842–1844," *Rhode Island History,* XXXVI (May, 1977), 35–41.

Swan, Bradford F. "The Providence Town Papers," *Rhode Island History,* XI (July, 1952), 65–70.

Taylor, Philip K. "Little Rest [Kingston, R.I. prior to 1825]," *New England Magazine,* XXXIV (Apr., 1903), 129–143.

Thomas, John L. "Romantic Reform in America, 1815–1860," *American Quarterly,* XXII (1965), 656–81.

Thompson, Mack E. "The Ward-Hopkins Controversy and the American Revolution in Rhode Island: An Interpretation," *William and Mary Quarterly,* 3rd Ser., XVI (July, 1959), 363–375.

Towles, John Ker. "Factory Legislation of Rhode Island," *American Economic Association Quarterly,* 3rd Ser., IX (Nov., 1908), 1–119.

Trimble, William. "Diverging Tendencies in New York Democracy in the Period of the Locofocos," *American Historical Review,* XXIV (Apr., 1919), 396–421.

————. "The Social Philosophy of the Locofocos Democracy," *The American Journal of Sociology,* XXVI (May, 1921), 705–715.

Warren, Charles. "Earliest Cases of Judicial Review of State Legislation by Federal Courts," *Yale Law Journal,* XXXII (Nov., 1922), 15–28.

Webster, William C. "A Comparative Study of the State Constitutions of the American Revolution," *Annals of the American Academy of Political and Social Science,* IX (1897), 380–420.

Weiner, F. B. "Notes on the Rhode Island Admiralty, 1727–1790," *Harvard Law Review,* XLVI (Nov., 1932), 44–90.

Welles, Arnold. "Father of Our Factory System, Samuel Slater," *American Heritage,* IX (Apr., 1958), 34–39, 90–92.

Wesley, Charles W. "Negro Suffrage in the Period of Constitution-Making, 1787–1865," *Journal of Negro History,* XXXII (Apr., 1947), 143–168.

Wiecek, William M. "Popular Sovereignty in the Dorr War — Conservative Counterblast," *Rhode Island History,* XXXII (May, 1973), 35–51.

Williamson, Chilton. "The Disenchantment of Thomas W. Dorr," *Rhode Island History,* XVII (Oct., 1958), 97–108.

————. "Rhode Island Suffrage Since the Dorr War," *New England Quarterly,* XXVIII (March, 1955), 34–50.

Williamson, Jeffrey G. "Ante-Bellum Urbanization in the American Northeast, 1820–1870," *Journal of Economic History,* XXV (Dec., 1965), 592–608.

Wood, Henry Trueman. "William Bridges Adams," *Dictionary of National Biography,* I, 108–109.

Wright, Benjamin F. "The Early History of Written Constitutions in America," in *Essays in History and Political Theory in Honor of C. H. McIlwain.* Edited by Carl Wittke. Cambridge: Harvard Univ. Press, 1936.

Zevin, Robert B. "The Growth of Manufacturing in Early Nineteenth-Century New England," *Journal of Economic History,* XXV (Dec., 1965), 680–682.

III. UNPUBLISHED WORKS

Appleton, Marguerite. "The Relations of the Corporate Colony of Rhode Island to the British Government." Doctoral dissertation, Brown University, 1928.

Benson, Susan Porter. " 'A Union of Men and Not of Principles:' The Rhode Island Antimasonic Party." Master's thesis, Brown University, 1971.

Brown, Maude O. "The *Providence Patriot and Columbian Phenix, 1802* to 1835." Unpublished research paper, RIHS, 1975.

Cohen, Joel Alden. "Rhode Island and the American Revolution: A Selective Socio-Political Analysis." Doctoral dissertation, University of Connecticut, 1967.

Colasanto, Robert M. "All the King's Men: The Jackson Party in Rhode Island, 1828–1838." Senior honors essay, Department of History, Rhode Island College, 1971.

Coyle, Franklin Stuart. "The Survival of Providence Business Enterprise in the Revolutionary Era, 1770–1785." Master's thesis, Brown University, 1960.

Crane, Theodore R. "Francis Wayland and Brown University, 1796–1841," Doctoral dissertation, Harvard University, 1959.

Crowe, Beryl Lee. "The Dorr Rebellion: A Study of Revolutionary Behavior." Master's thesis, University of California, 1961.

Davis, Thomas M. "The Traditions of Puritan Typology." Doctoral dissertation, University of Missouri, 1968.

Dennison, George Marshel. "The Constitutional Issues of the Dorr War: A Study in the Evolution of American Constitutionalism." Doctoral dissertation, University of Washington, 1967.

Flynn, Theresa A. "The Dorr War." Master's thesis, Rhode Island College, 1931.

Freeman, Donald McKinley. "South County Reaction to the Dorr Rebelion as Illustrated by Elisha Reynolds Potter." Master's thesis, University of Rhode Island, 1955.

Gettleman, Marvin E. "Political Opposition and Radicalism in the Dorr Rebellion." Unpublished paper presented at the Annual Meeting of the Organization of American Historians in Philadelphia, April 18, 1969.

Gilbane, Brendan Francis. "A Social History of Samuel Slater's Pawtucket, 1790–1830." Doctoral dissertation, Boston University, 1969.

Hubbard, Clifford Chesley. "Constitutional Development in Rhode Island [1636–1926]." Doctoral dissertation, Brown University, 1926.

Langer, Kenneth Thomas. "Elisha Reynolds Potter, Sr.: Politician." Master's thesis, University of Rhode Island, 1957.

Lindemann, Robert A. "Important Factors in the Colonial History of Rhode Island Influencing Her Participation in the Revolutionary Movement." Doctoral dissertation, University of Indiana, 1952.

Longhorn, Milton. "The Rise of the Merchant Class in Rhode Island." Doctoral dissertation, University of Wisconsin, 1936.

Lough, George J. Jr. "The Champlins of Newport: A Commercial History." Doctoral dissertation, University of Connecticut, 1977.

Lowney, Charlotte. "The Heyday and Death of Lotteries in Rhode Island, 1820–1842." Master's thesis, Brown University, 1965.

Lowther, Lawrence Leland. "Rhode Island Colonial Government, 1732." Doctoral dissertation, University of Washington, 1964.

McCann, John B. "A Study of the Mill Worker in the Blackstone Valley, 1820–1830." Master's thesis, Providence College, 1931.

MacInnes, John Blanchard. "Rhode Island Bills of Public Credit, 1710–1755." Doctoral dissertation, Brown University, 1952.

McKiernan, Donald E. "The Debtor-Creditor Struggle in Rhode Island, 1781–1790." Master's thesis, Rhode Island College, 1967.

Mullen, Walter F. "Rhode Island and the Imperial Reorganization of 1763–1766." Doctoral dissertation, Fordham University, 1965.

Newton, Anne Mary. "Rebellion in Rhode Island: The Story of the Dorr War." Master's thesis, Columbia University, 1947.

Nylander, Jane Cayford. "The Sullivan Dorr House in Providence, Rhode Island." Master's thesis, University of Delaware, 1961.

O'Toole, Dennis Allen. "Exiles, Refugees, and Rogues: The Quest for Civil Order in the Towns and Colony of Providence Plantations, 1636–1654." Doctoral dissertation, Brown University, 1973.

Polishook, Irwin H. "Rhode Island and the Union, 1774–1790." Doctoral dissertation, Northwestern University, 1961.

—————. "Unorthodoxy in Massachusetts: A History of the Banishment of Roger Williams from Massachusetts and Its Consequences." Master's thesis, Brown University, 1958.

Reed, John William. "The Rhetoric of a Colonial Controversy: Roger Williams versus the Massachusetts Bay Colony." Doctoral dissertation, Ohio State University, 1966.

Reilly, James F. "Moses Brown and the Rhode Island Antislavery Movement." Master's thesis, Brown University, 1951.

Reinitz, Richard M. "Symbolism and Freedom: The Use of Biblical Typology as an Argument for Religious Toleration in Seventeenth Century England and America." Doctoral dissertation, University of Rochester, 1967.

Richards, John J. "History of the Collapse of Compulsory Militia Service in Rhode Island, 1836–1842." Manuscript, Rhode Island Historical Society, ca. 1930.

Rider, Sidney S. "The Development of Constitutional Government in Rhode Island. . . ." Manuscript in 27 scrapbooks, Rhode Island Historical Society.

Rudolph, Richard H. "The Merchants of Newport, Rhode Island, 1763–1786." Doctoral dissertation, University of Connecticut, 1975.

Still, Bayrd. "State Constitutional Development in the United States, 1829–1851." Doctoral dissertation, University of Wisconsin, 1933.

Stoughton, Robert Wetmore. "The Philosophy of Dorrism." Master's thesis, Brown University, 1936.

Sullivan, Thomas Joseph. "From Federalist to Whig: The Political Career of Tristam Burges." Master's thesis, University of Rhode Island, 1964.

Sweet, Edward F. "The Origin of the Democratic Party in Rhode Island, 1824–1836." Doctoral dissertation, Fordham University, 1971.

Thornton, William Barrie. "Henry Bowen Anthony: Journalist, Governor, and Senator." Master's thesis, University of Rhode Island, 1960.

Tormey, Dorothea Jane. "The Providence Association of Mechanics and Manufacturers: The First Thirty Years." Master's thesis, University of Rhode Island, 1957.

Vaccaro, Ralph George. "The Politics of David Howell of Rhode Island in the Period of the Confederation." Master's thesis, Columbia University, 1947.

Walsh, Sister Mary Edward, R.S.M. "The Irish in Rhode Island From 1800 to 1865." Master's thesis, The Catholic University of America, 1937.

Whitney, Herbert Allen. "The Narragansett Region: Concentrations of Population, 1635–1885." Doctoral dissertation, University of Michigan, 1962.

Withers, Richard Eugene. "Roger Williams and the Rhode Island Colony: A Study in Leadership Roles." Doctoral dissertation, Boston University, 1966.

Index

Acote's Hill, 346, 346n, 347–49
Adams, John, 136
Adams, John Quincy, 210, 219, 240
Adams, William B., 250
Address to the People of Rhode Island, 255–56, 256n, 257, 257n
Alabama, 184
Aldrich, George B., 338n
Aldrich, Wilmarth N., 352
Alexander Champion and Thomas Dickason v. Silas Casey, 163n
Algerine Convention, 351
Algerine Law, 324, 324n, 326, 327, 328n, 329, 336–38, 342, 352–53, 361–62
Allen, Crawford, 340
Allen, Philip, 81, 369, 369n, 371
Allen, William, 331–32
Allen, Zachariah, 81, 340
Almy, Jonathan, 189
American Anti-Slavery Society, 310
American Party, 370
American Revolution, 36n, 49, 53–54, 57–71, 94, 94n; and apportionment controversy, 63–71; and R.I. renunciation of allegiance, 59, 59n, 60n; and War for Independence, 61; as a conservative movement, 62–63; British occupation of R.I., 74; causes for revolt against British rule, 51; Declaration of Independence, 57; development of two-party politics prior to, 50; effects of, 71–73; French assistance in, 61n, 71; political and constitutional changes produced by, 60–73; political factions and, 63n; principles of, 123–24; reaction to Lexington and Concord, 58–59; revolutionary movement, 58; R.I. ratifies Declaration of Independence, 60; taxes during, 63–71; war costs during, 68, 128–29, 131n, 135–37, 140. *See also* Articles of Confederation; Paper money.
American System, 187, 246
Ames, Fisher, 120n, 134n
Ames, Samuel, 253n, 340, 347, 360, 366, 367, 375
Andros, Edmund, 27
Angell, Joseph K., 249, 254, 254n, 255–56, 256n, 260, 260n, 264, 269, 273, 287, 288, 326n
Annapolis Convention, 107

Anthony, Burrington, 330–31, 335, 337
Anthony, Henry Bowen, 276, 276n, 366, 368; and nativist causes, 277, 319, 321–22, 373n, 374n
Anti-Catholicism. *See* Roman Catholics, sentiments against.
Antifederalism. *See* Antifederalists.
Antifederalists, 106, 110, 112–13, 114n, 115, 117, 117n, 118, 118n, 119, 120n, 121, 124, 126, 128n, 131, 131n, 132, 134, 134n, 135–36, 141n, 174–75. *See also* Paper money.
Antimasons, 246, 259, 266n, 272
Antinomians, 16, 253
Antislavery, 37n, 71–72, 72n, 124–26, 131n, 278, 310, 312, 314, 332, 370
Antunes, Joseph, 35
Aquidneck Island (island of Rhode Island), 19, 21; early settlement of, 16.
Arkwright, Sir Richard, 145
Arnold, Benjamin, Jr., 126n, 309, 311
Arnold, Lemuel, 236, 266n, 273, 328n, 367–68
Arnold, Peleg, 108, 175, 182n
Arnold, Welcome, 81, 120n
Articles of Confederation, 74–75, 108, 122, 244. *See also* Confederation Congress.
Ashurst, Sir Henry, 30
Atherton Company, 22, 23n
Atwell, Samuel Y., 253n, 265, 267n, 302–03, 303n, 304, 309, 311, 316, 324, 324n, 326–27, 355–56, 361

Bacon, Sir Francis, 96
Baker v. Carr, 376
Balch, William J., 282, 303
Ballou, Ariel, 247, 309, 352
Ballou, Levi, 126n
Bank Act of 1836, 278–79, 279n
Bankhead, Col. James, 343, 346, 349

Barrington (R.I.), 105n, 130, 203n, 212, 264n, 265n, 267, 312
Bartlett, David, 177n
Battle of Saratoga, 339
Baylies, Francis, 239–40
Beckford, F. L., 354n
Bell, Jared, 277, 293, 293n
Bellingham (Mass.), 350
Bellomont, Earl of. *See* Coote, Richard.
Benton, Thomas Hart, 331
Bicameralism, 39
Bicknell, Joshua, 203n
Bill of Rights (U.S.), 112, 115, 115n, 123, 131, 192
Bill of Rights (R.I.), 238, 264, 310–11, 320, 372; in *Digest of 1798,* 173; in early R.I., 20; proposed in 1824, 203, 203n
Blackstone, Sir William, 96
Blackstone Canal, 150
Blackstone River, 145, 148, 154, 349
Blackstone Valley, 148–50, 274n
Blake, Gen. Joseph A., 356
Blanchard, Claude, 61
Block Island (New Shoreham, R.I.), 47, 64, 105n, 113, 114n, 265n, 284n
Blodget, Col. Leonard, 338n, 340–41
Blodgett, William, 350
Borden, Luther N., 362
Boston (Mass.), 246, 249
Bourn Amendment, 375–76
Bourne, Benjamin, 93, 113, 115, 142
Bowen, Henry, 258
Bowen, Jabez, 69, 81, 107, 121, 142
Bradford, William, 61, 113
Brayton Law, 376, 376n
Bridgham, Samuel W., 191, 200, 219n
Brinley, Francis, 30
Bristol (R.I.), 66, 85–86, 110, 121, 128, 129–30, 130n, 148, 165, 177, 180, 182, 197, 199,

Bristol (R.I.) (*cont.*)
202, 224, 241, 252n, 258, 267,
274n, 318, 340–41, 346, 367
Bristol County, 43n, 164–65, 191–
92, 207, 267
Brown, David, 239, 272, 337
Brown, Dr. John A., 269, 270n,
299, 299n, 309, 326, 331
Brown, John (of Hopkinton), 130
Brown, John (of Providence),
111n, 130n, 136, 142, 167–68,
241
Brown, John Carter, 321–22
Brown, Moses, 124–25, 125n,
131n, 132, 142, 146
Brown, Nathan A., 253
Brown, Nicholas, 35, 78n, 81, 104,
111n, 130n, 142
Brown, William J., 325
Brown, William W., 347
Brown University (Rhode Island
College), 109, 347
Brownson, Orestes A., 302, 357,
357n, 358n
Bryant, William Cullen, 336
Bull, Henry, 202, 208
Burges, Tristam, 231, 231n, 232,
234, 243n, 253n, 270, 280,
324n
Burges, Walter S., 336, 345, 348–
49, 355n, 361, 363, 377
Burgess, Thomas M., 341, 346, 349
Burgess, Welcome, 203
Burke, Congressman Edmund,
348, 358–59, 360n, 361
Burnaby, Rev. Andrew, 52
Burrill, George R., 168, 172, 176–
78, 186, 239, 291, 377
Burrill, James, Jr., 165, 169
Burrillville (R.I.), 149, 154n, 201,
252n, 324n
Burroughs, William, 276

Calhoun, John C., 332–33, 374
Canada, 375
Carlile, Francis Y., 234
Carpenter, Thomas F., 298, 298n,
326, 326n, 352–54, 356, 357n

Carrington, Edward, 202, 208,
328n
Carter, Col. Charles W., 338n,
340
Carter, John, 131
Catholics. *See* Roman Catholics.
Causin, John, 358
Central Falls, 158
Channing, William, 97, 98
Charles I (king of England), 17
Charles II (king of England), 22,
54, 62, 94
Charlestown (R.I.), 68, 70n, 82,
83n, 105n, 115, 120n, 125n,
154, 168, 172n, 255, 255n,
265n, 283
Charter of 1643, 17–18, 21–22;
unites Providence, Portsmouth,
and Newport, 17–18
Charter of 1663, 14, 21–54, 57n,
62, 62n, 63, 64, 94, 103, 104,
105, 151, 174, 176, 189, 201;
and slavery, 36n; attempts to
reform, 154n, 162–72, 176,
177, 177n, 178, 179n, 184,
185n, 186, 187–90, 192–94,
194n, 196, 198, 200–12,
239, 247–48, 253–54, 256,
261–67, 274, 302, 309–79;
attempts to rescind, 27–31;
suffrage provisions of, 23. *See
also* Religious freedom; Suffrage, demands for reform.
Charterites, 314–20, 322n, 324,
327–28, 331, 337, 339, 344,
344n, 347, 362. *See also* Law
and Order faction.
Chepachet (R.I.), 343–44, 346,
348–49
Childs, Francis, 87, 127n
Childs, Joseph, 265, 273
China trade, 249
Chipman, Nathaniel, 290–91, 305
City of Newport v. Horton, 38n
City of Providence v. Moulton,
38n
Clark, John Innes, 101n, 112,
118

Clarke, John, 21, 23n, 26n; commissioned to obtain royal charter, 22
Clarke, John H., 369n
Clarke, Joseph, 60, 70
Clay, Henry, 236, 359n
Clifford, Nathan, 363
Cleveland, Chauncey, 344
Coddington, William, 16, 17, 21; attempts feudal domain, 17
Code of 1647. See Portsmouth Assembly.
Coke, Sir Edward, 94, 99
Collins, Amos, 177
Collins, Charles, 271, 273, 302n
Collins, John, 83, 108, 111, 111n, 113, 115–16, 117n, 119n, 135, 174
Columbian Phenix (Providence), 179–80
Commerce. See United States Constitution.
Comstock, Job, 116, 126, 126n
Conanicut Island. See Jamestown.
Concord (Mass.), 57, 58
Confederation Congress, 60, 73, 100n, 107, 126
Congdon, Charles T., 297n, 299n
Congress. See Confederation Congress; Continental Congress; United States Congress.
Connecticut, 23n, 28, 61, 61n, 62n, 78, 127, 134, 154, 184, 187–88, 190, 331–32, 344, 346, 348–49; claims to Narragansett Country, 22, 23n
Constitution. See Rhode Island Constitution; United States Constitution.
Constitutional Convention (U.S.), 93, 99n, 100, 107–08, 108n, 109, 109n, 124, 125n, 127. See also United States Constitution.
Constitutions (R.I.). See Algerine Constitution of November 1842; Constitutional Party; Landholders' Constitution;

People's Constitution; Rhode Island Constitution.
Constitutional conventions (R.I.), 68–70, 70n, 71, 162, 165, 166–68, 171, 177, 177n, 178, 178n, 184–86, 188, 189, 195, 198, 200–02, 202n, 203–12, 239, 241, 247–48, 254, 257, 261–63, 263n, 264–69, 272, 288, 290–91, 294, 303–04, 328, 377. See also Algerine Convention; Landholders' Convention; People's Convention.
Constitutional Party, 254, 258, 258n, 259–60, 260n, 261, 263, 264, 266–67, 267n, 269–70, 270n, 271, 271n, 272, 272n, 273, 273n, 274n, 277–78, 283–86, 286n, 287, 287n, 288, 288n, 295, 299, 302n, 303, 304, 318
Continental Congress, 58n, 74, 92, 108. See also Second Continental Congress.
Cooke, Nicholas, 58–59, 59n
Cooley, Franklin, 322
Coote, Richard (Earl of Bellomont), 29–33, 40
Cornbury, Lord. See Hyde, Edward.
Corry, Rev. John, 274, 274n
Cotton, John, typological debate with Roger Williams, 10, 11
Country Party, 83, 85, 87, 89–91, 98, 101, 102, 103, 106, 108, 108n, 113, 115, 116–17, 117n, 119, 119n, 133, 136, 194n
Court of Common Pleas, 41, 84, 91, 189, 264, 267
Court of Equity, 42
Court of General Sessions, 41, 267n
Courts. See Judiciary.
Coventry (R.I.), 70, 70n, 83n, 105, 110, 189, 197, 199, 259, 267, 286
Cranston (R.I.), 83n, 165, 177, 177n, 247n, 252n, 378n
Cranston, Henry Y., 189, 253n, 351, 358

Cranston, Robert B., 189, 273,
283, 366
Cranston, Samuel, 31
Cranston Street Arsenal, 339–40
Crawford, William, 210
Cromwell, Oliver, 21, 22; confirms
patent of 1643, 18n, 22n
Cross, Joseph, 255, 255n
Crompton (R.I.), 154
Cumberland (R.I.), 83n, 102, 130,
130n, 150, 177, 177n, 246–47,
252n, 254, 257, 263, 267, 312,
344

Danforth, Walter R., 188, 322
Daniels, David, 247, 253n, 254,
269, 326n, 344
Dartmouth, Earl of, 31n, 53
Decatur, Stephen, 36n
Declaration of Independence, 57,
60, 62, 134, 221, 238; ratified
by R.I., 108
Deference, in colonial politics, 50,
50n
Democracy, 17, 19, 51–53, 61,
61n, 73, 79, 101n, 121–23, 140,
219, 230, 236, 253
Democratic Republicans (Republicans), 175, 177–79, 179n,
180–81, 181n, 182, 182n, 188,
191, 231, 234, 241, 251, 281,
305, 318
Democrats, 241, 243–46, 248n,
253, 258–59, 261, 265–66, 270–
73, 273n, 274n, 276n, 277,
280–84, 287n, 293, 293n, 294,
298n, 299, 300n, 302, 314, 317,
326, 328, 328n, 332–33, 336,
344, 348, 351n, 352–54, 357,
358–59, 361n, 366–69, 369n,
370, 370n, 371, 375–77. See
also Equal Rights Democrats.
Denham, Daniel, 189
Despean, John S., 338n
Devol, Gilbert, 96, 98
DeWolf, James, 177, 180–81, 241,
258, 258n, 261, 263n, 265
DeWolf, William, 202

Dexter, John S., 126n
Dexter, Samuel, 190
Dexter Training Grounds, 339
Diamond Hill (R.I.), 344
Digest of 1719, 32–34
Digest of 1798, 172–73, 174n
Digest of 1822, 195
Dillingham Petition, 300
Diman, Byron, 328n, 368
Dixon, Nathan F., 202, 208–10,
253n, 273, 328n
Dominion of New England, 27–28,
30
Dorr, Ebenezer, 249
Dorr, Henry, 316
Dorr, Lydia (Allen), 249
Dorr, Sullivan, 249, 340, 367
Dorr, Sullivan, Jr., 340
Dorr, Thomas Wilson, 54, 170–71,
181n, 186, 202, 249–51, 254,
254n, 259, 260n, 261–62, 265,
268–71, 271n, 273, 278, 279n,
281, 286–88, 288n, 298, 298n,
309, 311–12, 315, 320n, 321–
23, 324n, 325n, 326, 326n,
329, 346, 352–54, 354n, 355n,
357–59, 359n, 360–63, 365–66,
369–71, 373n, 375, 377–78;
and Address to the People of
R.I., 255–56, 256n, 257n; and
banking proposals, 278–80,
313; and immigration, 255;
and militarism, 336–42, 344n,
346–48; and reform convention
of 1834, 253–56; and suffrage
reform, 260–65, 271, 277, 287–
88, 288n, 300n, 304–05, 311;
arrested, 355; as delegate to
People's Convention, 305; as
leader of reform movement,
264, 278, 304n, 305n; as
People's governor, 327, 329,
330–32, 334–41, 344–45, 348–
49, 355–56, 359, 362, 367;
death of, 371; drafts People's
Constitution, 305, 310, 314;
early reform beliefs, 250–52;
elected to Assembly, 260;

Dorr, Thomas Wilson (*cont.*)
exiled, 340–43; political conversion of, 282–85, 287, 287n; political rights restored, 371; released from prison, 367–68; returns to R.I., 344–45, 348; second exile, 348, 351; tried for treason, 338n, 355–57, 362, 364. *See also* Dorr Rebellion; Dorrites; Constitutional Party; People's Constitution; People's Convention; People's Legislature; Suffragists.

Dorr Liberation Society, 368

Dorr Rebellion, 154n, 171, 195, 297n, 305, 309–51, 353, 359, 360n, 365, 370–71, 373n; as treasonable act, 331, 337, 338n, 355–56

Dorr Troop of Horse, 328

Dorrites, 188, 190, 202, 246, 287n, 293n, 317–18, 321–23, 326–27, 335n, 339, 342, 346, 347, 350–52, 354, 356, 358–60, 362–67, 369, 369n, 375–76; militia units, 344; raid arsenal, 338n, 338–41. *See also* Dorr, Thomas Wilson; People's Constitution; People's Convention; People's Leglislature; Suffragists.

Douglass, Frederick, 312

Doyle, Thomas, 254

Dudley, Joseph, 28, 30

Duff, Henry J., 275n, 312, 360

Durfee, Job, 113, 114n, 131n, 193, 202, 203n, 208, 230n, 317–18, 326, 335, 355–56, 364–65, 369n

D'Wolf, Col. Henry, 340–41, 348

Dyer, Elisha, 347, 371

Earle, Caleb, 202, 203n

East Greenwich (R.I.), 102, 105n, 148, 154, 182, 191, 202, 349, 351

Easton, Nicholas, 102

Eaton, Levi C., 326n

Edes, Peter, 86–87, 89, 103, 131, 131n

Eddy, Samuel, 218

Education, 178, 203, 206, 206n, 278, 311

Elections, 10, 38, 39n, 40, 42n, 51–52, 52n, 53n, 58, 108, 110, 113–14, 175n, 178–79, 180n, 181–83, 183n, 191–93, 199–200, 205–06, 207n, 210, 212, 218–20, 220n, 230–34, 236, 236n, 247, 259, 259n, 260n, 266, 269n, 270n, 271, 293n, 296–98, 298n, 315, 323–24, 326–27, 327n, 351, 354, 354n, 359, 366–68, 369n; and frauds and abuses, 48–49, 52, 265, 270, 284n, 314–15. *See also* Suffrage.

Elizer, Isaac, 35

Ellery, William, 116–17, 132n, 134–36, 137n, 138, 142

Ellsworth, Oliver, 134, 136, 137n

Emerson, Ralph Waldo, 291

England, 17–19, 28, 38, 45, 57n, 60, 62n, 63n, 94, 123, 129, 146, 251, 375. *See also* Parliament; Privy Council.

Equal Rights, 160, 250, 265, 280–89, 282n, 298–99, 305, 310–12, 317, 319–20, 352–53, 359, 369, 371, 375. *See also* Equal Rights Democrats and Locofocos.

Equal Rights Democrats, 277, 280, 280n, 281–82, 293, 298, 313. *See also* Democrats.

Evans, George Henry, 368n

Ex Parte Dorr, 368n

Ex post facto laws, 173

Exeter (R.I.), 68, 70n, 105n, 154, 243

Fall River (R.I., later Mass.), 154, 275, 275n

Federal Hill (Providence), 337, 339

Federalism. *See* Federalists.

Federalists, 106, 109–13, 113n,
114n, 115, 118n, 119n, 121,
124, 127–28, 130–31, 130n,
134–35, 139–42, 168, 172,
175–82, 185–86, 191, 196,
219, 225, 227, 251, 280
Fenner, Arthur, 113, 113n, 115–
16, 174–75, 176n, 178, 179n
Fenner, James, 178, 179, 179n,
181, 201n, 220, 234, 236, 266n,
271n, 298n, 328, 328n, 351–54,
357, 359, 366–68
Ferrari, Francis, 36n
Field, David Dudley, 250
First Social Reform Society, 294
Fitton, Rev. James, 275n
Fones, John, 30
Fort Adams, 275, 328, 328n, 343
Foster (R.I.), 64n, 67, 70n, 102,
105n, 110, 154, 197, 199, 264n
Foster, Theodore, 133n, 134, 137n,
162
Foundry Legislature, 329–30, 337,
339. See also People's Legis-
lature.
Fowler, Christopher, 202, 203n,
206–07
France, 71
Francis, John, 136–37
Francis, John Brown, 234, 234n,
235n, 241, 243–45, 254, 259,
259n, 260n, 272, 274n, 284n,
287n, 298, 315, 325, 332, 342,
352, 357, 360n, 366n, 369,
373n
Franklin, James, 47n
Freebody v. Brenton, 44
Freeman. *See* Suffrage.
Frieze, Jacob, 286n, 287n, 327,
327n

Garrison, William Lloyd, 312
Gaspee. See H.M.S. *Gaspee.*
General Assembly, 29, 32–33, 35,
39–48, 52, 52n, 53n, 57n, 58,
58n, 60, 64, 66–71, 74–77, 81n,
83–84, 84n, 87–88, 93–105,
108–111, 115, 115n, 123, 133,

135, 162–67, 170–71, 176–78,
180, 182, 182n, 186–90, 192–
98, 200–01, 209n, 218, 221,
223–24, 226, 230n, 231–33,
235n, 239, 242, 243n, 256, 260–
61, 267n, 270, 292, 298, 320,
324, 327, 333, 344–45, 347,
351, 360, 367, 369n, 370n, 374,
377; and Board of Councillors,
328–29, 346–47; and powers of
towns, 37n, 38n; apportionment of delegates to, 53–54,
54n, 63–71, 101n, 103n, 103–
05, 151, 154n, 162n, 163, 166–
69, 171, 174, 184, 186, 191,
194–95, 197–200, 200n, 203–
08, 217, 231, 247–48, 253, 256–
57, 259, 262, 263–68, 272, 274,
285, 294, 301, 312–15, 317,
319–20, 374–76; Grand Committee of, 175–76, 179n, 183,
183n, 205, 365n, 368; powers
in colonial R.I., 37, 37n, 38–
39; powers under Charter of
1663, 24; reacts to Negro petition for suffrage, 301; re-
nounces allegiance to king, 59,
59n, 60n
General Court of Trials, 40. *See
also* Portsmouth Assembly.
George III (king of England), 53,
59, 62
Gibbs, William C., 191–93, 219n,
366
Glocester (R.I.), 67, 69, 83n, 102,
105n, 110, 113, 165, 212, 265,
302, 344
Goddard, William G., 186, 317,
322, 358, 366
Goodwin, Henry, 98
Gordon, John, 298n, 356
Gorton, Samuel, 16, 18
Greeley, Horace, 299n
Green, Theodore Francis, 169, 377
Greene, Albert C., 202, 258
Greene, Nathanael, 58
Greene, William, 175
Greenville (R.I.), 349

Habeas corpus, 173, 368n
Haile, Levi, 261, 262, 263, 265, 318
Hallett, Benjamin F., 202n, 222n, 223n, 224, 234, 246, 359, 361, 363, 366n
Hamilton, Alexander, 134n, 318
Harrington, Charles C., 254
Harris, John S., 246, 309, 335, 338n, 352, 354n
Harris, William, 249
Harrison, William Henry ("Tippecanoe"), 297–98
Hartford Convention, 190
Hawkins, Serjeant William, 96
Hazard, Benjamin, 190, 202, 225, 227, 230, 233, 245, 253n, 257n, 261–63, 263n, 265, 265n, 266, 273, 301
Hazard, Edwin, 349
Hazard, Jonathan J., 82, 83, 115–16, 120n, 121n
Hazard, Joseph, 96, 98
Hazzard, Jeffrey, 243
Hibernian Orphan Society, 274
Hill, Hiram, 326n, 344n, 354n
Hines, Joseph, 190
H.M.S. *Gaspee,* 31, 31n, 53
Hodges, Almon D., 347, 350, 367, 368n
Hodges, James L., 241
Holden, Thomas, 61
Hopkins, Samuel, 125
Hopkins, Stephen, 35, 50, 59n
Hopkinton (R.I.), 68, 70, 70n, 103n, 105n, 130, 130n, 154, 177, 191
Hoppin, William W., 371
Horsmanden, Lord Daniel, 31n, 53
Howard, Jesse, 283
Howell, David, 73, 77, 96–99, 104, 126, 127n
Howell, Jeremiah B., 179n
Howland, James, 72
Howland, John, 93n
Hubbard, Henry, 348
Huguenots, 36n

Hull, Edward, 113, 114n
Huntington, Benjamin, 132n, 134
Huntington, Jabez, 332
Hutchins, John, 187
Hutchinson, Anne, 16
Hutchinson, Thomas, 53
Hyde, Edward (Viscount Cornbury; Lord Cornbury), 30, 31

Illinois, 158, 184, 358
Immigration, 160, 254–55, 265, 274–75, 275n, 312, 345n; encouraged in R.I. colony, 24. *See also* Suffrage.
Impost duties, 75–79, 79n, 121, 133. *See also* Tariffs.
Independence. *See* Declaration of Independence; Rhode Island Independence Day.
Independent Company of Cadets, 168, 178
India Point (Providence), 348
Indiana, 158, 184
Indians, 8, 14, 16–18, 172n. *See also* Narragansett Indians.
Industrialization, 145, 197; and constitutional reform movements, 150–151, 209; and cotton, 146–50, 258n; and distribution of wealth, 150, 150n; and manufacturing, 147–49; and metals, 149–50; and population, 150, 150n, 151, 154, 154n, 158; and steam power, 148, 150, 154n; and suffrage, 183; and suffrage reform, 220, 226, 230; and wool, 147; effects of, 291
Iredell, James, 100
Irish, 160, 254, 274, 275, 276n, 277, 298n, 312, 317, 319, 321–22, 322n, 345, 356, 360, 369, 369n, 371, 374n, 375. *See also* Immigration; Nativism; Roman Catholics; Suffrage.
Irish, George, 258

Jackson, Andrew, 219, 236–37, 240, 243, 243n, 276, 281, 341

Jackson, Charles, 367–68, 369n
Jackson, George W., 276n
Jackson, Richard, Jr., 175, 179
Jamestown (Conanicut Island,
    R.I.), 21, 64, 128, 130, 256,
    267, 312, 358
Jefferson, Thomas, 179, 182, 226,
    230, 276
Jeffersonians. *See* Democratic
    Republicans.
Jenckes, Joseph, 44–45
Jenckes, Thomas Allen, 351n
Jews, 34–35, 36n, 71n; in New-
    port, 34n. *See also* Lopez,
    Aaron; Elizer, Isaac; Lucena,
    James.
Johnston (R.I.), 70n, 165, 247n,
    248n, 252n, 259, 349
Jones, Josiah, 188
Jones, William, 179, 181, 182,
    220, 298n
Joslin, Joseph, 309, 337
Joy, Benjamin, 272
Judiciary, attempts to reform, 170,
    186, 200n, 203, 205, 208–09,
    209n, 217–18, 248, 253, 256,
    264, 266–67, 267n, 278, 313,
    374; in colonial R.I., 40–43.
    *See also listings by individual
    courts.*

Keach, Eddy, 324n
Kelley, Abby, 312
Kelby, Alexander, 350
Kent, Chancellor James, 228,
    250
Kent County, 43n, 61, 69n, 191,
    192, 207, 235n, 267
Kentish Guards, 349
King, Dr. Dan, 255n, 283, 284
King, Samuel Ward, 248n, 259,
    259n, 286, 298, 325–27, 332–
    35, 340–43, 346–49, 353, 357,
    360n, 364–65
King William's War, 28
King's County, 41, 63. *See also*
    Washington County.
Knight, Nehemiah, 182, 196, 199,

219, 220n, 232n, 240, 242, 255,
    258–59, 259n, 274n, 280, 286
Know-Nothings, 369n, 371
Knowles, James Davis, 185–87,
    239, 291
Knowles, John P., 326n
Knowles, Joseph, 276

Landholders' Convention, 315–16,
    320, 323, 345
Landholders' (Freemen's) Con-
    stitution, 275n, 320, 320n, 321,
    321n, 322–24, 327, 351, 372–
    74
Larned, William G., 286
Law and Order faction, 286,
    286n, 287n, 317–20, 323, 325–
    27, 333–35, 342, 344–45, 349–
    50, 351n, 352–53, 354n, 358,
    359n, 360n, 363–66, 366n,
    367–68, 370–72, 374. *See also*
    Charterites.
Leigh, Benjamin Watkins, 228
Lexington (Mass.), 57–58
Liberty of conscience. *See*
    Religious freedom; Williams,
    Roger.
Lippitt (R.I.), 154
Little Compton (R.I.), 110, 128,
    130, 130n
Little Rest (Kingston), 68, 69,
    242
Locke, John, 71, 99n, 281
Locofocos, 277, 280–81, 293–94,
    294n, 296, 298, 310, 313, 320,
    332, 353, 357
Lonsdale (R.I.), 247
Lopez, Aaron, 35, 36n
Louisiana, 220n
Low, Samuel, 354n
Loyalists, 45n, 63, 72. *See also*
    Newport Tory Junto.
Lucena, James, 35, 35n, 36n
Luther, Martin, 361–63
Luther, Rachel, 361, 363
Luther, Seth, 222n, 238, 238n,
    239, 246n, 252, 270–71, 291,
    302

Luther v. Borden, 318, 361–65, 365n, 377

Maclay, William, 137
McCarty, George, 300
McClernand, John A., 358
McLane, Louis, 148–49
McNeill, William Gibbs, 347–50
Madison, James, 100n, 117n, 127, 179, 182
Maine, 184
Man, George F., 326n
Man, Samuel F., 368
Manning, James, 109
Manufacturers' and Farmers' Journal, 187–88, 191–93, 198–200, 202, 207, 212, 233–34, 276, 286n
Marchant, Henry, 74, 92, 111–12, 112n, 113, 142
Marsh, Metcalf, 247, 247n, 268–69, 273, 286, 288, 288n, 303, 354
Marshall, John, 100
Martin, Josiah H., 350
Maryland, 15, 107, 358
Mason, Otis, 263, 269, 273
Massachusetts, 28, 29, 53, 58, 58n, 69, 78, 120n, 136, 184, 187, 190, 239–41, 275n, 341, 346, 348–49
Massachusetts Bay Colony, 8, 9, 23n, 25
Massachusetts Sentinel, 127
Mathewson, Elisha, 202
Mathewson, Noah, 126n
Merry, Barney, 221
Microcosm (Providence), 233–34
Middletown (R.I.), 64, 83n, 105n, 128–30, 258, 312
Melville, David, 189
Miller, John, 187, 234, 276n
Miller, Wiliam, 239, 272
Mississippi, 184
Missouri, 184, 331
Mitchell, William, 239
Money. *See* Paper money.
Moore, Ely, 336

Montesquieu, 96
Morris, Robert, 79n
Mowry, Daniel, 165
Mowry, Enos, 177, 178n
Mumford, Paul, 92, 92n, 93, 96, 98

Narragansett Bay, 14, 18, 23n, 145, 154, 340
Narragansett Country, 36n; conflicting claims in, 22
Narragansett Indians, 345. *See also* Indians.
Narragansett Proprietors, 30–31. *See also* Atherton Company.
National [Land] Reform Association, 368n
National Republicans, 236, 241–42, 248n, 258, 259n, 260n, 266n
Nativism, 276–77, 295, 312, 314, 319–22, 327n, 347, 369n, 370–71, 373, 374n, 375. *See also* Immigration; Roman Catholics.
Navigation Acts, 57n
Negroes, 71, 296, 296n, 314, 324–25, 331, 345, 360, 372n, 374n; and emancipation act of 1784, 71–72; and slave code, 36n; and suffrage, 300–01, 301n; as slaves, 36n, 369; denied franchise, 195, 311; granted vote, 345, 372; slave trade and U.S. Constitution, 112; statutes prohibit sale of, 72n. *See also* Antislavery; Slave trade.
New Age and Constitutional Advocate (Providence), 299, 299n
New Bedford (Mass.), 299n
New Deal, 377
New England Association of Farmers and Mechanics, 238, 246
New England Confederation, land claims of, 17
New Era, 277, 293, 293n
New Hampshire, 29, 110, 250, 331, 348, 351, 355, 365

New Jersey, 27n
New Shoreham. *See* Block Island.
New York, 29, 76n, 110, 119,
    123n, 132n, 158, 184, 228,
    228n, 240–41, 244n, 250, 276,
    280, 282, 293–94, 294n, 331–
    32, 335–36, 341, 348–49, 358,
    368
New York Tribune, 299n
Newport (R.I.), 18–19, 23, 37n,
    49n, 52, 53n, 64, 81, 83, 85–
    86, 90, 92, 102–03, 103n, 105n,
    108, 110–11, 117, 125–30, 132,
    134, 135n, 138, 140, 151, 162–
    64, 168, 172, 178, 182, 190–
    92, 197, 201–04, 208–10, 212,
    221, 225, 245, 252n, 261, 267,
    274n, 275, 283, 301–02, 304–
    05, 309, 312, 328, 333, 337,
    341, 344, 346, 351; consolida-
    tion with Portsmouth, 17;
    decline after Revolution, 72,
    73n. *See also* Charter of 1643;
    Newport County; Newport
    Tory Junto.
Newport County, 41, 41n, 69, 154,
    172, 189, 191–93, 206, 267,
    340, 355
Newport Herald, 87, 131
Newport Tory Junto, 31, 31n
Niger, Alfred, 300
Nightingale, Joseph, 101n
North, Lord, 31n
North Carolina, 111, 131, 131n,
    220n, 244n
North Kingstown (R.I.), 39n,
    70n, 102, 177n, 197, 199, 201,
    255, 267
North Providence (R.I.), 105n,
    150, 165, 202, 203n, 221, 247n,
    252n, 254, 257, 257n, 261, 267,
    312, 349
*Northern Star and Constitutional
    Advocate* (Warren), 285

Ohio, 100n, 158, 331
O'Sullivan, John L., 250, 236,
    357

Owen, Samuel, 113, 116, 126,
    126n

Pabodie, William, 182n
Page, John, 138n
Paine, Thomas, 75
Panic of 1837, 283n, 287
Paper money, 31, 44–45, 45n, 70,
    70n, 80n, 83n, 84n, 100, 101–
    06, 116–17, 117n, 118, 118n,
    126, 128, 133, 140; and Anti-
    federalism, 118–21; and force
    acts, 101–02; and lodge money,
    84, 87–88, 90, 98n, 119n; and
    political coercion, 90–91; and
    Revolutionary debt, 80–81,
    81n, 82, 88–91; and *Trevett
    v. Weeden* case, 93n; and U.S.
    Constitution, 119n; attempts to
    depreciate, 101, 101n; contro-
    versy over, 80–91; controversy
    over test acts, 101–02; effect
    on town-country relations, 90.
    See also Country Party; Land-
    holders' Party.
Parliament, 17, 18n, 31n, 34, 38,
    63n, 94
Parmenter, David, 315
Parsons, C. W., 157
Pawtucket (Mass.), 350, 354
Pawtucket (R.I.), 150, 158 221,
    261, 275, 284, 349–50
Pawtucket Chronicle, 257n, 286n
Pawtucket Falls, 145
Pawtuxet River, 148, 150, 154,
    349
Pawtuxet Valley, 148, 227
Pearce, Dutee J., 189, 192n, 202,
    203n, 208–10, 210n, 231 231n,
    232, 234, 283, 284n, 302, 309,
    311, 314–15, 326n, 330–31,
    335, 337, 338n, 348, 352
Peckham, William, 181n, 259,
    259n, 260n, 272, 273, 278, 283,
    302n
Penn, William, 30
Pennsylvania, 81n, 132n, 137, 158,
    241, 376n

People's Constitution, 207n, 305,
310, 310n, 311–21, 324, 324n,
326, 327, 327n, 331, 335, 337–
38, 341, 353, 358, 361–64, 370,
374–75, 378
People's Convention, 309–10, 312,
314, 316
People's election of 1842, 326–27,
327n
People's Legislature, 311, 328,
337, 340, 343, 343n, 346, 348,
350. See also Foundry
Legislature.
Phenix (R.I.), 154
Philadelphia (Pa.), 75, 100, 105,
107–08, 108n, 109, 124
Phillips, Peter, 60
Phips, William, 28
Pierce, Horace A., 338n
Pirates, 29, 30
Pitman, John, 181, 202, 203n,
208, 317, 324–26, 335, 363–64
Polk, James K., 355n, 363
Portsmouth (R.I.), 16–19, 23, 64,
68, 83, 105n, 113, 114n, 128–
30, 130n, 131n, 138, 204, 265,
267. See also Charter of 1643.
Portsmouth Assembly, 19, 20;
enacts Code of 1647, 20;
establishes General Court of
Trials, 20
Portuguese, 35, 36
Potter, Americus V., 371
Potter, Elisha R., Jr., 181, 256n,
273n, 315, 325, 327n, 330–31
Potter, Elisha R., Sr., 163, 167,
179, 195–203, 208, 219, 220n,
225, 230, 230n, 231n, 232,
234, 234n, 235n, 242, 242n,
243, 243n, 245, 259n, 261–62,
265–66, 333–35, 345, 345n,
352, 357–58, 367, 369
Potter, Sheriff Roger, 337, 338n,
341
Preston, Jacob, 358
Preston, William C., 332
Privy Council, 29n, 38; appeals
to, 25, 25n, 43–44, 44n

Providence (R.I.), 14–19, 23, 26,
37n, 49n, 58n, 66, 68, 72, 81,
83, 85–86, 89, 101–04, 108,
112–13, 121, 128–30, 132,
132n, 136, 138, 140, 148–50,
158, 162, 165–71, 179–82,
190–91, 193, 194n, 195, 197,
200, 202, 203n, 208, 212, 222,
222n, 223, 227, 234, 234n, 237,
237n, 239, 241, 245, 247, 249–
50, 252, 252n, 254–57, 261,
263–64, 267, 271–74, 275n,
288, 300, 305, 312, 321, 336–
37, 340–41, 344–45, 347, 371,
374–76. See also Charter of
1643; Providence City Council; Providence Town Meeting.
Providence Abolition Society, 126,
126n
Providence American, 212
Providence and Stonington Railroad, 347
Providence Association of Mechanics and Manufacturers, 129
Providence Bank v. Alpheus
Billings and Thomas G. Pittman, 194n, 245n
Providence Beacon, 217
Providence City Council, 247
Providence County, 41, 41n, 164–
65, 168, 191–92, 206–07, 235n,
267, 347, 355, 358
Providence Express, 348–49
Providence Gazette, 67, 131, 163,
188
Providence Journal, 276, 276n,
294, 319, 321–22, 346, 351n,
354, 369, 369n
Providence Morning Courier, 286,
286n
Providence Patriot, 188, 196
Providence Town Meeting, 132,
166
Providence Workingmen's Asso-
ciation, 249
Purdy, Elijah F., 336
Puritanism, 126; covenant the-
ology, 9, 10; principle of

Puritanism (*cont.*)
non-separation, 8; social and
political arrangement of, 10;
typology of, 10; view of Ten
Commandments, 11

Quakers, 72n, 124–25, 125n, 131n.
See also Antislavery.
Queen Anne's War, 28
Quincy, Josiah, 196

Randall, Charles, 246, 269, 273,
284, 286–87
Randall, Dexter, 253n, 352
Randolph, Edward, 27–28, 28n,
30
Randolph, John, 228
Randolph, Richard K., 328n, 333,
342
Rathbun, George, 358
Rathbun, Joshua B., 321
Religious freedom, 9, 12, 13, 15,
15n, 16, 16n, 17–18, 22, 26,
27n, 33, 33n, 36, 121, 173–74,
205, 278, 310; and *Digest of
1719*, 32; guaranteed by
Charter of 1663, 25–26. *See
also* Suffrage.
Republican Herald (Providence),
230, 294, 300n
Republican Party, 370–71, 375–77
Revere, Paul, 249
Reynolds v. Sims, 376
Rhode Island, autonomy prior to
American Revolution, 54; basis
for government, 26; boundaries
of, 24; codification of law, 31;
colonial governor of, 24;
colony as federal common-
wealth, 20; democratic rule in,
19; disunity in early colony of,
17; founding by religious exiles,
16; governmental organization
based on Charter of 1663, 23–
24; judicial antecedents, 20;
reaction to federal union, 75–
80; threat of union with Connecticut, 28. *See also* Aquid-

neck Island; Charter of 1643;
Charter of 1663; Elections;
General Assembly; Williams,
Roger.
Rhode Island American, 185,
233–34
Rhode Island Constitution of
November 1842 (Algerine
constitution), 351–52, 364,
367, 372–78; amendments to,
370n, 374–76, 376n, 377–78,
378n; and Bourn Amendment,
375. *See also* Charter of 1663.
Rhode Island Independence Day,
59n
Rhode Island Republican, 191,
210–12
Rhode Island Suffrage Association,
282, 294–96, 298n, 299, 302–
04, 314, 327n
Rhodes, Nathan C., 264, 272
Rice, Emanuel, 327n
Rich, Robert (Earl of Warwick),
17
Richards, Lawrence, 239, 272
Richmond (R.I.), 68, 70, 70n,
105n, 154, 172n, 265n
Richmond, William E., 187, 195n,
198, 202, 203n, 208, 291
Richmond Enquirer (Va.), 224
Ripley, George, 250
Rivers, Thomas, 254–55, 265,
273
Robbins, Asher, 197, 201–02, 208,
232, 232n, 253n, 301, 302n
Robbins, Christopher, 193, 203
Robinson, Christopher, 247, 255,
256n, 269, 273
Robinson, Martin, 271
Rochambeau, Jean Baptist
Donatien de Vimeur, Comte de,
61n, 71
Roman Catholics, 33, 36n, 71,
71n, 274, 274n, 275, 275n,
298n, 312, 322, 357n; and R.I.
citizenship, 35; granted full
citizenship, 71; sentiment
against, 33–34, 34n, 276–77,

Roman Catholics (*cont.*)
295n, 319–22, 327n, 345, 371.
See also Irish; Nativism.
Rotch, William, 125n
Royal Commissioners (1665), 33n, 46
Rush, Richard, 241

St. John the Baptist Church (Tiverton), 275
St. Joseph's Church (Newport), later renamed St. Mary's, 275
St. Mary's Church (Pawtucket), 275
St. Patrick's Church (Providence), 274n, 275
Sts. Peter and Paul Church (Providence), 274n, 275
Sands, Ray, 113, 114n
Sanford, Peleg, 30
Sayles, John, 126n
Sayles, Welcome B., 337, 338n, 354
Scituate (R.I.), 64n, 66–67, 70n, 102, 105n, 110, 154, 154n, 165, 202, 212, 255, 264n, 267, 312
Scott, Gen. Winfield, 350
Scott, Larned, 247
Second Continental Congress, 59–60, 60n
Seekonk River, 145
Separation of church and state, 9–13, 16, 18, 23n, 26n, 174
Sessions, Darius, 58
Seward, William, 349
Shay's Rebellion, 69
Sheldon, James, 126n
Shenton, Daniel, 189
Sherwood, John, 31n
Simmons, James F., 273, 274n, 298, 332, 346, 351–52, 367–68
Slamm, Levi, 282, 293n, 336
Slater, Samuel, 146–47
Slatersville (R.I.), 154, 246–47
Slave trade, 36, 112, 124–25, 125n, 258n
Slavery. *See* Antislavery; Negroes.
Slocum, Giles, 131n

Smith, Elisha G., 353
Smith, Henry, 175
Smith, John (of Providence), 171
Smith, Perry, 331
Smith, Richard, Jr., 30
Smith, William, 255–56, 256n, 257n, 269, 273, 309, 354n
Smith's Hill (Providence), 342–44
Smithfield (R.I.), 70n, 83n, 85, 103n, 105n, 148, 150, 154, 165, 177, 177n, 178, 197, 246–47, 247n, 252n, 256–57, 267, 285, 301, 312, 344
Smuggling, 120n
Snow, Edwin, 157
South Carolina, 332
South Kingstown (R.I.), 36, 39n, 68, 70, 70n, 83n, 111, 114n, 125, 136, 149, 154, 163–64, 167–68, 172n, 178, 182, 195–99, 202, 259, 259n, 262, 267, 272
Spear, William S., 210n, 217
Spencer, Ambrose, 228
Spencer, John C., 343, 346
Sprague, Amasa, 356
Sprague, Jedediah, 338n
Sprague, William, 182n, 235n, 236, 266n, 327, 327n, 331–32, 342–43, 346, 352, 357, 360n, 366n
Stamp Act, 31n, 57n, 94
Stanton, Joseph, Jr., 115–16, 125n, 126, 126n, 133n, 134
Staples, William R., 318
State House (R.I.), 328–29, 336
State v. Dorr, 362
States rights, 76, 79–81, 122, 330
Sterne, John, 259
Stiness, Philip B., 288, 352
Story, Joseph, 317–18, 324, 335, 335n, 363
Strong, Caleb, 136, 137n
Suffrage, 160, 183, 204, 205, 236–37; and apportionment issue, 154n; and land requirements, 48n, 48–49, 180–81;

Suffrage (*cont.*)
demands for reform, 151, 170, 180–82, 185–86, 189–90, 192, 195, 195n, 203–05, 209–10, 217–48n, 252–65n, 270–75n, 277, 282, 287–88, 293–303, 311, 313, 315–17, 320–21, 326, 369, 370n, 372; and immigrants, 254–55, 265, 274–77, 312, 314–15, 322, 360, 369–71, 373, 375; in colonial R.I., 19, 46–50; qualifications of freemen, 46–50; religious restrictions on, 33; in Charter of 1663, 23, 24
Suffragists, 311, 314–18, 321, 323–35, 337, 339, 341, 344–45, 349, 351, 353–54, 358n, 359, 361, 361n. *See also* Constitutional Party; Dorrites.
Sugar Act, 31n
Superior Court (R.I.), 35, 42, 42n, 43, 43n, 44, 61, 92, 92n, 95, 98; and special session to hear *Trevett v. Weeden,* 92, 92n, 93
Supreme Court (R.I.), 38n, 91, 98–99, 208, 217–18, 245n, 266, 287n, 317, 355, 355n, 364, 368n, 371, 374, 377
Swansea (Mass.), 362

Tallmadge, Nathaniel, 332
Tammany Hall, 281, 336–37
Taney, Roger B., 364–65, 365n
Tariffs, 134–35, 234, 244. *See also* Impost duties.
Taunton (Mass.), 239
Taxes, and paper money controversy, 81–83, 85, 88–89, 89n, 92n
Taylor v. Place, 99, 375
Test Act, 33–34
Thomas W. Dorr v. Rhode Island, 363
Thurston, Benjamin B., 293n, 324n

Tilden, Samuel J., 336
Tilley, Charles N., 269, 273, 283
Tillinghast, Joseph, 273, 283, 346
Tillinghast, Thomas, 96, 98
Tillinghast, William I., 239–40, 242, 246–47, 247n, 249, 252, 259, 259n, 264, 272, 287
Titus, Jonah, 246, 337, 352
Tiverton (R.I.), 83n, 128, 130, 154, 172, 203n, 246, 275, 275n, 321
Tories. *See* Loyalists; Newport Tory Junto.
Towns, declining, 151, 151n, 154, 157–58, 160, 172n, 191, 194, 206, 212, 267; expanding, 151, 151n, 152–54, 154n, 160, 191, 198, 201, 207, 212, 213n, 227, 252, 267, 312, 345, 374; static, 151, 151n, 154, 154n, 160, 191, 198, 206, 212. *See also listings for individual municipalities.*
Treadwell, Francis C., 368, 368n
Treaty of Paris (1783), 60
Trevett, John, 92–93, 95, 97
Trevett v. Weeden, 90–101, 126
Turner, George, 356, 361
Tyler, John, 298, 325–26, 328, 330–31, 333–34, 342–43, 346, 358–59, 360n, 364–65
Typology (Biblical). *See* Williams, Roger.

United States Chronicle (Providence), 105, 131, 162
United States Circuit Court, 163n, 335, 362
United States Congress, 74–76, 79–81, 85, 109, 111–12, 115, 115n, 117n, 119–20, 120n, 122, 125, 131–32, 132n, 135–36, 137n, 232, 283, 293, 353, 358, 360–61, 364–65, 375n. *See also* Confederation Congress; Second Continental Congress.

432

United States Constitution, 79, 87, 100, 106, 108–09, 111n, 117n, 118, 118n, 120n, 183, 238, 296, 325; adoption of, 83n; amendments to, 114–15, 115n, 123; and economic factors, 119–21; economic reasons for adoption, 133–40, 142; and interstate commerce, 129; and protective tariffs, 129–30; and question of direct taxation, 119, 120, 120n, 123n, 129, 135, 140; and real versus personal property interests, 139, 139n, 140–41, 141n, 142, 142n; antislavery objections to, 124–26, 131n; proposed R.I. amendments to, 114–15, 115n, 117n, 119–20, 120n, 122–23, 123n, 125; R.I. ratification of, 105–16, 118–19, 121, 128–42, 145, 374n. See also Antifederalists; Bill of Rights (U.S.); Constitutional Convention; Federalists.

United States Supreme Court, 194n, 245n, 317–18, 353, 361–65, 365n, 366n, 368, 376–77

Updike, Daniel, 112n, 113, 114n, 202

Updike, Wilkins, 208, 226, 230n, 243, 374–75, 375n

Van Buren, Martin, 240–41, 273, 279n, 297–98, 345n

Vane, Sir Henry, 21

Varnum, James Mitchell, 92–101, 108, 139n

Vermont, 290

Verin Case of 1638, 16n

Virginia, 36n, 57n, 110, 132n, 138n, 220, 224, 228, 228n, 332–33

Wales, Samuel H., 309

Walker, Robert J., 363

Wallace, William A., 376n

Walsh, "Big Mike," 336, 348

Wanton, Joseph, 31n, 45n, 58–60, 63

War of 1812, 146, 158, 184

Ward, Henry, 58, 60

Ward, Samuel, 35, 50, 107

Ward-Hopkins controversy, 50–51

Warren (R.I.), 85–86, 128, 130, 148, 165, 224, 239, 246, 252n, 257, 261, 270, 274n, 284, 340, 344, 346, 353, 362

Warwick (R.I.), 18–19, 23, 37n, 70n, 83n, 105n, 130, 130n, 131n, 150, 154, 202, 227, 234, 241, 267, 272, 312, 349

Warwick, Earl of. See Rich, Robert.

Washington, George, 59, 121, 131–32, 132n

Washington County, 63, 68, 70, 149, 154, 164, 167–68, 172, 191–92, 206, 255n, 267

Waterman, John R., 199n, 202, 232, 287, 309, 352

Wayland, Rev. Francis, 227, 347

Webster, Daniel, 241, 318, 330, 334–35, 343, 343n, 363–64

Weed, Thurlow, 349

Weeden, John, 92, 92n, 93, 96–97, 100. See also Trevett v. Weeden.

Weeden, John H., 253n, 261–65, 269, 273, 284

Weeden, Wager, 309, 326

West Greenwich (R.I.), 69n, 70n, 201, 264n, 265n, 376

West Warwick (R.I.), 150, 154

Westerly (R.I.), 68, 70, 70n, 105n, 130, 154, 202, 208, 210, 349

Western lands, 77

Wheaton, Henry, 179, 179n

Wheaton, Seth, 179

Wheaton, William T., 264

Wheeler, Bennett, 131, 162, 188

Wheeler, Col. Jonathan M., 340

Whigs (English), 34, 243n, 244, 276n

Whigs, 241, 245–46, 252, 258–61,

Whigs (*cont.*)
263, 265, 266n, 270, 272–77,
280–81, 283–84, 293n, 294,
297, 297n, 298, 300n, 314, 317–
18, 325–26, 328, 328n, 332–33,
349, 351–55, 357, 359, 366–70,
376n
Whipple, John, 242, 250, 253n,
273, 318, 325, 335, 342, 363–
64, 365n
Whipple, Thomas, 259, 259n,
260n
White, Aaron, Jr., 246, 326n, 336,
341, 354, 354n, 363
Wilbour, Isaac, 175–76, 179n, 218
Wilbur, Peleg, 328n
Wilkinson, Abraham, 202, 203n
Williams, John, 126n
Williams, Roger, 7–8, 16, 21, 126,
173–74, 185, 249, 298n, 369;
and land purchases from Indians, 14, 18; and liberty of
conscience, 12–13, 26; and
settlement of Providence, 14–
15; and "soul liberty," 11; as
political theorist, 7–8; banished
from Mass. Bay, 8–9; counter-
acts divisive forces in colony,
21–22; disagrees with Puritan
theology, 8, 10–11; early political views, 15; influence on
Founding Fathers, 13, 13n;
influence on royal Charter of
1663, 13–14; opinion of Charter
of 1663, 26n; religious creed
of, 12; secures patent of 1643,
17–18; settlement at Providence, 14; traditionalist views
of, 12, 15n; typological debate
with John Cotton, 10–11;
typological method, 9–13. *See
also* Providence; Religious
freedom; Separation of church
and state.
Winthrop, John, 14n
Winthrop, John, Jr., 22, 23n
Woodbury, Levi, 331, 365, 365n
Woonsocket Falls (R.I.), 154,
158, 246–47, 275, 340, 344,
346, 349–50
Woonsocket Patriot, 286n
Worcester (Mass.), 343n
Workingmen's Party, 253, 272
Wright, Silas, Jr., 331

About the Author

Patrick T. Conley is a Professor of History at Providence College. He graduated from Providence College, *magna cum laude* (1959) and received his master's and doctorate in American History from the University of Notre Dame (1961, 1970). In 1973 he earned a Juris Doctor from Suffolk University Law School. Professor Conley served as volunteer chairman of the Rhode Island Bicentennial Commission (ri76), chairman of the Cranston (R.I.) Charter Review Commission, and secretary of the 1973 Rhode Island Constitutional Convention where he was primary sponsor of the amendment establishing procedures for the convening of constitutional conventions and streamlining the process of constitutional revision. He also drafted the campaign financial disclosure clause of the new suffrage amendment. Dr. Conley has published numerous articles in the fields of history, government and law. Recently he co-authored *Catholicism in Rhode Island: The Formative Era*.